Human and Machine
Problem Solving

Human and Machine Problem Solving

Edited by

K. J. Gilhooly

University of Aberdeen
Aberdeen, United Kingdom

Plenum Press • New York and London

Library of Congress Cataloging in Publication Data

Human and machine problem solving.

Includes bibliographies and index.
1. Problem solving. 2. Problem solving—Data processing. 3. Cognitive science. I.
Gilhooly, K. J.
BF449.H86   1989   153.4'3   88-31628
ISBN 0-306-42962-4

© 1989 Plenum Press, New York
A Division of Plenum Publishing Corporation
233 Spring Street, New York, N.Y. 10013

Printed in the United States of America

Contributors

J. L. ALTY, Turing Institute, George House, 36 North Hanover Street, Glasgow G1 2AD, United Kingdom

I. BRATKO, E. Kardelj University, Faculty of Electrical Engineering, and J. Stefan Institute, 61000 Ljubljana, Yugoslavia

M. T. H. CHI, Learning Research and Development Center, University of Pittsburgh, Pittsburgh, Pennsylvania 15260

M. R. B. CLARKE, Department of Computer Science, Queen Mary College, University of London, London E1 4NS, United Kingdom

BENEDICT DU BOULAY, School of Cognitive Sciences, University of Sussex, Brighton BN1 9QN, United Kingdom

MICHAEL W. EYSENCK, Department of Psychology, Royal Holloway and Bedford New College, University of London, Egham, Surrey TW20 OEX, United Kingdom

R. A. FROST, School of Computer Science, University of Windsor, Windsor, Ontario N9B 3P4, Canada

ANGUS R. H. GELLATLY, Department of Psychology, University of Keele, Keele, Staffordshire ST5 5BG, United Kingdom

K. J. GILHOOLY, Department of Psychology, University of Aberdeen, Aberdeen AB9 2UB, United Kingdom

DENNIS H. HOLDING, Department of Psychology, University of Louisville, Louisville, Kentucky 40292

RICHARD E. MAYER, Department of Psychology, University of California, Santa Barbara, California 93106

P. Reimann, Psychology Institute, University of Freiburg, D-7800 Freiburg, West Germany

J. C. Thomas, AI Laboratory, NYNEX Corporation, White Plains, New York 10604

Preface

Problem solving is a central topic for both cognitive psychology and artificial intelligence (AI). Psychology seeks to *analyze* naturally occurring problem solving into hypothetical processes, while AI seeks to *synthesize* problem-solving performance from well-defined processes. Psychology may suggest possible processes to AI and, in turn, AI may suggest plausible hypotheses to psychology. It should be useful for both sides to have some idea of the other's contribution—hence this book, which brings together overviews of psychological and AI research in major areas of problem solving.

At a more general level, this book is intended to be a contribution toward comparative cognitive science. Cognitive science is the study of intelligent systems, whether natural or artificial, and treats both organisms and computers as types of information-processing systems. Clearly, humans and typical current computers have rather different functional or cognitive architectures. Thus, insights into the role of cognitive architecture in performance may be gained by comparing typical human problem solving with efficient machine problem solving over a range of tasks.

Readers may notice that there is little mention of connectionist approaches in this volume. This is because, at the time of writing, such approaches have had little or no impact on research at the problem-solving level. Should a similar volume be produced in ten years or so, of course, a very different story may need to be told.

Thanks are due to the following people who helped solve the problem of producing this book: to the secretarial staff of my department for expert word processing and reprocessing; to P. Bates, for many of the figures; to Professor E. A. Salzen, my head of department, for providing a good working environment at Aberdeen; to Professors

Sanford and Oatley, and P. J. O'Donnell, who provided me with facilities to work on this book during a visiting fellowship at the Psychology Department of Glasgow University; to Ben du Boulay, for much advice; and to Ken Derham, senior editor at Plenum Press, who greatly assisted the transition from initial proposal to final product.

                                                                  K. J. Gilhooly

Aberdeen

Contents

CHAPTER 3

Human Nonadversary Problem Solving

RICHARD E. MAYER

CHAPTER 4

Adversary Problem Solving by Machine

M. R. B. CLARKE

CHAPTER 5
Adversary Problem Solving by Humans

DENNIS H. HOLDING

CHAPTER 6
Machine Expertise

J. L. ALTY

CHAPTER 7
Human Expertise

P. REIMANN and M. CHI

CHAPTER 8
Machine Inference

R. A. FROST

CHAPTER 9
Human Inference

ANGUS R. H. GELLATLY

CHAPTER 10
Machine Learning

I. BRATKO

Chapter 11
Human Learning

Michael W. Eysenck

Chapter 12
Problem Solving by Human–Machine Interaction

J. C. Thomas

CHAPTER 13
Human and Machine Problem Solving: A Comparative
Overview

K. J. GILHOOLY

Human and Machine
Problem Solving

1

Human and Machine Problem Solving

Toward a Comparative Cognitive Science

K. J. GILHOOLY

1. INTRODUCTION

During a long history the topic of problem solving has been approached from three main angles. In order of antiquity, there have been *normative* approaches, which have sought to prescribe optimal means of solving various types of problems, such as problems in reasoning or in game playing. Next, there have been *psychological* studies, which have attempted to understand problem-solving processes in humans and other animals. Most recently, with the advent of *computer science*, considerable effort has been invested in automating problem-solving processes in a number of task areas. These efforts form part of the field of *artificial intelligence* (AI), which attempts to construct programs that can carry out complex performances hitherto the preserve of humans and other organisms.

Recent psychological analyses of human problem solving and AI

K. J. GILHOOLY • Department of Psychology, University of Aberdeen, Aberdeen AB9 2UB, United Kingdom.

syntheses of computer problem solving both involve viewing problem solving as a form of information processing. Thus, both humans and suitably programmed computers are seen as flexibly manipulating symbols in order to solve problems. Viewing natural and artificial information processing as essentially the same is the perspective of the recently emerged discipline known as *cognitive science* (for an introductory treatment of cognitive science, see Gardner, 1985). Cognitive science takes as its topic knowledge acquisition and use *in general*, whether by artificial or natural systems.

This volume is intended as a contribution toward a *comparative* cognitive science of problem solving in which the differing information-processing procedures followed by human and machine may be compared and contrasted, with a view to developing general principles applicable both to natural and artificial problem solving.

In the remainder of this chapter, I will first consider the general area of problem solving and discuss definitions and classifications of problem types and solving processes. Second, I will discuss psychological and machine approaches to problem solving separately from each other. Third, the interaction of human and machine perspectives will be outlined. Finally, I will suggest some issues and questions that may be borne in mind while you are reading the substantive chapters. These questions and issues will be returned to in the overview chapter that closes this book.

2. PROBLEM SOLVING

2.1. PROBLEMS

"Problems" come in an unending variety of forms, and any general definition of the term is bound to be rather abstract. Many years ago the Gestalt psychologist Karl Duncker (1945, p. 2) offered a still serviceable definition when he wrote that "a problem exists when a living organism has a goal but does not know how this goal is to be reached."

2.1.1. Definitions

Duncker's definition might be rephrased in cognitive science terms by saying that "a problem exists when an information-processing system has a goal condition that cannot be satisfied without a search process." This definition is sufficiently broad to encompass both natural

information-processing systems (Duncker's "organisms") and computers under program control. It is clear that a goal condition may or may
not signal the existence of a problem. If a solving method can be accessed and applied without search, then there is no problem. So, a
numerate adult human does not find "18/3 = ?" a problem, nor even
"18729/3 = ?" Similarly, a suitably programmed computer could evaluate the preceding expressions without a search process being invoked.
On the other hand, to find a good move in a given chess position
would normally be a problem requiring search, although its difficulty
may vary from solver to solver. (By "difficulty" here, I mean the amount
of processing effort required to solve.) A chess expert familiar with a
given type of position may well be able to propose a suitable move
with little or no search, while a novice may require considerable search
(and usually not find such a good solution). Similarly, a given position
may constitute a difficult problem for one chess-playing program but
not for another.

2.1.2. Classifications

Most, perhaps all, problems can be described as having a three-
part structure (Reitman, 1965). The three main components are a starting state, a goal condition, and a set of actions that can be used to
transform the starting state in order to meet the goal.

Although problems will be as variable as goal conditions, starting
states, and action sets can be, certain classificatory dimensions and di-
chotomies have been proposed in computing science and psychology
and have been found useful over the years.

One such distinction is that between *well-* and *ill-defined* problem
components (Reitman, 1965). To take a paradigm case: A problem is
well defined if all components are completely specified; i.e., the starting state, the goal state, and the actions available are all specified. For
example, a chess problem is well defined. It has a specified starting
state, a definite goal, and a strictly defined set of available actions.
Completely well-defined problems are probably found only in the realms
of the formal sciences, and in games and pastimes. In other areas of
life, problems tend to be more or less ill defined in one or more components; e.g., the problem of improving the educational value of a lec-
ture course is an everyday problem in higher education but is clearly
ill defined. How educational value is to be measured and by how much
it is to be improved are not specified, nor are the means available to
transform the starting state spelled out. In practice, most research in
both psychology and computing has focused on rather well-defined

problem solving. This is reasonable since the problem interpretation stage is less "problematic" with well-defined problems.

A second useful distinction is between *adversary* and *nonadversary* problems (Nilsson, 1971). In nonadversary problems, solvers are faced with nonresponsive materials that are not trying to defeat the solver's purposes. In adversary problems, a rational opponent must be faced who is trying to undo the solver's attempts. Thus, adversary problems have an additional layer of complexity compared with nonadversary problems (Winston, 1984).

A third distinction that has come to be of increasing importance in problem-solving research generally is that between *semantically rich* and *semantically impoverished* domains (Bhaskar & Simon, 1977). To a large extent, this distinction refers to the solving system's view of the problem area. A problem is semantically rich for solvers who bring considerable relevant knowledge to the task. So, if someone has just been introduced to the game of Go, a particular problem in the game would be semantically impoverished for that person, but not for a Go master. Many artificial puzzles used in human and machine studies of problem solving—e.g., missionaries and cannibals (Amarel, 1968; Thomas, 1974), Tower of Hanoi (Anzai & Simon, 1979; Ernst & Newell, 1969), 8-puzzle (Doran & Michie, 1966; Ericsson, 1975)—are semantically impoverished for most subjects. As will be seen in Chapters 6 and 7, more recent research in both human and machine problem solving has focused on semantically rich problem areas, such as game playing, medical diagnosis, geological prospecting, and political analysis.

2.1.3. Problem Areas Addressed

In the chapters that follow, a number of different types of problems will be discussed from the human and machine perspectives. These will include well-defined adversary and nonadversary problems (Chapters 2, 3, 4, and 5), semantically rich problems (Chapters 6 and 7), logic problems (Chapters 8 and 9), and learning problems (Chapters 10 and 11). Since the latter two areas have not so far been discussed, they will now be introduced.

The particular area of logic considered in this book is deductive inference. This area is a source of well-defined, nonadversary, and—for most human subjects—semantically impoverished problems. It involves using rules of great generality to generate and check putative inferences from premises assumed to be true.

Learning is an interesting form of problem solving in that the goal is *internal* and is to modify the subject's or system's knowledge rather than bringing about some external state of affairs. It may also be noted that learning is a typical by-product of problem solving in that solving a particular problem provides a basis for generalization to other problems as well as a learning experience specific to that problem.

2.2. SOLVING

Necessarily, much of the time spent in solving problems is spent failing to solve! Ideally, the whole process of detecting and responding to problems would be referred to by some other expression, such as "problem attempting" or "problem processing." However, usage over the years has come to dictate that "problem solving" refers to the whole process from problem detection through various attempts to problem solution or problem abandonment. In the present discussion, then, "problem solving" refers to the overall process of responding to a problem.

A few broad steps are generally discerned in problem solving. These are the following:

1. Detecting that a problem exists; realizing that there is a discrepancy between the current situation and a goal and that no way is known to reach solution without search. In the machine case, the top-level goals are set by the programmer or user; unexpected subproblems may be uncovered as solution attempts proceed. In the human case, top-level goals are presumed to be set by socialization pressures and are an important source of individual and cross-cultural differences. In the course of working toward the top-level goals, numerous specific subgoals arise and provide targets for problem solving.

2. Formulating the problem more completely. How are the starting conditions to be defined and represented? How are the goals to be defined and represented? What relevant actions are available? A problem formulation is an internal representation of the problem components, and solution attempts are made within this representation.

Two broad ways of representing problems are (a) in state space terms and (b) in problem reduction terms (Nilsson, 1971). In the state space approach, the solver typically works forward from the starting state representation and explores alternative paths of development as these branch out from the starting state. Within the state space approach, the solver may also work backward by inverse actions from goal states toward the starting state. A resulting successful sequence could then be run forward to reach a goal state from the starting state. Indeed, both forward and backward exploration may be tried in various mixtures within the same problem attempt. In the problem reduction approach, the overall problem is split up into subproblems. For example, if the goal state involves a conjunction of conditions (achieve

X and Y and Z), then problem reduction would seek to achieve each condition separately (either by further problem reduction or by state space search). A key method within problem reduction is means–ends analysis, in which subgoals are set up for achievement such that those subgoals would lead to achievement of higher-level goals. Problem and subproblem reduction continue until subgoals are reached that can be immediately solved because a method is already known for them. Usually, there are alternative ways to reduce problems and so search plays a role in developing alternative reductions. (These techniques are discussed more fully in Chapter 2.)

3. Given a representation and a choice of approach (state space or problem reduction), attempts can begin. Although in the case of well-defined problems, computers may in theory continue until solution or until all possible move sequences have been exhausted, humans usually give up—or at least set problems aside temporarily—long before all possible state action or problem reduction sequences have been explored. That is to say, *stop rules* are invoked. Different types of stop rules can be readily imagined (Simon, 1967). For example, one type of rule would be to stop exploring within a particular representation if solution has not been reached by a certain time and return to the problem formulation stage to produce a revised formulation for further exploration. A second type of rule would be to accept a "good enough" problem state rather than continue exploration for an optimal state [i.e., Simon's (1967) "satisficing" notion]. A third type of rule would be to only stop if an optimal solution is reached, i.e., a "maximizing" rule. In the human case, rules for temporarily setting problems aside are probably used; however, this topic does not seem to have been researched. A further type of stop rule would be an "abandon" rule, i.e., a judgment that further reformulation and/or exploration would not be worthwhile and the problem should be left unsolved. Intuitively, this would seem to involve rather complex assessments of the chances of succeeding or failing and of the cognitive and other costs of continuing work or abandoning the problem. Again, this type of stop rule appears to have been little researched in either the human or the machine case.

3. PERSPECTIVES

3.1. Psychological Perspective

Psychology aims at understanding human problem solving. Thus, psychological approaches are *analytic*. They seek to represent real processes in terms of manageable interrelated concepts. In other words, the aim is to construct a model, or at most a small number of models, that will make human problem solving intelligible to humans.

The processes studied are manifestly *fallible* in that human problem solving is prone to many errors, false starts, apparent inconsistencies, and failures to progress ("getting stuck").

In devising analyses, psychologists can assume, barring accidents and illness, that the physical substrate underlying human problem solving (the nervous system) is *fixed*. Evolutionary processes are too slow to noticeably affect contemporary psychology! (However, damage to the nervous system by accident or disease can leave the person with highly specific impairments coupled with otherwise normal functioning. See Chapter 11 for some examples.)

Although the nervous system is fixed, it clearly permits very flexible processing and has an important capacity for *learning* or self-improvement within the bounds of its fixed architecture. It is widely accepted (e.g., Card, Moran, & Newell, 1983) that the main fixed characteristics of human information processing are a limited-capacity short-term or working memory system, a virtually unlimited long-term memory system, relatively slow transfer of information to long-term memory, with rapid recognition but problematic recall. These features shape the strategies followed in human problem solving. For example, a strategy involving a large load on working memory is not likely to be used, nor is a strategy requiring perfect recall from long-term memory on the basis of minimal cues.

Human information processing at the level of problem solving is generally assumed to be *serial* even though the brain is evidently a parallel system. Parallel processes seem to be most usefully invoked in theories of perception and recognition, while at higher levels seriality seems to emerge, probably to facilitate control. Recent theoretical developments in psychology have sought to explain many phenomena in perception and (elementary) learning in terms of massively parallel activity among large numbers of interconnected units, and this "connectionist" approach has been extended, albeit tentatively, to sequential thought processes (Rumelhart, Smolensky, McClelland, & Hinton, 1986). However, while this approach to thinking is too recent to evaluate fairly, at least one friendly critic (Norman, 1986) has pointed out a number of problems and has argued for a "supervisory" sequential system to account for problem solving and the more deliberate complex forms of learning. (The general issue of parallel thought streams is also discussed in Section 3.3 of this chapter.)

Finally, it may be noted that psychological approaches are *empirical* as well as theoretical. Indeed, it has been argued that cognitive psychology tends to be too empirical, with insufficient concern for general unifying theories (Newell, 1973). The recently emerging approach to thinking as a form of "mental modeling" may provide a useful framework for future general theorizing (Gilhooly, 1987; Johnson-Laird, 1983).

3.2. MACHINE PERSPECTIVE

Many machines have been devised in order to reproduce and amplify desirable characteristics of human actions. So, for example, machines have been devised to lift ever larger weights, faster and more cheaply; to dig deeper, faster, cheaper; to move people and goods faster, cheaper, further; and so on. In the realm of information-processing machines, important aims are to increase accuracy, consistency, speed, and economy.

An essential aim of the machine approach, then, is to achieve *accurate* processing (as compared with human fallible processing). Thus, the machine approach to problem solving is essentially *synthetic* and seeks to construct processes that can assist or even replace and exceed human operators. This aim contrasts with the emphasis on analysis in psychological research.

Particular computers have fixed hardware, although add-ons are possible that can considerably modify the original. However, in the computer world, hardware characteristics tend to change rapidly. This contrasts with the fixed nervous system "hardware" with which the psychologist deals. In computers both memory capacity and speed of basic operations have increased dramatically in a few years. Furthermore, the serial (Von Neumann) architecture, which has dominated developments so far, may soon give way—or at least yield some space to—the highly parallel machine designs and prototypes now receiving increased attention and effort (Hillis, 1985). (It may be noted that the promise of such machines has undoubtedly helped fuel the connectionist approach in psychological theorizing.)

Thus, approaches to machine problem solving will reflect changes in hardware. For example, searches in chess can become wider and deeper in fixed time because of improvements in memory and speed; also, with suitable programming, a highly parallel machine could tackle many subproblems of an overall problem simultaneously, and so produce a solution much more rapidly than could a serial machine.

Just as psychological theories and models need to be tested, so also do AI programs. Although there are empirical approaches to testing and developing machine problem-solving techniques (e.g., Doran

& Michie, 1966) in which programs are tested on a range of problems within their domain and adjusted to improve performance measures, formal approaches are also used. Sometimes it is possible to prove that a certain procedure is bound to solve a class of problems (i.e., be algorithmic) or even to be an optimal algorithm. The existence of such proofs obviates any need for empirical exploration of the techniques concerned. Since humans are by no means restricted to following optimal paths, the role of formal analyses in the study of human problem solving, in contrast, is likely to be limited to providing normative baselines against which performance can be measured.

3.3. Interaction of Human and Machine Perspectives

Machine analogies have strongly shaped current psychological approaches to human thinking. The approach that has dominated the psychological study of thinking since the mid-1960s is that of the information-processing school. This school has roots in 1940s developments in cybernetics (Weiner, 1948), information theory (Shannon & Weaver, 1949), and game theory (Von Neumann & Morgenstern 1944), and gathered momentum with the increased salience of computing theory and practice in the early 1950s. The year 1956 is generally accepted as the start of the "information-processing revolution" in psychology, since that year saw a number of seminal publications in the new mold, such as the Bruner, Goodnow, and Austin study of concept learning and the Newell, Shaw, and Simon computer model of problem solving. The information-processing approach is directly derived from an analogy between human thinking and computer program execution. In both cases it is argued that symbols are being manipulated; symbol manipulation is realized in one case by electronic means, and in the other case by neurological means. The human nervous system thus is regarded as analogous to computer hardware and is seen as storing and executing programs for internal and external actions that are analogous to computer programs.

One possible drawback with the machine analogy for human thinking is that, until recently, most computers have been strictly serial (Von Neumann) devices, and it is difficult to maintain that the nervous system is similarly strictly serial. At least at the level of perception, attention, and recognition memory, nervous system activity is most plausibly described as highly parallel. However, at the level of thinking, there is remarkably little indication of truly parallel activity. There are a few possible counterexamples, such as "incubation" phenomena, which have sometimes been taken to indicate a parallel stream of unconscious thought coexisting alongside the main conscious stream. The notion of incubation in thinking derives from self-reports by artists and scientists and was largely popularized by Wallas (1926) in a stage analysis of problem solving. In Wallas's analysis, if an initial stage of conscious work (Preparation) is unsuccessful, then it is followed by a period in which the problem is not consciously worked on (Incubation). Incubation is followed by Inspiration, the occurrence of an idea for solution, which then must be further tested in a final stage, Verification. However, incubation phenomena have proven difficult to produce reliably in laboratory settings, and so little is known of the conditions favoring such effects. Even if incubation effects occur, they may be due to beneficial forgetting of misleading directions of search rather than to unconscious work taking place in parallel to the conscious stream of thought. Indeed, Simon (1966) has shown how such effects might be obtained even with strictly serial models of thinking.

If thinking can be fully described as symbol manipulation according to rules, then, since any such process (whether serial or parallel) can be simulated on a serial computer, the computer can provide the "final metaphor" for thinking (Johnson-Laird, 1983, p. 10). This conclusion is not, of course, particularly restrictive, because there is ample scope for many detailed models within the computer metaphor.

However, the underlying assumption, that thinking can be fully described as symbol manipulation according to rules, has been questioned, notably by the philosopher John Searle (1980). Searle has argued that since thought is meaningful and meaning can never reside merely in symbols, then thinking cannot be fully understood simply as symbol manipulation. In Searle's view, then, a robot equipped with an impeccable natural language understanding program would not truly "understand" language because it would only be manipulating symbols. The argument is bolstered by inviting the reader (assumed not to know Chinese) to consider himself or herself hand-simulating such a program to deal with Chinese language inputs and produce Chinese outputs. Would the hand-simulator truly understand Chinese? Intuitively, it would seem not. However, a counterargument is that the broader context of processing must be considered, in that symbols relate to sensory inputs and motor outputs as well as to each other. Meaning, it may be argued, resides in systems as wholes, not in surgically isolated symbols or symbol strings.

Overall, the machine-inspired information-processing approach to the study of human thinking is likely to be dominant for many years to come, and within this approach numerous frameworks, theories, and models can and will flourish and compete.

Have there been many influences on machine problem-solving programs from human studies? It is tempting, though oversimplifying, to reply "none" to this question. The traffic seems to have been nearly all one way—from the better-defined area of computing to the less well-defined area of psychology. A scan of the chapters in this volume will not show any great influence of human studies on developments in machine problem solving. This one-sidedness is probably inevitable, since useful analogies are always from the known to the unknown. Machine approaches and solutions are necessarily known and thus provide analogies for the unknown human processes. Human processes are rarely known in detail and so only rather general influences from human to machine studies may be apparent. For instance, analyses of human problem solving indicated wide use of means–ends analysis (Duncker, 1945), and this was noted as an influence on early studies of problem reduction in machine problem solving (Newell, Shaw, & Simon, 1958).

4. SOME ISSUES

The substantive chapters have been contributed by experts in their particular areas. While you are reading them, questions of a comparative nature will be worth bearing in mind, and some suggested issues are now listed.

1. In each area, what have been the mutual influences of human and machine studies?
2. Within and across areas, do general principles emerge that apply to both human and machine problem solving?
3. In each area, to what extent are problems of real-life scale and complexity dealt with, as against circumscribed and well-defined tasks?
4. In each area, have machine and human studies focused on similar or different issues?
5. Are connections and continuities discernible across areas, as well as between human and machine approaches within areas?

5. REFERENCES

Amarel, S. (1968). On representation of problems of reasoning about actions. In D. Michie (Ed.), *Machine intelligence* (Vol. 3). Edinburgh: Edinburgh University Press.
Anzai, Y., & Simon, H. A. (1979). The theory of learning by doing. *Psychological Review, 86*, 124–140.

Bhaskar, R., & Simon, H. A. (1977). Problem solving in sementically rich domains: An example from engineering thermodynamics. *Cognitive Science, 1,* 193–215.

Bruner, J. S., Goodnow, J. J., & Austin, G. A. (1956). *A study of thinking.* New York: Wiley.

Card, S., Moran, T., & Newell, A. (1983). *The psychology of human computer interaction.* Hillsdale, NJ: Erlbaum.

Doran, J. W., & Michie, D. (1966). Experiments with the graph traverser program. *Proceedings of the Royal Society, 294*(14), 235–259.

Duncker, K. (1945). On problem solving, *Psychological Monographs, 58* (Whole No. 270), 5.

Ericsson, K. A. (1975). Instruction to verbalise as a means to study problem-solving processes with the 8-puzzle: A preliminary study. *Reports from the Department of Psychology, 458,* University of Stockholm, Sweden.

Ernst, G. W., & Newell, A. (1969). *GPS: A case study in generality and problem-solving.* New York: Academic Press.

Gardner, H. (1985). *The mind's new science: A history of the congnitive revolution.* New York: Basic Books.

Gilhooly, K. J. (1987). Mental modelling: A framework for the study of thinking. In D. N. Perkins, J. Lochhead, & J. Bishop (Eds.), *Thinking.* Hillsdale, NJ: Erlbaum.

Hillis, W. D. (1985). *The connection machine.* Cambridge, MA: MIT Press.

Johnson-Laird, P. N. (1983). *Mental models.* Cambridge: Cambridge University Press.

Newell, A. (1973). You can't play 20 questions with nature and win. In W. G. Chase (Ed.), *Visual information processing,* New York: Academic Press.

Newell, A., Shaw, J. C., & Simon, H. A. (1958). Elements of a theory of human problem-solving. *Psychological Review, 65,* 151–166.

Nilsson, N. J. (1971). *Problem solving methods in artificial intelligence.* New York: McGraw-Hill.

Norman, D. A. (1986). Reflections on cognition and parallel distributed processing. In J. L. McClelland, D. E. Rumelhart, & the PDP Research Group, *Parallel distributed processing* (Vol. 2). Cambridge, MA: MIT Press.

Reitman, W. (1965). *Cognition and thought.* New York: Wiley.

Rumelhart, D. E., Smolensky, P., McClelland, J. L., & Hinton, G. E. (1986). Schemata and sequential thought processes in PDP models. In J. L. McClelland, D. E. Rumelhart, & the PDP Research Group, *Parallel distributed processing* (Vol. 2). Cambridge, MA: MIT Press.

Searle, J. (1980). Minds, brains and programs. *Behavioral and Brain Sciences, 3,* 417–57.

Shannon, C. E., & Weaver, W. (1949). *The mathematical theory of communication.* Urbana: University of Illinois Press.

Simon, H. A. (1966). Scientific discovery and the psychology of problem solving. In R. G. Colodny (Ed.), *Mind and cosmos: Essays in contemporary science and philosophy.* Pittsburgh: University of Pittsburgh Press.

Simon, H. A. (1967). Motivational and emotional controls of cognition. *Psychological Review, 74,* 29–39.

Thomas, J. C., Jr. (1974). An analysis of behavior in the hobbits-orcs problem. *Cognitive Psychology, 6,* 257–269.

Von Neumann, T., & Morgenstern, O. (1944). *Theory of games and economic behavior.* Princeton: Princeton University Press.

Wallas, G. (1926). *The art of thought.* London: Jonathon Cape.

Weiner, N. (1948). *Cybernetics.* New York: Wiley.

Winston, P. H. (1984). *Artificial Intelligence.* (2nd ed.). New York: Addison-Wesley.

2

Nonadversary Problem Solving by Machine

BENEDICT DU BOULAY

1. INTRODUCTION

Almost all artificial intelligence programs can be said to be doing some form of problem solving whether it be interpreting a visual scene, parsing a sentence, or planning a sequence of robot actions. In this chapter we shall adopt a rather more specialized meaning for the term and regard it as covering the study of the properties of algorithms (1) for conducting search and (2) for construction and manipulating plans of action.

By "nonadversary" problem solving we mean problem solving in a context where there is no opponent and where it is only the unyielding nature of the problem itself that needs to be overcome. Thus, we exclude chess and other multiagent games but include recreational puzzles such as Rubik's Cube or the 8-puzzle. We also exclude "cooperative" problem solving where two programs (or a program and a human) join forces to solve a problem. Thus, for our purposes, the only knowledge and the only goals that have to be taken into account are those of the problem solver or planner itself.

Search is one of the central issues in problem-solving systems. It

BENEDICT DU BOULAY • School of Cognitive Sciences, University of Sussex, Brighton BN1 9QN, United Kingdom.

becomes so whenever the system through lack of knowledge is faced with a choice among a number of alternatives, where each choice leads to the need to make further choices, and so on until the problem is solved. Playing chess is a classic example of this situation. Other examples are the attempt to diagnose a malfunction in some complex piece of machinery or determining how best to cut material to make an item of clothing with the minimum of waste. Thus, interpreting a visual scene and parsing a sentence can be regarded as searches for a plausible interpretation of possibly ambiguous visual or aural data, and making a plan can be regarded as a search in a space of plans to find one that is internally coherent and achieves the given goals.

Where the number of possibilities is small, the program may be able to carry out an exhaustive analysis of them all and then choose the best. In general, however, exhaustive methods will not be possible and a decision will have to be made at each choice-point to examine only a limited number of the more promising alternatives. In chess, for example, there are just too many possibilities for a program (or a person) to imagine every possible move, each of the possible corresponding replies, further moves in response, and so on to the anticipated conclusion of the game. But deciding what counts as "promising" is sometimes very hard. A good chess player is good precisely because, among other skills, he or she has an eye for plausible ways to proceed and can concentrate on these. Although it is easy to design problem-solving programs that are good at keeping track of choices made and choices yet to be explored, it is hard to provide programs with the common sense that can cut through such a welter of possibilities to concentrate its main analysis on the small number of critical choices.

Some problems that at first sight require a solution based on search—Rubik's Cube, for example—turn out on further study to be soluble by special-purpose methods that are essentially deterministic in character. The degree of search needed in the solution of other problems, such as the traveling salesman problem (i.e., the determination of the shortest circular route linking a given set of cities so that each city is visited once only), can also be enormously reduced by special methods and by relaxing some constraint in the problem—for example, that an "acceptable" solution be found rather than the "best" solution.

The first part of this chapter is concerned with problems where simplifying techniques are not known and search, either systematic and exhaustive or partial and heuristic, must be employed. The second part of the chapter then considers search within the domain of planning programs. The treatment in both cases is elementary, and more detailed descriptions can be found in Barr and Feigenbaum (1981), Charniak and McDermott (1985), Nilsson (1980), or Rich (1983).

The objective of this chapter is to give a sense of the way that artificial intelligence (AI) construes the terms *problem solving* and *planning*. So, the chapter does not provide an exhaustive list of AI problem-solving and planning systems but rather indicates the kinds of issue that workers in AI have grappled with and introduces a vocabulary to address these notions.

There is a tension in AI between the investigation of general-purpose methods that can be applied across domains and the discovery and exploitation of the special knowledge, heuristics, tricks, and shortcuts that can be applied in particular domains to improve performance. This chapter is concerned with general-purpose methods. It should be noted, however, that these general-purpose methods often provide the framework into which the available domain specific knowledge may be attached.

In many ways the problem solvers and planners referred to here are easily outstripped in performance by knowledgeable humans. But this is the state of play at present. What AI has done is to emphasize that even such impoverished tasks as finding one's way using a map or planning how to construct some simple object hide a wealth of issues that belie our apparently effortless human ability to succeed at such tasks.

1.1. PROBLEM-SOLVING SYSTEMS

Many problem-solving systems have the following features:

1. A knowledge base containing information about the current state of the problem in hand.
2. A set of operators for transforming the knowledge base in some way.
3. A control strategy or means of deciding which operator to use at any particular point during the solution of the problem, and a way of deciding when the problem is solved or unsolvable.

Consider a robot chef that could plan and then cook a meal. The knowledge base might initially contain the goal to produce supper. The final state of the knowledge base would be a fully worked out plan for the meal which indicated every ingredient that would be needed and all the necessary cooking and preparation actions. The operators would split the goal to produce some complicated meal into its constituent parts. So the main goal of planning a meal might be split by one operator into the simpler goals of planning a starter and planning a main course and planning a dessert. An alternative operator at this point might ignore the starter, another might ignore the dessert, and yet another might subdivide the meal in another way entirely. The control strategy would decide between the various operators available at each point, possibly abandoning one putative plan if it led to an impossible situation, such as the need for an unobtainable ingredient. The control strategy would also ensure that bits of a plan were all coordinated properly.

Consider a program to solve the 8-puzzle. This is a puzzle where there are 8 numbered tiles that can slide in a 3 by 3 square framework containing 9 spaces. One tile can be slid at a time into the single unoccupied space in the framework. In most versions of the puzzle the tiles are set in some disorganized order at the start and the problem is to rearrange them into order by sliding one tile at a time (and not taking them out of the framework!).

In a program to solve the 8-puzzle (see Figure 1) the knowledge base would contain a representation of the tiles in the frame and the operators would be the moves available at the particular point in play. Here a solution would be a completed sequence of tile moves that brought the puzzle to the required state. The control strategy would make sure that, in general, it was the tiles that were out of place that were moved (though of course it might be necessary to temporarily move tiles that were already in the right place), because it would be these misplaced tiles that would necessarily have to be moved as part of any solution.

The amount of search involved in a problem can be reduced if there is a method of estimating how effective an operator will be in moving the initial problem state toward a solution—e.g., a method for choosing "promising" moves in chess or choosing which tile to slide in the 8-puzzle. A great deal of attention has been given to methods of making such estimates and to the repercussions of such estimates on control strategy.

Occasionally the amount of search can be reduced dramatically by representing the problem in a new way—that is, by looking at it from a different viewpoint (see, e.g., Amarel, 1981). Planning programs, for example, can usually reduce search by first considering only the most important factors of a problem before going on to consider the details once the main issues have been sorted out. In general, the representation of the problem by the program is determined by the programmer, and even these "hierarchical" planners have their notion of "importance" built in. Getting a program to decide for itself what counts as important or determine the best way to view a problem is extremely difficult. Getting a program to automatically reorientate its view of a problem in the way suggested is, alas, beyond the state of the art.

1.2. STATE SPACE SEARCH AND PROBLEM REDUCTION

Many search problems fall into one or the other of two classes, depending on the action of the operators involved. In some problems each operator takes the problem state or situation and transforms it into a *single* new problem state. For example, in the 8-puzzle each move transforms the arrangement of the tiles to give a new arrangement. Here the problem is to find the sequence of operators (moves) that in total transforms the initial state of the frame of tiles to a concluding state. This is called state space search.

By contrast, problem reduction involves the use of operators that break down a complex problem possibly into *several* simpler, possibly independent, subproblems, each of which must be solved separately. The meal-planning system alluded to earlier is an example of this kind of system. Each subproblem may itself be broken down into sub-sub-problems, and so on, until "microproblems" are met which either can be solved immediately without further decomposition or are seen to be definitely insoluble.

In both state space approaches and problem reduction there may be a variety of operators that, in principle, can apply at any particular point. Thus, in the 8-puzzle (a state space example) there is always a choice of at least two tiles that could be moved at each stage; in undertaking a mathematical integration (a typical problem reduction example) there will be typically be a number of methods available, each of which will subdivide the larger integration problem into smaller ones in a different way.

State space search involves searching what may be thought of as an "or graph." Here a "graph" should be thought of as a network of nodes linked by arcs, like a road network linking cities. Each node in the graph represents a state of the problem and each arc from a node represents an operator that could be applied to that state. It is called an or graph (as opposed to an and/or graph, see below) because the branching paths from each node represent alternatives (hence "or"). The problem for the system is to find a path (possibly the shortest path) linking the node representing the starting state with the node representing the final (or goal) state.

By contrast, problem reduction involves the search of an and/or graph where each node now represents only a part of the problem to be solved and each arc links a problem to a subproblem. Arcs from a node are bunched into groups. Each group of arcs from a node represents a particular way of decomposing the problem and is one of the alternative operators that can be applied to that node. Since each group is an alternative, it can be regarded as the "or" part of the graph. Within each group, the various arcs link to nodes representing the subproblems that need to be solved using that particular operator. Thus, within a group the arcs are in an "and" relation to each other, because all the subproblems must be solved. The problem for the system in this case is to find the interconnected paths that link the node that represents the starting state with all the nodes that represent the ultimate decomposition of the problem into its simplest subproblems.

1.3. Blind Search and Heuristic Search

The totality of all possible nodes in a problem is known as its *search space*. It is important to distinguish the complete search space for a problem (i.e., all possible nodes and arcs) from that part of the space that any particular system explores in its attempt to find a solution (i.e., those nodes and arcs actually considered). Usually only a portion of this space is or can be explored. Chess, for example, has been estimated to have around 10^{120} nodes, and even draughts has around 10^{40}. The reader may care to compute how long such spaces might take to explore even working at the rate of a million nodes per second.

Some control strategies work by exploring the search space *forward* from an initial state toward a solution. Such methods are also sometimes called *data-directed*. An alternative strategy is to work *backward* from a goal or final state toward either soluble subproblems or the initial state, respectively. Such a control strategy is called *goal-directed*. Problem reduction systems often work in this way. Sometimes a mixture of both forward and backward strategies is employed, in the hope that working forward and backward will successfully meet in the middle.

Where the search space is small, systematic (but blind) methods can be used to explore the whole search space. These include *depth-first search*, where, for each new node encountered, one of the arcs from it is explored. Only if a dead end is reached does the system return to the most recent choice-point and try a different arc. This method is easy to implement but can be dangerous in that the system may spend a long (or infinite!) time fruitlessly exploring a hopeless path. A variation on this method, called *bounded depth-first* search, sets a limit on the depth to which exploration is allowed.

Breadth-first search is another systematic but blind method. Here all the arcs from a node are explored before one moves on to explore any arcs from the new nodes encountered. The advantage of this method is that it is guaranteed to find a solution by the shortest path (if one exists), but it can be computationally expensive, especially if each node is bushy, i.e., has many arcs coming out of it. These systematic but blind methods can be applied to either state space representations or problem reduction.

Most systems are limited by either time or space constraints to explore only a portion of the search space, choosing only certain of the alternatives available. Such systems depend on knowledge of the problem domain to decide what might be promising lines of development. They will have some measure of the relative merits either of the different nodes or of the available operators to guide them. Search that is so guided is called *heuristic* search. The methods used in such search are called *heuristics*. These terms often carry the connotation of inexactness and fallibility and are contrasted with algorithms, which are bound to work. Again, both state space search and problem reduction search can be conducted using heuristics.

1.4. GRAPHS AND TREES

Some of the above discussion may give the impression that the search space of nodes and arcs is a preexisting artifact that the program explores. Occasionally this is true, but in most cases the problem-solving program explores the space by "growing" it as it goes. Thus, it is often reasonable to picture a problem-solving program as if it were a walker, without a map but with a notepad, searching for a particular village in a maze of country roads. As the search proceeds, the traveler keeps a record of which roads and villages have already been encountered but can have no foreknowledge of what lies ahead.

By choosing one node in the graph as a starting point (whether working forward or backward) and by applying the available operators, the program grows a solution *tree* rather than a graph. That is, each node explored points back to one node only, the one from which it was produced. The production of a tree rather than a graph makes it straightforward to extract a solution path, traced from the node representing the solution back to the starting node. Depending on the particular problem and on the way the program is implemented, this tree may or may not contain the same node at different points. Reencountering a node during search indicates that the program has found a loop in the search space. For example, if this happens while solving

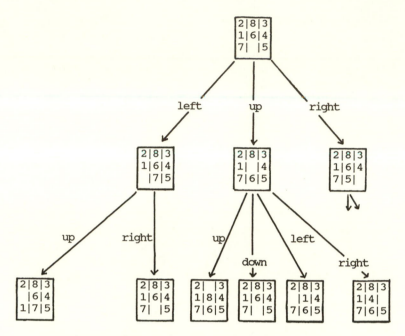

FIGURE 1. Portion of the search tree for the 8-puzzle.

the 8-puzzle, it means that the program has found a set of moves that takes it to exactly the same position as has been met before.

In Figure 1 each node represents the state of the eight tiles in the 8-puzzle. The operators are named "left," "right," "up," and "down" and correspond to "moving" the blank space in the frame in the direction named by the operator. It may seem silly to think in terms of moving a nonexistent blank, but it is just this kind of adjusted perspective on a problem that often provides the crucial leverage.

The properties of a desirable solution will vary with the type of problem. For some, any solution will do; for others, only the least-cost, or shortest-path, solution is wanted. In others again, it may be desired to find a solution with as little computation as possible whether or not that solution turns out to be cheap to implement. Different kinds of heuristics will be needed to allow for these different situations.

2. STATE SPACE REPRESENTATION

In this section we describe an algorithm that will search the OR graphs associated with state space problems. The method is based on the graph traverser developed by Doran (1968) and his colleagues. Note that the discussion is now concerned with a method for searching rather than the properties of the space being searched.

2.1. THE GRAPH TRAVERSER

A general algorithm for solving state space problems involves maintaining two lists of nodes, named TRIED and UNTRIED. TRIED holds the nodes that have already been visited—that is, those nodes to which all the relevant operators have been applied. UNTRIED holds the nodes yet to be explored. Search is controlled by the way that new nodes are added to UNTRIED. UNTRIED is maintained as an ordered list and the algorithm always picks the first node on it as the next one to explore. So everything depends on way that this list is ordered and the way that new nodes are inserted into it.

It is also assumed that a node representing a state of the problem includes a pointer back to its parent node and also, for some problems, the numerical worth of the state.

Recall the analogy of the traveler in the maze of roads. For the sake of this example, every road junction is given a name and at each junction there is a signpost displaying the names of junctions immediately ahead down each of the roads. We should imagine that the traveler is trying to find a particular road junction. The list TRIED holds the names of the junctions that the traveler has already visited, and the list UNTRIED holds the names of junctions that the traveler has noted from the signposts but has not yet actually visited. The analogy breaks down if pushed too far, especially in the case of breadth-first search, as we shall see.

Search starts with the list TRIED empty and the list UNTRIED containing a single node representing the initial state of the problem. Search continues until either the goal node is encountered or the list UNTRIED is empty, indicating that there are no more possibilities to be explored. At each stage a node is taken from the list UNTRIED, the nodes that it connects to are placed back in the list UNTRIED and the node itself is moved to the list TRIED.

In the next section we show how changing the way that new nodes are inserted into the list UNTRIED in the above algorithm produces either blind or heuristic search. For example, if the nodes immediately leading from the current node are placed at the beginning of UNTRIED, then we get depth-first search; if they are placed at the far end, we get breadth-first search; and if they are placed in order of our best guess about their merit (to be explained), then we get heuristic search.

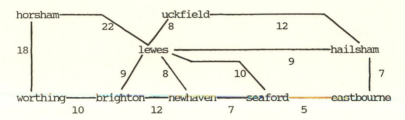

FIGURE 2. Simple map to be searched.

2.2. BLIND SEARCH

Let us apply the graph traverser to demonstrate a variety of blind search techniques. Imagine that the problem is to find a route from one town to another given only local information about how towns are interconnected. The map in Figure 2 shows a fragment of such a network. We must emphasize that the program cannot "see" this overall view of the map (as you can) and must work simply with information about which town is connected to which town. Imagine that the problem is to find a route from Brighton to Hailsham. Our representation for a state of the problem can simply be a three-element structure containing the name of the town we are currently exploring, the number of arcs traversed so far from the start, and the name of the town we have just come from, e.g.,

[lewes 1 brighton]

It is useful to include the third element—i.e., town just come from—in order to be able to reconstruct the route back to the start from the goal if need be, in this case Brighton. The number of arcs traversed so far is used to control the search process. In the example, Lewes is 1 arc away from Brighton, the starting town for the current problem. A starting state could be represented as follows, where "start" is a dummy town name

[brighton 0 start]

Expanding a node or state such as [lewes 1 brighton] involves determining a list of all the towns that are connected to Lewes, with the number of arcs increased by 1, and the pointer back set to Lewes—e.g., the expansion of [lewes 1 brighton] is

[[horsham 2 lewes][uckfield 2 lewes][newhaven 2 lewes]
[seaford 2 lewes][hailsham 2 lewes][brighton 2 lewes]]

Notice that we have included the road back to Brighton, although it makes no sense to go straight back to Brighton having just come from there. There will have to be a loop-detecting mechanism to make sure that the system does not fruitlessly search in circles.

2.2.1. Breadth-First Search

In breadth-first search all the nodes at a particular distance from the start node (measured in number of arcs) are explored before exploring nodes further away. That is, "siblings" of a node are dealt with before "children." In the example based on Brighton, then, all the nodes immediately reached from Brighton are checked to see if any of them are Hailsham. Then each of these nodes (Lewes, Worthing, Newhaven) are themselves explored, and so forth, gradually moving further out from Brighton one arc at a time in each possible direction until Hailsham is encountered (rather quickly in this tiny example!).

To produce this method of search in the graph traverser, list UN-TRIED should have states with a low value for the number of arcs placed earlier on it than states with a high value. In this example it is as if we trace out the repercussions of traversing each arc from the start, then each arc from the towns that we reach, gradually moving outward one arc at a time. It is a little difficult to sustain the analogy of the single traveler used earlier. We have to think of the traveler being able to clone himself or herself at each node and each clone exploring the next arc (and producing further clones). The advantage of this strategy is that if the goal can be reached at all, the path from it back to the start is guaranteed to consist of the smallest possible number of arcs. The disadvantage is that, for large search spaces, very many states may have to be explored in order to reach this happy conclusion, and so the lists TRIED and UNTRIED may grow very large. In Figure 3 showing breadth-first search, the set of arcs "a," "b," "c" is produced before any of the arcs "d," "e," "f," "g." Whether arc "a" is produced before arc "b," or arc "d" before arc "e," is not important for our current purposes.

2.2.2. Depth-First Search

In depth-first search the "first child" of each node is explored first. We can arrange this by making sure that states with a high value for

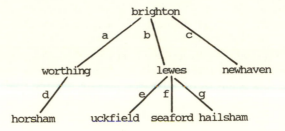

FIGURE 3. Breadth-first search.

the number of arcs traversed so far are placed early in UNTRIED. In the Brighton example this would involve choosing one of the arcs from the start, then one of the arcs from the resultant town, then one of the arcs from there, and so on, moving further and further away from the start on each expansion.

The advantage of depth-first search is that we might strike it lucky and quickly hit upon the town we seek. The disadvantage is that we may explore fruitless paths. Obviously, in the tiny example used these distinctions are academic, but in a large search space the issue becomes much more important.

In Figure 4, depth-first search causes Horsham to be checked next after Worthing (i.e., arc "b" after arc "a"), and only later is Lewes checked (arc "c").

2.2.3. Bounded Depth First

It is easy for depth-first search to explore a hopeless path forever. To control this, a depth limit is sometimes set. This can be incorporated into the state expansion process so that if the state it is given is already at the maximum depth, no further states are yielded.

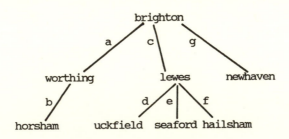

FIGURE 4. Depth-first search.

2.2.4. Uniform Cost

So far we have assumed that all arcs are of equal value or cost. In many situations, including the current example, this is not the case. Here it is reasonable to regard each arc as labeled with a distance, representing the distance between towns. We could then seek the shortest distance between two towns, for example, rather than just seeking any linking route. The representation of states could be changed so that rather than storing the number of arcs traversed so far, it stores the total distance traveled so far. The expansion process should then be changed so that it computes the total distance traveled from the start for each new state rather than the total number of arcs, so that for example, expanding (see Figure 2)

[lewes 9 brighton]

would yield on expansion

[[horsham 31 lewes][uckfield 17 lewes][newhaven 17 lewes]
[seaford 19 lewes][hailsham 18 lewes][brighton 18 lewes]]

This indicates that Horsham is 31 miles via Lewes from the starting point, Brighton, and Uckfield is 17 miles away. Note that Brighton is 18 miles from Brighton going via Lewes! A uniform cost strategy to find the goal of, say, Eastbourne tries Uckfield or Newhaven before Horsham (say) simply because these two towns yield the shortest distance so far (and it uses the naive principle that whatever route is shortest so far ought to be the first to be tried). The program has no knowledge of the topology and thus no particular reason to believe that Uckfield or Newhaven is any closer to Eastbourne than Horsham is. Uniform cost search can be achieved by placing nodes on UNTRIED in the order of their distance from the start. Notice that this method does not make any estimate of the direction or distance of the goal. But, like breadth-first search, it is bound to find the shortest route (in miles) if one exists, though it may take a long time to find it if the search space is large.

2.3. HEURISTIC SEARCH

When we search for a route between two cities on a map, we do not follow one of the unintelligent, systematic, blind methods described above. Rather we bring other information to bear that cuts down the amount of search. For example, we might select the next intermediate city if it seems to be in the right general direction of the goal. The search methods described earlier all relied only on information about how far an intermediate node was *from the start node.* Heuristic methods require not only this but also information about *distance to the goal.* Where this distance can be estimated exactly little or no search need be done because it will be clear how best to proceed. In general, this will not be the case, and we have to make the best estimate we can in the circumstances.

The basic idea is that the value associated with a node should be based on the estimated total distance to the goal via that node. In the map-searching example the estimated distance to the goal could be inferred approximately either by looking up the straight-line distances between the towns or by computing them via their map coordinates.

If such calculation is possible, we then arrange for the node expansion process to estimate the distance yet to go and include this as part of the representation of the state. New nodes are placed on UNTRIED in the order determined by this estimated distance, so that it will be the node that seems to be nearest to the goal that is expanded next. This is known as *best-first* search. The function that computes the worth of a node is called an *evaluation function.*

The above method thus uses heuristics to decide which node to expand next. That is, there is no guarantee that the estimate of distance yet to go is accurate. For example, using tables of straight-line distances may be a bad idea when searching for shortest road routes through mountainous country.

Heuristics can be applied to other parts of the search process, for example, by deciding not to expand certain nodes on the basis of global information. In our examples we have always assumed that if a node could be expanded, then *all* the available operators should be used, so producing all the children of the node. A more selective method might decide that some operators look more promising than others and only apply the more (or the most) promising ones. The ones not selected could be returned to later if need be. This is called partially expanding a node and was the method adopted in the original graph traverser program.

2.3.1. A* Algorithm

An evaluation function based on an accurate measure of the distance to the node in question plus an underestimate of the distance still to go leads to a search method called the A* algorithm.

In this method the evaluation function computes the sum of the distance from the start to the node in question plus an estimate for the remaining distance to the goal. That is

$$\text{value(node)} = \text{dist\_from\_start(node)} + \text{est\_dist\_to\_goal(node)}$$

Here the evaluation function applied to a node estimates the distance between the start and the goal for the path passing through that node.

There is an important result in search theory that depends on the way we estimate the distance still to go. This is that if we always *underestimate* the distance still to go, then search will find the shortest route if one exists. Clearly the most radical underestimate of distance still to go is to set it to zero. In this case the computed value of a node is just its distance from the start and the search method is equivalent to breadth first or uniform cost.

The more accurately we can estimate the distance still to go, while always returning an underestimate, the more focused the search will be and the fewer nodes explored.

2.3.2. Bidirectional Search

As search moves out from the start node the resultant search tree grows ever more branches. For instance, if each node has 3 children, then there will be 3 children (of the start node), 9 grandchildren, 27 great-grandchildren, and so on. We may be able to control this increase somewhat if we are in the fortunate (and unusual) position of being able to focus the search through the use of a clever evaluation function. Starting from the goal and trying to find a path back to the start has the same problem in that the further one moves back, the more nodes there are to consider. Some programs have tried to reduce the total number of nodes to be considered by simultaneously working forward from the start and backward from the goal in the hope of meeting somewhere in the middle. There are then two search trees being generated, but since each is likely to be half the depth of a single tree reaching from start to goal (or vice versa), for fewer nodes should be needed to be explored. Such methods have had limited success in that the two trees do not necessarily meet in the middle but only near either the goal or the start, thus partly nullifying the value of the method.

3. PROBLEM REDUCTION REPRESENTATION: AND/OR GRAPHS

In a problem reduction representation each of the available operators that might be applied to the problem description split (or reduce) the problem into several simpler (it is hoped) subproblems. Further operators are applied to reduce these subproblems until only trivial sub-sub . . . subproblems remain that can be solved immediately without further reduction.

Integrating a mathematical expression can be considered as an example of this process and can be pictured as an and/or graph. The "or" branches indicate alternative possibilities (i.e., more than one operator might apply to that particular part of the problem). The "and" branches represent the fact that the problem has been split and that *all* the subproblems have to be solved independently in order to solve the main problem.

3.1. BLIND SEARCH

Blind, systematic, and exhaustive methods can be applied to problem reduction representations just as they can to state space representations. Such methods suffer from much the same drawbacks as have already been discussed, with an extra overhead in that rather more information needs to be stored. The graph-traverser algorithm described in the previous section can be modified to suit and/or graphs.

3.2. HEURISTIC SEARCH

Where search spaces are large, blind exhaustive methods are inapplicable and further information needs to be exploited to guide the search process. Heuristics can be used to guide the choice of operators at each possible "or" branch to increase the likelihood that an overall solution will be found. Where an optimal solution is required (rather than simply any solution, so long as it is arrived at quickly) some kind of definition of optimality must be made. Now a solution path will be an and/or tree rather than simply a linear list of operators as derived in a state space search. So, either the cost of such a tree could be defined in terms of the longest path in the tree from root to tip, or it could be defined in terms of the total number of arcs in the tree. This provides two different measures of optimality. We might use the former if we had a system that could undertake certain subgoals in parallel and we were interested in finding a solution that had the fastest execution time, since this time would be dominated by total length of the tree. The latter might be better when we have to take account of the cost of every arc traversed in the solution.

As with state space search, an evaluation function can be employed to guide the choice of operator based on some kind of estimate of the "distance" or cost yet to go to the solution. Again, so long as the estimate of the cost of the solution of the remaining part of the problem is underestimated, an algorithm similar to the A* algorithm can be found that is guaranteed to find the least cost solution.

3.3. MEANS/ENDS ANALYSIS

And/or graphs can be searched either forward or backward, so in principle bidirectional search is possible as in state space representations. Means–ends analysis can be considered as a variant on bidirectional search inasmuch as it explicitly compares the current state of the problem with the final desired state and notes any differences. Each difference is then used to guide the choice of operator that might reduce this difference and thus take the problem nearer to a solution. This method was employed in the General Problem Solver (GPS; Ernst & Newell, 1969), an early and highly influential AI program. Other chapters in this collection comment on the psychological plausibility of this general-purpose problem-solving method. Of course, for any class of problems the system has to be primed with the appropriate table of differences and their associated, preferred operators.

The efficiency of this method depends on the accuracy with which an operator can be linked to a difference and the likelihood that application of such an operator will not introduce more differences than it removes. Typically, search will still need to be undertaken because the linking between a difference and its preferred operators can only be advisory, and any choice may have to be undone in the light of later events.

4. PLANNING

Planning systems form that class of problem solvers whose "problem" is to construct some sequence of actions to achieve a stated goal. Typically, this consists of a sequence of robot movements or manipulations intended to build some structure or mechanism. Clearly, some of the examples of problem-solving systems we have already considered fall into this category. Thus, an unexecuted solution to the 8-puzzle is an ordered sequence of tile moves, i.e., a plan. However, knowledge-based planning systems normally tackle more complex domains than this and employ methods that go beyond those already described.

The process of constructing a coherent sequence of actions will usually require search as first one possibility is evaluated and then another, so many of the techniques described earlier are employed in the planning systems discussed below.

1. The actions that may be incorporated into plans will have both more complex preconditions and more complex effects than simply moving a tile in a frame.
2. Actions may interfere with each other in a variety of ways; e.g., one action may make a subsequent action impossible to perform because it undoes some precondition or it consumes some resource (e.g., time, tools, or materials) needed by later actions.
3. The system may search not in a space of states of the world (as in the 8-puzzle) but in a space of states of partial plans. Such systems move "up" a level, but they may still exploit any of the problem-solving methods, considered earlier, at this higher level. "Moves" in the space now correspond not to actions that will later be executed but to refinements of a current partial plan of actions into a new partial plan. For example, such a refinement may not introduce any new action to the partial plan but may consist of a reordering of the actions already considered. Furthermore, the partial plan may be constructed not in terms of eventual actions but in much higher-level terms, which only further consideration and refinement will turn into potentially executable actions.

This kind of metalevel reasoning enables an intelligent analysis by the system of, for example, undesirable interactions between actions and their elimination, consideration of the plan at different levels of abstraction, and so on.

Historically, AI planning systems have frequently exercised their skills in the apparently simple "blocks world," where the goal is to achieve some spatial configuration of blocks via an actual or simulated robot that can push, pull, lift, and generally manhandle single blocks. There have been three good reasons for this focus on an apparently impoverished domain. First, crucial issues such as goal interactions are highlighted. Second, working in a simple domain has allowed progress where a full frontal attack on a complex domain would not. Third, working in a simple domain provides some help in separating out the general domain-independent issues (which can be reapplied elsewhere) from issues that are specific to that class of problems.

Where real robots manipulating real objects are concerned, extra complexity is introduced by unexpected side effects of actions (e.g., knocking into something), by failure to complete actions successfully (e.g., dropping a block that was to be stacked or failure to get a bolt started in a tapped hole), or by third parties who make unforeseen changes to the robot's environment.

Recent AI systems have attempted to move beyond hypothetical blocks worlds to plan in more realistic industrial/commercial settings where issues of plan monitoring, real physical constraints and tolerances, or time and resource management issues become much more important. We are also beginning to see the gap narrowing between what are essentially the qualitative reasoning approaches of AI and the more traditional numerically based methods of operations research.

This section simply provides a broad overview of the issues. For more detailed discussion the reader should consult the texts referred to at the start of this chapter or read Tate (1985), which provides an excellent short summary of all the main issues.

4.1. THEOREM-PROVING APPROACHES

It is possible to pose the problem of finding a plan in theorem-proving terms. In this approach, the "givens" are the current state of the world, the "to prove" is the desired state, and each individual step in the proof corresponds approximately to an action that might be carried out. The goal is to construct a proof demonstrating that the final desired state is indeed reachable, via a sequence of legal moves, from the original state. In some ways this is rather like an algebraic proof that a certain expression is indeed derivable from some other expression.

Theorem-proving methods generally introduce variables that stand for objects in the world as well as variables that stand for situations of the world. The axioms (or "givens") of such a system state the relations that hold between states of the world and actions that effect those states. Logical implication is used to represent the way that one state can be derived from a preceding state. The theorem to be proved usually consists of a statement about the relations that are required to hold in the world state that the plan is expected to achieve. The system then exploits its inference mechanism(s), typically resolution, to determine a plan to achieve this desired state. The plan will typically contain a nested sequence of functions where each function corresponds to a single action in the plan. It will show how the final desired state can be "derived" from the initial state via a sequence of actions.

Using such methods, an initial state (i.e., "state-1") might be something like on(block-*a*, table,state-1) & on(block-*b*, block-*a*,state-1) &

clear(block-*b*,state-1)

with a final state ("state-*X*") such as

on(block-*a*,table,state-*X*) & on(block-*b*, table,state-*X*) &

clear(block-*a*,state-*X*) & clear(block-*b*,state-*X*)

"State-*X*" is the final state. The intended meaning of an expression such as "on(block-*a*, table,state-1)" is that a block named "block-*a*" is resting on the "table" in "state-1," the starting state. The intended meaning of "clear(block-*b*, state-*X*)" is that the top of "block-*b*" is free of obstructions in state-*X*, the final state.

A suitable inference rule might be that in any state if a block is on another block and the first block is clear (i.e., it has nothing on top of it), then a new state is possible in which the first block is lifted up by the robot ·prior to be being placed elsewhere.

Such an approach is powerful in the sense that the full expressive power of (say) predicate calculus is available to express starting and desired states as well as effects (and noneffects, see later) of actions. The drawback is that search spaces are usually large and, unless metalevel reasoning is used, such systems tend to conduct their search for a proof of the theorem at a single level, thus exacerbating the combinatoric issues. Detailed examples of this approach are given in Nilsson (1980) and Kowalski (1979).

4.2. STRIPS-like Systems

STRIPS-like systems are less expressive than full predicate calculus but generate much smaller search spaces. In such systems each action that may form part of a plan is expressed as an operator. Such an operator has a set of preconditions (i.e., an expression of what must be true in the world in order that the operator may be applied), an "add list" (i.e., a list of facts that are made true by the application of the operator), and a "delete list" (i.e., a set of facts about the world that will no longer be true once the operator has been applied).

Pickup is an example of such an operator

PICKUP *x*
preconditions: block(*x*), handempty, clear(*x*), on (*x,y*).
delete list: on(*x,y*), handempty.
addlist: holding(*x*), clear(*y*).

The operator refers to variables x, y that will be bound to whatever objects are relevant at the time the operator is to be applied. We can read such an operator as saying that the robot can pick up an x if it is a block and if it is clear of other objects and if its hand is empty. Once it is picked up, the robot is then holding x, the object that was supporting x is now clear, the robot hand is no longer empty, and x is no longer on top of what it was before. The operator also assumes that y will be clear after the operator is applied—an unwarranted assumption if a block can support more than a single block directly on its upper surface.

The underlying representational assumption in such systems is that facts that are not explicitly deleted using the "delete list" of an operator are presumed to remain true after the application of that operator. This crucial simplification reduces the search space, but it is only reasonable for rather simple, "loosely coupled" worlds—i.e., where interactions between objects and between actions and objects can be predicted and stated easily and exactly. In the predicate-calculus-based systems, mentioned earlier, it is necessary to provide "frame axioms" that explicitly state which aspects of the world are unaffected by each action (these extra axioms help to enlarge the already extensive search spaces associated with unguided theorem-proving methods).

A STRIPS-like system is supplied with a set of facts that denotes the initial state of the world and a second set of facts (which may contain existentially quantified variables) that denotes the desired state of the world. The planning system searches through its repertoire of operators in the attempt to find a sequence of application that will transform the first set of facts into the second. The constraint is that each operator in the sequence can be applied only if its preconditions are met. Thus, some operators will play a facilitating role in the plan by getting the world into a suitable state where some more crucial operator can apply. In the example given above, it may be necessary to apply other operators in order to clear the top of a block so that the robot can lift and stack it elsewhere.

Given such a representation, the search for a suitable operator sequence may be conducted in a variety of ways. The system may reason forward from the initial state, reason backward from the final state, or apply means–ends analysis in the attempt to reduce the difference between the initial and goal state. Reasoning backward using operators requires the system to determine what conditions would be needed in order that a particular operator could be applied. This in its turn leads to the generation of subgoals that consist of operator sequences whose role is to make true the preconditions of the given operator.

Theorem-proving techniques may still be employed, not so much to derive the plan directly but to reason about states of the world. For example, these techniques may determine that a particular hypothesized intermediate state of the world is impossible (e.g., that the robot's hand is both empty and grasping something) or may compute more complex descriptive relations about the world from simpler ones (e.g., that if block A is directly on top of block B, it is "above" it).

Where there is more than a single goal to achieve, there is always the possibility that achieving one goal may interfere in some way with the achievement of the other. In the easier cases these "goal interactions" can be resolved by dealing with the goals in an appropriate order (e.g., obtaining the ingredients before cooking the meal). In harder cases achieving one goal precludes achieving the other (e.g., eating one's cake and having it).

The original STRIPS system (Fikes & Nilsson, 1971) had only a limited ability to cope properly with goal interactions such as occur when trying to change the world of Figure 5a into that of Figure 5b.

The goal state could be expressed as

$$on(A,B) \ \& \ on(B,C)$$

The STRIPS system was called "linear" because it worked on the assumption that the subgoals of a problem could be tackled independently (and thus, for example, in the order in which they happen to be given in the goal state) and their interactions ignored. However, if the system starts working on the goal "on(A,B)" first, it can be achieved by taking "C" off "A" and then placing "A" on "B." Now it starts on the second goal of achieving "on(B,C)." In order to do this it must remove "A" from on top of "B" (the standard constraint being that only one block can be grasped and moved at a time) and then place "B" on top of "C." Thus, dealing with the second goal undoes the actions that achieve the first goal.

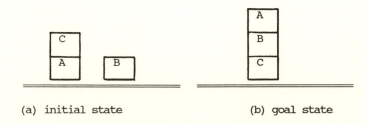

(a) initial state   (b) goal state

FIGURE 5. A problem involving goal interaction.

Doing things in the other order is no better and leads to the same kind of difficulty (i.e., placing "B" on "C" as the first move in order to achieve the second of the two goals). The problem could be solved by STRIPS but the plan would contain redundant actions.

What is needed is a more global view of the task, one that makes less immediate commitment to a particular order of actions and can reason about such interactions. This example shows only a very simple interaction in a very simple world, but it is symptomatic of the kinds of difficulty faced by planning systems.

Notice that STRIPS-like systems are essentially concerned with a search through a space of states of the world. Each operator in the eventual plan transforms the world in some way that takes it closer to the desired goal state. Such systems can be refined in a number of ways. One is to have the system record useful "sequences" of operators that achieve some standard configuration and then search for such configurations and employ these "macrooperators" as a way of reducing later search spaces. A more important refinement is to make the planner search through a space of partial plans rather than through a space of states of the world to be operated on by the plan. This move up to the metalevel can dramatically reduce the size of the search space.

4.3. HIERARCHICAL AND NONLINEAR PLANNERS

Hierarchical planners consider the planning problem at a number of different levels, which are ordered either by difficulty or by generality. Such systems try to plan for the most difficult goal first or the most wide-ranging goal, only moving "down" a level once the most difficult part or the most general part of the problem is solved. For example, consider the problem of planning a complex journey to another country. It is obviously more sensible to consider global issues about (say) flight times before worrying about the more contingent details of how one will get to the airport in time for the flight. STRIPS-like systems (and early predicate-calculus-based systems) tended to treat all actions as equally important and might spend fruitless time considering plans for how to get to the airport before dealing with flight times. If consideration of the problem at this higher level shows that it is impossible, failure can be reported earlier before effort is wasted on the details. Furthermore, if the system can form a partial plan that successfully deals with the problem at some level of generality, it can then move down a level and try to incorporate the new details into the already partially specified plan. Some systems allow reconsideration of the more global levels if failures of planning are encountered at the detailed stages.

A second way of reasoning about plans rather than reasoning about world states is employed by those "nonlinear" planners that adopt a "least commitment" approach concerning the ordering of actions within a plan (see, e.g., the Noah system, Sacerdoti, 1977). A partial plan may contain several actions that need to be carried out but without (as yet) committing the plan to a particular sequence for those actions. An example would be the plan needed to achieve the world state shown in Figure 5, considered earlier. Special mechanisms ("critics" in the Noah system) are used to transform the partial ordering into a particular sequence. Such methods can themselves be applied hierarchically first to the most general or difficult actions and then at each succeeding level of detail.

The metalevel reasoning described above does not solve all the problems. Indeed, it shifts them "up" a level in the hope that the search space in the metalevel is smaller than that at the action level and that guidance derived from metalevel considerations will radically constrain exhaustive searches at lower levels. However, where there are a number of alternative ways that a partial plan might be adjusted, the system will still have to make some choice, and recover from that choice if it turns out to be misconceived. In other words, there is still a search problem. Various mechanisms beyond those so far described have been employed, such as dependency-directed backtracking and reason maintenance systems (also known as truth maintenance systems). Both these mechanisms explicitly store links between conclusions and the assumptions on which they are based so that the repercussions of later evidence can be sensibly exploited (e.g., if a wrong choice turns out to have been made, the system can reason about exactly why the choice was wrong, rather than systematically searching all alternative earlier choices in the expectation that one of these must have been the wrong one). For a review of these issues and an analysis of the computational complexity of "planning," the reader is referred to Chapman (1987).

5. CONCLUSIONS

This chapter has attempted to give a sense of the kinds of issues that have concerned a strictly AI approach to problem solving and planning. These have included state space and problem reduction methods, blind and heuristic search, goal interactions, and metalevel reasoning. This chapter has made virtually no reference to human problem solving and planning, which are dealt with in other chapters in this collection, though it might be noted that the AI techniques described have been applied specifically to the issue of modeling human problem solving (e.g., GPS) and (to an extent) human planning (e.g., Wilensky, 1983).

ACKNOWLEDGMENTS. I thank Allan Ramsay and Ken Gilhooly for critical comments on an earlier draft of this paper.

6. REFERENCES

Amarel, S. (1981). On representations of problems of reasoning about actions. In B. L. Webber & N. J. Nilsson (Eds.), *Readings in knowledge representation.* Los Altos, CA: Tioga.

Barr, A., & Feigenbaum, E. A. (1981). *The handbook of artificial intelligence* (Vol. 1). Los Altos, CA: William Kaufmann.

Chapman, D. (1987). Planning for conjunctive goals. *Artificial Intelligence, 32*(3), 333–377.

Charniak, E., & McDermott D. (1985). *Introduction to artificial intelligence.* Reading, MA: Addison-Wesley.

Doran, J. (1968). New developments of the graph traverser. In E. Dale & D. Michie (Eds.), *Machine intelligence* (Vol. 2). Edinburgh: Oliver and Boyd.

Ernst, G., & Newell, A. (1969). *GPS: A case study in generality and problem solving.* New York: Academic Press.

Fikes, R. E., & Nilsson, N. (1971). STRIPS: A new approach to the application of theorem proving to problem solving. *Artificial Intelligence, 2,* 189–208.

Kowalski, R. (1979). *Logic for problem solving.* New York: North-Holland.

Nilsson, N. J. (1980). *Principles of artificial intelligence.* Los Altos, CA: Tioga.

Rich, E. (1983). *Artificial intelligence.* New York: McGraw-Hill.

Sacerdoti, E. D. (1977). *A structure for plans and behavior.* New York: Elsevier.

Tate, A. (1985). A review of knowledge-based planning techniques. *Knowledge Engineering Review, 1,* 2.

Wilensky, R. (1983). *Planning and understanding.* Reading, MA: Addison-Wesley.

3

Human Nonadversary Problem Solving

RICHARD E. MAYER

The purpose of this chapter is to examine briefly the nature of human nonadversary problem solving. A related purpose is to determine how an information-processing model of problem solving—inspired by and implemented on computers—can serve as the basis for a theory of human problem solving. The chapter consists of three parts: an introduction, which defines key terms and concepts in human nonadversary problem solving; a body, which explores six major characteristics of human nonadversary problem solving; and a conclusion, which summarizes the implications for a theory of human problem solving.

1. INTRODUCTION

1.1. DEFINITIONS

What is a problem? A problem solver has a problem when a situation is in one state, the problem solver wants the situation to be in a different state, and the problem solver does not know an obvious way to eliminate obstacles between the two states. In short, a problem con-

RICHARD E. MAYER • Department of Psychology, University of California, Santa Barbara, California 93106.

sists of three components: the given state, the goal state, and obstacles that block movement from the given to the goal state.

An important implication of this definition is that a problem always exists relative to the problem solver. Another way to make this point is to say that the same situation may be a problem for one person but not for another person. For example, $3+5=$ _____ is likely not to be a problem for an adult who has a memorized answer; i.e., the adult has no obstacles between the givens and the goal. In contrast, $3+5=$ _____ is likely to be a problem for a young child who has not yet memorized the number facts; the child may use a strategy for deriving the answer, such as reasoning that "I can take 1 from the 5 and give it to the 3. Then, 4 plus 4 is 8."

A distinction can be made between well-defined and ill-defined problems. A well-defined problem has a clearly specified given state, goal state, and operators that may be applied to problem states. For example, solving an algebra equation such as $X+2=4(X-2)$ is a well-defined problem for most adults since they can clearly specify the given state (i.e., the equation), the goal state (e.g., $X=$ _____), and the legal operators (i.e., adding the same number to both sides, adding the unknown to the both sides, etc.). An ill-defined problem lacks a clear specification of one or more of the given state, the goal state, or the operators. For example, writing a chapter on problem solving can be an ill-defined problem because the goal state and the legal operators are not easy to specify.

Another important distinction can be made between routine and nonroutine problems. Routine problems are familiar problems that, although not eliciting an automatic memorized answer, can be solved by applying a well-known procedure. Although the problem solver does not immediately know the answer to a routine problem, the problem solver does know how to arrive at an answer. For example, the problem 888×888 is a routine problem for most adults. In contrast, nonroutine problems are unfamiliar problems for which the problem solver does not have a well-known solution procedure and must generate a novel procedure. For example, suppose you were given a full glass of water and asked to pour out half of the water; if you have never solved a problem like this before, this is a nonroutine problem. (One solution procedure is to tilt the glass until the water line forms a diagonal going from one corner of the top to the opposite corner of the bottom.)

The Gestalt psychologists (Duncker, 1945; Katona, 1940; Wertheimer, 1959) have pointed out that routine problems require "reproductive thinking"—applying already known solution procedures to the initial problem state—while nonroutine problems require "productive thinking"—generating a creative or novel procedure. These authors argue that school tasks tend to emphasize routine problems rather than nonroutine problems, i.e., mechanical thinking rather than creative thinking. This chapter focuses on nonroutine problems, and to some extent on ill-defined nonroutine problems.

What is problem solving? Problem solving is cognitive processing that is directed toward solving a problem. In short, the definition of problem solving consists of three components: (1) Problem solving is cognitive in that it occurs internally in the mind or cognitive system, (2) problem solving is a process in that operators are applied to knowledge in memory, (3) problem solving is directed in that the cognitive activity has a goal (Mayer, 1983).

This definition is broad enough to include many cognitive activities that involve conscious cognitive control, including aspects of learning and remembering, or language comprehension and production. For example, if you were asked to summarize the foregoing paragraph, that would be an act of problem solving. Problem solving is also involved in many nondirect retrieval tasks, such as naming all the states that border Texas. In contrast, many cognitive activities that involve automatic processing or undirected thinking are excluded by this definition. For example, decoding of printed words into sounds is an automatic cognitive process for most adults and hence cannot be considered problem solving. Daydreaming is not problem solving because it does not have a goal (although some scientists have introspected that great insights have come through daydreaming).

This definition of problem solving involves three main theoretical entities: symbols, operators, and control. Symbols are used to represent the initial and goal states of the problem, operators are applied to the various states of the problem to generate new states, and control refers to metacognitive processes such as planning and monitoring a solution procedure.

1.2. TYPES OF PROBLEMS

A major division used to organize this book is a distinction between adversary and nonadversary problems. Adversary problems involve two or more players who compete against one another in a game, such as chess or checkers. Nonadversary problems, such as solving a puzzle or finding a cure for a disease, do not involve competition against opposing players in a game. Orthogonal to the foregoing distinctions between well-defined versus ill-defined problems and routine versus nonroutine problems, the universe of possible nonadversary problems can be broken into several categories: transformation problems, arrangement problems, induction problems, deduction problems, divergent problems.

In transformation problems, an initial state is given, and the problem solver must determine the proper sequence of operators to apply in order to transform the given state through a series of intervening states into the goal state. An example is the Tower of Hanoi problem: Given three pegs (peg A, peg B, and peg C) with a large, medium, and small disk on peg A (with the large on the bottom and the small on top), the goal is to have the three disks on peg C (with the large on the bottom and the small on top), by moving only one disk at a time and never placing a larger disk on top of a smaller disk or moving a larger disk that has a smaller disk on top of it. Algebra equations and water jar problems are other examples.

In arrangement problems, all the elements of the problem are given and the problem solver must determine how to organize the givens in order to satisfy the goal. An example is a matchstick problem (Katona, 1940): Given nine matchsticks, make four triangles. Anagrams and cryptarithmetic are other examples.

In induction problems, a series of instances is given and the problem solver must induce a rule or pattern that describes the structure of the problem. An example is an oddity problem in which you must choose the item that does not belong (Kittel, 1957): *gone start go stop come.* Other examples include series completion and analogy problems.

In deduction problems, premises are given and the problem solver must apply the appropriate rules (e.g., logic) to draw a conclusion. An example is Wason's (1966) card-turning problem: Given four cards with A, D, 4, and 7, respectively, on one side, which ones would you turn over to test the premise "If a card has a vowel on one side, then it has a number on the other side"? Other examples include categorical, linear, and conditional syllogisms.

In divergent problems, the problem solver is given some situation and asked to generate as many possible solutions as possible. An example is the brick problem: List all the possible uses for a brick. Other examples include listing all possible hypotheses for "who done it" in a mystery story.

1.3. ANALYSIS OF PROBLEM SOLVING

Problem solving can be analyzed into two major phases: representation and solution. Representation involves moving from a statement or presentation of the problem in the world to an internal encoding of the problem in memory. More specifically, representation involves

TABLE 1. A Model of Problem Solving

PROBLEM PRESENTATION
—(apply representational processes)→
PROBLEM REPRESENTATION
—(apply solution processes)→
PROBLEM SOLUTION

---

mentally encoding the given state, goal state, and legal operators for a problem. Solution involves filling in the gap between the given and goal states. More specifically, solution involves devising and carrying out a plan for operating on the representation of the problem.

Table 1 summarizes a straightforward analysis of the problem-solving process that could serve as a framework for both human and machine problem solving. The capitalized words represent states and the arrows represent transitions between states. First, the problem-as-presented is converted into some cognitive representation, by applying representational processes to the presented problem. The input to the representational process could be a statement of the problem in words; the output could be a representation of the given state, the goal state, and all legal operators for producing intermediate states. Second, the solution procedures are applied to the cognitive representation, eventually yielding the problem solution.

The representation and solution processes may be analyzed, respectively, as building a problem space and using procedures for searching for a path through the problem space (Newell & Simon, 1972). The input to the solution process is a cognitive description of the problem (including the given state, goal state, intermediate states, legal operators) and the output is a search path (i.e., application of a series of operators) between the given and goal states. The search through the problem space (i.e., the connections among the given, goal, and all intervening states) is controlled by a set of procedures, such as a means–ends analysis strategy.

Can a straightforward information-processing model be applied to human nonadversary problem solving? To answer this question, consider the following problem:

Construct four equilateral triangles using six toothpicks.

According to our model, the first step is to convert the words of the problem into some cognitive representation such as that summarized in the following:

Given: Six sticks on tabletop
Goal: Four equilateral triangles
Operators: Moving sticks around on tabletop

The next step is to apply operators that will convert the given state into the goal state. For example, one frequent attempt is to use four sticks to make a square and then lay the other two sticks as diagonals. Unfortunately, this is an unacceptable solution because the four triangles created by these moves are not equilateral. After spending 5 to 10 minutes on the problem, many problem solvers give up. A correct solution requires that the problem solver use three dimensions rather than just two—that is, the problem solver must change his representation of the problem givens and allowable operators. For example, you can construct a pyramid with one equilateral triangle as a base and three equilateral triangles as sides.

This example points out several challenges to (or constraints on) the straightforward model of problem solving presented in Table 1. First, humans often distort the problem to be consistent with their expectations. For example, a problem solver may encode the term *equilateral triangle* as *triangle*, since most puzzle problems involve general shapes such as square, circle, triangle. Thus, the process of comprehending each of the propositions in the problem-as-presented can involve distorting the problem. Second, humans focus on inappropriate aspects of the problem. For example, a problem solver may make the assumption that the problem must be solved in two-dimensional space rather than in three dimensions. This approach to the problem puts blinders on the problem solver's search for solution. Third, the problem representation changes during problem solving. As the problem solver sees that the problem-as-represented is difficult to solve, the problem solver can change the representation to allow for more kinds of operators, such as moving the sticks in three dimensions or breaking the sticks. Fourth, the problem solver may apply procedures rigidly. For example, if the problem solver has just solved a series of geometry puzzle problems that each involve constructing diagonals, the problem solver is likely to apply a similar procedure in this problem. Fifth, problem solving involves insight, intuition, and creativity. In this problem, some problem solvers may report having "aha" experiences in which the pieces of the problem fit together. Sixth, the control of the problem-solving process is influenced by the problem solver's beliefs about problem solving. A problem solver who believes that all problems are solved within 5 minutes will give up if he or she has not solved the problem within 5 minutes. As you can see, the first three observations focus mainly on representation and the last three focus mainly on solution processes.

The straightforward analysis of problem solving appears to require some modifications in light of these six observations and corresponding research findings. To the extent that findings contradict the straightforward information-processing model, they constitute challenges to applying the model to human problem solving. Similarly, when Gilhooly (1982) compared a simple information-processing model with data from a number of studies on thinking, he concluded that while useful up to a point, it could not cover all the data, and would require replacement by a more elaborate model. The next section examines these six challenges to the model of problem solving summarized in Table 1.

2. CONSTRAINTS ON A MODEL OF HUMAN NONADVERSARY PROBLEM SOLVING

2.1. Humans Systematically Distort the Problem To Be Consistent with Prior Knowledge

When a person is verbally presented with a problem, the first step may be to translate the words of the problem into some internal cognitive representation. The process of going from words to mental representation involves more than straightforward decoding of the words; it also involves using one's prior knowledge. One kind of prior knowledge is knowledge of problem types or what Mayer (1982, 1987) has called "schematic knowledge."

For example, Riley, Greeno, and Heller (1982) asked elementary school children to listen to an arithmetic word problem and then repeat it. Errors in immediate recall may be used to diagnose possible encoding errors. For example, one problem was:

> Joe has three marbles.
> Tom has five more marbles than Joe.
> How many marbles does Tom have?

One of the most common errors in recall was to change a sentence that asserted a relation into a sentence that assigned a value to a variable. For example, when this happened, the second sentence would be recalled as "Tom has five marbles."

Corresponding results have been obtained in adults. Mayer (1982) read a series of algebra story problems to adults and asked them to recall them from memory. For example, one problem was as follows:

> A river steamer travels 36 miles downstream in the same time that it travels 24 miles upstream. The steamer's engines drive in still water at a rate of 12 miles per hour more than the rate of the current. Find the rate of the current.

The most common error in recall was to change relational sentences into assignment sentences. When this happened in the river steamer problem, the second sentence was remembered as "The steamer goes 12 miles per hour in still water."

These kinds of results suggest that humans use schemas for representing sentences in story problems. Apparently, some people do not have as effective schemas for relational sentences as for assignment sentences. Thus, a relation is occasionally encoded as an assignment.

Similarly, humans may have a limited set of schemas for problem types. For example, Riley et al. (1982) identified three types of arithmetic word problems: cause/change problems (such as "Joe has 3 marbles. Tom gives him 5 more marbles. How many marbles does Joe have now?"), combination problems (such as "Joe has 3 marbles. Tom has 5 marbles. How many do they have altogether?"), and comparison problems (such as "Joe has 3 marbles. Tom has 5 more marbles than Joe. How many marbles does Tom have?"). Although all three problem types require the same kinds of arithmetic computation, young children found combination and comparison problems to be more difficult than cause/ change. Results suggested a developmental trend in which students begin by interpreting each problem as a cause/change problem, and eventually learn to discriminate among problem types.

Mayer (1982) and Hinsley, Hayes, and Simon (1977) obtained similar results with older problem solvers. For example, Mayer (1982) found that when students erred in recalling a problem, they tended to change it from an uncommon version to a more typical version of the problem. Hinsley et al. presented an ambiguous problem (about cars driving along intersecting roads) that could be interpreted as a distance-rate-time problem or a triangle problem; when subjects made mistakes they tended to misread information in a problem in a way that was consistent with their schema. For example, one subject who interpreted the problem as a "triangle problem" misread "4 minutes" as "4 miles" and assumed this was the length of a leg of the triangle.

In summary, problem solvers use their prior knowledge—such as schematic knowledge—to guide their interpretation of the presented problem. This process can result in distortions that change the problem to be more consistent with the problem solver's prior knowledge. Distortions in the representational process can lead to the problem solver's working on a problem that is different from the one that was actually presented.

2.2. HUMANS FOCUS ON INAPPROPRIATE ASPECTS OF THE PROBLEM

When a problem is presented in words, a problem solver may represent the givens, goals, and operators in a way that is consistent with the problem statement but which limits the process of problem solution. The problem solver, for example, may place limits on the problem-solving operators that were not part of the problem statement or may define the goal or given state in a narrower way than is necessary.

For example, consider the bird problem presented by Posner (1973, pp. 150–151):

> Two train stations are 50 miles apart. At 2 P.M. one Saturday afternoon two trains start toward each other, one from each station. Just as the trains pull out of the stations, a bird springs into the air in front of the first train and flies ahead to the front of the second train. When the bird reaches the second train it turns back and flies toward the first train. The bird continues to do this until the trains meet. If both trains travel at the rate of 25 miles per hour and the bird flies at 100 miles per hour, how many miles will the bird have flown before the trains meet?

The problem solver may represent the goal of the problem as determining the sum of the distances that the bird flies on each trip between the trains. In contrast, the problem solver may represent the goal of the problem as determining the amount of time the bird flies and then converting that to a measure of miles flown. The former representation leads to much difficulty, while the latter makes the problem simple.

As another example, consider the old monk problem presented by Hayes (1978, p. 178):

> Once there was a monk who lived in a monastery at the foot of a mountain. Every year the monk made a pilgrimage to the top of the mountain to fast and pray. He would start out on the mountain path at 6 A.M., climbing and resting as the spirit struck him, but making sure that he reached the shrine at exactly 6 o'clock that evening. He then prayed and fasted all night. At exactly 6 A.M. the next day, be began to descend the mountain path, resting here and there along the way, but making sure that he reached his monastery again by 6 P.M. of that day.

Given this information, your job is to prove or disprove the following assertion: Every time the monk makes his pilgrimage there is always some point on the mountain path, perhaps different on each trip, that the monk passes at the same time when he is climbing up as when he is climbing down.

One way to represent this problem is to think of the monk climbing up from 6 A.M. to 6 P.M. on one day and climbing down from 6 A.M. to 6 P.M. on the next day. In contrast, you could think of the problem as one monk climbing up and one climbing down on the same day, both beginning at 6 A.M. and ending at 6 P.M. Although the for-

mer representation leads to great difficulty, the latter makes clear that
the ascending and descending paths must cross at some time during
the day.

The wording of a problem can affect a problem solver's tendency
to represent the problem in a useful way. For example, Maier and Burke
(1967) found that most subjects missed the following problem:

> A man bought a horse for $60 and sold it for $70. Then he bought it back
> again for $80 and sold it for $90. How much did he make in the horse
> business?

In contrast, all subjects correctly answered the problem when it was
worded as follows:

> A man bought a white horse for $60 and sold it for $70. Then he bought a
> black horse for $80 and sold it for $90. How much money did he make in
> the horse business?

As you can see, when subjects are encouraged to represent the problem as two separate transactions, they perform better than when they
represent it as a series of three transactions on the same horse.

Finally, consider the nine-dot problem, in which you are given nine
dots arranged as below:

```
•   •   •

•   •   •

•   •   •
```

Your job is to draw four straight lines, without lifting your pencil from
the paper, so that each dot is touched by one of the lines.

Adams (1974) suggests that problem solvers represent this problem in a way that creates "conceptual blocks." For example, some
problem solvers represent the problem as saying that the lines cannot
go outside the square, i.e., they create a self-imposed boundary or limit
on acceptable solutions. In contrast, the correct answer requires drawing lines that extend beyond the boundaries of the square. In an important series of experiments summarized by Weisberg (1986), simply
telling problem solvers to go outside the square did not make the problem trivially easy. Thus, helping students not to focus on inappropriate
aspects of the problem does not ensure that they will immediately solve
the problem.

In summary, the initial representation that a problem solver creates can limit the subsequent search process. Thus, initial representation is not a trivial or automatic process, but rather a crucial step that
can affect the solution process. There may be several forms for representing the givens, goals, and operators; each may be consistent with
the problem statement, but some may limit the ensuing search process.

2.3. HUMANS CHANGE THE PROBLEM REPRESENTATION DURING PROBLEM SOLVING

Once a problem has been translated from words into some internal representation, the problem representation does not necessarily remain static during the ensuing problem solution process. As the search process progresses, the problem solver may reformulate the original representation of the problem. Thus, representation and solution are interactive processes that are influenced by one another.

Duncker's (1945) tumor problem provides a classic example of how problem solving requires successive reformulations of the problem. Consider the following problem:

> Given a human being with an inoperable stomach tumor, and rays that destroy organic tissue at sufficient intensity, by what procedure can one free him of the tumor by these rays and at the same time avoid destroying the healthy tissue that surrounds it?

Duncker (1945) presents the thinking-aloud record (or protocol) of a subject who is solving the tumor problem, which is presented in abbreviated form below:

> 1. Send rays through the esophagus.
> 2. Desensitize the healthy tissue by means of chemical injection.
> 3. Expose the tumor by operating.
> 4. One ought to decrease the intensity of the rays on their way; for example—would this work?—turn the rays on at full strength only after the tumor has been reached.
> 5. One should swallow something inorganic (which would allow passage of the rays) to protect the healthy stomach walls.
> 6. Either the rays must enter the body or the tumor must come out. Perhaps one could alter the location of the tumor—but how? Through pressure? No.
> 7. Introduce a cannula.
> 8. Move the tumor toward the exterior.
> 9. The intensity ought to be variable.
> 10. Adaptation of healthy tissue by previous weak application of the rays.
> 11. I see no more than two possibilities: either to protect the body or to make the rays harmless.
> 12. Somehow divert . . . diffuse rays . . . disperse . . . stop! Send a broad and weak bundle of rays through a lens in such a way that the tumor lies at the focal point and thus receives intense radiation.

In this example, Duncker notes that the subject continually changes how he represents the givens and goals of the problem. The subject seems to deal with general or functional representations of the goal before moving on to specific solutions. For example, the subject deals with general goals, such as "avoid contact between rays and healthy tissue," which suggest more specific goals, such as "displace tumor toward surface," which suggest specific solutions, such as "use pressure." The subject seems to move from one general representation to another, including "avoid contact between rays and healthy tissue," "desensitize healthy tissue," and "lower intensity of the rays on their way through the healthy tissue." It is through reformulating this general representation of the goal that the subject comes to represent the goal as "give weak intensity in the periphery and concentrate in the tumor," which leads to the specific solution of "use lens."

According to Duncker, problem solving does not involve applying solution procedures to one's specific representation of the problem. Instead, the problem representation is continually changing, moving from general descriptions of the goal and givens to more specific descriptions. The process of problem solution is not a phase of problem solving that follows neatly after the problem has been represented; instead, problem solution is tied to the process of successively reformulating the problem representation.

2.4. HUMANS APPLY PROCEDURES RIGIDLY AND INAPPROPRIATELY

Once a person has acquired a set of well-practiced procedures, these can be applied to many problems. However, well-learned procedures can be misapplied, i.e., used in situations where they are not appropriate or where they should be modified. Rigidity in problem solving occurs when the problem solver applies well-practiced but inappropriate procedures.

A classic example of rigidity in problem solving comes from the Luchins (1942) water jar problems. Suppose that you are given three empty jars of various sizes and an unlimited supply of water; your job is to use these jars to produce a certain amount of water. For example, if you are given empty jars of 21, 127, and 3 units each and asked to produce 100 units of water, you could fill the 127-jar and scoop out 21 and 3 and 3. If you were given 14, 163, and 25 and asked to produce 99, you could fill the 163 and scoop out 14 and 25 and 25. If you were given 18, 43, and 10 and asked to get 5 you could fill the 43 and scoop out 18 and 10 and 10. If you were given 9, 42, and 6 and asked to get 21, you could fill the 42 and scoop out 9 and 6 and 6. If you were given 20 and 59 and 4, and asked to get 31, you could fill the 59 and scoop out 20 and then 4 and 4. Now, suppose that the next problem is to get 20 units of water using jars of size 23, 49, and 3. Luchins found that most students used the procedure, fill the 49 and subtract 23 and 3 and

3. In contrast, a simplier solution is to fill the 23 and scoop out 3—a procedure used by most students who do not receive the previous five problems. These results suggest that past use of a procedure (such as the $b-a-2c$ procedure for the water jar problems) can blind the problem solver to more efficient, but less frequently used, procedures (such as $a-c$ for the sixth problem).

Another example of rigid application of procedures occurs when students use the keyword approach to solving arithmetic word problems (Briars & Larkin, 1984; Mayer, 1987). In the keyword approach, children add the numbers in a problem when it contains an expression such as "altogether" and subtract the smaller from the larger number in a problem when it contains a word such as "difference." For example, consider the following problem:

> John has 5 marbles. Susan has 3 more marbles than John. How many do they have all together?

A child using the keyword approach would carry out the procedure, 5 plus 3 equals 8. As you can see, blind application of procedures that worked previously in similar situations can lead to errors on new problems.

In summary, automaticity of problem-solving procedures can lead to rigidity in the problem solution process. Although a problem solver may know how to apply a given operator, the problem solver may not know the conditions under which it is or is not appropriate to apply the operator. Humans may tend to select procedures that are familiar, well practiced, or just used in similar problems—even when such procedures are not appropriate.

2.5. HUMANS ARE INTUITIVE AND INSIGHTFUL AND CREATIVE

In some cases, when a problem solver is presented with a novel problem, the problem solver must generate a creative solution. A novel (or nonroutine) problem is one that the problem solver has never seen before, and a creative solution is an action that the problem solver has never used before. Where does a creative solution come from? According to behaviorist theories of problem solving, the problem solver generalizes from a similar problem or engages in random solution attempts (Weisberg, 1986). According to Gestalt theories of problem solving, the problem solver must have insight into the problem, i.e., see how the parts of the problem fit together in new ways (Katona, 1940; Kohler, 1925; Wertheimer, 1959). Thus, for behaviorist theories the same processes are involved in solving routine and nonroutine problems, while for Gestalt theories, nonroutine (or creative) problem solving involves qualitatively different thinking than routine problem solving.

As an example of the role of insight, consider Wertheimer's (1959) parallelogram problem: Given a parallelogram of height h and base b, find the area. If you have already learned the formula for parallelograms, area = height × base, then this problem simply requires a blind application of the rule—what Wertheimer calls "reproductive thinking." In contrast, if you know how to find the area of rectangle but you do not know how to find the area of a parallelogram, then this is a novel problem for you and requires a creative (insightful) solution. One insight is to see that the triangle on one side of the parallelogram can be cut off and placed on the other side, producing a rectangle with sides b and h. Since you know how to find the area of a rectangle, the problem is all but solved. Here, the problem solver has insight into the structure of parallelograms; that is, the problem solver sees the relationship between parallelograms and rectangles. Van Hiele (1986) argues that this kind of problem solving is based on intuitive thinking.

As another example, consider Polya's (1965, p. 2) pyramid problem:

> Find the volume F of the frustrum of a right pyramid with square base, given the altitude h of the frustrum, the length a of a side of its upper base, and the length b of its lower base.

If you do not know the formula for finding the volume of the frustrum of a right pyramid, then this is a novel problem that requires a creative solution. Polya assumes, however, that you do know the formula for finding the volume of a pyramid. One insight is seeing that you could create the full pyramid by adding a smaller pyramid to the top of the frustrum; then, to get the volume of frustrum you could subtract the volume of the smaller pyramid from the volume of the full pyramid.

In summary, these examples point to role that insight plays in creative problem solving. Unfortunately, the Gestalt psychologists and even contemporary Gestalt-inspired theorists (Van Hiele, 1986) do not offer clear definitions of insight. However, these observations give some rationale for supposing that qualitatively different solution processes may be involved in routine versus nonroutine problems. For example, in a recent review, Weisberg (1986) offered a reasonable compromise between a "genius" view—which holds that creative problem solving is a mysterious and unanalyzable process—and the "behaviorist" view—which holds that the same processes are involved in routine and non-routine problem solving; the compromise is that while routine and nonroutine problem solving may be different from one another, both can be studied and analyzed scientifically.

2.6. Humans Let Their Beliefs Guide Their Approach to Problem Solving

Finally, the sixth observation concerns the role of what Schoenfeld (1985a,b) calls "control" of the problem solution process. Humans decide which problems are the ones they should try to solve, which procedures to use, whether the procedures are working or need to be replaced, whether the problem is worth continued attention, etc. One kind of knowledge that affects the control of problem solving is the belief system of the problem solver. Beliefs about problem solving include ideas about what are reasonable ways to solve problems, when it is appropriate to stop working on a problem, etc.

Consider the following problem from Schoenfeld (1983, 1985a,b):

> You are given two intersecting straight lines and a point P on one of them. . . . Show how to construct, with straightedge and compass, a circle that is tangent to both lines and that has the point P as its point of tangency to one of them.

In Schoenfeld's study, no students ever derived a solution to the problem using mathematical proof. Instead, all students used trial-and-error construction; when they were asked why a particular construction works, they responded, "It just does."

Schoenfeld concluded that students believe "proof is worthless for discovery" and thus do not think of using proof even though they are capable of doing so. Schoenfeld (1985b, p. 372) lists three beliefs that many of his students seemed to possess:

> Belief 1: Formal mathematics has little or nothing to do with real thinking or problem solving. Corollary: Ignore it when you need to solve problems.
>
> Belief 2: Mathematics problems are always solved in less than 10 minutes, if they are solved at all. Corollary: Give up after 10 minutes.
>
> Belief 3: Only geniuses are capable of discovering or creating mathematics. Corollaries: If you forget something . . . you won't be able to derive it on your own. Accept procedures at face value, and don't try to understand why they work.

Some other widely held beliefs of mathematical problem solvers (Silver, 1985) are the following: There is always one correct way to solve any mathematical problem; mathematics is not applicable to solving real-world problems; mathematics problems can be solved using only a few basic operations and can always be solved in only a few minutes.

As an example of how specific beliefs affect problem solving, consider the taxicab problem (Kahneman & Tversky, 1973; Shaughnessy, 1985; Tversky & Kahneman, 1980):

> A cab was involved in a hit-and-run accident at night. Two cab companies, the Green and the Blue, operate in the city . . . 85% of the cabs are Green and 15% are Blue. A witness identified the cab as a Blue cab. The court tested his ability to identify cabs . . . the witness made correct identifications in 80% of the cases and erred in 20% of the cases. What is the probability that the cab involved in the accident was Blue rather than Green?

Shaughnessy (1985, p. 404) summarizes a study in which some students say that the probability is 100% that a Blue cab was involved in the accident. One subject "just believed it was a Blue cab"; another subject said, "Oh, the witness was right. It was a Blue cab." These subjects simply do not seem to believe in the concept of probability; for them, events either happen or don't happen.

In summary, the problem solver's beliefs about problem solving can affect the process of problem solution. The persistence of the problem solver, the problem solver's selection of solution procedures, and even the problem solver's decision to approach a certain problem are influenced by the problem solver's beliefs. This observation points out that problem solving involves more than purely cognitive events.

3. CONCLUSION

The foregoing examples have provided some challenges to the straightforward picture of problem solving suggested by the information-processing model. More specifically, these examples have called into question four implicit premises of the information-processing model summarized in Table 1: atomization, componentialization, mechanization, and concretization.

The first premise concerns the atomization of problem-solving elements. In the information-processing approach, the problem is represented as a given state, a goal state, and a set of operators that can produce intermediate states. The atoms in this analysis of the problem are states and actions for transforming states. These can be clearly specified for well-defined problems. However, our examples show that determining the atoms for ill-defined problems is often the crucial part of problem solving rather than the starting point. Further, consistent with the "mental chemistry" theory, the atoms may change as they are combined during the problem-solving processes.

The second premise concerns componentialization of problem-solving processes. In the information-processing approach, problems are first translated into internal representations; then, operators are sequentially applied to create a series of new problem states. However, our examples show that representation and solution are interactive processes; i.e., the problem representation is continually reformulated during the process of problem solution.

The third premise concerns the mechanization of problem solution processes. In the information-processing approach, a problem-solving strategy such as means–ends analysis is used to guide the solution process. This is an algorithm that requires no insight, no invention, no intuition. Yet our examples show that many problems require general strategies that are much less algorithmic and more intuitive than means–ends analysis.

The fourth premise concerns the concretization of problem-solving states. In the information-processing approach, each concrete action results in movement from one concrete state to another. However, our examples have shown that thinking sometimes occurs at a general or a functional level rather than at the level of specific problem states. Problem solvers may sometimes find a functional solution before hitting upon a specific course of action.

Each of these four implicit premises underlying the information-processing approach must be carefully examined in light of our current understanding of human problem solving. It would be convenient if we could use the same framework to describe human and machine problem solving; for example, it would be convenient if an information-processing model inspired by, and implemented on, machines could also be applied to human problem solving. However, this chapter has shown some of the constraints that need to be considered before a unified theory of human and machine problem solving can be created.

ACKNOWLEDGMENT. Preparation of this chapter was supported by Grant MDR-8470248 from the National Science Foundation.

4. REFERENCES

Adams, J. L. (1974). *Conceptual blockbusting*. New York: Freeman.

Briars, D. J., & Larkin, J. H. (1984). An integrated model of skill in solving elementary word problems. *Cognition and Instruction, 1*, 245–296.

Duncker, K. (1945). On problem solving. *Psychological Monographs, 58*(5, Whole No. 270).

Gilhooly, K. J. (1982). *Thinking: Directed, undirected, and creative*. London: Academic Press.

Hayes, J. R. (1978). *Cognitive psychology: Thinking and creating*. Homewood, IL: Dorsey Press.

Hinsley, D., Hayes, J. R., & Simon, H. A. (1977). From words to equations. In P. Carpenter & M. Just (Eds.), *Cognitive processes in comprehension*. Hillsdale, NJ: Erlbaum.

Kahneman, D., & Tversky, A. (1973). On the psychology of prediction. *Psychological Review, 80*, 237–251.

Katona, G. (1940). *Organizing and memorizing*. New York: Columbia University Press.

Kittel, J. E. (1957). An experimental study of the effect of external direction during learning on transfer and retention of principles. *Journal of Educational Psychology, 48*, 391–405.

Kohler, W. (1925). *The mentality of apes*. New York: Harcourt, Brace & World.

Luchins, A. S. (1942). Mechanization in problem solving. *Psychological Monographs, 54*(6, Whole No. 248).

Maier, N. R. F., & Burke, R. J. (1967). Response availability as a factor in problem-solving performance of males and females. *Journal of Personality and Social Psychology, 5*, 304–310.

Mayer, R. E. (1982). Memory for algebra story problems. *Journal of Educational Psychology, 74*, 199–216.

Mayer, R. E. (1983). *Thinking, problem solving, cognition*. New York: Freeman.

Mayer, R. E. (1987). Teachable aspects of problem solving. In D. Berger, K. Pezdek, & W. Banks (Eds.), *Applications of cognitive psychology*. Hillsdale, NJ: Erlbaum.

Newell, A., & Simon, H. A. (1972). *Human problem solving*. Englewood Cliffs, NJ: Prentice-Hall.

Polya, G. (1965). *Mathematical discovery* (Vol. 2). New York: Wiley.

Posner, M. I. (1973). *Cognition*. Glenview, IL: Scott, Foresman.

Riley, M. S., Greeno, J. G., & Heller, J. I. (1982). Development of children's problem-solving ability in arithmetic. In H. Ginsberg (Ed.), *The development of mathematical thinking*. New York: Academic Press.

Schoenfeld, A. H. (1983). Beyond the purely cognitive: Belief systems, social cognitions, and metacognitions as driving forces in intellectual performance. *Cognitive Science, 7*, 329–363.

Schoenfeld, A. H. (1985a). Metacognitive and epistomological issues in mathematical understanding. In E. A. Silver (Ed.), *Teaching and learning mathematical problem solving: Multiple research perspectives*. Hillsdale, NJ: Erlbaum.

Schoenfeld, A. H. (1985b). *Mathematical problem solving*. Orlando, FL: Academic Press.

Shaughnessy, J. M. (1985). Problem-solving derailers: The influence of misconceptions on problem-solving performance. In E. A. Silver (Ed.), *Teaching and learning mathematical problem solving: Multiple research perspectives*. Hillsdale, NJ: Erlbaum.

Silver, E. A. (1985). Research on teaching mathematical problem solving: Some under-represented themes and needed directions. In E. A. Silver (Ed.), *Teaching and learning mathematical problem solving: Multiple research perspectives*. Hillsdale, NJ: Erlbaum.

Tversky, A., & Kahneman, D. (1980). Causal schemata in judgment under uncertainty. In M. Fishbein (Ed.), *Progress in social psychology*. Hillsdale, NJ: Erlbaum.

Van Hiele, P. M. (1986). *Structure and insight*. Orlando, FL: Academic Press.

Wason, P. C. (1966). Reasoning. In B. M. Foss (Ed.), *New horizons in psychology*. Harmondsworth, UK: Penguin.

Weisberg, R. (1986). *Creativity: Genius and other myths*. New York: Freeman.

Wertheimer, M. (1959). *Productive thinking*. New York: Harper & Row.

4

Adversary Problem Solving by Machine

M. R. B. CLARKE

1. INTRODUCTION

Methods of problem solving by machine have been discussed in a previous chapter. In principle, the adversary makes very little difference; adversary problem-solving graphs are just special cases of AND/OR graphs (Nilsson, 1980). Nevertheless specialized techniques have been developed, many of them highly efficient problem-independent search procedures.

Distinction is necessary between cases of two or more adversaries and between situations of perfect and less than perfect information. Chess is a two-person game of perfect information because each state of the game is completely visible to both players; negotiating for a used car is a two-person game of imperfect information; poker and the European Economic Community are n-person games of imperfect information.

In spite of the obvious relevance of adversary problem solving to economic and military strategy, most published work concerns either domain-independent techniques or games and other idealized and unworldly problems. The reason for this is not that the importance of

M. R. B. CLARKE • Department of Computer Science, Queen Mary College, University of London, London E1 4NS, United Kingdom.

real-life problems is unappreciated, rather that it is more productive to study simple problems before complex. Games epitomize most of the issues involved in real-world problem solving without the often irrelevant complications of the real-world environment.

Because of the stimulus provided by organized competition between programs and machines—and also because the game seems to be of about the right complexity to test existing techniques—much of the available literature is about chess, and therefore much of this chapter as well. However, as an experimental setting in which to study adversary problem solving, chess is open to criticism for the comparative complication and inelegance of its rules and apparatus. Supporters of chess as an object of scientific study would say that in practice these are only minor programming inconveniences to be balanced against the deep principles required for good play and lack of mystery that surrounds them. One advantage possessed by games with simpler rules than chess is that they can often be parameterized to provide a natural continuum of difficulty, although the same effect can be achieved to some extent by looking at progressively simpler endgames in chess or small localized problems in Go. Neither chess nor Go can represent situations of uncertainty unless a model of suboptimal opposing play is included.

We start by looking at an area in which considerable progress has been made, that of domain-independent search techniques.

2. SEARCH TECHNIQUES FOR TWO-PERSON GAMES

Human players know that when analyzing a position to decide on a move they look ahead. "If I go there he might go there, I then have to go there and he plays there and wins, so I can't do that. But suppose I play here. . . ." This branching tree of possibilities from the current position is a fundamental notion in machine problem solving.

Figure 1 shows a representation of the analysis process diagrammed, as is the convention, by an inverted tree whose root, at the top, is the current position—P, say. The three branches from P show possible moves to "successor" positions (nodes of the tree) P_1, P_2, P_3. Nodes at which the first player is to move are indicated by squares, with circles for the second player. From P_1 the second player has a choice of moves giving rise to positions P_{11}, P_{12}, P_{13}, etc. In practice, the number of moves in each position (called the branching factor) will vary from node to node, as will the number of moves played (depth) before the game ends. For simplicity suppose that in this case the game

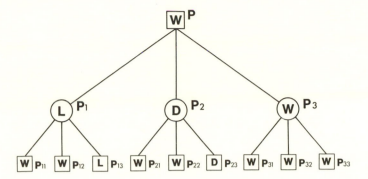

FIGURE 1. Example game tree.

ends after one move on each side, with the result in each case shown from the "square" player's point of view; i.e., P_{11} is a win for "square" and hence a loss for "circle," and so on. Clearly, if P_1 actually arises, then "circle" will choose to move to P_{13}, which is a win for him. Therefore P_1 can be labeled as a loss for "square." Similarly, P_2 is a draw and P_3 is a win, so the actual position P for which this analysis is being carried out is a win for the player to move, and the winning move is to P_3.

Note now that if we assign the value +1 to a win, 0 to a draw, and −1 to a loss for the player to move at P, then we can describe what we have done in terms of maximizing and minimizing. The player to move at P (call her MAX now) always chooses the move that maximizes, the other player (MIN) the move that minimizes the value. This method of deducing the value of P by alternately minimizing and maximizing is the minimax algorithm.

3. MINIMAXING WITH AN EVALUATION FUNCTION

So far we have assumed that we can see ahead to the end of the game, where the tips of the tree are terminal in the sense that the game can go no farther and a definite result has been obtained. But the minimax rule (Figure 2) is equally applicable to numerical values other than +1, 0, −1. Suppose now that we cannot see ahead to the end, but that we can look ahead a certain distance and then rank positions numerically according to how promising they are for MAX. The method is the same. MAX looks ahead to P_1 and then considers each of MIN's moves to P_{11}, P_{12}, P_{13}, P_{11} she values at 10, P_{12} at 11, P_{13} at −4. Clearly, MIN would choose P_{13} value −4, so the value of P_1 with MIN to move is −4;

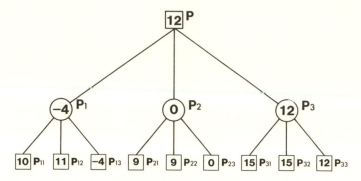

FIGURE 2. Minimaxing.

MAX then "backs up" this value to P as the best that has been achieved so far in the analysis, and starts work on P_2. Eventually P_3 is evaluated at 12, and this is the best that is available to MAX from P, so P is finally evaluated at 12.

Note that this procedure is "depth-first" in that MAX explores all moves from P_1 before looking at any from P_2 and that this enables the value at P to be updated by comparing the value of the ith successor P_i with the best obtained from $P_1 \ldots P_{i-1}$. For the procedure to terminate, there must be some rule for stopping and applying the evaluation function, otherwise the search would go on forever down the leftmost branch, the first to be explored.

4. THE ALPHA–BETA ALGORITHM

The next step toward the search algorithms that are actually used in practice comes with noticing that many of the branches explored by the minimax procedure are redundant in the sense that they cannot affect the value finally returned. Consider part of a search tree, Figure 3a, in which the nodes a and b represent positions already analyzed and labeled with their backed-up values while x and y are positions whose values are not yet completely determined because the tree below the dotted branch at y has yet to be searched. If x is a MAX node we have $x = \max(a, y)$ and $y \leq b$, so if $b \leq a$, then $y \leq a$, and we know that $x = a$ whatever happens down the dotted branch, which can therefore safely be pruned from the tree. This is called a "shallow cutoff." A more subtle argument shows that cutoffs can occur deeper in the tree if information about the best value currently achieved for MAX is carried

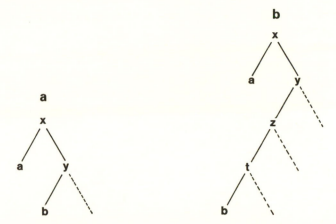

FIGURE 3. Alpha–beta pruning: (a) shallow cutoff; (b) deep cutoff.

forward. Consider Figure 3b, where again a and b are fully determined, while x, y, z, and t are in the process of being evaluated. We now have $x = \max(a,y)$, $y \leq z$, $z \geq t$, $t \leq b$. Suppose $z = t$. Then $z \leq b$, so if $b \leq a$ then $x = a$, and the dotted branch from t can be pruned. On the other hand, if $z > t$ then the branch from z to t could never be chosen. Either way, the dotted branch from t is irrelevant and need not be searched—a "deep cutoff."

The size of the tree that has to be searched in order to calculate the minimax value can therefore be reduced if the current backed-up value is passed down for comparison from each position to its successors, and this value can of course be improved as the search proceeds, leading to more and more cutoffs. Two bounds are required, one for MAX and one for MIN. Traditionally these have been denoted by α and β, and the method of search that utilizes them is known as the alpha–beta algorithm. It was first described by Newell, Shaw, and Simon (1958) and since then has been subjected to intensive refinement and analysis.

With evaluation functions that can be linearly ordered, and hence represented by a single number, the minimax procedure can be expressed more succinctly in negamax form by valuing terminal nodes from the point of view of the side to move and calculating the value of all nonterminal nodes as the maximum of the values of their successors with sign reversed. With this simplification, which avoids treating MAX and MIN nodes separately, the alpha–beta algorithm takes the following simple form, where eval(P) is a function that returns the terminal evaluation of the position P:

```
function evaluate (P: position; α,β:value; d:depth):value;
var v:value;
begin if d = maxdepth then return eval(P)
   else begin generate_successors(P,S);
      for i: = 1 to number_of_successors do
      begin v: = -evaluate (S[i], -β, -α, d + 1);
         if v > α then α = v;
         if α ≥ β then return (α)
         end;
         return (α);
      end;
end;
```

The interval defined by the bounds α and β is called the search window. It can be shown that, if the minimax value of position P is denoted by $mm(P)$, the value $ab(P,\alpha,\beta)$ returned by an execution of evaluate $(P,\alpha,\beta,0)$ satisfies

$$
\begin{array}{ll}
ab(P,\alpha,\beta) <= \alpha & \text{if } mm\ (P) <= \alpha \\
ab(P,\alpha,\beta) = mm(P) & \text{if } \alpha < mm(P) < \beta \\
ab(P,\alpha,\beta) >= \beta & \text{if } mm\ (P) >= \beta
\end{array}
$$

Thus, if maxval denotes some value larger than any terminal evaluation, evaluate $(P, -\text{maxval}, +\text{maxval}, 0)$ is guaranteed to return the minimax value of P while searching in many cases a considerably smaller tree. If every position has exactly n successors, called the branching factor, and the tree is searched to constant depth d, then the minimax procedure clearly evaluates n^d terminal nodes. It can be shown (Slagle & Dixon, 1969) that, with the best possible ordering of successors, the alpha–beta algorithm given above makes, for even d, $2n^{d/2} - 1$ terminal evaluations, or, to put it another way, can search with perfect ordering to nearly twice the depth for the same amount of work as minimax. To illustrate the effect of the cutoffs, Figure 5 shows an example (taken from Baudet, 1978). The negamax tree is as shown in Figure 4.

The alpha–beta algorithm searching the same tree left to right would give the tree shown in Figure 5, where dotted branches and nodes in black represent cutoffs and positions not evaluated. Note that the values backed up to some internal nodes are not the same as with the minimax method, but if a sufficiently large search window is used, the value at the root is correct.

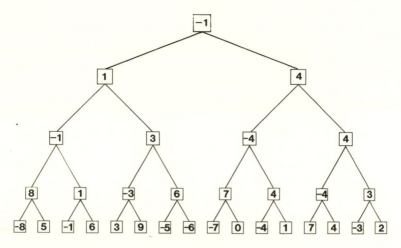

FIGURE 4. Negamax tree.

5. REFINEMENTS OF THE BASIC ALPHA–BETA RULE

In practice, many refinements of the basic alpha–beta algorithm are used, among the most effective being searching with a narrow window, iterative deepening, and the use of transposition tables.

An execution of evaluate $(P,\alpha,\beta,0)$ is guaranteed to return the minimax value of P only if the window (α,β) encloses this value. In theory,

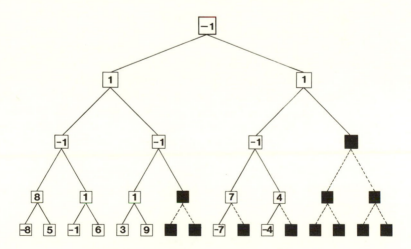

FIGURE 5. Alpha–beta search of tree in Figure 4.

searches that fail high or low should be repeated with a modified window. In practice, it is usually the best move rather than the value that is required, and if only one move fails high it is guaranteed to be the best, while the narrow window gives many more cutoffs that compensate for the occasional ambiguous result and repeated search.

Iterative deepening (Slate & Atkin, 1977) starts from a shallow maximum depth setting, which is increased while time and/or space allow, the main variation from each iteration being used to order branches in the next iteration, again with aim of generating the maximum number of cutoffs. Further refinements can be found in Campbell and Marsland (1983) and Frey (1983).

In many cases the possibility of transposing moves, playing the same moves in a different order, means that what we have hitherto imagined as a tree is not a tree but a graph. There may be several ways of reaching the same position. In order to avoid wasting time reevaluating positions over which considerable search effort may already have been expended, positions that have already been completely searched can be stored together with their value and any other relevant information. Thousands of positions are likely to be involved, and hashtable techniques are used to make the method cost-effective.

All the search algorithms discussed so far have been directional; that is to say, there is an ordering of the terminal nodes; imagine them laid out left to right, such that the algorithm never evaluates a node to the left of one previously examined. The SCOUT algorithm (Pearl, 1980) is one of several possible modifications of alpha–beta in which, if the first line to a terminal node is in fact the minimax best line, the rest of the tree is searched with a minimal window, but if a minimal window search in a subsequent subtree fails high, then a recursive call is made with a modified window. Clearly, in some circumstances, nodes may be reexamined, so algorithms of this type are in general nondirectional. Another nondirectional algorithm is Stockman's (1979) SSS* procedure, which is a more general AND/OR graph searching method that can be shown never to evaluate a terminal node that alpha–beta prunes. A survey of these procedures and other variants on the basic alpha–beta pruning rule is given by Campbell and Marsland (1983).

6. THEORETICAL ANALYSES OF ALPHA–BETA AND ITS VARIANTS

Alpha–beta and its variants have been the subject of intense theoretical analysis as well as practical improvement in recent years. Obvious questions to ask are: How much more efficient is alpha–beta than minimaxing? Is it the best possible algorithm for adversary tree search-ing? How much difference does good ordering make? More fundamen-tally, one can also question the whole rationale behind minimaxing.

The belief that look-ahead combined with minimaxing imprecise terminal evaluations helps in distinguishing good from bad moves is entrenched in game-playing practice, but why should backing up im-precise estimators result in a more precise estimate? Two plausible ar-guments can be made in support. First, by searching you get both nearer the end of the game and to more stable positions, both situations where the evaluation function can be presumed more reliable. Second, the backed-up value combines information from all nodes on the search frontier and so should be a more reliable evaluation than one based on a single node. Nau (1980) argues that the second argument is fallacious by producing instances of search trees where searching deeper consis-tently gives worse evaluations. It is generally believed that the distri-bution of values in typical game trees prevents this happening in actual practice, but the question is by no means resolved and there may be other arguments both for and against minimax. Pearl (1983) gives the example shown in Figure 6.

Suppose the terminal values measure the probability that MAX can force a win from the corresponding position. Should he choose to move to P_1 or P_2? The minimax method would give P_1 the value 0.3 and P_2 the value 0.2, and so lead MAX to choose P_1. Assuming, however, that the terminal probabilities are independent, the probability that P_1 is a win for MAX is 0.12, whereas the probability that P_2 is a win is 0.16, and so on a betting basis, maximizing the expected gain, P_2 is to be

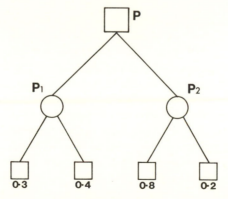

FIGURE 6. A possible counter-example to minimax.

preferred. If the product rule is used, these questions of pathology do not arise, but strong assumptions have had to be made about independence of probabilities. However, if MIN is assumed to agree with MAX's estimate of the probabilities, then MIN can be predicted to choose the 0.3 branch from P_1 and the 0.2 branch from P_2, which appears to justify the minimax rule. It is not yet clear that there is any paradox and the question probably cannot be resolved until the decision-theoretic framework is more completely defined.

As mentioned above, Slagle and Dixon (1969) showed that the number of terminal nodes examined by alpha–beta must be at least $2n^{d/2} - 1$ but may in the worst case be the entire set of n^d terminal nodes. Perfect ordering is unlikely to be achieved in practice, so what happens with random ordering of terminal values? Pearl has shown that the equivalent branching factor of the alpha–beta algorithm, for trees in which the terminal node values are randomly distributed with the uniform continuous valued distribution, is given by $r = s/(1-s)$, where s is the positive root of the equation $x^n + x - 1 = 0$. Since Pearl (1980) has also shown that this quantity bounds any directional algorithm below, the alpha-beta algorithm is asymptotically optimal. The parameter s is about $n/\ln(n)$ and for realistic values of n is close to $0.93n^{0.75}$. It can be shown that SSS* always examines strictly fewer nodes than alpha–beta, although the magnitude of this improvement has not been accurately evaluated. However, SSS* and alpha–beta have been shown to be asymptotically equivalent.

7. OTHER PROBLEM-INDEPENDENT ADVERSARY SEARCH METHODS

All the algorithms discussed so far have been variants or generalizations of the alpha–beta pruning method. The B* algorithm, developed by Berliner (1979) and Palay (1982), is a method of determining the best move by associating with each node in the tree optimistic and pessimistic values that bound the true values. The algorithm works by showing that the pessimistic value of one of the successor positions of the root is greater than the optimistic value of all the other immediate successors. The move to that position is then guaranteed to be the best, even if the true backed-up values have not been precisely determined. The B* algorithm gives considerable flexibility in the choice of searching strategy, and Berliner conjectures that it comes closer to capturing the technique of human tree searching than the other methods considered. Palay (1982) compares several rules for making decisions about which subtree to search and discusses these issues in more detail than is possible here.

8. SELECTIVE SEARCH, EVALUATION FUNCTIONS, AND QUIESCENCE

Up to here we have assumed that some procedure is available for generating a set of successors to a given position—the so-called move generator—but we haven't said anything about which moves are generated or how the decision to terminate forward look-ahead and make an evaluation is taken in practice. In fact, these questions are all related, but for the moment we consider them as separate.

In any position a certain set of legal moves is available for the player to move. We will call a search based on this full set of legal moves at every internal node of the tree a full-width search, and we have seen above that if on average there are n legal moves, then a search to depth d makes n^{kd} terminal evaluations where $0.5 < k \leq 1$, depending on how effective the alpha–beta pruning is. Suppose now that we only look at a fraction $0 < p < 1$ of the legal moves then for the same amount of work we can search to depth D given by $n^{kd} = (pn)^{kD}$, i.e., $D = d\{\log(n)/\log(pn)\}$. So that if, for example, out of 32 legal moves we always choose the best 8, we can look 60% further ahead. We will call a search based on a subset of the full set of legal moves a selective search.

Potentially, of course, selective search is unreliable because the subset of moves chosen may not contain the move that would be selected by a minimax evaluation of the full-width tree. Note that this selection of a subset has nothing to do with alpha-beta pruning as defined above. The algorithms discussed in the previous section are all risk-free improvements on straight minimax and can be applied to any search whether full-width or selective.

Selection is usually done on a heuristic basis by trying to implement rules that seem to be used by human experts or perhaps by applying static evaluation to depth one successor positions. Because of their limited computational resources, human players, beginner or expert, perform selective search all the time. Expert players, however, have a selection function that is both more reliable and more stringent than that of beginners and can thus look much further ahead for the same amount of work. This does not necessarily mean that we have to simulate human experts to construct programs that play well. Just as the numerical algorithms that are used in computing are not the same as those used for hand calculation, so the algorithms used for effective move selection in a computer program may well be different from those of the human expert—even if we could say unambiguously what those were. In fact, Beal (1987) has shown that a certain game-independent search algorithm called null-move quiescence search, when used with a chess evaluation function consisting only of material balance, can select not only captures but checks, threats to capture, and many other types of tactical move in chess.

This brings us to the subject of quiescence. For many games, static evaluation at terminal nodes makes sense only if the position is stable enough for the features included to be relatively permanent. Since—in chess, for example—material balance must be the major component of an evaluation function, terminal positions have to be tactically quiescent if major blunders are to be avoided. Assigning a static value to tactically volatile positions is difficult because of hung pieces, pins, X-ray attacks. No algorithm is known, and almost certainly none exists, that can do this accurately without search. A point here is that human notions of quiescence may be irrelevant or dangerous to implement because many of the positions that are reached in a full-width search are rather bizarre from a chess player's point of view.

One might think that the ideal solution would be to apply a specialized procedure for finding combinations (see below), and only if this fails to come up with anything to use positional criteria such as pawn structure, king safety, control of open files, and strong squares. Unfortunately, such a solution is computationally infeasible, and most programs resort to a more limited analysis of captures, checks, and threats. Captures tend to die out, checks are less convenient. Many series of checks are useless but they often go on a long time.

So, in practice, even the full-width search programs do not just stop at a fixed depth and apply static evaluation. The full-width search is terminated by a selective search to quiescence based on the static evaluation function. The latter, of course, is entirely game-dependent. For chess it will certainly include material balance, together with measures of center control, pawn structure, and king safety. For Go it will measure groups already captured, together, perhaps, with some mathematically defined notion of influence.

9. A SHORT HISTORY OF GAME-PLAYING PROGRAMS

Almost before the digital computer was a reality, Shannon (1950) and Turing (1950) had invested much time in thinking how it might be programmed to play chess, a considerable (and typical) leap of imagination at a time when all other applications were mathematical. The tree-searching and evaluation paradigm originated with Shannon (1950), but, although several programs were written, all those for nontrivial games were weak until Samuel's (1967) justly celebrated draughts (checkers) program. For its time, Samuel's program was a tour de force. Playing at near championship level, it set a pattern of development that is still continuing. The basis of his program was an alpha–beta search with an evaluation function that was a weighted sum of numerically coded features of the position with adjustable weights that could be used to reflect their relative importance. In most of today's programs the weights are empirically set by the programmer to fine-tune performance (or correct positional naiveties). Getting the program to adjust its own weights automatically is often suggested but much less often implemented. The problems are lack of stability and knowing which component of the evaluation contributed most to the blunder that one wants to avoid in the future. Samuel recognized and tackled these difficult problems, even with some measure of success. Draughts is a simpler game than chess or Go, and probably about as difficult as Othello (see below). It may well be true that the techniques used today for chess would lead to a superhuman draughts machine.

The next significant development was Greenblatt's (Greenblatt, Eastlake, & Crocker, 1967) chess program. This was the first to play a reasonably good game of chess and to take part in tournaments against human players. There followed a period of steady development stimulated by the organization of regular American, European, and world computer chess championships. The first world championship was won by a Russian program called Kaissa (Arlazarov & Futer, 1979), but, surprisingly, comparatively little chess programming seems to be done in the USSR, although when any work is published it is of high quality and very innovative.

Up to about 1980 most of the successful chess programs were based on full-width alpha–beta searches tailored with ever-increasing ingenuity to ever more powerful machines. Slate and Atkin (1977) were the most successful team in this era. At about this time chess machines began to appear and to be widely marketed. These were conventional programs of the Greenblatt, Slate, and Atkin type but programmed in the assembler for the microprocessors that had become widely available.

Ken Thompson (one of the originators of the widely used UNIX operating system) had been competing with a conventional chess program but now built a machine called Belle that was a new departure, featuring hardware move generation, tree searching, and evaluation. Consisting of about 1700 chips and driven by an LSI-11 that contains the chess programs, interface, opening books, and operating system software, it can search about 160,000 positions per second. The move generator consists of an 8×8 array of specially constructed circuits that transmit and receive signals propagated by the units representing neighboring squares. Material balance and pawn structure is also kept track of by hardware. Full details are given in Condon and Thompson (1983).

CRAY BLITZ is a full-width search-based program, with no special hardware but running on one of the world's most powerful computers, that uses most of the methods described above such as alpha–beta with iterative deepening and large transposition tables to avoid repeating searches previously evaluated. The CRAY X-MP system allows multitasking on four processors, and considerable experiment has gone into finding the best way to utilize this effectively.

The latest special-purpose chess machine is that being developed by Hans Berliner's group at Carnegie Mellon. The core of the machine (Berliner, 1986) is a hardware move generator consisting of 64 specially designed chips, one for each square on the board, that compute in parallel all moves to that square together with enough information about material balance and centrality to order moves for the search routines. The remainder of the machine is similar to Belle. At the time of writing, HITECH is the strongest chess program ever, playing at an Elo rating of about 2400, although CRAY BLITZ has beaten it on occasion.

Programs to play games other than chess have appeared spasmodically in the literature. Apart from Samuel's draughts program mentioned above, there have been several attempts at Go and Othello, some of which are described more fully below. For several years Hans Berliner has also been developing a program to play backgammon, which, unlike chess and Go but like bridge and poker, involves an element of chance. The latest version of the program employs almost no search and depends almost entirely on very finely tuned heuristics. Described in Berliner (1980), it plays at world championship level.

10. EXAMPLE OF IMPLEMENTATION METHOD FOR CHESS

The brief history given above shows that, with the stimulus of competition, chess-playing programs have reached a particularly high state of development. Having seen how sophisticated the state-of-the-

```
111 112 113 114 115 116 117 118 119 120
101 102 103 104 105 106 107 108 109 110
091|092|093|094|095|096|097|098|099|100
081|082|083|084|085|086|087|088|089|090
071|072|073|074|075|076|077|078|079|080
061|062|063|064|065|066|067|068|069|070
051|052|053|054|055|056|057|058|059|060
041|042|043|044|045|046|047|048|049|050
031|032|033|034|035|036|037|038|039|040
021|022|023|024|025|026|027|028|029|030
011 012 013 014 015 016 017 018 019 020
001 002 003 004 005 006 007 008 009 010
```

FIGURE 7. Method of mapping the chessboard for fast move generation.

art programs are, it might be interesting as a concrete example of implementation to see how one could go about writing a minimal chess program of one's own.

Assuming for simplicity that a full-width selective alpha–beta search is to be used, and neglecting the practically important interface aspects such as move input and board display, there are two main issues to be addressed—namely, board representation/move generation and quiescence/evaluation. Leaving aside purpose-built hardware, two main methods of position representation have been developed; the choice depends to some extent on the word length of the machine and what bit operations are available. For a simple machine-independent program in a high-level language, a convenient and reasonably efficient method is that shown in Figure 7.

Imagine the 8×8 chessboard embedded in a one-dimensional array, called Board, say, of length 120. The numbers in Figure 7 are array indices, so the square e4, for example, corresponds to the array element Board[56]. Now give each piece a unique code—white pawn = +1, black pawn = −1, white knight = +2, etc.; let empty squares be denoted by zero and squares off the edge of the board by integers larger than +6 (the code for the white king). Legal moves can now be generated for each piece representing the directions in which it can move. For example, king moves can be obtained by adding −11, −10, −9, −1, +1, +9, +10, or +11 to the king's present address. The eight possible offsets for the knight are −21, −19, −12, −8, +8, +12, +19, +21. We now see why the enlarged board can be 12×10 rather than 12×12. Consider a knight on the square whose algebraic notation is a4, board index 52 in this mapping. Adding in turn the eight offsets given above, we get 31, 33, 40, 44, 60, 64, 71, 73. Of these 31, 40, 60, and 71 will contain piece codes greater than $+6$, i.e., be marked as off the edge of the board. Note how addresses 40 and 60 have been used in this case; the board "wraps around," which saves some storage—significant if many positions have to be stored or copied.

For the long-range pieces successive increments of each possible offset are tried until an obstructing piece or a square off the edge is encountered. The geometrically possible moves can thus be generated quite simply, but now one has to consider the other complications of the full game, such as the *en passant* capture, castling, and not being able to leave the king in check. The current possibility of castling and *en passant* capture can be indicated by using the spare locations off the edge of the board as flags to record the current legality of these moves. Checks and pinned pieces are more of a problem. It takes a long time to radiate out from the king's square to see if, for example, a move by some other piece has left him in check. Bearing in mind that the move concerned is quite likely to be pruned by the tree-searching algorithm, a better solution may be to generate the superset of pseudolegal moves and, if a move comes to be made, only then to see if it leaves the king in check.

A completely different way to represent the board and generate moves was first proposed by Adelson-Velskii, Arlazarov, Bitman, Zhivotovskiy, and Uskov (1970), and varieties of it have been used in some of the fastest programs, particularly those with convenient word-length and low-level bit operations.

Suppose we assign one bit of a 64-bit word to each square of the board. Each word can then represent a set of squares; for example, all the squares next to the white king can be represented by a single word in which the bit for each of the relevant squares is set to 1 and all the rest to zero. Move generation can be done as follows. Suppose we have 64 words, each of which represents all the squares accessible to a knight currently on a given square, and we now want to generate all geometrically possible (pseudolegal) moves for a white knight on $e4$. We take the word whose bits represent all the white pieces and logically "and" the negation of this with the word representing the possible moves of an $e4$ knight. The resulting bit map gives the $e4$ knight moves that are not to a square occupied by another white piece.

Assuming that the alpha-beta algorithm described above is to be used, the important parameter in determining performance of the program is the evaluation function. Clearly, it has to include material balance. What goes on top of that will determine how "sensibly" from a chess point of view the program plays.

11. KNOWLEDGE-BASED SELECTIVE SEARCH

One way to improve the efficiency of search is to move the emphasis away from fast-search algorithms and concentrate only on analyzing those moves that according to the semantics of the game are relevant to improving the position. The current chess programs may look at 10 million positions before deciding on a move; a chess master may only look at 10 or at most 100. Clearly, he uses his knowledge of chess to drastically reduce the branching factor. Pruning of this kind is potentially hazardous, but so is terminating a full-width search after 9 ply when the position calls for 20. The stimulus of competition will ensure that search-based programs are developed as long as improvements in computer architecture make this productive, but in parallel to these developments, there have been some attempts to more or less directly simulate human knowledge-based search. As far as chess is concerned, the first attempt seems to have been by Zobrist and Carlsson (1973), who used a method of representing patterns input by a chess master. The program played a full but mediocre game.

The next attempt to reproduce human reasoning was by Hans Berliner (1974), who undertook an analysis of causality in tactical sequences. Berliner's program CAPS II did use search, but instead of just returning numbers back up the tree, it attempted to abstract data from the analysis so that if the evaluation was adverse the reason could be deduced. Squares critical to the transport of pieces were remembered, and the program tried to deduce from these data whether a particular move could be blamed for the result. It did moderately well at generating defenses to deep threats but could not ultimately compete even on its own ground with the search-based programs and thus has not been developed.

Pitrat (1977) describes a program that aims to find a combination in a given position by generating plans based on observed features of the position, such as pieces that are unprotected or immobile because pinned. Plans cannot always be carried out immediately, and in such cases the program looks for moves that make them possible. It was tested and performed reasonably convincingly on a small number of tactical problems but was again no better than the full-width search-based programs being developed at the same time.

The most recent attempt to implement knowledge-based search is that of Wilkins (1982). His program PARADISE (PAttern Recognition Applied to Directing SEarch) is, like Berliner's and Pitrat's, a program for finding chess combinations, i.e., forced sequences that lead to mate or

gain of material. The program has a knowledge base of about 200 production rules. Production rules are a common implementation technique in artificial intelligence. Each rule is of the form *if* condition *then*
action. In PARADISE each condition is a combination of features of the
position and, when triggered, can be viewed as searching for all instances of the condition in the position. For each instance that is found,
the action part of the rule posts "concepts" in a database of information accessed by the reasoning part of the program. For example, in
one of the rules the condition part matches defensive pieces that are
trapped, and the action part posts the suggestion to attack this piece
in the global database. This information may then be used by another
rule higher up the abstraction hierarchy to build up an understanding
of the position and generate a plan of attack. This is the static analysis
phase. Plans are characterized in four ways: THREAT, which specifies
what the plan aims to win; SAVE, which specifies what counterthreats
it prevents; LOSS, which specifies what it gives up; and LIKELY, which
is an estimate of its probable success measured by the number of un-
forced moves available to the defense. The plans generated are then
evaluated by a best-first search, which keeps track of unsearched alternatives and their expectations as it proceeds. Full details are in Wilkins
(1979), a summary with examples in Frey (1983). The program has been
tested on a number of well-known tactical problems. It performs well
on examples for which its production rules are relevant, typically examining tens of nodes in a few minutes in a humanlike pattern of
analysis. There is no reason to think that adding new rules will significantly increase the branching in the search or the total processing time,
provided that the patterns are carefully designed for efficient matching.

The three contributions in this area of knowledge-based search that
have been described are all in their way carefully thought-out pieces of
work, yet one is left with the impression that they are complicated and
ad hoc. Clearly, there is plenty of scope for further work in this area,
but until search-based programs show signs of reaching a plateau, im-
petus is lacking for radical alternatives.

12. EXACT PLAY IN CHESS ENDGAMES

We have seen how computers can be programmed to play a complete game of chess quite well, but certainly not perfectly. Not even
the best human players are consistently perfect; indeed, it is doubtful
if we will ever know for the initial position in chess what the best move

is and whether the theoretical result with perfect play is a win for White, a draw, or a win for Black.

There is, however, one part of the game where perfect play is not only theoretically but practically possible—in simple endgames. Take, for example, the mate with king and rook against king. Not only is this known to be a win for the stronger side but elementary texts give the most efficient method of achieving it from any configuration of the pieces.

It was realized recently that simple endgames were one area where computers could be used for completely correct computation of the value of chess positions. The technique, which has been called retrograde enumeration, essentially consists of working backward from terminal positions of known value. Taking king and rook against king as an example, a mapping is constructed from positions to integers taking advantage of any symmetries that exist for the pieces under consideration. For example, in this case there are no pawns so the board can always be rotated to bring the white king into a triangle of at most 10 squares. Since $10 \times 64 \times 64 = 40,960$, every possible position can be coded as an integer in the range 0–40,959. (Actually there are also other symmetries that can be used to reduce this to 32,896.)

In this case White on the move always wins, so the aim is to label each White-to-move position with the number of moves to mate with optimal play on both sides. The method is as follows: First, label all terminal positions with their value. Those in which White can mate on the move can be labeled wins at depth zero; many will be illegal or impossible—for example, because Black is in check or the rook is on top of the king—and these must be marked accordingly. Most positions will be unlabeled. Now the simplest method is to look at every unlabeled position in turn and try to evaluate it with a two-ply minimax. Those in which White can force transformation to a depth-zero win can be labeled as wins at depth two; the remainder cannot yet be labeled. The process is then iterated until no more positions can be evaluated. The resulting database can then be used to drive an interactive program that plays the endgame perfectly against a human or machine opponent, or more productively perhaps as a research tool for investigations into data compression, induction of rules from examples, concept formation, etc. (Michie, 1980; Thompson, 1986). It is worth noting also that genuine contributions to chess knowledge have come as a by-product of work such as this (Clarke, 1977; Michie, 1980).

Although programs that use databases such as this play perfectly, the approach is clearly limited to endings with very few pieces on either side. All the four-piece endings (including kings) have been computed, as have some with five (Thompson, 1986).

13. OTHER NONPROBABILISTIC GAMES

Compared with chess, Go has appeared only infrequently in the literature. The main reasons for this seem to be partly cultural (there are fewer players and the principles of expert play are not easily translated into Western terminology) and partly that Go programs have been isolated efforts not benefiting from the stimulus of competition and development over long periods that chess has enjoyed.

Go is played on the grid-points of a 19 × 19 board that is initially empty. The two players, Black and White, place stones of those colors alternately on unoccupied points. Broadly speaking, the aim is to fence off as much territory as possible with your own stones while avoiding having them surrounded and captured by the opponent. However, there is no space here to give an illustrative game or indeed much idea of the vast experience and subtlety of reasoning required to play well. Good references for beginners are Iwamoto (1976) and Fairbairn (1977).

Whereas in the middle of the game in chess there are about 30 legal moves, in Go there may be two or three hundred, and it seems clear that full-width look-ahead, however efficient, is always going to be inappropriate, except possibly at the end of the game. While knowledgeable tree pruning and heuristics may ultimately be proved necessary for grandmaster play in chess, they are clearly essential right from the start in Go.

One approach is to search the subtree of moves relevant to satisfying a predetermined goal. This is the method adopted by Reitman and Wilcox (1979), whose program is probably the most well developed to date. Their tactical analyzer maintains a goal stack for each color, and in each new position arising during the search, new subgoals are added or deleted according to whether or not satisfying them will contribute to achieving higher-level goals. The moves examined in the search are those that impinge on the most recently added subgoal for the side to move. This is similar to the methods used by Berliner (1974), Pitrat (1977), and Wilkins (1979) in their investigations of tactical play in chess.

Lehner (1983) has shown that a similar goal-directed look-ahead can be used for strategic planning. As in chess, but to a far greater extent, plans can be formulated in Go simply on the perceptual characteristics of a position, without any look-ahead, but, because of unexpected side effects, such a purely perceptual analysis is usually inadequate for evaluating the plan; look-ahead is necessary, even at the strategic level, and for strong play this search has to allow for tactical side effects as well.

A primary concept in Go is the notion of "influence" exerted by a stone on a neighboring position, and also the notion of a group of stones. The program of Sander and Davies (1983) attempts to model these concepts. An earlier program of Zobrist (1970) worked by matching local configurations to stored patterns.

Othello is another member of the Go family of board games that involve the capture of territory by surrounding the opponent's pieces. It is played on an 8 × 8 grid with a set of disks that are white on one side and black on the other. Starting from an initial configuration in which each player has two disks in the center, each side in turn moves by placing a disk on the board with the player's color facing up. The disk must be played on a vacant square, and it must surround one or more of the opponent's disks by enclosing them along one or more of the eight horizontal, vertical, or diagonal directions. The opponent's captured disks are turned over to the player's color; thus, disks are never taken off the board, they just change color. If such a capture cannot be made, the player loses his turn. Usually the game ends when the entire board has been filled, which normally takes $64 - 4 = 60$ moves, or earlier if neither side can play. The winner is the one with the more disks showing, but in tournaments the winning margin can also be significant.

Combinatorially the game is clearly not as complex as chess or Go, and full-width fixed-depth search together with a carefully developed evaluation function will probably give superhuman performance. Rosenbloom (1982) describes such a program and compares various evaluation strategies. Similar in design to the currently successful chess programs, his program plays Othello at world championship level.

14. GAMES OF IMPERFECT INFORMATION, GAME THEORY

All the games we have discussed up to this point have been games of perfect information. Both players have full access to the current state of all the relevant variables. Hardly any adversarial situations in real life have this property. Games of imperfect information are in two main categories. Those where the uncertainty lies in the contents of opponents' hands and/or their strategy (pattern of play in certain situations), and those with random moves that depend on the throw of dice, etc. In these situations statistical decision theory rather than, or possibly combined with, minimax look-ahead is the basic algorithmic tool.

One game that combines most of these characteristics is poker. Findler and his colleagues have for many years been using poker as the setting in which to study and compare decision-making, problem-solving, and learning techniques. Poker shares many important features of decision-making with real-life problems. Findler (Findler, Sicherman, & McCall, 1983) summarizes these as the following:

A. A likely state of nature based on subjective probability and plausible but not necessarily rational actions by the other participants.
B. The player can manipulate information either by buying it or by giving out, possibly misleading, information of his own.
C. Each player has limited financial resources to be managed optimally in the long run. His strategy is the visible projection of his resource management style.
D. Both tactical (short-term) and strategic decisions are made on the basis of probability and expected utility.

The long-term goal of Findler's work is to investigate how decisions should be made under conditions of uncertainty and risk. Like many realistically large problems, poker cannot be solved by the mathematical theory of games—an effective analysis has to use computer simulation. For details see the many papers referenced in Findler et al. (1983).

15. CONCLUSION—LIKELY FUTURE TRENDS

Most of the significant developments over the last 20 years have been in search techniques and special-purpose hardware for playing chess. Comparatively little has been done on knowledge representation and scarcely anything on learning. The imminent advent of parallel hardware will, if anything, lead to even more intensive investigation of parallel minimax and its variants. It is possible, but see Berliner (1986), that these developments will take us near to world championship level for chess. So although the development of search algorithms is far in advance of knowledge-based work, there will still not be much incentive to stimulate human thinking in chess. Go is another matter entirely—the search space is so large that highly selective search is essential. My forecast for Go is that some of the techniques from the rapidly developing science of computer vision will be applied to the problem of isolating significant features of a position and using these, supplemented by efficient but local tactical analysis, in a fairly direct simulation of human patterns of reasoning.

Another probable development is increasing interest in multiperson games and the underlying logic of adversarial reasoning, where recent developments (e.g., Halpern & Moses, 1986) in the logics of knowledge and belief have a clear application to reasoning about an opponent's statements and deductions.

16. REFERENCES

Adelson-Velskii, G. M., Arlazarov, V. L., Bitman, A. R., Zhivotovskiy, A. A., & Uskov, A. V. (1970). Programming a computer to play chess. *Russian Mathematical Surveys, 25,* 221–262.

Arlazarov, V. L., & Futer, A. L. (1979). Computer analysis of a rook end-game. In E. W. Elcock & D. Michie (Eds.), *Machine intelligence* (Vol. 9). New York: Wiley.

Baudet, G. M. (1978). On the branching factor of the alpha–beta pruning algorithm. *Artificial Intelligence, 10,* 173–199.

Beal, D. F. (1989). Null-move quiescence search. *Advances in computer chess 5* (in press).

Berliner, H. J. (1974). Chess as problem-solving: The development of a tactics analyzer. Doctoral dissertation, Computer Science Department, Carnegie-Mellon University.

Berliner, H. J. (1979). The B* tree search algorithm: A best-first proof procedure. *Artificial Intelligence, 12,* 23–40.

Berliner, H. J. (1980). Backgammon computer program beats world-champion. *Artificial Intelligence, 14,* 205–220.

Berliner, H. J. (1986). Computer chess at Carnegie-Mellon University. In D. F. Beal (Ed.), *Advances in computer chess 4.* Oxford: Pergamon Press.

Campbell, M. S. & Marsland, T. A. (1983). A comparison of minimax tree search algorithms. *Artificial Intelligence, 20,* 347–367.

Clarke, M. R. B. (1977). A quantitative study of king and pawn against king. In M. R. B. Clarke (Ed.), *Advances in computer chess 1.* Edinburgh: Edinburgh University Press.

Condon, J. H., & Thompson, K. (1983). Belle chess hardware. In M. R. B. Clarke (Ed.), *Advances in computer chess 2.* Edinburgh: Edinburgh University Press.

Fairbairn, J. T. (1977). Invitation to Go. Oxford: Oxford University Press.

Findler, N. V., Sicherman, G. L., & McCall, B. (1983). A multi-strategy gaming environment. In M. A. Bramer (Ed.), *Computer game-playing, theory and practice.* Chichester: Ellis Horwood.

Frey, P. W. (1983). *Chess skill in man and machine.* New York: Springer-Verlag.

Greenblatt, R. D., Eastlake, D. E., & Crocker, S. D. (1967). The Greenblatt chess program. *Proceedings of the AFIPS Fall Joint Computer Conference, 31,* 801–810.

Halpern, J., & Moses, Y. (1986). A guide to the logics of knowledge and belief. *Proceedings, AAAI-86.* Los Altos, CA: Morgan Kaufman.

Iwamoto, K. (1976). *Go for beginners.* New York: Pantheon.

Lehner, P. E. (1983). Strategic planning in Go. In M. A. Bramer (Ed.), *Computer game-playing, theory and practice.* Chichester: Ellis-Horwood.

Michie, D. (1980). A prototype knowledge refinery. In M. R. B. Clarke (Ed.), *Advances in computer chess 2.* Edinburgh: Edinburgh University Press.

Nau, D. S. (1980). An investigation into the causes of pathology in games. *Artificial Intelligence, 19*, 257–278.

Newell, A., Shaw, J., & Simon, H. A. (1958). Chess-playing programs and the problem of complexity. *IBM Journal of Research and Development, 2*, 320–335.

Nilsson, N. (1980). *Principles of artificial intelligence*. Palo Alto: Toga.

Palay, A. J. (1982). The B* tree search algorithm—New results. *Artificial Intelligence, 19*, 145–163.

Pearl, J. (1980). *SCOUT: A simple game-searching algorithm with proven optimal properties*. Loss Angeles: Cognitive Systems Laboratory, School of Engineering and Applied Science, University of California.

Pearl, J. (1983). Game-searching theory: Survey of recent results. In M. A. Bramer (Ed.), *Computer game-playing, theory and practice*. Chichester: Ellis Horwood.

Pitrat, J. (1977). A chess combination program which uses plans. *Artificial Intelligence, 8*, 275–321.

Reitman, W., & Wilcox, B. (1979). Modelling tactical analysis and problem solving in Go. *Proceedings of the Tenth Annual Pittsburgh Conference on Modelling and Simulation*, 2133–2148.

Rosenbloom, P. S. (1982). A world championship level Othello program. *Artificial Intelligence, 19*, 279–320.

Samuel, A. L. (1967). Some studies in machine learning using the game of checkers—Recent progress. *IBM Journal of Research and Development, 11*, 601.

Sander, P. T., & Davies, D. J. M. (1983). A strategic approach to the game of Go. In M. A. Bramer (Ed.), *Computer game-playing, theory and practice*. Chichester: Ellis Horwood.

Shannon, C. E. (1950). Programming a computer for playing chess. *Philosophical Magazine, 41*, 256–275.

Slagle, J. R., & Dixon, J. (1969). Experiments with some programs which search game trees. *Journal of the Association for Computing Machinery, 16*, 189–207.

Slate, D. J., & Atkin, L. R. (1977). Chess 4.5—The Northwestern University chess program. In P. W. Frey (Ed.), *Chess skill in man and machine*. New York: Springer-Verlag.

Stockman, G. (1979). A minimax algorithm better than alpha-beta? *Artificial Intelligence, 12*, 179–196.

Thompson, K. (1986). Retrograde analysis of certain endgames. *ICCA Journal* (September).

Turing, A. M. (1950). Computing machinery and intelligence. *Mind, 59*, 433–460.

Wilkins, D. E. (1979). Using patterns and plans to control search. *AIM-329*, Computer Science Department, Stanford University.

Wilkins, D. E. (1982). Using knowledge to control tree searching. *Artificial Intelligence, 18*, 1–51.

Zobrist, A. L. (1970). Feature extraction and representation for pattern recognition and the game of Go. Ph.D. thesis, University of Wisconsin.

Zobrist, A. L., & Carlsson, F. R. (1973). An advice-taking chess computer. *Scientific American, 228*, 92–105.

17. FURTHER READING

There are several collections of survey and research-level articles on computer game playing, as well as many nontechnical popular books. Among those referenced in this chapter are the following:

Beal, D. F. (Ed.). (1986). *Advances in computer chess 4*. Oxford: Pergamon Press.

Bramer, M. (Ed.). (1983). *Computer game-playing, theory and practice*. Chichester: Ellis Horwood.

Clarke, M. R. B. (Ed.). (1977). *Advances in computer chess 1*. Edinburgh: Edinburgh University Press.

Clarke, M. R. B. (Ed.). (1980). *Advances in computer chess 2*. Edinburgh: Edinburgh University Press.

Clarke, M. R. B. (Ed.). (1983). *Advances in computer chess 3*. Oxford: Pergamon Press.

Frey, P. W. (1983). *Chess skill in man and machine*. New York: Springer-Verlag.

Newborn, M. (1975). *Computer chess*. New York: Academic Press.

Conference proceedings and journals in artificial intelligence also usually have a few papers, and occasionally whole issues, on computer game playing. Among these are the proceedings of the International Joint Conference on Artificial Intelligence, Nos. 1–9 (published biennially by a variety of publishers, 1973–1987) and the journal *Artificial Intelligence* (Elsevier).

5

Adversary Problem Solving by Humans

DENNIS H. HOLDING

1. ADVERSARY GAMES

If problem solving consists of the search of a problem space (Anderson, 1985), then the presence of an adversary vastly complicates that search. Instead of finding a linear sequence of operators that will transform the initial problem state successively from one subgoal to another until the final goal state is achieved, adversary problem solving faces us with an expanding set of possibilities. If we make any one move, our opponent can make several replies; we can respond to each of these replies, but each response will engender a further set of replies. Hence, the search tree grows exponentially. A complete solution to the problem is often beyond our reach, and beyond the resources of a computer, with the result that our decisions must be based on heuristic principles.

Many real-life situations show these characteristics. Bargaining for a used car, coaching the tactics of a basketball team, planning a course of therapy, or conducting a battle—all involve the consideration of moves and countermoves. If A offers this, executes this, says this, or deploys this, then B might respond in 1, 2, 3, . . . N ways, and A must be ready with a reply to each response. However, the structure of these

DENNIS H. HOLDING • Department of Psychology, University of Louisville, Louisville, Kentucky 40292.

problems is most clearly seen in the conduct of games, and it is in the area of games that most of the analytic research has been conducted. Much of this work has been concerned with the contribution of memory to expertise, although the current chapter will emphasize the analysis of search trees.

1.1. GAMES RESEARCH

Chess provides the best stereotype of an adversary game, but some work has also been reported on the games of Go and gomoku (or "pegity"), on bridge, and on the sports of basketball and volleyball. Unfortunately, the nonchess studies have concentrated on issues other than those arising from the search tree. In the case of Go, which is played by adding "stones" to a grid so as to surround opposing forces, it has been confirmed that a beginner and a master differ in their memory for briefly presented positions. Reitman (1976) used both a copying and a memory task, comparing the patterns of stones placed between glances back to the copied board with those placed from memory. There was some overlap, but no exact correspondence between the two sets of pattern placements. Furthermore, the patterns indicated by the penciled circles of a Go master as forming the basic units, or "chunks," used in memorizing the positions were overlapping rather than separate. Of course, the master remembered the positions extremely well.

It has been shown by Eisenstadt and Kareev (1975) that players encode the patterns of stones differently according to whether they believe the patterns to have arisen from Go or from gomoku. The two games gave rise to different levels of accuracy in memory, and to different kinds of errors, showing that memory for the patterns is partly determined by an overall game schema. With respect to gomoku, Rayner (1958a) made a number of useful observations. He showed that learning to play gomoku (pegity), whose object is to place five stones or pegs in a line, depends on learning the appropriate strategies. The most effective offensive patterns are cross-lined configurations, because these minimize the chances of defensive moves by the adversary. The learning process exhibited successively fewer failures to construct crossed-line patterns, together with fewer failures to defend against these attacks, as shown in Table 1. These changes were paralleled by increased times necessary to calculate the sequences.

The game of bridge was investigated by Engle and Bukstel (1978), who again showed that players of different levels of expertise differed in their memory for structured hands of cards. The unskilled players were poorer at memorizing, and tended to attach more importance to

TABLE 1. Frequencies of Crossed-Line Strategies
in Pegity[a]

	Trial		
	1	3	5
Successful construction	3	8	6
Failures to construct	22	7	5
Successful defense	17	6	7
Failures to defend	15	10	12

[a]Adapted from Rayner (1958a).

the honor cards than to the number sequences within suits. Charness (1979) has also found memory differences in bridge, confirming that these do not occur with unsorted hands. The better players excelled at planning the play of contracts, at rapid bidding, at the incidental learning of problem hands, and at memory for briefly seen hands.

In sports, Allard, Graham, and Paarsalu (1980) have shown further memory differences dependent on skill. When basketball scenes were structured, during offensive play, varsity players remembered the details of the scenes far better than did nonplayers, although this did not happen with the relatively unstructured scenes of turnovers and rebounds. It has also been shown (Allard & Starkes, 1980) that volleyball players are quicker at detecting the presence or absence of the ball in game scenes than are nonplayers or other athletes. The finding provides some indication that factors other than memory may be important in distinguishing players of differing levels of skill.

1.2. MEMORY AND SKILL

The emphasis on rote memory found in the research on nonchess games arises as a result of the strong theoretical position adopted by Chase and Simon (1973) with respect to chess. In earlier research, de Groot (1965) had failed to find search differences between stronger and weaker players but did find differences in memory for briefly presented chess positions. Grandmaster and master players were able to reproduce about 93% of the pieces after exposures of only 3 to 4 seconds, whereas a class player could remember only 51%. Jongman (1968) made the suggestion that strong players literally recognize large parts of these game positions on the basis of patterns already in long-term memory, simply filling their short-term memory with references to these existing categories.

Chase and Simon (1973) similarly proposed that chess patterns were composed of smaller "chunks," which could be committed to memory without overload by masters who had learned a sufficient vocabulary of subpatterns. These authors had attempted to identify the characteristics of chess chunks by using the comparison of memory and copying tasks. In this work those pieces that were replaced together, either between glances in copying or between pauses in remembering, were taken to define the chunks. If the names or labels for such chunks were to be held in short-term memory as appropriate, the results of a computer simulation (Simon & Gilmartin, 1973) implied that between 10,000 and 100,000 subpatterns would be needed to duplicate the performance of a master. However, if separately counted White, Black, and transposed patterns are regarded as equivalent, these figures reduce to between 1000 and 10,000 patterns (Holding, 1985). In any case, the memory performance of the master must reflect considerable prior learning.

Explaining the master's feats of short-term memory in this way seems to imply further conclusions regarding long-term memory. However, the novelty of Chase and Simon's (1973) theoretical position lay in reversing the apparent causal sequence. Having established that memory performance depends upon chess expertise, they proceeded to hypothesize that skill at chess depended on memory. Specifically, the authors suggested that the long-term memory of the master contained both familiar patterns and plausible moves associated with those patterns. The two kinds of information were linked in a production system, wherein the necessary conditions would be satisfied by familiar patterns and the corresponding action would consist of bringing plausible moves to attention.

This account appears unsatisfactory on several grounds. The chunking account of short-term memory is weakened by the findings that interpolated tasks do not interfere with chess memory. Charness (1976) found that various mental tasks carried out during the retention interval had no effect on memory by experienced players, while Frey and Adesman (1976) showed that neither counting backward nor remembering other chess positions had any effect. In both cases, the chess information appears to have been processed directly into long-term memory. It can also be shown that the accuracy of chess memory depends on the level of processing. Goldin (1978) found that memory was good following demanding tasks, such as choosing moves or evaluating positions, but poor following superficial tasks, such as counting the pieces. Similarly, Lane and Robertson (1979) found that semantic orienting instructions produced good retention after the incidental learning of chess positions, even though short-term memory was inhibited by an interfering task. A final complication is provided by Reynolds (1982), who showed that chess memory may depend less on the meaningfulness of the positions than on the degree of spatial focusing that they exhibit.

1.3. The Need for Alternative Explanations

More serious objections can be made to the theory that memory determines skill. For example, the subpatterns forming the chunks identified by Chase and Simon (1973) seem incapable of generating the moves required in the positions they represent since the chunks are too small and scattered to provide the necessary interaction between the pieces. Furthermore, the theory leaves out of account several important determinants of chess skill, such as verbal knowledge, search strategies, and evaluation judgments. In all, Holding (1985) lists 40 objections of various kinds to the theory as it stands. Probably the most cogent of these are several demonstrations that skill differences and memory differences may vary independently.

One example of the discrepancy between memory performance and chess expertise comes from the work by Charness (1981a) on age differences in move selection. Fortunately, there exists for chess a systematic, numerical rating scale that reliably differentiates standards of performance (Elo, 1978), which could be used in Charness's work to match players of different ages before they were given a brief memory task. After seeing chess positions for 4 seconds each, a group averaging 54 years of age were able to replace only 24% of the pieces correctly. A younger group, averaging 20 years of age, were correct with 35% of the pieces, which is half again as much. These differences in the ability to memorize positions are apparently due to problems in encoding the positions into familiar chunks since measures of consolidation and retrieval did not differentiate the players. Nevertheless, although the older players had greater difficulty in accessing the appropriate patterns in long-term memory, their skill ratings were ensured as equivalent by the design of the experiment and thus did not vary with the memory scores.

A direct approach to the problem of memory and skill was taken by Holding and Reynolds (1982). Players of different U.S. Chess Federation (Elo) rating strengths were asked to memorize random arrangements of pieces that, unlike meaningful chess positions, are known to elicit equal memory performance from players regardless of their level of expertise. Next, the players chose the best continuation moves that they could find in studying those positions. The value of these chosen moves was assessed by comparing them with the best lines of play

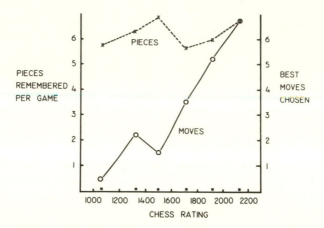

FIGURE 1. Skill differences in move choice despite no differences in memory scores. (From Holding & Reynolds, 1982.)

discovered by the authors during exhaustive analysis, with the results shown in Figure 1. The memory scores are virtually flat, and unrelated to playing strength, but the number of best moves chosen nevertheless rises with playing strength (correlating at .75). Hence, differences in memory for the subpatterns contained in the positions cannot account for the demonstrated differences in chess skill.

Similar effects have since been reported by Saariluoma (1985). In three experiments, players of differing strengths were tested for their speed in identifying whether or not a king was in check, in counting the number of minor pieces (bishops and knights) on the board, and in their memory for briefly exposed positions. Again the differences in playing strength were not reflected in memory for random positions, although they were quite evident in real positions, and again the differences persisted in chess-related tests. All players were somewhat slower to react in the random positions, but the relative skill differences in detecting checks and counting minor pieces were equivalent to those in real positions. As before, it must be concluded that skilled performance is not determined by memory for specific chess configurations.

2. DEALING WITH THE ADVERSARY

If we abandon the idea that chess skill relies on specific memories, while of course retaining the idea that remembered knowledge may inform the search process, the way is clear to explore the characteristics of human search. As noted above, the presence of an adversary makes for an expanding search tree. In chess, there are 20 opening moves for White and for Black, so that there are already 400 possibilities going into White's second move. The number of possible, legal moves increases thereafter, and a corrected estimate (Holding, 1985) shows 7.5 million positions attainable after White's third move and 225 million after Black's. A practical estimate of the entire tree, based on de Groot's mean of 32 moves per position and Holding's (1980) count of 78 plies per game, reveals a total of 32^{78} branches. This figure represents a magnitude of 10^{117}, which is quite close to the 10^{120} often suggested, and is a very large number indeed.

Of course, a human problem-solver will occupy himself with only a tiny fraction of these possibilities. A typical search tree by an average player, and the chess position on which it is based, are shown in Figures 2 and 3. The ways in which human players deal with search requirements have been elucidated in a number of experiments, to be described below. Furthermore, it will be necessary to discuss chess knowledge, which, in human play as in some experimental computer programs, can be shown to facilitate the search process. It will also become clear that evaluation judgments play a key part in determining the efficiency of search, just as evaluation functions play a key part in tree search by computers. In many cases it will become evident that human cognitive processes are more similar to the comparable computer operations than is often supposed. However, the alternate plies in a search tree are those deriving from an adversary, and predicting the moves of an adversary may constitute an instance where human and computer methods diverge.

FIGURE 2. The chess position used to obtain the protocol plotted in Figure 3. (After Black's 15th in Fischer–Petrosian, Candidate's Match, Buenos Aires, 1971.)

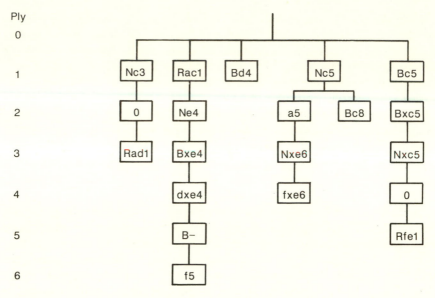

FIGURE 3. Search tree generated by average (1610) player in response to the position shown in Figure 2.

2.1. PREDICTING OPPONENT MOVES

It makes very little difference to a computer, apart from minor technical adjustments, whether it is calculating moves for itself or its opponent. However, human players are very much identified with their own side in a game and may therefore have to overcome various biases in predicting for the opponent. At the simplest level, there is a problem because the opponent's piece layout is upside down, which is bound to affect the player's perception of the situation on the board. In any case, there seems to be a tendency for asymmetry in forecasting the moves for one side or the other.

One kind of evidence was provided by Cleveland (1907), who made a number of observations on people learning to play the game. He classified progress into a number of stages, beginning with learning the moves and ending with the development of "position sense." The latter development of skill was partly associated with the ability to predict opponent moves, which seemed rather poor during the early stages of progress. Rayner (1958b) found very similar results in children learning to play pegity (gomoku), although there were some complications. At the age of 5, the children tended to play "monologues," completely disregarding their opponents' moves. However, by age 7 they switched strategies, regarding the stopping of the opponent as the main object of the game. Thereafter the balance was somewhat rectified, but the proportion of stopped attacks, which implies consideration of the opponent, gradually increased from age 11 through adulthood.

By the time that higher levels of skill have been achieved, there seems to be an increased regard for the opponent. In Holding's (1979) data on chess evaluation, the effect appeared as a heightened judgment of the value of the opponent's position in a number of test games. When seated as White, tournament chess players tended to overestimate the value of the Black position; when they were seated as Black, the reverse effect occurred. The data were also analyzed in terms of relative "winningness," with similar results. When seated on the winning side of a test position, the players overestimated the defensive chances of the losing side; when seated on the losing side, they overestimated the attacking values of the winning side.

Some of the eye movement data collected by Tikhomirov and Poznyanskaya (1966) bear on the same issue. As the visual search of a chess position by a strong player proceeds, the greatest proportion of moves considered are those of the opponent. During the first 35 seconds of inspecting a position, the observed ratio of 6 opponent moves to 1 own move was overwhelming. The ratio dropped to 7:4 in the next 70 seconds, and changed to 6:3 in the final 20 seconds, but it is clear that considering the moves available to an opponent has a very high priority for players at the master level.

2.2. The Opponent's Intentions

There is some evidence that the way in which tree search progresses depends upon anticipating the plans of the adversary. The approach taken by Tikhomirov and Terekhov (1967) was to make recordings of the hand movements of blind players during move choice. These players were accustomed to handling the pieces while considering moves, so that the records showed something of their normal decision processes, and the experimenters were also able to make use of verbal reports by the players. Some aspects of the records seemed to be connected with hypothesis testing. For example, if a sequence of moves appeared highly predictable, as in a series of forced exchanges, the finger movements tended to involve fewer squares on the board. The squares required by the planned moves were visited more often, and lingered over longer, to the neglect of areas of the board peripheral to the action.

One aspect of these effects on search size concerns the accuracy of

TABLE 2. Variation in Search Size Depending on Agreement with Expectation of Opponent Moves[a]

	Objectively			
	Coincident		Discrepant	
Subjectively	Squares contacted	N contacts	Squares contacted	N contacts
Coincident	20	44	20	46
Discrepant	37	149	45–47	450–890

[a]From Tikhomirov and Terekhov (1967).

predictions based on plans or themes. If the opponent made a move consistent with an opponent plan, the sequence was predictable and the number of squares searched was restricted. As Table 2 shows, this was true when the opponent move was subjectively judged to be coincident with his apparent intentions, whether or not there was an objective discrepancy. However, as the experimenters were aware of the intentions of the opponent, it was also possible to examine objective coincidence or discrepancy. When a move was subjectively viewed as discrepant from the opponent's intentions, the search was widened to include more squares, even if the move was objectively coincident. However, the broadest search occurred when the opponent move was really discrepant.

There are other reasons why a human player might broaden or deepen his search, depending on the outcomes he encounters during the search process. Remember, as evident in the earlier discussion of computer play, that obtaining and comparing the outcomes or evaluations is the central objective of forward search. However, before considering these issues in detail, it is necessary to recount the basic findings concerning human search.

3. CHARACTERISTICS OF THE SEARCH PROCESS

The first statistics on human search were those by de Groot (1965), who recorded verbal protocols from players while they were thinking out loud during move choice. There were no substantial differences in the search depth data from five grandmasters and five experts, who explored to average maximum depths of 6.8 and 6.6 plies, respectively. This finding was largely responsible for the abandonment of the idea that better play consisted of thinking further ahead, and hence for the later concentration on memory factors in chess skill.

However, it should be noted that the separation between these players' levels of skill was relatively small, as was the number of players tested, and the data were obtained from a single test position with some idiosyncratic features. In any case, the overall mean depth of search was apparently 5.3 plies for the grandmasters and 4.8 for the experts. Bearing in mind the exponential growth of the search tree, it should be noted that an increase of 0.5 ply in search depth represents a considerable expansion of choice and an appreciably more powerful search. Some of the other statistics are also interesting. The grandmasters considered an average of 35.0 moves, involving 4.2 different lines of play, against 30.8 moves with 3.4 different lines by the experts. Furthermore, the grandmasters thought faster, taking 9.6 minutes (against the experts' 12.8 minutes) to decide on a move, and mentioning 3.5 (against the experts' 2.5) moves per minute.

Later work using the same test position has shown appreciably greater maximum depths of search attained by strong players. A player tested by Newell and Simon (1965) recorded a depth of 9 plies, for example, while an expert investigated by Wagner and Scurrah (1971) pushed the depth out to 15 plies. Although many more moves come into consideration early in the search process, so that the mean depth is usually much less than the maximum, the same player recorded a mean depth of 6.8 plies for an endgame position.

3.1. Problem Behavior Graphs

Following the procedure used by Newell and Simon (1965), the protocol data may be systematized in the form of problem behavior graphs. An example is shown in Figure 4, which makes use of the same data represented in Figure 3. Whereas in Figure 3 the results are organized as a tree of moves, Figure 4 preserves the order in which the different variations were mentioned.

As Figure 4 shows, the protocol is divided into a number of *episodes*, each of which begins with a *base move* and continues until an overt or implied evaluation is made of the resulting position. The end of an episode is the *terminal node*, and alternatives later than the base moves are *branches*. The base moves or later moves may be *unique* or *repeated*, and repeats may be *immediate* or *delayed*. Some moves may be unstated but *implied*, while others may be simply skipped altogether and are known as "no-moves" or *null moves*. A count of *total moves* is

Episode	Ply						
	0	1	2	3	4	5	6
E 1		Nc3 ?					
E 2		Rac1 +					
E 3		Bd4 +					
E 4		Nc3 −					
E 5		Nc5	a5	Nxe6	fxe6 −		
E 6		Rac1	Ne4	Bxe4	dxe4	B−	f5 −
E 7		Nc5 +					
E 8		Nc3	0	Rad1 +			
E 9		Bc5	Bxc5	Nxc5	0	Rfel +	
E 10		Bd4 ?					
E 11		Nc5	Bc8 +				
E 12		Bc5 +					

FIGURE 4. Problem behavior graph representing the protocol shown as a tree in Figure 3. Some of the derived statistics are as follows: time—8.5 minutes; episodes—12; unique base moves—5; immediate repeats—0; delayed repeats—7; other moves—15; null moves—2; implied moves—1; total moves—27; mean depth per episode—2.25 plies; maximum depth—6 plies.

taken to include all of the component nodes, whether repeated, implied, or null. Figure 4 shows the representative statistics that can be derived from these categories.

When these figures are obtained for a sample of players facing a variety of chess positions, there is no room for doubt that differences in playing strength are accompanied by different amounts of forward search. Charness (1981b) compared 34 players whose USCF ratings varied from 1283 to 2004 (from Class D to Expert), finding systematic increases in the depth, breadth, and speed of search. Regardless of age, which was also a factor in the experiment, the average maximum depth of search was 5.7 plies. However, this figure changed by 1.4 plies for each standard deviation (nominally 200) in rating points. The regression analyses therefore give a maximum depth of 3.6 plies at a 1300 rating, for example, which would rise to nearly 9 plies at the expert level of 2000. Essentially similar findings were obtained by Holding and Reynolds (1982), given that the test positions were random.

This sharp increase in maximum depth is partly reflected in the other measures. For mean depth of search over all branches of the tree, the average of approximately 3 plies drops to 2.3 plies at the 1300 level, and rises to 4.1 at the 2000 level. The mean depth would extrapolate to 5.7 plies at the grandmaster level, which is surprisingly close to the de Groot (1965) figure. Apart from these changes in depth of search, there are differences in the times taken and the number of moves explored. An average young player, for example, would take about 8 minutes to explore for a move. During this time he would examine just over 4 different base moves, in approximately 9 episodes, looking at a total of 33 moves altogether. In comparison, an expert of the same age would take 12 minutes—half again as long, but still examining moves at the same rate—looking at 4 different base moves but, in 12 episodes, examining 49 total moves.

There are clearly substantial differences due to playing skill. The Charness (1981b) data also showed some age differences, which are, however, less relevant to our present purposes. The older players tended in general to take less time, and to examine somewhat fewer base moves and total moves. Notice, though, that where their skill level was equivalent, it appeared that the moves they selected were equally good. At any age, increasing skill is associated with deeper and broader exploration of the search tree.

3.2. PROGRESS THROUGH THE TREE

As we have seen, players do not progress systematically through the move tree. There are more separate episodes than there are base moves, because certain moves are repeatedly investigated. De Groot (1965) noted that many of these episodes, particularly those involving delayed repeats, had the effect of extending the search. This tendency was called "progressive deepening," although the protocols show many instances of broadening as well. Later work has shown that what happens depends in large part on the evaluation reached at the end of a search episode. As one might expect, what a player does when he encounters a good line of moves is often different from what he does after an unfavorable continuation.

After analyzing the protocols, Newell and Simon (1965) generated a set of rules for predicting the progress of search. The most important of these stated that the analysis of any base move is independent of the analysis of others, regardless of interruptions, and that the first episode of any base move will involve normal moves, while later episodes will contain increasingly unusual moves. Less often applicable rules are that expansion of the search tree may be restricted to considering only those opponent moves that favor the searcher, and that a check is often made for alternative base moves before selecting a move for play. The most critical rule is the "win-stay/lose-shift" rule: "If the evaluation of an episode is favorable, then analysis of the base move is continued, whereas if the evaluation is unfavorable, then a different move is chosen for analysis."

Work by Scurrah and Wagner (1970) confirms most of the rules but, unfortunately, throws doubt on the win-stay/lose-shift principle. In their protocols, the player often failed to shift to a new base move on encountering a negative evaluation. The next line move was often a self-move, rather than an opponent move, and it appeared that players were more likely to persist with an unfavorable line early in the search process, only shifting when all plausible continuations had been exhausted. The same data (Wagner & Scurrah, 1971) showed an interesting effect due to varying the amount of search time made available by the experimenters. In a set of test positions examined by the same expert player, the number of total moves increased with search time, but the absolute number of different moves was approximately constant at 50 to 60 per game. Hence, the proportion of different moves, which is an index of the breadth of search, went down as search time increased. Apparently, the search becomes shallower but broader when time is short.

Further elucidation of the win-stay/lose-shift principle was provided by Reynolds (1981), who entitled it the "homing heuristic." The use of this heuristic seems to depend on the strength of the player. When de Groot's (1965) protocols were reexamined, the evaluative statements were classified as positive, negative, or neutral, and the direction of subsequent search was noted, with the results shown in Table 3. The cases that comply with the homing heuristic are those where search size increases after a negative evaluation, decreases after a positive evaluation, or does not change after a neutral evaluation. The pro-

TABLE 3. Proportional Changes in Search Size after Negative, Positive, or Neutral Evaluations[a]

	Evaluation					
	Grandmasters and masters			Experts and class players		
	−	+	=	−	+	=
Increase	.46	.18	.36	.42	.29	.29
Decrease	.34	.49	.17	.37	.27	.37
No change	.19	.33	.48	.33	.50	.17

[a]From Reynolds (1981).

portions of these cases, underlined in the table, are clearly higher for the grandmasters and masters than for the experts and class players.

4. PLANS AND KNOWLEDGE

The search process by human or computer need not consist of a blind, full-width examination of all the branches of the tree within an attainable depth of ply. After earlier computer experiments using plausible-move generators to reduce the size of the exponential tree, the most successful mainframe programs of the last decade have employed full-width search. However, as will be evident from the preceding chapter, there are now several programs that attempt to use chess knowledge in more "intelligent" search. For example, the speed chess program written by Church and Church (1977) largely dispenses with forward search by identifying chess goals and then computing plans to achieve these goals. More recently, Frey and Atkin (1979) have proposed methods for using conditional evaluation functions that will give some direction to computer play. In a first phase of move selection, there would be a static analysis to discover key patterns; once these patterns were identified, then modified evaluations would be used to direct the course of search in the light of the identified goals. Again, the PARADISE program by Wilkins (1980), which uses only small amounts of search in order to explore plans, attains the goals identified by consulting a knowledge base.

4.1. USING PLANS

Since computer programmers have attempted to introduce plans and goals in the belief that human players calculate with their help, it is unfortunate that there is so little information on human goal-directed search. It is at least clear from the verbal protocols that human players do consider plans at various levels of abstraction. The 1610 player, whose search tree was illustrated earlier as Figure 3, shows several kinds of planning activity.

During his first appraisal of the situation, and before mentioning any specific move sequences, the player gives some short-range suggestions: "The knight has to be moved to a more central position. . . . Another plan might be to seize the open file by moving the Q rook." At a later point, after episode 4 (in Figure 4), he develops another idea: "I think White should attack the isolated pawn with, maybe, the indirect threat of Radl." This idea later reappears in episode 8 of the problem behavior graph. The player also conceives of a long-term strategy for his opponent, after the long variation in episode 6: ". . . f5 would support the pawn; that way, Black would have some control in the center and his bishop would be able to move, someplace—it would give him somewhat of a K-side attack, maybe some sort of pawn storm." Many similar instances of planning, again at several levels of generality, can be extracted from sources such as the de Groot (1965) protocols.

The advantages of formulating plans are several. The existence of a plan tends to integrate a series of moves and, by giving a direction to selectivity, can potentially restrict the otherwise enormous volume of forward search to a few lines that satisfy the objectives of the plan. Having a plan entails formulating a goal, either short-term or long-term, and this enables the player to search backward from a desired position as well as forward from an existing position. The presence of a clear goal will both expedite and change the process of evaluation, because a terminal node can be directly evaluated in terms of the extent to which it meets the goal objective. The danger, of course, is that adherence to a plan may cause the player to miss other promising moves.

Highly skilled chess players who write chess advice are almost unanimous in recommending the use of plans. Perhaps the most extreme position in this regard has been adopted by Krogius (1976), who favors the idea that even a bad plan is better than no plan at all. However, these ideas remain untested. No experimentation exists on the way in which plans might influence the course of human move selection. As a result, explication of the planning process as applied to move search must come from the design of computer programs.

Bratko (1984), for example, describes an endgame program that initially investigates whether White has a win. Perhaps this can be achieved by pawn promotion, which becomes a first plan for consideration, but the system must now find counterplay by Black. Two alternatives might present themselves—stopping the White pawn, or prompting the Black pawn. Although the first scheme does not work, the second gives a predicted draw, and so White must now modify the initial plan. Up to this point the search has involved only a few nodes. The new modification is a composite plan—promote the White pawn while stopping the Black pawn. Investigating this possibility involves a somewhat larger search, but a search that is still restricted by the need to look only at those moves that impinge on Black's best counterplan. In this way, the program economically achieves forecast goals, using move constraints to identify the means.

4.2 Using Knowledge

The part played by specialized chess knowledge in reducing the scope of the search process is potentially very large. Berliner (1984), whose HITECH program recently won the 1986 Computer Chess Championship, argues that knowledge has the property of projection ability. Tactical knowledge might replace a 9-ply search for the win of a pawn, positional knowledge a 25-ply search, and strategic knowledge a 45-ply search. An example is presented by the "square of the king," an endgame principle that defines the area within which a king can stop an opposing passed pawn. Knowledge of this principle will be equivalent to a search of between 2 and 10 plies. In addition, chess knowledge applied at the terminal nodes of a search will greatly enhance the efficiency of an evaluation function.

Human players, particularly expert players, possess vast stores of verbal knowledge, quite apart from any pattern information. This is hardly surprising since there is other evidence that verbal abilities are prominent in highly skilled players. As many as 96% of the 180 titleholders surveyed by Elo (1978) had proficiency in more than one language, and between 40 and 50% had professions like journalism that require verbal skills. Highly rated chess players are also extremely good at memorizing game sequences, and differences in verbal recall distinguish different levels of skill. In Chase and Simon's (1973) data, players at three levels of expertise were tested on short-term memory for verbally dictated 20-ply sequences, and on long-term memory for a complete 50-ply game. Table 4 reproduces the percentage errors for the dictated sequences, and the errors to criterion made in learning the whole game; for comparison, Table 4 also shows the percentage errors

TABLE 4. Memory for Sequences or Positions by Players of Different Strengths[a]

	Beginner	Class A	Master
Dictated			
20-ply sequence (STM) (percent errors)	43	6	1
Whole game (LTM) (errors to criterion)	94	13	4
Visual			
Briefly displayed (percent errors)	67	51	19

[a]Based on data from Chase and Simon (1973).

made in reproducing briefly exposed, quiescent test positions. Although the memory-skill theory discussed in Section 1.2 above was based on the findings for briefly exposed positions, it is obvious that the differences between players are just as great when verbally dictated move sequences are to be remembered.

Players do rely in part on rote memory for games, using their own past games and those reported in the chess literature. Such specific knowledge can be put to use in many phases of the game. Players also rely on specific knowledge of opening theory, which codifies systems of attack and defense, and conserves search time in the early stages of a game. If one wishes, lines in such well-worn openings as the Ruy Lopez can be memorized to a depth of 15 to 20 moves, or more, although most players content themselves with perhaps 6 to 10 moves over a broad selection of opening variations. Such knowledge is often thought to be most useful when the underlying themes can be generalized, so that departures from a known line can be adequately met.

General knowledge of chess principles can also be used to advantage, in middle game and endgame play. As Cleveland (1907) concluded, the skilled player approaches the middle game like an inventor—he knows what has to be done, and surveys his stock of "pulleys, cranks and gearing" in order to accomplish the task. Forks, pins, and skewers exemplify extremely general plans and techniques that are part of the repertoire of any skilled player. In addition, there are a number of principles, or even algorithms, like the square of the kind mentioned above or the Lucena "bridge" for queening a pawn with K, R, and P against K and R, that bear on the endgame. Such knowledge is a part of the stock in trade of all serious chess players.

4.3. KNOWLEDGE AND SKILL

One recent experiment (Pfau and Murphy, 1988) has attempted to quantify the amounts of verbal knowledge available to players at different levels of skill. Multiple-choice questions were administered to 59 players whose USCF ratings extended from 882 to 2494. There were 75 questions in all, bearing on knowledge pertaining to the opening, middle game and endgame. A typical question about the opening was:

> 5. Smyslov's Variation of the Queen's Gambit Accepted is characterized by:
>   (a) B-N5   (b) P-KN3   (c) P-K3   (d) B-K3   (e) QN-Q2.

A question concerning middle game principles was:

> 33. Generally, the best way to answer a wing attack is to:
>   (a) counterattack on the same wing.

    (b) defend on the attacked wing.
    (c) counterattack on the opposite wing.
    (d) strengthen one's position on the opposite wing.
    (e) counterattack in the center.

Finally, an endgame question is represented by:

14. Triangulation is a technique used to:
    (a) encircle the K in an attack.
    (b) relieve a cramped position.
    (c) gain a couple of tempi.
    (d) win the opposition in K and R endgames.
    (e) win the opposition in K and P endgames.

(Note—the correct answer is (e) in each of these examples.)

The players were also given problem positions to test for tactical and positional judgment, and were given the standard memory task for briefly presented positions. The correlations were then obtained between USCF chess rating, the knowledge, skill, and memory tests, and various measures of playing history and personal characteristics.

The most important result for present purposes was that verbal knowledge proved to be a significant predictor of chess skill. The USCF rating and knowledge scores correlated at .70, which indicates an appreciable effect of chess knowledge. The scores suggest that an expert (2000) player would possess about 55% more knowledge of this kind than an average (1500) player. The two diagram tests, for tactical and positional judgment, correlated at about the same level; this is hardly surprising since these tests directly tap the kind of behavior that determines the chess ratings. On the other hand, the brief memory scores gave a correlation of only .44 with chess rating. Furthermore, using the memory scores in a combined regression equation did not significantly improve the prediction due to chess knowledge. Apparently, chess knowledge is a better predictor of chess skill than is the ability to recognize and classify chess patterns in memory.

5. EVALUATION FUNCTIONS

The value of chess knowledge is most crucial in its application to the evaluation of positions. The search process as a whole is designed to select the best available move by projecting ahead to potential positions, comparing their values at the terminal nodes, and backing up the resulting values to the decision node by a minimax procedure. If this process is to be efficient, the terminal evaluations must be reliable and accurate. Hence, the success of full-width search programs such as CHESS 4.5 and its descendants (Slate & Atkin, 1977) depends heavily on the use of an elaborate evaluation function. There is no point in looking ahead if the value of the resulting positions cannot be evaluated.

It can be shown that a poor evaluation function may actually worsen the prediction achieved by forward search. Nau (1982), for example, has examined circumstances in which search trees may develop "pathology." If the evaluations supplied at the terminal nodes are sufficiently poor, the results of forward search may be paradoxical, with deeper searches yielding worse predictions than shallower searches. It is obvious that errors in calculating piece exchanges will have serious effects, but it should be noted that inaccuracies in positional evaluation may also become compounded, thus leading to errors in move choice.

5.1. Material and Positional Evaluations

Most computer evaluation functions lay heavy emphasis on counts of material balance, with positional considerations playing a secondary role. However, the analysis of game characteristics made by Holding (1980) shows that piece captures are the exception. Out of 11,656 plies that were played in 100 recorded games, only 21% involved captures of pieces or pawns. Furthermore, in most cases these captures were made as part of reciprocal exchanges, so that even fewer of the cases represented changes in material balance. Only 4.5% of all plies contained materially unbalancing captures. Hence, since captures of any kind occur at a rate of only 1 in 5 plies, and material gains at a rate of only 1 in 22 plies, it is apparent that positional rather than material evaluation will be required at the majority of terminal nodes.

Human players show instances of both kinds of evaluation in their protocols. The ends of some search episodes are punctuated by statements like "and that wins the exchange" or "leaving Black a pawn up." In many more cases the evaluations are based on positional considerations, in comments such as "but the bishop at e7 is not controlling anything" or "now White has unconnected rooks, at least" or simply "I like Black's position." Thus, positional judgments by players may range all the way from analytic statements, based on the kinds of principle recommended by chess texts, to purely global statements of opinion.

As Cleveland (1907) recognized, in concluding that a sense of position is the "culmination of one's whole development," human skill depends on accurate evaluation. Players at different levels differ in their abilities to calculate piece exchanges and, more important, in their abilities to forecast positional advantages. Although calculating a series of exchanges is the simpler task, Hartston (1976) even proposes a formula for the value of any combination to the average club player, based on the likelihood of errors. The value rises in direct proportion to the expected gain of material but is taken to decrease rapidly as calculation progresses, in proportion to the square of the number of moves that must be seen ahead.

The kinds of consideration that must be borne in mind for positional evaluation have been summarized by Horowitz and Mott-Smith (1973) in the form of a numerical system. Their "point-count chess" scheme awards points for center control, better development, more space, strong outposts, the bishop pair, the "minor" exchange, half-open files, file control, rooks on the seventh, and a number of pawn features such as a mobile pawn wing, passed pawns (especially when outside or protected), advanced pawns, pawn majorities (particularly when offside), advanced chains, and pawn salients, as well as for having the better king. In contrast, points are lost for various weaknesses of pawns or squares, for backward, doubled, isolated, or hanging pawns, for a hanging phalanx, crippled majority wing, weak-square complex, holes in the position, cramped position, bad bishop, or king in the center. To a great extent, the stronger players appear to take these considerations into account when making positional judgments.

5.2. Judgment and Skill

Work on skill differences in evaluation has mostly relied on global judgments. Holding (1979) developed a numerical scale in which a value of 10 was used as the baseline, and values up to 20 represented successively greater advantages for whichever side was winning. These values were linked with verbal anchors such as 13-advantage; 16-won, with best play; 18-crushing advantage. Since the weaker side is assumed to take a value of 10, the numbers may be viewed as advantage ratios for the White or Black sides. "Black 16" may be interpreted as 1.6 in favor of Black, or, alternatively, all scores may be compared in terms of relative advantage for White (Black, 0.4).

Fifty chess players were asked to evaluate the advantage ratios in five middle games and five endgames, chosen from quiescent positions in world-class games. The simple errors, in which players mistakenly said that White or Black was winning or drawing, were sufficient to show substantial differences between the different playing classes. (The classes span 200 points each, from USCF ratings of 1000 to 2000.) The evaluation errors are shown in Figure 5, where they decrease by a factor of 2 from class E to class A. In addition, it was clear that the differ-

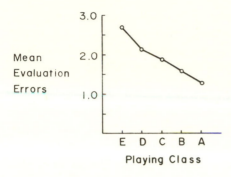

FIGURE 5. Errors in evaluating wins or draws by different classes of player. (Based on data from Holding, 1979.)

ent classes of player used the scale with differing discrimination. The better players used higher values, on the average, while the judgments made by the weaker players were more restricted. The mean advantage ratio judgments descended regularly: class A, 12.6; B, 12.1; C, 11.7; D, 11.6; E, 11.0. A detailed analysis showed that these differences were more apparent in the endgame than in the middle game, and in the more drawish examples of the middle game.

Two of the test positions, illustrated by Holding (1981), were particularly diagnostic of chess skill. Both were quiet positions in which there were no obvious winning moves. Perhaps as a result, the average players assumed that the positions were drawn, while the weaker players gave the win to the wrong side. In the middle game example, class A players (strongest) correctly gave winning chances to Black (at 1.4), class C (average) gave a draw at 0.4, and class E (weakest) gave White the advantage at 1.2. In the endgame example, where White had an edge, the figures were similar: class A, 1.1; class C, 1.0; and class E, 1.1 for Black.

Further analysis confirmed that human players do not carry out an entirely static analysis. Horowitz and Mott-Smith (1973) distinguish between "pictorial" and "dynamic" features in making the point count. For example, it is inadvisable to give a positional credit for a rook controlling an open file (pictorial) if that control can be successfully opposed (dynamic), or to give a demerit for a bad bishop (pictorial) that could be readily exchanged off (dynamic). Human players appear to have incorporated dynamic features into their "static" evaluations in cases where certain move sequences were salient. In one game position most players rated Black's advantage anomalously low, and it turned out that this occurred because they tended to select the wrong move continuation—a minor piece exchange that dissipated the advantage.

This finding was followed up by a count of the instances in which players chose the correct (actual game) move or an incorrect move. Only the above-average players made a sufficient number of correct moves to justify an analysis, but, for these players, it was clear that the move choice influenced the evaluation. When the winning side in a test position has the move, then choosing the correct move should enhance the evaluation, but when the losing side is on the move, choosing the best move should lower the apparent advantage for the winner. There was, in fact, a significant increase when the winner's advantage was favored by the chosen move, compared with a decrease when the chosen move favored the opponent. Hence, although the evaluations are required in order to make a choice of move, the choice of move partially determines the evaluation. Human evaluation processes appear to be partly recursive, with selective search-and-evaluation components providing dynamic contributions to the overall evaluation. As Holding (1985) points out, the dynamic components may be readily and perhaps automatically supplied by the search of small subtrees.

5.3. COMPARISON WITH COMPUTERS

The evaluation judgments secured by Holding (1979) were compared with those offered by computer evaluations at three levels of elaboration. The simplest was an early Shannon-type count of the relative mobility of the White and Black pieces. A second program was chosen as intermediate in its level of sophistication. In this case the evaluation depended on "square control," a measure of the relative chess values of the pieces occupying and attacking each of the squares on the board, which expresses the relative power of the White and Black formations. Reynolds (1982) found that stronger players tend to focus their interest on those squares, whether empty or not, that are impinged upon by the most pieces, and this program shows similar characteristics. Finally, the positional component of the CHESS 4.5 program was taken as the best available example of a complex, knowledge-based function. This program (Slate & Atkin, 1977) incorporates most of the common textbook principles, such as kind defense, varieties of pawn structure, development of knights and bishops, rook connection or file control, and queen mobility and attack potential. The results of applying this function broadly approximate the use of the point-count system.

When correlations were run on the evaluations for the test positions, it appeared that the three computer measures were somewhat interrelated. Although one might expect mobility to contribute toward all three functions, the mobility score correlated only at .40 with square control, and at .58 with the complex CHESS 4.5 score. On the other hand, the square control measure correlated as highly as .75 with the CHESS 4.5 score, despite the fact that one function considers only attack values while the other includes a wide range of chess principles. With the effects of mobility partialed out, the two more advanced functions still correlated at .69, which suggests that both programs are producing fairly similar results by divergent methods.

The most interesting correlations were those between the players and the computer programs, reproduced in Table 5. For this purpose the players were divided into upper and lower skill groups, separated at the average rating of 1500. The two groups of players evidenced somewhat different tendencies. Note first, in Table 5, that only the 1500− players showed a significant correlation with the mobility score, in line with the assumption that this is a relatively primitive measure. The correlations for the stronger (1500+) players rise in concert with the level of complexity of the three computer functions, although the figure obtained for the 1500− players actually decreases on square control. However, the highest correlations for both stronger and weaker players are with the CHESS 4.5 function.

The extremely high (.91) correlation between CHESS 4.5 and the stronger players is rather surprising, until one remembers the level of play attained by the computer. The implication appears to be that both human and computer are operating in analogous ways. In other words, the result is an indirect confirmation of the idea that, like those of CHESS 4.5, the human judgments are at least implicitly based on the kinds of chess principle that give rise to the point count.

TABLE 5. Correlations between Human Judgments and Selected Computer Evaluations[a]

Players	Computer types		
	Mobility	Square control	Chess 4.5
1500+	.44	.58[b]	.91[c]
1500−	.68[b]	.63[b]	.80[c]

[a]From Holding (1979).
[b]$p < .05$.
[c]$p < .01$.

6. PROJECTING AHEAD

Computers have no difficulty in performing evaluations at the intermediate or terminal nodes during search, simply updating the positions as necessary. Human players, on the other hand, often seem overloaded by the process, and may be incapable of accurate evaluation at the search depths they manage to achieve. It seems reasonable to assume that the representations they construct for unseen positions, whether by visualization or by verbal or symbolic methods of encoding, may sometimes be inadequate to support the complete evaluation process. It also seems likely that the necessary ability to project ahead will vary with the degree of playing skill. There are some indications that this is the case.

6.1. FOLLOWING ONE LINE OF MOVES

Research on the forward evaluation of anticipated chess positions has to overcome two major obstacles. One problem arises from the nature of the human search process, which tends to be highly selective and highly variable between different individuals. Hence, if uncontrolled search is permitted, it is impossible to make direct comparisons between players. A second source of difficulty is that no absolute criterion exists for determining the accuracy of evaluations; one cannot assume that a computer-based function will be as accurate as an experienced player, and one cannot simply use the judgments of the strongest players without biasing the results. A provisional solution to the first problem is to control forward search by dictating a fixed subset of move variations. As for the second, one answer is simply to limit the problem to investigating how well different classes of player can foresee their own later evaluations.

In an experiment by Holding and Pfau (1985), players at various skill levels made preliminary evaluations of middle game test positions taken from actual games. The experimenters then dictated pairs of moves, using chess notation, without the moves being made on the board. After each move pair (2 plies), the players had to give a revised evaluation, using the scale described earlier in this chapter. The process was continued for 6 plies, which is approximately the maximum search depth for an average player. At this point the players were asked to recommend the best-seeming continuation move, again based on the anticipated but unseen position. Finally, the pieces were moved into their terminal positions by the experimenter, and the subjects were asked

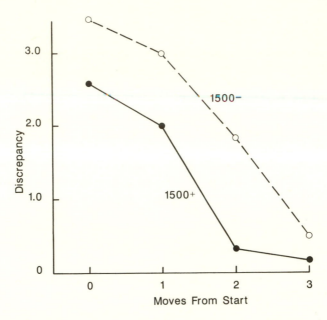

FIGURE 6. Discrepancies between direct evaluations of a final position and evaluations made while thinking ahead for different numbers of moves, for players above and below average playing strength. (From Holding & Pfau, 1985.)

to make direct, visual evaluations of the positions they had earlier foreseen.

Scoring the suggested moves in accordance with their correspondence with actual grandmaster play provided an independent measure of skill, which agreed fairly well ($r = .49$) with the USCF ratings. However, there were some discrepancies among the younger players, apparently due to the rapid fluctuation of their chess ratings. In consequence, the subsequent analyses were again based on a simple split between the 1500 − and 1500 + categories of player. The main score of interest was the discrepancy between the direct evaluations of each final position and those made at each juncture of the look-ahead procedure. The results for the most discriminating game sequence (from Black's 16th to White's 19th in Tal–Szymczak, Lublin, 1974) are shown in Figure 6.

The data illustrate several clear effects. For both sets of players the initial evaluations are considerably at variance with the true state of affairs, presumably because the players underestimate the force of Tal's attack. However, these discrepancies become rapidly reduced as the dictated game progresses. Both groups seem to develop an under-standing of the state of affairs obtaining after White's third move in the sequence. At the same time, there are constant differences at each move pair between the higher and lower groups of players. The 1500 – players remain about one advantage ratio point less accurate than the 1500 + players throughout most of the sequence, although the discre-pancy is substantially lowered by the time the final position has been reached. The 1500 + players show virtually no discrepancy after the second move, appreciating the forthcoming position two plies ahead of its announcement.

6.2. ANTICIPATION THROUGH A TREE

If stronger players can see ahead more clearly, one might expect their advantage to accumulate as the look-ahead progresses. This effect was not found in the last experiment, presumably because the players were following only a single line of moves. A more realistic comparison would use a complete tree of variations, which might yet be predeter-mined in order to avoid uncontrolled differences between individuals. Projecting ahead through a tree of moves would be expected to show progressively increasing differences between stronger and weaker players, and would form an appropriate task for investigating other phenomena such as minimaxing by human players.

Some of my recent work (Holding, in press) has utilized predeter-mined game trees. Sixteen players of different skill levels were asked to give successive evaluations for the unseen nodes of a practice tree and two test trees. As in the previous experiment, the test trees were 6 plies deep. One game (from White's 32nd move in Gligoric–Kavalek, Skopje, 1972) was extremely tactical, with imminent mating threats, while the other (from Black's 15th move in Fischer–Petrosian, Candi-dates' Match, 1971) required more strategic, positional consideration. To keep the experiment within the bounds of subject tolerance, the branching factor was limited to 2 and branching occurred only at alter-nate nodes, for White in one and Black in the other, yielding 8 terminal nodes and 29 total nodes. As an example, Figure 7 shows the more tactical game tree. The moves selected at each branch were based on the extensive analysis of the games provided by Euwe and Meiden (1978).

Again, as before, after the moves were dictated and evaluated, the players were asked to make direct evaluation judgments of the up-dated terminal positions. To check on the relationship between evalu-ation and skill, these judgments were compared with the assessments

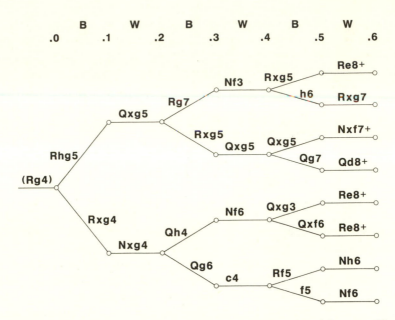

FIGURE 7. Binary tree based on analysis by Euwe and Meiden (1978) of the game Gligoric–Kavalek, Skopje, 1972.

made by a senior master (Dennis Gogel). The 1500− group were significantly worse than the 1500+ group, underestimating the winning side's advantage by as much as 5.1 points, against an underestimate of 1.8 points by the 1500+ players. The relationship shown as a group difference also held good in correlating the individual scores, at −.76, confirming that as USCF rating goes up, evaluation error goes down.

A more important score is the anticipation error throughout successive branches of the tree. However, the discrepancies between the projected evaluations of unseen positions and the direct evaluations of terminal positions cannot be as simply calculated in this experiment as in the previous case, because each binary tree requires 8 direct, terminal evaluations. In this experiment, the minimax values of the direct evaluations were used at the appropriate nodes. Thus, if a player gave an anticipated evaluation of 14 for White at one of the nodes at ply 5, where Black is on the move, and the following direct evaluations are 15 and 11 for White, it is assumed that Black would have chosen the 11, so that a discrepancy of 3 would be recorded. These discrepancy scores were averaged at each ply, with the results shown in Figure 8, where the tactical game is again used as an example.

It is obvious from Figure 8 that the error scores for the higher-rated

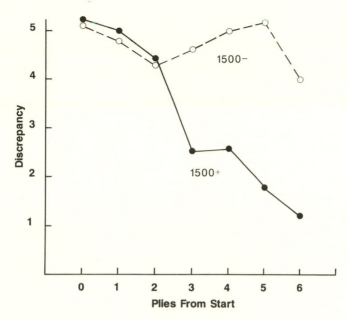

FIGURE 8. Discrepancies between anticipation and direct evaluation for the tree shown in Figure 7, comparing players above and below average in playing strength.

1500+ group are descending virtually as before. As compared with Figure 6, there is a slight increase in the absolute values of error, but the trend is the same. As the position changes toward its final pattern, the stronger players increasingly recognize the potential in the game. However, the weaker 1500— players show the predicted divergence, apparently beginning to improve but then becoming lost in the maze of variations. The statistics for the combined data of the experiment confirm what is seen in the graph. There is a significant difference between playing classes, a significant difference across successive plies, and a significant interaction between players and plies.

6.3. HUMAN MINIMAXING

The data provide further opportunities to determine how consistently human players utilize their trees. One form of inconsistency would be an overall failure to choose the implied best move. In other words, a player might choose Rhg5 as the best move although his evaluation scores yield R × g4 as the best solution. As it happens, the players were asked at the end of the forward judgment task, and before making the direct evaluations, which of the two initial moves they would choose.

For scoring, their anticipatory terminal evaluations were backed up through the tree to give a minimax solution that was then compared with the chosen move. Only one of the 1500+ players showed an inconsistency, but six of the 1500− players did, which is of course a significant difference.

A more detailed examination of inconsistencies within the tree consists of analyzing the discrepancies ply by ply. What these scores provide is an estimate of how well the players foresee the short-range consequences of successive choices. At each ply, the greater of the two succeeding values for White, or the lesser of the two for Black, can be subtracted from the evaluation for that node. These differences may be used as algebraic scores, but it is more instructive for present purposes to neglect the sign of the differences. Table 6 shows the results treated as absolute error, again taking the data from the tactical game as an illustration.

The results shown in Table 6, although reduced in amount, are similar in outline to those derived from the direct, visual judgments as in Figure 8. By and large, the stronger players seem to decrease their error over successive plies, while the weaker players do not. Evidently the discrepancies from direct judgment are partly due to inconsistencies within the tree itself. There is an overall difference in the amount of error made by the 1500+ versus the 1500− players, which is reflected in the means: 1500+, 1.1 per ply; 1500−, 1.8 per ply. As before, the difference is apparent in the individual scores, with the correlation reaching −.76. Stronger players are clearly more consistent in their judgments throughout the game tree, just as they foresee the eventual outcomes better and evaluate them more accurately.

7. HUMANS VERSUS COMPUTERS

As we have seen, even strong human players commit some errors in handling the search process, showing discrepancies between their

TABLE 6. Inconsistencies (Mean Advantage Points) with Minimax
Evaluations at Successive Plies within the Search Tree[a]

Players	Ply					
	0	1	2	3	4	5
1500+	1.5	0.9	1.8	1.5	1.1	1.0
1500−	3.5	1.6	1.6	2.3	2.8	2.6

[a]Based on the tactical game used in Figure 8.

direct and foreseen evaluations and inconsistencies in backing up their own foreseen values. Computers, of course, do not. The kinds of errors that computers may be said to commit are those due to design philosophy rather than to execution, except where there is some identifiable component malfunction. The point is theoretically trivial, but of some practical significance for the design of chess programs since, for example, the designer need not concern himself with miscalculation of variations, and also for the person playing against a computer, who cannot afford to hope for an error to save the game. Our main concern, though, is to decide whether there are any fundamental differences in the approaches to chess play taken by human and computer players.

7.1. KNOWLEDGE, SEARCH, AND EVALUATION

There can be no clear conclusions concerning the comparison of human and computer play, if only because there exist many different types of computer program. Human players make use of chess knowledge, as we have seen above, but so too do many computer programs. Virtually all current programs utilize a data bank of opening knowledge, and some, like the recent versions of Belle, contain many thousands of the opening variations available in the *Encyclopedia of Chess Openings*. Human chess knowledge is also applied to the middle game and endgame phases of the game, where some differences exist. The use of chess knowledge in the later stages of the game has not typified the larger mainframe full-width search programs, although of course there are several other programs that make much greater use of knowledge.

Human players employ a selective search, rather than full-width search. Similarly, many prominent computer players such as the Greenblatt program used plausible-move generators to restrict search width and, although this approach has fallen into disrepute because the initial move selection was often deficient, there has recently been a return to more selective search practices. Then too, many programs such as CRAY BLITZ use forms of variable-depth procedure in which a quiescence search is added to an exhaustive fixed-depth search. This is not too unlike the iterative deepening used by human players, perhaps differing more in degree than in kind. What Hartston (1986) has in mind when accusing computer chess of "artificial stupidity" is the lack of a goal-directed search, and the absence of chess knowledge as applied to the planning process. However, human players do not always use these methods, while some computer programs already incorporate them.

Human knowledge is also valuable in guiding the evaluation of

chess positions, both in providing a basis for positional pluses and mi-
nuses and in determining the conditional values of specific positional
features and material advantages. Some programs incorporate a fair
amount of chess knowledge in the evaluation function, although there
is always a trade-off in allocating processing time between elaborate
evaluation and ply searching. Most programs use conditional evaluation to the extent of changing the weightings when entering the endgame, and, as mentioned above, Frey and Atkin (1979) have presented
much more detailed recommendations for conditionalization.

Nevertheless, it cannot be denied that most of the programs with
which players are familiar are still prone, if decreasingly so, to make
what are disparaged as "computer moves." Often these seem pointless, or directed only at short-term goals. Some examples of the kinds
of move that programmers hope to avoid can be gleaned from the game
shown in Figure 9, a Sicilian Defense played by Bobby Fischer against
an unspecified computer and reported by Adams (1980). The computer
gets a somewhat inferior development coming out of the opening, and

Computer-Fischer

1. e4 c5 2. Nf3 d6 3. d4 cxd4 4. Nxd4

Nf6 5. Nc3 a6 6. Be2 e5 7. Nb3 Be7

8. Be3 0-0 9. Qd3 Be6 10. Nbd7 11. Nd5

Rc8 12. Nxe7+ Qxe7 13. f3 d5 14. Nd2

Qb4 15. Nb3 dxe4 16. Qd1 Nd5 17. Ba7

b6 18. c3 Qe7 19. fxe4 Ne3 20. Qd3

Nxf1 21. Qxa6 Ne3 22. Bxb6 Qg5 23. g3

Ra8 24. Ba7 h5 25. Qb7 h4 26. Kf2 hxg3+

27. hxg3 f5 28. exf5 Rxf5+ 29. Ke1 Raf8

30. Kd2 Nc4+ 31. Kc2 Qg6 32. Qe4 Nd6

33. Qc6 Rf2+ 34. Kd1 Bg4 35. Bxf2 Qd3+

36. Kc1 Bxe2 37. Nd2 Rxf2 38. Qxd7

Rf1+ 39. Nxf1 Qd1 mate.

FIGURE 9. Sicilian defense played by Fischer (Black) against a computer (White). (Reported
by Adams, 1980.)

its aggressive 12. N×e7+ does not really pay. On move 14, the computer plays Nd2, only to have to retract it again (15. Nb3) on the next move. Fischer then uses the temporary win of a center pawn to improve his position, and the computer proceeds to trap its own bishop (17. Ba7), subsequently allowing a knight fork (19. . . . Ne3). In responding oddly to this disaster it again pins its bishop (24. Ba7), generating idle threats on the queen's wing while Fischer prepares a mating attack. As the program succumbs, it is still playing irrelevantly (38. Qxd7), taking an innocent knight far from the scene of action.

7.2. Experimental Comparisons

The modern programs that compete in the World Computer Chess Championship do not make many mistakes as blatant as those recorded in Figure 9. However, identifiable differences remain in their styles of play. Kopec and Bratko (1982) have argued that the computer's ability to undertake high-speed search of thousands or millions of nodes should make for an advantage in sharp, tactical positions, while games by human players should be distinguished by their use of chess knowledge concerning useful move sequences or themes. The pawn-lever theme, in which a pawn is pushed to provide an eventual improvement in pawn structure or damage to the opponent's pawn structure, was selected as the test vehicle.

Examples of tactical or pawn-lever play were given to 35 human players and to 17 different computer programs. Nearly all of the problems contained a single best move, and the scoring reflected whether the correct move was mentioned as a first or later choice. The computer programs scored better than the human players on the tactical positions and, as predicted, scored better on the tactical positions than on the lever positions. In later work with 8 computer programs Kopec, Newborn, and Yu (1986) found a somewhat diminished effect, perhaps because the new problems did not clearly differentiate tactical from positional considerations. Nevertheless, the overall superiority of the computers remained in tactical play.

The later work also investigated the analogue of multiprocessing, inquiring whether human players can improve their play by working in pairs. The paired performance was better—in most cases, it amounted to a gain in playing strength of approximately 200 rating points. It was also shown that players can improve their performance when given more time (30 seconds to 8 minutes) for analysis of the problems. The really strong players were far better than the intermediate level players on the longer tests, although they were barely superior at the shorter time intervals.

7.3. PLAYING AGAINST COMPUTERS

There are several sources of advice for human players tackling computer opponents, although much of the advice is becoming outdated. One very simple strategy that is rarely available was demonstrated by Tom Martinak in a match by masters against four highly rated computers (NUCHESS, BELLE, CRAY BLITZ, and DUCHESS). As reported by Resnick (1983), the player simply replayed, move by move, an earlier first-round win by another player, while the computer simply repeated its earlier loss. Clearly, memory for game sequences can be a valuable human asset. Other players obtained successes by more sophisticated means, such as playing into rook endings, playing for the good versus the bad bishop, and playing for open middle game positions.

The comments of David Levy (1978), who had successfully upheld his challenge against computer chess programs, afford several useful pointers. One consideration is the factor of long-range positional planning, in which chess programs are generally weak. However, his overall strategy is described as "do-nothing-but-do-it-well." In other words, refrain from embarking on tactical complications since, as we have seen, it is in this area that chess programs excel, while human players are prone to miscalculation. Furthermore, the strategy also implies a long-range attempt to reach an endgame safely, since computer endgames, uninformed by chess knowledge, have until recently been notoriously weak in this phase of the game.

The detailed recommendations by Hearst (1977) include studying the computer's weaknesses and, again, concentrating on positional rather than tactical play. A common computer weakness is the tendency to grab material whenever it is offered, and a player can sometimes extricate himself from a tight position by exchanging off the attacking pieces. The human player may also capitalize on this tendency by offering sacrifices, with a fair confidence that they will be accepted, although it pays to be very certain that the sacrifice is sound. In general, the policy of formulating long-range plans, and developing threats as subtly as possible, can be expected to pay off. A final recommendation is again to play for an endgame, in the hope of using superior chess knowledge.

8. OVERVIEW

If indeed the principal difference between human and computer lies in the human ability to use chess knowledge in formulating long-term plans, it is particularly unfortunate that the research literature contains so little that is relevant to planning. At the applied level, as it happens, it is also true that there is little information on the human conduct of endgames. Although this chapter has reviewed a broad array of research findings, there are a number of other gaps in our empirical knowledge of game skills that should be mentioned before attempting to summarize the available research information.

8.1. UNRESOLVED ISSUES

A brief selection may be taken from the unresolved issues identified by Holding (1985). For example, little is known about aptitudes for chess and related games. It is often assumed that chess requires high spatial ability, but there is little to bear this out. It is relatively clearer that verbal processes are involved at various stages of chess memory and computation, but there is room for more explicit investigation of these processes, and for an elaboration of the details of chess knowledge. The study of errors in chess has been completely neglected, so that a typology of errors is needed along with a description of the players and situations that provoke various errors.

There are subsidiary questions concerning how people visualize and view the board, and an enormous variety of possible questions involving memory. Compared with the issues concerning short-term memory, reviewed above, long-term memory has been virtually neglected. However, skilled players remember hundreds of games, and we should ask how these memories interact with chess processing and how this form of memory distinguishes different levels of skill. Again, to what extent it is valuable to memorize explicit algorithms, like the procedure for mating with K, N, and B, needs determining. A different topic is that of cuing for position memory, by placing pennies or some of the pieces on the board, a technique that has provided some interesting but fragmentary results that could be pursued further. Then too, the part played by empty squares in the organization of chess memory and attention requires further research.

As far as plans are concerned, a direct demonstration is needed to show that plans do in fact affect chess behavior. If so, we need to know how many of the moves are planned, by players of different strengths, and what levels of planning are used over what length of move sequence. It is also necessary to distinguish between goals and the means of achieving them, to discover whether these have the same weight in determining skill, and to investigate what forms are taken by the board goals. In some instances a goal might consist of a set configuration, although, more often, the goal might be a sequence of moves such as eliminating a bad bishop. Obviously, a number of issues also arise from the work on search processes reviewed earlier, and the interaction between search and evaluation processes requires further attention. A good model of the fine structure of the human search process is necessary in order to integrate the findings in this area.

Apart from explicating the differences between static and dynamic evaluation, work is needed to reveal the details of evaluative judgments. Good and poor players may or may not use the explicit features of the point-count type of system, for example, and may or may not make their evaluations conditional on different board goals. Again, there are probably differences in the extent to which good and poor players can discount salient but temporary features of the positions to be evaluated. Finally, there are unresolved questions concerning the ways in which players integrate, configurally or by summation, the partial evaluations from specific board features that make up the overall evaluations.

8.2. Conclusions

Despite these gaps in our knowledge, the available research has established a good deal of information. Much of the work is represented in the SEEK model (search, EVALUATE and KNOW) proposed by Holding (1985), which includes the main dimensions along which chess skill seems to be differentiated. The SEEK approach stresses that move choice, which is central to playing skill, is made by reference to the consequences of different move alternatives. These consequences are provided by explicit or implicit search and evaluation, both of which may be supported or supplanted by appropriate chess knowledge. Hence, for human as for computer, the central activity consists of thinking ahead.

In more detail, the work reviewed above has shown that skill differences may underlie, but do not result from, differences in short-term memory. Memory for briefly exposed positions is resistant to interference, and dependent both on level of processing and on features of organization such as chess meaning or spatial concentration, but appears to have an almost incidental relationship to chess mastery. There are, however, other differences in long-term memory for games and for chess theory that seem to play an important part in determining expertise.

Confronting an adversary exacerbates the problem of predicting the consequences of alternative moves, and is differently handled by players at different levels of practice. Beginners are poor at predicting for the adversary, as are young children, but masters appear to concentrate more on opponent moves than on their own moves. Children tend to make more mistakes when attacking, but players at all tournament levels tend to overestimate the opponent's chances. Reading the opponent's intentions helps to determine the extent of search, so that predicted replies yield narrower searches than do unexpected replies.

Other search statistics, often derived from problem behavior graphs, reveal a number of differences between players. Good and poor players differ in their mean and maximum depths of search, in the total number of moves they examine, and in the amount of time spent searching. There are also skill differences in the way that players progress through the tree. All players tend to return to reinvestigate certain sequences, although stronger players do this more often. In many cases this maneuver is accompanied by a tendency to deepen the search after a positive evaluation while broadening it after a negative, although players often fail to react to a negative outcome, particularly when the next move is their own. On the other hand, there is evidence that this decision procedure is more often adopted by stronger players. In addition, there is a tendency toward broadening search when time is short.

The evidence from verbal protocols shows that players do entertain plans, although evidence on their function is lacking. In fact, the most useful information on the process of planning is that deriving from the computer literature. However, research shows that good and poor players differ in the amount of verbal knowledge that they possess, which ranges from rote memory for entire games and organized knowledge of opening variations, to a generalized knowledge of middle game principles and themes, and to a detailed knowledge of explicit algorithms for accomplishing frequently encountered goals. Such differences in knowledge are better statistical predictors of chess skill than are differences in short-term memory.

Players of different levels of skill vary in their gross evaluations of whether the White or Black side is winning, and in the amount of discrimination they show between different positions. Their evaluations are partly dependent on move choice. Only the weaker players use mobility as a criterion, but the comparison with computers suggests that all players tend to use explicit chess features in their judgments.

Stronger players project their evaluations ahead more accurately when following a single line of moves, improving their accuracy as the position develops. When confronted with a binary tree, the weaker players fail to improve their anticipation, although the stronger players improve as before, with the result that the gap between good and poor players becomes progressively wider. Finally, stronger players show better agreement with the minimax values of their later evaluations, and fewer inconsistencies throughout the search tree. Search by the stronger player is therefore distinguished by a clearer appreciation of the consequences of alternative lines of play.

9. REFERENCES

Adams, J. (1980). Fischer in the Philippines. *British Chess Magazine, 100,* 398–400.

Allard, F., Graham, S., & Paarsalu, M. E. (1980). Perception in sport: Basketball. *Journal of Sport Psychology, 2,* 14–21.

Allard, F., & Starkes, J. L. (1980). Perception in sport: Volleyball. *Journal of Sport Psychology, 2,* 22–33.

Anderson, J. R. (1985). *Cognitive psychology and its implications* (2nd ed.). New York: Freeman.

Berliner, H. J. (1984). Search vs. knowledge: An analysis from the domain of games. In A. Elithorn & R. Banerji (Eds.), *Artificial and human intelligence.* New York: Elsevier.

Bratko, I. (1984). Advice and planning in chess endgames. In A. Elithorn & R. Banerji (Eds.), *Artificial and human intelligence.* New York: Elsevier.

Charness, N. (1976). Memory for chess positions: Resistance to interference. *Journal of Experimental Psychology: Human Learning and Memory, 2,* 641–653.

Charness, N. (1979). Components of skill in bridge. *Canadian Journal of Psychology, 33,* 1–16.

Charness, N. (1981a). Visual short-term memory and aging in chess players. *Journal of Gerontology, 36,* 615–619.

Charness, No. (1981b). Search in chess: Age and skill differences. *Journal of Experimental Psychology: Perception and Performance, 2,* 467–476.

Chase, W. G., & Simon, H. A. (1973). The mind's eye in chess. In W. G. Chase (Ed.), *Visual information processing.* New York: Academic Press.

Church, R. M., & Church, K. W. (1977). Plans, goals and search strategies for the selection of a move in chess. In P. W. Frey (Ed.), *Chess skill in man and machine.* New York: Springer-Verlag.

Cleveland, A. A. (1907). The psychology of chess and learning to play it. *American Journal of Psychology, 18,* 269–308.

de Groot, A. D. (1965). *Thought and choice in chess.* The Hague: Mouton.

Eisenstadt, M., & Kareev, Y. (1975). Aspects of human problem solving: The use of internal representations. In D. A. Norman & D. E. Rumelhart (Eds.), *Explorations in cognition.* San Francisco: Freeman.

Elo, A. (1978). *The rating of chessplayers, past and present.* New York: Arco.

Engle, R. W., & Bukstel, L. (1978). Memory processes among bridge players of differing expertise. *American Journal of Psychology, 91,* 673–689.

Euwe, M., & Meiden, W. (1978). *Chess master and grandmaster.* London: Allen & Unwin.

Frey, P. W., & Adesman, P. (1976). Recall memory for visually presented chess positions. *Memory and Cognition, 4,* 541–547.

Frey, P. W., & Atkin, L. R. (1979). Creating a chess player: Thoughts on strategy. In B. W. Liffick (Ed.), *The Byte book of Pascal.* Peterborough, NH: Byte Publications.

Goldin, S. E. (1978). Effects of orienting tasks on recognition of chess positions. *American Journal of Psychology, 91,* 659–671.

Hartston, W. R. (1976). *How to cheat at chess.* London: Hutchinson.

Hartston, W. R. (1986). Artificial stupidity. In D. F. Beal (Ed.), *Advances in computer chess 4.* Edinburgh: University of Edinburgh Press.

Hearst, E. (1977). Man and machine: Chess achievements and chess thinking. In P. W. Frey (Ed.), *Chess skill in man and machine.* New York: Springer-Verlag.

Holding, D. H. (1979). The evaluation of chess positions. *Simulation and Games, 10,* 207–221.

Holding, D. H. (1980). Captures and checks in chess: Statistics for programming and research. *Simulation and Games, 11,* 197–204.

Holding, D. H. (1981). Psychologists analyze the role of memory. *Chess Life, 36,* 30–31.

Holding, D. H. (1985). *The psychology of chess skill.* Hillsdale, NJ: Erlbaum.

Holding, D. H. (in press). Evaluation factors in human tree search. *American Journal of Psychology.*

Holding, D. H., & Pfau, H. D. (1985). Thinking ahead in chess. *American Journal of Psychology, 98,* 271–282.

Holding, D. H., & Reynolds, R. I. (1982). Recall or evaluation of chess positions as determinants of chess skill. *Memory and Cognition, 10,* 237–242.

Horowitz, I. A., & Mott-Smith, G. (1973). *Point count chess.* London: Allen & Unwin.

Jongman, R. W. (1968). *Het oog van de meester.* Amsterdam: Van Gorcum.

Kopec, D., & Bratko, I. (1982). The Bratko–Kopec experiment: A comparison of human and computer performance. In M. R. B. Clarke (Ed.), *Advances in computer chess 3.* Oxford: Pergamon.

Kopec, D., Newborn, M., and Yu, W. (1986). Experiments in chess cognition. In D. F. Beal (Ed.), *Advances in computer chess 4.* Oxford: Pergamon Press.

Krogius, N. (1976). *Psychology in chess* (K. Young & B. Cafferty, Trans.). Dallas, TX: Chess Digest.

Lane, D. M., & Robertsons, L. (1979). The generality of the levels of processing hypothesis: An application to memory for chess positions. *Memory and Cognition, 7,* 253–256.

Levy, D. (1978). Man beats machine. *Chess Life and Review, 33,* 600–603.

Nau, D. S. (1982). An investigation of the causes of pathology in games. *Artificial Intelligence, 19,* 257–278.

Newell, A., & Simon, H. A. (1965). An example of human chess play in the light of chess-playing programs. In N. Weiner & J. P. Schade (Eds.), *Progress in biocybernetics.* Amsterdam: Elsevier.

Pfau, H. D., and Murphy, M. D. (1988). Role of verbal knowledge in chess skill. *American Journal of Psychology, 101,* 73–86.

Rayner, E. H. (1958a). A study of evaluative problem solving: I. Observations on adults. *Quarterly Journal of Experimental Psychology, 10,* 155–165.

Rayner, E. H. (1958b). A study of evaluative problem solving: II. Developmental observations. *Quarterly Journal of Experimental Psychology, 10,* 193–206.

Reitman, J. (1976). Skilled perception in Go: Deducing memory structures from inter-response times. *Cognitive Psychology, 8,* 336–356.

Resnick, P. (1983). Humans beat machines. *Chess Life, 38,* 8.

Reynolds, R. I. (1981). *Search heuristics of chessplayers of different calibres.* Paper presented to the Southern Society for Philosophy and Psychology, 73rd Annual Meeting, Louisville, KY.

Reynolds, R. I. (1982). Search heuristics of chess players of different calibers. *American Journal of Psychology, 95*, 383–392.

Saariluoma, P. (1985). Chess players' intake of task-relevant cues. *Memory and Cognition, 13*, 385–391.

Scurrah, M., & Wagner, D. A. (1970). Cognitive model of problem solving in chess. *Science, 169*, 209–291.

Simon, H. A., & Gilmartin, K. (1973). A simulation of memory for chess positions. *Cognitive Psychology, 5*, 29–46.

Slate, D. J., & Atkin, L. R. (1977). The Northwestern University chess program. In P. W. Frey (Ed.), *Chess skill in man and machine.* New York: Springer-Verlag.

Tikhomirov, O. K., & Poznyanskaya, E. D. (1966). An investigation of visual search as a means of analyzing heuristics. *Soviet Psychology, 5*, 3–15.

Tikhomirov, O. K., & Terekhov, V. A. (1967). Evristiki cheloveka [Human heuristics]. *Voprosy Psikhologii, 13*, 26–41.

Wagner, D. A., & Scurrah, M. J. (1971). Some characteristics of human problem-solving in chess. *Cognitive Psychology, 2*, 454–478.

Wilkins, D. (1980). Using patterns and plans in chess. *Artificial Intelligence, 14*, 165–203.

6

Machine Expertise

J. L. ALTY

1. THE AUTOMATION OF PROBLEM SOLVING— CONTINUING A TRADITION

Problem solving using machines is not new. The activity has been going on for many centuries. However, it was only in the 19th century that real progress on the design and production of machines that could solve a variety of problems was achieved. Babbage designed his difference engine in the 19th century and put it to practical use for the Admiralty. Later he designed the analytical engine but was never able to acquire enough funding to complete it (Morrison & Morrison, 1961). The analytical engine was an impressive system having many of the components of the modern-day digital computer. However, it was based upon mechanical engineering properties, and the tolerances required in its production could not be achieved at that time. It is important to remember this long history of the mechanization of problem solving. It puts present-day artificial intelligence efforts into perspective. Expert systems are, in a way, a continuation of a tradition going back to Babbage.

Automation of problem solving always requires two steps—a representation of the problem-solving process in some form, and an implementation of some or all of these steps exploiting the physical properties of a device or physical material. Babbage's engines required the

J. L. ALTY • Turing Institute, George House, 36 North Hanover Street, Glasgow G1 2AD, United Kingdom.

problem to be restated as a sequence of operations (the program), which were then executed on the mechanical device. The analytical engine provided a major advance in that the steps required for problem solution could be stored in the system itself and then executed automatically. Modern digital computers now provide the technology to do this.

The digital computer was a great advance in that it could handle a wide variety of problems. This led many early workers in artificial intelligence into believing that a general-purpose problem-solving strategy could be implemented on one of these machines. However, early attempts at this approach, such as the general problem solver (Ernst & Newell, 1969), revealed serious difficulties in the approach. Seemingly straightforward problems (in human terms) proved extremely difficult to solve, most attempts at problem solution resulting in combinatorial explosions. It was quickly realized that human beings did not solve problems in this way (in fact, humans are not usually very good general-purpose problem solvers) but rather solved problems by utilizing knowledge about the problem domain itself. This realization gave rise to the knowledge-based approach to problem solving.

In fact, traditional computing approaches had always used this knowledge-based approach. Programs that produced salary advice notes or stock control records have always relied heavily upon a knowledge of the problem built into the program. Such programs were useless for solving any other type of problem. Programming languages such as COBOL and FORTRAN therefore can be regarded, in a sense, as knowledge representation systems.

When artificial intelligence rediscovered the knowledge-based approach, however, it brought added insight to the representation of the problem solution process—the ideas of explicit knowledge representation and the separation of control knowledge. These new insights were crucial and distinguish a FORTRAN program containing a considerable amount of expert knowledge from an expert system. In simple terms, explicit knowledge representation means storing the knowledge in the computer as far as possible in its original form.

2. PROBLEM-SOLVING KNOWLEDGE REPRESENTATION

Given a problem to be solved, the knowledge required to solve it can be collected together in a box, as shown in Figure 1. Such knowledge will be of many types—guesses, hunches, experience. There may be a number of ways of solving the same problem using different subsets of this knowledge. In trying to automate the problem-solving pro-

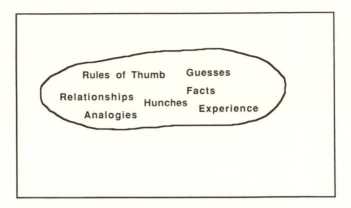

FIGURE 1. The knowledge to solve a problem.

cess, it is unlikely that we will be completely successful. Usually a part of the solution process remains with the human being—often the difficult, judgmental parts of the process. This gives rise in any attempt at automation to the automation boundary (or human–computer interface). The position of this boundary will depend upon the nature of the problem. In some cases—say, salary-slip production—automation will be almost complete. In other cases—say, personnel selection—the human part may still be quite large. However, as traditional computing techniques have improved, the boundary has moved inexorably reducing the human part. If we redraw Figure 1 by reordering the knowledge in it by some measure of complexity, we obtain Figure 2.

The complexity measure is deliberately rather vague. "Straightforward knowledge" covers knowledge such as facts and relationships, which can be relatively easily represented in traditional programs. "Expertise" is that peculiar type of knowledge that we generally ascribe to experts in a particular field and will be defined more closely shortly. "Common sense" knowledge is shown as having the greatest complexity and this might, at first sight, seem rather odd. Yet common sense is rather special and might be described as the "expertise of living." It is extremely wide ranging, utilizing a vast knowledge base of experience.

Figure 2 shows the progression of the automation boundary over the years as computing techniques have become more extensively used. Traditional computing is now coming up against the problem of representing expert knowledge and is beginning to find that traditional representation techniques are inadequate. To justify this assertion we need to examine what expert knowledge is.

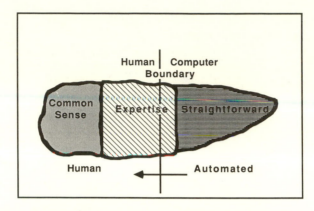

FIGURE 2. Problem-solving knowledge ordered by complexity.

3. THE NATURE OF EXPERT KNOWLEDGE

Although it is difficult to be precise about the nature of human expert knowledge, we can make some statements about it. First, it is often inexact. Indeed, the higher the level of the expertise, the more inexact it becomes. Real experts rarely use calculators, more usually manipulating sets of symbols and probabilities. It is also often incomplete, the gaps in the data being filled in by intuition, experience, or reasoning about relationships. One of its most significant properties is that it is not always correct. Experts are sometimes just plain wrong! The definition of an expert might even be "someone who gets it wrong less than most people." Expert knowledge is also rarely a complete description of the problem space, often involving the use of a set of incompatible and incorrect models. Expertise might also be defined as knowing when to use which of a set of incorrect models.

An important aspect of experts and expertise is the importance of explanation or justification (Teach & Shortliffe, 1985). Because experts do not always reach the correct conclusion, their clients are entitled to ask for an explanation of the advice given, or a justification for a recommended action. The clients then have to make up their own minds as to whether or not to accept the advice given. Usually, clients cannot escape the legal consequences of actions resulting from implementing an expert's advice, so they must be able to check the situation with the expert and have an explanation in a language that they understand.

Finally, an important property of expertise is that it is continuously changing. Experts are repeatedly updating their knowledge. Failures are used to modify and improve performance. There is no end point. Experts cannot declare a time when their expertise is complete.

4. KNOWLEDGE REPRESENTATION

We do not know how knowledge is represented in the human brain, but we can define some characteristics that will be important in representing problem-solving knowledge. Clearly, we will have to represent facts, such as "an Alfa-Romeo is a car" or "Peter is a man." Furthermore, we must be able to represent relationships between these facts, such as "Peter owns an Alfa-Romeo." In reality, relationships can be very complex, such as the management structure of a large organization or the structure of a huge organic molecule. Facts and relationships are obviously important, but they have limited value in themselves. It is the sort of knowledge we find in the data division of a COBOL program. It is not capable of solving problems. To solve problems we need knowledge that acts upon the facts and relationships and creates new ones. Such knowledge is equivalent to the procedure division of a COBOL program.

The procedural knowledge of a FORTRAN or COBOL program can be represented in a variety of constructs, but it can be shown that such knowledge can always be represented as a set of rules of the form

if conditions *then* actions

The conditions are conditions of the static knowledge and the actions change the static knowledge. By successively applying the rules the static knowledge base is changed until a required solution is achieved. Thus, if we had two facts, such as "The sky is red" and "It is dusk," and a rule of the form

"if the sky is red *and* it is dusk *then* the shepherds will be delighted"

we could create the knowledge that "the shepherds are delighted."

In any real problem-solving activity there will be many such rules, and at any time a number of rules will have their *if* conditions satisfied. The difficulty is which rule should be executed? This is a problem of control and involves a further type of knowledge required in problem solving. What should be done next? In the traditional approach the control knowledge is rather primitive. Programming statements are usually ordered in some way, and the control strategy is "if the next activity is not defined try the next programming statement."

The problem-solving activity can therefore be represented as a set of facts, relationships, rules, and control, and we can identify all these types in traditional computing.

5. PROBLEMS WITH THE TRADITIONAL APPROACH

As has already been pointed out, the traditional programming languages conveniently separate out knowledge into static and active elements. COBOL makes this very explicit and most traditional languages rely on this distinction. Human knowledge does not fit into this neat classification, and problems occur particularly in learning. Let us take the earlier example concerning shepherds. The rule "*if* the sky is red at dusk *then* the shepherds are delighted" is true whether or not we ever apply it. It can be regarded as static knowledge about the world—a sort of conditional fact. More important, we have to consider it in this way if we are in a learning situation. Let us assume that the sky is red at dusk and we come across some exceedingly disgruntled shepherds. Clearly, our rule (or conditional fact) is in error. Under questioning the shepherds reveal that they have not been paid! We now need to learn by modifying our rule to "*if* the sky is red at dusk *and* the shepherds have been paid *then* the shepherds will be delighted." In this learning process the rule becomes a data and is edited by some higher-level rule. The "active" knowledge has become "static" knowledge. The distinction made in traditional programming languages between data and program therefore not only is incorrect but also removes from them the capability of learning new rules.

A second problem of traditional knowledge representation comes from the available data structures and the ways in which they are manipulated. Indices are used in profusion—array subscripts, record numbers—and these are manipulated in *do* loops or *for* loops that manipulate the index. The control strategy is so based upon the statement order that it is almost impenetrable by anyone other than the programmer who wrote it. No wonder there are serious problems in program maintenance. Traditional programmers are effectively "knowledge butchers." The knowledge required to solve a problem is hacked and distorted until it fits the traditional representation scheme. It may then do the job required but cannot be easily recognized as doing it. This often means that the persons who supplied the knowledge (the domain experts) cannot recognize the representation of their knowledge in the programming language, and they certainly cannot debug it when errors occur. The knowledge is there but it has become implicit. The programming maintenance problem becomes particularly serious when the representation of expertise is considered. Because expert knowledge is continually changing, we could be faced with an impossible maintenance situation.

The issue of explicit knowledge is not only confined to the way in which we represent the procedures; it also involves the control strategy itself. If we are to successfully explain the actions of the program, we need to represent the control (or reasoning) strategy explicitly as well. If a traditional program were asked why it did a particular action, in most cases it would reply, "because it was next." Ideally, we would like the control strategy to mimic as far as possible that of the expert.

Another problem with traditional programming concerns the extensive use of algorithms. Most expertise does not fit conveniently into this framework. Experts do not have fixed ways of solving problems. Their solution strategy varies as the solution progresses, and the choice of the next step is often based upon its appropriateness in bringing the current state nearer to the ultimate goal. To do this experts make extensive use of heuristics. They also use heuristics to determine which heuristic to use. Heuristics are effective in handling large search spaces where algorithmic approaches suffer from a combinatorial explosion.

6. ARCHITECTURES FOR REPRESENTING MACHINE EXPERTISE

We can therefore list some important properties that we would require in any program simulating human expertise:

- The knowledge should be stored in an explicit form.
- The reasoning should be as "natural" as possible.
- The system should be able to provide explanation of its behavior.
- The system should be able to handle uncertainty.
- The system should be capable of incremental updating.

There are a variety of architectures for representing human expertise in machines which, in part, can meet these requirements. We will consider two main approaches—the rule-based approach (and a development called the blackboard approach), and frame-based abduction (or set-covering technique).

6.1. THE PRODUCTION SYSTEM APPROACH

This is described in more detail in the chapter on machine inference. Briefly, a production system consists of a *database* of facts and
relationships, a set of *if . . . then* rules known as *productions* and a
control mechanism that decides which one of a set of applicable rules to
execute. The *if* part is a set of conditions in the database, and the *then*
part alters some facts or relationships in the database. Figure 3 below
illustrates the key components. The system can operate in two modes
known as forward and backward chaining. In forward chaining mode
(sometimes known as data-directed) the set of rules that can "fire" at
a particular instance is determined (called the conflict resolution set),
and one rule is chosen by the control strategy and fired. The cycle is
repeated until the goal is reached. In backward chaining mode (often
called goal-directed) the set of rules that, if fired, would have produced
a possible goal is determined. One is selected and the *if* conditions now
become new goals.

The process is repeated until a situation is reached where all the *if*
conditions are satisfied (possibly by asking the user) and the goal is
therefore proved. Otherwise, another goal is chosen and the process
repeated. It is now common to call the facts, relations, and productions
the *knowledge base*, and the control system the *inference engine*.

Production systems are convenient architectures for implementing
expert systems. The reasoning mechanism is flexible (forward or backward) and the expertise stored as rules is in a reasonably explicit form.
They therefore satisfy two important characteristics mentioned ear-

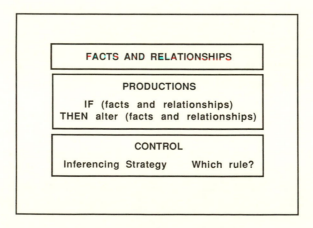

FIGURE 3. A production system.

lier—that the knowledge should be explicit and that the reasoning mechanism should as far as possible mimic the expert. These two properties also provide a mechanism for at least partially satisfying the third requirement—that the system should be able to provide explanations of its behavior. When a user of the system asks, *"How* did you reach that result?"* the system can provide a trace of the rules fired and the output will be reasonably explicit. Alternatively, the user can ask, *"Why* are you asking me this?"* and the system can quote the current rule. Repeated use of *why* takes the user back up the reasoning path.

A key part of any production system is how the control strategy is implemented. One popular method is to order the rules in order of priority and then fire the first rule that can be fired. After this the strategy is repeated from the top of the rule set again. This strategy, however, violates one of our principles—that of having an explicit reasoning mechanism. If the user asks, *"Why* did you fire that rule?"* the only answer the system can give is "because it was the first I could fire." In a priority system most of the crucial strategy knowledge is contained in the rule order.

A better way is to use "metarules," which are rules about rules. A metarule can be used to choose which particular rule should be fired from a conflict resolution set. The user can now ask *why* and get a more meaningful answer. Metarules are a convenient way of representing the control strategy in an explicit manner and enable the inference engine to be considerably simplified and made more general. This is an important consideration when we discuss the concept of expert system shells.

The production system approach can also provide the other two requirements outlined earlier, the facility for incremental updating and a mechanism for handling uncertainty. If the rules are designed carefully, using unique *if* conditions and metarules, the ordering of the rules is immaterial. This means that rules can be added very easily giving an incremental updating capability. Uncertainty can be handled by adding "certainty factors" to the rules and data, and these can be propagated using a variety of mechanisms.

The rule-based approach is based upon deductive logic. In Section 7 we discuss three approaches to implementing expert systems using a production systems approach—MYCIN, XCON, and PROSPECTOR.

6.2. MULTIPLE EXPERTS AND MIXED REASONING STRATEGIES

There are many problems for which a single expert does not have the knowledge to solve a problem by himself. In such cases, a collection of experts working cooperatively will often be successful. This concept has been used to develop an approach called the "blackboard" architecture. A set of experts each work on their own subproblem but communicate their intermediate results via a blackboard. Some experts utilize the output of other experts as input to their problem-solving process and their output is used in turn by others. The approach was first used in the development of the HEARSAY speech understanding system (Erman, Scott, & London, 1984) but has more recently been applied to problems such as sonar detection and protein molecule identification. The individual experts in these systems are often rule-based. A more detailed examination of the HEARSAY system is given in Section 8.

6.3. The Set-Covering Approach (or Frame Abduction)

The frame-based abduction technique is actually based upon a well-known approach in operational research—the set-covering technique. The domain-specific knowledge is collected into sets or frames (Minsky, 1975) and sets of hypotheses are generated to explain the observations. These are then tested by examining their ability to describe what has been observed and new questions are then generated to assist between the choice of competing hypotheses. As a result, new information is generated and the cycle repeated. It is said that the knowledge required for this approach is relatively easy to collect since it occurs naturally in frames. It also works well when multiple causes are a possibility. INTERNIST, for example, can diagnose multiple disease situations. The INTERNIST system is described in Section 9.

6.4. Multiple Paradigms

It is possible, of course, to use a combination of the techniques outlined above. Such a knowledge-rich approach is exemplified in the use of sophisticated artificial intelligence workstations such as those provided by Symbolics, Texas Instruments, or Xerox. These systems are based upon the object-orientated approach exemplified in the SMALLTALK system (Goldberg & Robson, 1983). Knowledge is collected together in frames that can embody methods as well as factual information. These frames are connected in the form of a hierarchy. The lower-level frames in the system are objects. Objects communicate by passing messages to each other. Values can be active in that a change to them will send a message to another object.

Methods in frames can be rule-based, and frames, by definition, can be used to collect together sets of information. An example of such a system is the COMPASS expert system for telephone switch maintenance, which is described in Section 10.

7. THE RULE-BASED APPROACH—MYCIN, PROSPECTOR, AND XCON

A large number of successful expert systems have been created using the rule-based approach. To illustrate the approach we will examine three rather early examples, two of which are no longer used in anger (MYCIN and PROSPECTOR). However, the systems have been extensively reported on and have been used as models for many subsequent systems; thus, they have considerable pedagogical value. They also cover a wide range of techniques—uncertainty with backward chaining in MYCIN, uncertainty based upon Bayesian statistics and the use of inference networks in PROSPECTOR, and forward chaining with metarules in XCON.

7.1. THE MYCIN SYSTEM

MYCIN (Shortliffe, 1976) was developed at Stanford University to assist physicians with the diagnosis and treatment of infectious diseases. It tries to establish the cause of the disease (i.e., the bacterium) and then prescribes treatment. The factual knowledge is stored as a set of triples (with a certainty factor) of the form

CONTEXT—PARAMETER—VALUE (0.8)

A context is some real-world entity, such as a patient; a parameter is some attribute of the context (e.g., age); and the value is its actual value (e.g., 24 years). The certainty factor of the triple varies between -1 (false) and $+1$ (true). An example of a triple might be

ORGANISM1—IDENTITY—PSEUDOMONAS (0.8)

meaning "the identity of organism1 is Pseudomonas with a certainty of 0.8." The reasoning process instantiates triples and manipulates uncertainties. At the commencement of the consultation many triples will be incomplete.

A typical production rule in MYCIN is shown in the following:

if   1.   it is not known whether the organism was able to
               grow aerobically
and   2.   the site of the culture is blood
or   the lab has attempted to grow the organism an-
               aerobically
and   3.   the organism was able to grow anaerobically
then   there is evidence that the aerobicity of the organism
               is facul (0.5) or anaerobic (0.2).

These rules are encoded in LISP, but a translation facility exists to enable a rule to be viewed in its original English form. Normally, backward reasoning is employed, the rules are repeatedly applied using
domain-dependent knowledge to decide which rules to consider, until
the goal triple(s) is instantiated. Some rules instantiate triples by asking
questions of the physician. The certainty factor of a triple is calculated
from the certainty factor of the premise, the certainty factor of the rule,
and the triple's original certainty factor if it existed already (Shortliffe
& Buchanan, 1975). For a simple account of how this is done see Alty
and Coombs (1984).

    The inference engine is guided by domain-dependent knowledge
in the form of a context tree. A typical tree is shown in Figure 4. The
tree is a form of template, and the actual triples that are instantiated
during the consultation mimic the tree. Explanation facilities are provided via *how* and *why*.

    Below is an annotated example taken from an actual consultation
(user input is given in italic type):

Is ORGANISM1 a streptococcus?
No. The identity of ORGANISM1 is E. coli (.7),   MYCIN simply lists the
    Klebsiella pneumoniae (.4), Pseudomonas   ORGANISM1 triples
    (.22), Proteus nonmirabilis (.19), Salmonella   in order of cer-
    (.02).   tainty.

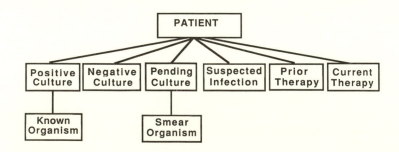

FIGURE 4. A MYCIN context tree.

Why did you rule out streptococcus as a possibility for ORGANISM1?

Rule 33 could have been used to determine that the identity of ORGANISM1 is Streptococcus. However clause 2 of rule 33 [the morphology of organism is coccus] was already known to be false so the rule was never tried.

> Note the use of an English-like syntax. MYCIN identifies the rules that could have yielded this identity. It identifies the part(s) of the premise that were false.

How do you know that CULTURE1 *was from a sterile source?*

I used rule 189 to conclude that this blood culture was taken from a sterile site. This gave a cumulative c.f. of 1.0. The last question asked before the conclusion was made was 7.

> MYCIN lists the rule that instantiated this triple and indicates the last question asked.

What does GU *manipulation tell you about the identity of an organism?*

The rules listed below use whether the patient has had a GU manipulative procedure to conclude about the identity of the organism.

> MYCIN identifies those rules that have identity in the conclusion and GU procedure in premises

163, 166, 190. Which do you want to see?
166
Rule 166:

> The rule is displayed

if   1. the site of the culture is blood
and 2. the gramstain of the organism is gramneg
and 3. the morphology of the organism is rod
and 4. the portal of entry of the organism is urine
and 5. the patient has not had a GU procedure
and 6. cystitis is not a problem for which the patient has been treated
then   there is suggestive evidence (.6) that the identity of the organism is E. coli.

Note that this explanation follows directly from the production rule approach and the explicit storage of the rules. In fact, it is only a good explanation for another physician who understands the language, but the existence of a common language is true of many situations. With such a facility the domain expert can work with the system directly and suggest changes during development. It is also a very effective debugging tool.

MYCIN worked well within its limited domain. In a test with 10 random cases it attained a score similar to that of expert physicians. MYCIN was important because it became a model for many other expert system projects, such as SACON (engineering structural calculations; Bennett, Creary, Englemore, & Melosh, 1978), CLOT (blood disorders; Bennet & Goldman, 1980), and PUFF (respiratory intensive care; Aikins, Kunz, & Shortliffe, 1983).

7.2. THE XCON SYSTEM (R1)

Although based upon the production rule approach, XCON (previously known as R1; McDermott, 1982) exhibits some different characteristics than MYCIN. It is forward-chained and does not use uncertainty. It has also been most successful and is now used in a production environment. The objective of XCON is to take a list of system requirements for a computer system from a salesman and compute a working configuration of the components that make up the order. The history of the problem is interesting. DEC had tried to solve this problem a number of times, using conventional techniques, and had failed. This was because of the continuously varying knowledge required for the problem. The factory frequently makes changes to components either because of manufacturing difficulties or because of maintenance difficulties in the field. Furthermore, the designers are continually bringing out new devices and connections to extend the range. All these changes have an impact on the configuring process.

In 1978 Carnegie-Mellon University approached DEC and suggested that the problem might be attempted using knowledge-based techniques. The response was rather muted, but they were allowed to proceed with the development of a prototype. This was implemented in a production system language OPS4, later OPS5 (Forgy, 1981). The initial objective was to correctly configure 75% of orders for VAX computers. This was achieved with a few hundred rules. The next stage proved to be more difficult, and many rules were required to bring performance up to 95%. Now the system has over 3000 rules (though it does cover PDP11 computers as well), and it is in regular daily use.

Forward chaining can often lack focus. McDermott analyzed the configuring problem and found that it could be subdivided into six subproblems that involved no backtracking. The sequence was as follows:

- Determine if there are inconsistencies in the configuration.
- Put appropriate components into CPU cabinets.
- Put boxes in the Unibus expansion cabinets and the appropriate components in the boxes.
- Put frames in the Unibus expansion cabinets.
- Lay out the system diagram.
- Work out the cabling.

This was the order that had been observed in real experts. The rule-set can therefore be subdivided into six subsets or contexts. At the conclusion of a subtask, special rules generated the new context. These rules are effectively metarules.

OPS5 is a standard implementation of a production system in LISP. It does not therefore provide explanation facilities or uncertainty. Although it provides forward chaining backward chaining can be achieved by adjusting the problem. It has two conflict resolution strategies, LEX and MEA (XCON uses the latter). In MEA (means–end analysis) the strategy is (in order):

- Do not fire any rule-instantiations that have already fired.
- Use the first condition of the premise.
- Use the most recent instantiation.
- Use the most specific rule.
- Choose one at random.

The first condition prevents loops from occurring. The second condition is really the means–end analysis (the first *if* condition being a form of context marker so the rest of the conditions will be applied only to rules in the same context). If there is still a conflict, the most recent instantiations are chosen. If this still does not resolve the issue, more specific rules (i.e., more premise conditions) are chosen. Finally, if there is still a conflict, a rule at random is chosen from the remaining set. (For a more detailed account see Brownston, Farrell, Kant, & Martin, 1985.)

The facts in the knowledge base are essentially simple LISP lists. They are sets of attribute-value pairs. One member of the list may itself be a list. For example, the RK711 disk drive is represented as:

RK711-EA
    Class: Bundle
    Type: Disk drive
    Supported: Yes
    Component list: 1   070-12292-25
                        1   RK07-EA*
                        1   RK611

and the components mentioned will be further defined as lists of attribute-value pairs.

The rules are of three types—sequencing rules, operator rules, and information-gathering rules. The sequencing rules divide the rule-set into subsets and control the movement between subtasks. The operator rules check on constraints and place components in the configuration. The information-gathering rules access the database and provide the other two types of rule with information. Here is an example of an operator rule:

if   the most current active context is selecting a box and a module to put it in

and   the next module in the optimal sequence is known

and   the number of system units of space that the module requires is known

and   that box does not contain more modules than some other box on a different Unibus

then   try to put that module in that box

Note that the first condition is a context condition. The result of the MEA conflict resolution strategy is that this rule will be considered only in context. The explicit representation of the rules and the "natural" inferencing strategy mean that the domain experts can interact with the system and improve its performance. The output of XCON is continuously monitored by the experts and the rules modified to improve performance. This would be difficult to do in a conventional system. The system is now in regular daily use, and it is said that it pays for its development costs every few months.

It is interesting to note that the choice of VAX configuring at the outset was an arbitrary one. McDermott has suggested that if the alternative domain of PDP11 configuring had been chosen instead (and it was an option), the project would probably have foundered. The VAX problem had just the right level of complexity and was able to continue to satisfy management that the development was worth continuing. Once the VAX problem had been solved, the confidence it generated enabled management to justify the more difficult PDP11 problem (McDermott, 1981). There is a lesson here on initial choice of domain.

7.3. THE PROSPECTOR SYSTEM

PROSPECTOR (Duda et al., 1978) was developed by SRI International, in consultation with geological experts and the U.S. geological survey, to assist expert geologists in the evaluation of geological sites for certain deposits, in the evaluation of favorable geological resources in a region, and in selecting favorable drilling sites. It was developed over a decade between 1974 and 1984 and was implemented in LISP.

Geologists use highly specialized models when trying to determine the composition of a portion of the earth's surface. They examine the area for clues as to which of a number of models is most likely to describe the substructure below the surface. Once the appropriate model has been determined, it is a relatively easy task to make predictions about composition. Thus, they key expertise lies in model determination from a series of observations. PROSPECTOR uses a production sys-

tem architecture with some important extensions. Like MYCIN, it han-
dles uncertainty, but in a totally different way (Duda, Hart, & Nilsson,
1976). A rule in PROSPECTOR has the form:

if evidence *then* {to some degree} conclusion

These rules are put together into what is called an "inference net." The
conclusion of one rule can be the evidence of another, and the way in
which the rules can be fired is highly structured. The rules are simple,
often having only one *if* condition. Thus, a network is formed as in
Figure 5.

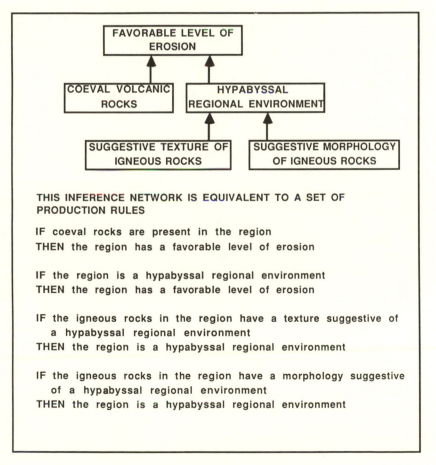

FIGURE 5. An inference network in PROSPECTOR.

Thus, much of the control structure is in the network itself. At the top of the diagram are goals (conclusions with no exit arcs). At the base of the network are questions (evidence with no arcs attached). The network shown in Figure 5 is actually taken from the middle of the network, so there would actually be further rules leading from "favorable level of erosion." The goals of the network are the different possible models of the earth's surface. There are about a hundred different models, though only a few are implemented in PROSPECTOR.

Uncertainty is handled in the following way. Each "space" (evidence or conclusion) is given a prior probability. This will be the probability of this space's being true in the absence of other evidence. All the goal model spaces, for example, will have a prior probability of being found somewhere on the earth. Question spaces will obtain a probability from the user. Each rule has associated with it a "rule strength," which consists of two numerical values called LN (logical necessity) and LS (logical sufficiency). These factors transmit changes in the probability of the evidence to the conclusion. The system works as follows:

- The goal with the highest probability is selected, and backward chaining takes place up the network until some questions are reached.
- The questions are answered with probabilities, and these cause changes to the probabilities of any conclusions directly connected to these question spaces.
- The changes in these conclusion spaces are changes in evidence for any rules emanating from these spaces, so these changes in turn cause changes in the conclusions of emanating rules.
- This continues until the changes are propagated right through the network to the goals and the cycle is restarted, but questions already asked are not asked again.
- Eventually, the probability of one goal rises significantly above the rest, and this is the conclusion of the consultation.

Probability propagation is achieved using Bayesian statistics (Konolige, 1979; for a simple treatment, see Alty & Coombs, 1984).

The prior probabilities and the LN and LS values constitute much of the expertise in the network and have to be supplied by the experts. The factor LS indicates how the probability of the conclusion is affected by knowing that the evidence is certain. LN indicates how the probability of the conclusion is affected by knowing that the evidence is false. Experts usually find it quite difficult to estimate these values.

In addition to the inference network, the spaces in it are connected together by a separate semantic network. This is geological knowledge such as "Pyrite and bomite are sulfides." This enables the questioning to be more realistic and avoids unnecessary questions, such as asking if sulfides are present when the system already knows that bomite is present.

Testing of PROSPECTOR showed that the system could accurately predict the location of mineral deposits. In 1980 at a test site near Washington, PROSPECTOR predicted the existence of molybdenum. Later drilling confirmed this prediction. The system was also the forerunner of a number of expert system shell-building tools, which are described in Section 10.

8. THE BLACKBOARD APPROACH (HEARSAY)

The HEARSAY system (Erman et al., 1984) was developed at Carnegie-Mellon University and is an attempt to apply symbolic reasoning techniques to signal processing. It recognizes words from a 1000-word vocabulary uttered as connected speech with about 90% accuracy. As a speech-understanding system it does not have a particularly remarkable performance, so its claim to fame resides in the type of architecture developed, known as a "blackboard" architecture. The basic idea is simple. A problem may not be solvable by a single expert but may be solvable if the expertise of a number of different experts is simultaneously employed. The experts communicate by means of a "blackboard."

When an expert finds something new, it is written on the board. It is immediately available to all and may trigger other experts to determine further new knowledge. The process continues until the problem is solved. The essential constituents are therefore a blackboard, or communications area, a mechanism for scheduling the experts, and a representation scheme for the expertise of the individual experts (often sets of production rules).

Figure 6 shows the knowledge sources (blackboard) and experts in . HEARSAY. The parameter level is the signal level for the speech utterance, and SEG produces a labeled segmentation from this. POM spots syllables, MOW creates words, and Parse attempts to parse word sequences. Word-seq-ctl and Word-ctl try to control the number of hypotheses created. Some experts (for example, MOW, POM, and SEG) are data-directed and use the knowledge at one level to influence a higher level. Other experts are goal-directed (e.g., Verify), while others operate at the same level (Predict and Stop, for example). RPOL communi-

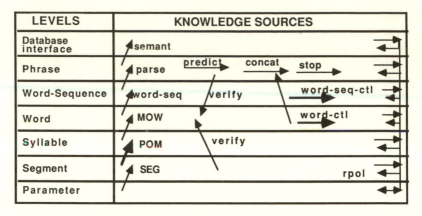

FIGURE 6. Knowledge sources and experts in HEARSAY.

cates between all levels and influences which expert will go next. The
blackboard architecture can therefore be viewed as the implementation
of a mixed forward–backward chaining strategy.

Effective problem solving in HEARSAY depends upon constructive
cooperation between the experts. Actions are constructive or competitive as to whether they support or compete with current hypotheses.
A process of selective attention is adopted to limit actions to those that
seem most promising. This selective attention is implemented using a
heuristic scheduler that calculates a priority for each action and executes the current highest priority action.

HEARSAY was not outstandingly successful in its chosen domain,
and a discussion of these deficiencies can be found in Lesser and Erman (1977). The technique has recently been applied in a number of
other domains (see Nii, 1986) and is expected to grow in importance.

9. THE SET-COVERING APPROACH (FRAME ABDUCTION)

The set-covering approach is based upon a formal theory of diagnostic inference (Reggia, Nau, & Wang, 1983) and is said to have many
of the normal diagnostic approach characteristics of human experts. A
disorder in a system usually presents itself in the form of symptoms.
Initially, human experts will probably be aware of only a few of these
symptoms. They construct a tentative hypothesis about the possible
causes, and the hypothesis is then tested by looking for more symptoms that ought to be present. Their presence or absence defines new

symptom and cause subsets, and the method is repeated. This is often termed a sequential hypothesis-and-test process (Elstein, Shulman, & Sprafka, 1978). The complete system consists of a knowledge base, an inference engine, and a user interface. Thus, architecturally it is similar to the rule-based approach, but the inference engine operates in quite a different manner.

9.1. THE INFERENCE MECHANISM

The inference mechanism can be described with the aid of Figure 7 (the treatment is based upon Reggia et al., 1983). Each disease d_i has a set of manifestations man(d_i) associated with it, and each manifestation m_j can be caused by a set of diseases causes(m_j). The complete sets D ($d_1, d_2, d_3, \ldots$) and M ($m_1, m_2, m_3, \ldots$) are the sets of all possible diseases and manifestations. No manifestation is also a disease. The relation $C = D \times M$ is the complete set of 2-tuples $<d_i,m_j>$ linking D to M. In many diagnostic situations we cannot be sure that the existence of a tuple $<d_k,m_1>$ will ensure that the manifestation m_1 must be present for disease d_k. Thus, the existence of a tuple implies only that the manifestation may be present. We can therefore formally define the sets man(d_i) and causes(m_j).

$$\text{man}(d_i) = \{m_j | <d_i,m_j> \in C\} \quad \text{for } d_i \in D$$
$$\text{causes}(m_j) = \{d_i | <d_i,m_j> \in C\} \quad \text{for } m_j \in M$$

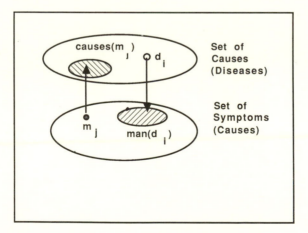

FIGURE 7. Causes and manifestations.

If there are multiple diseases, then the set of manifestations will be the union of the sets man(D) of man(d_1), man(d_2), man(d_3), etc., and for a given set of observed manifestations the possible causes are the union of the various causes(m_j) sets. As we have already stated, a manifestation need not be present for disease d_i even though $<d_i,m_j>$ exists. Thus, we will actually observe a set of manifestations $M+$ (which is less than the possible observable set).

A diagnostic problem is defined as $P = \{D,M,C,M+\}$. An explanation for this diagnostic problem P is a set of diseases E whereby $M+ \leq$ man(E) and $|E| \leq |D|$. In simple terms this means that a set of diseases E is an explanation for $M+$ provided the observed manifestations are within the set of possible observable manifestations and that E is the smallest set of diseases that could cause the manifestations $M+$. So if $\{d_1, d_2, d_3\}$ and $\{d_1\}$ could each account for $\{m_4,m_5,m_7\}$, then $\{d_1\}$ is the explanation. There could, of course, be a number of possible explanations with similar cardinality. Three simple data structures are used to construct and maintain a tentative hypothesis—manifestations, scope, and focus. The manifestations set is simply the set of manifestations observed so far, the scope set is the set of causes for which at least one manifestation is known to be present, and the focus set is a tentative solution for the manifestations already known (i.e., it is a set of valid explanations).

To illustrate the technique we will consider an example. Let us assume that a particular diagnostic problem is characterized as in Table 1. Clearly, a row in the table represents a *causes* set and a column represents a *man* set. Let us assume that initially manifestation m_3 is observed. Then the values of the three sets will be:

$$\text{mans}(m_3) \quad \text{scope}(d_1,d_4,d_5,d_6) \quad \text{focus}(d_1,d_4,d_5,d_6)$$

TABLE 1. A Causal Set

Cause	Symptom					
	m_1	m_2	m_3	m_4	m_5	m_6
d_1	0	1	1	0	1	0
d_2	1	0	0	1	1	0
d_3	1	1	0	1	1	0
d_4	0	1	1	0	0	1
d_5	1	0	1	1	0	0
d_6	1	0	1	0	0	1

Let us now assume that manifestation m_5 is also observed. The sets will then be

$$\text{mans}(m_3, m_5) \quad \text{scope(all diseases)} \quad \text{focus}(d_1)$$

Although (d_2, d_4) could be a cause of the observed manifestations (as can be a number of other pairs of diseases), they are not included in the focus because of the minimum cardinality rule.

Let manifestation m_1 now be found to be absent. This does not change the situation since the absence of a manifestation is not used to rule out a disease. Let manifestation m_6 now be observed. The new values are:

$$\text{mans}(m_3, m_5, m_6) \quad \text{scope(all diseases)}$$
$$\text{focus}(\ (d_1, d_4), (d_1, d_6), (d_2, d_4), (d_2, d_6), (d_3, d_4), (d_3, d_6)\ )$$

The focus has no single diseases since none can produce the observed symptoms; neither does it have explanations like (d_2, d_5, d_6) that can account for the symptoms but have a higher cardinality than 2 and are therefore rejected. Note that when a disease is eliminated from the focus, this is not permanent. More evidence can bring it back. The focus is actually decomposed into generators that are cartesian set products. Thus, the final focus above would actually be represented as

$$(\ (d_1, d_2) \times (d_4, d_6),\ (d_3) \times (d_4, d_6)\ )$$

This representation is more compact and is easily processed by explanation algorithms, but, most important, it does appear to be the way in which diagnosticians organize the possibilities during problem solving (Reggia et al., 1983).

9.2. System D—An Example

Figure 8 illustrates a frame from System D built using a "shell" called kms (Reggia, 1981). Knowledge is organized into frames called DESCRIPTIONS. A DESCRIPTION contains a summary of the manifestations of the disorder and other pertinent information. Some associations are causal (such as head pain), others are noncausal (for example, age), and these are clearly distinguished. A DESCRIPTION is essentially a description of the causes set we described earlier and the man set can be worked out from a collection of DESCRIPTIONS. The set of all these

```
MENIERE'S DISEASE <L>
  [ DESCRIPTION:
      AGE = FROM 20 TO 30 <L>;
      DIZZINESS= PRESENT
      [TYPE= VERTIGO;
      COURSE= ACTIVE AND PERSISTENT,
          EPISODIC [EPISODIC DURATION= MINUTES <L>, HOURS <H>;
          OCCURRENCE= POSITIONAL <H>, ORTHOSTATIC <M>,
          NON-SPECIFIC <L> ]   ];
      HEAD PAIN= PRESENT <L> [PREDOMINANT LOCATION =
      PERIAURAL];
      NEUROLOGICAL SYMPTOMS= HEARING LOSS BY HISTORY
      <H>,TINNITUS <H>;
      PULSE DURING DIZZINESS= MARKED TACHYCARDIA <L>;
      NEUROLOGICAL SIGNS= NYSTAGMUS [TYPE= HORIZONTAL,
      ROTATORY],
      IMPAIRED HEARING <H>        ]
```

FIGURE 8. A frame in System D.

frames also specifies the disease set D and the manifestations set M. The relationship C is also implicitly specified. The links between diseases and manifestations can have probabilities associated with them. These are shown in <> and mean <A>—always, <H>—high likelihood, <M>—medium likelihood, <L>—low likelihood, <N>—never. Elaborations are provided inside [. . .] that give more information on the association. The frame tells us (among other things) that Meniere's disease is uncommon, that it tends not to affect people between the ages of 20 and 30, that the dizziness is vertiginous in nature, and similar information.

The questions to the user are normally based upon the disorders currently in the focus. The system extracts from the DESCRIPTIONS the first attribute whose current value is not yet known. This will yield a set of possible attributes. From this set the attribute that appears in the most DESCRIPTIONS is selected and asked. This strategy serves to ensure that the questions most likely to discriminate between competing disorders are asked first. It also provides the designer with a mechanism for ordering the sequence in which questions are asked (i.e., put early questions at the head of a DESCRIPTION). Once a question is asked, a new focus is generated and the cycle begins again until no further questions remain. At this time the system enters a final phase in which the remaining disorders are ranked according to the weightings placed on the causal links using a simple scoring mechanism ($A = 4$, $H = 3$, . . . $N = 0$). The point that should be noted here is that this weighting process is context-dependent. The hypothesize-and-test cycle does use these weightings, but only to decide if a disease should be categorically rejected. If a symptom is always ($<A>$) present and is not observed, for example, the related disease will be rejected.

9.3. The internist System

The internist system (Miller, Pople, & Myers, 1982) is a powerful example of a system built using these techniques. The system has many similarities to System D but additionally uses a heuristic scoring procedure during the hypothesize-and-test cycle. It is generally regarded as one of the largest expert systems in existence and exhibits an impressive performance. It contains over 3500 manifestations and covers over 500 diseases. It was originally completed in 1974, but a more advanced version, caduceus, is at present under development.

In internist the link between a manifestation and its set of associated diseases (causes(m_j)) is called the evokes data structure. This link has a weighting factor of 0–5, indicating the strength of association. The inverse of this is the manifests relation (man(d_i)), which is also weighted with a factor of 1–5 related to the frequency of occurrence. Additional links exist by which disease entities and distinguished pathological states are interrelated—causal, temporal—and these links are weighted. The manifestations also have a number of other relations defined on them, such as its type (sign, symptom, and nature of laboratory test related to its cost and danger to the patient), its global importance (how important is it to account for the manifestation in the final diagnosis), and its relationship with other manifestations.

internist represents diseases as a hierarchically organized "disease tree" based upon organs of the body. The initial classification is by organ, such as liver or heart. There is then a further subdivision into disease areas, finally terminating with individual diseases. An example of how a portion of an internist disease tree might look is given in Figure 9.

The terminal node diseases take part in the evokes and manifests links. Each positive manifestation evokes not only the connected node but any higher-level nodes. A disease model (i.e., a set of possible diseases) is then constructed consisting of

- Manifestations not explained by the model.
- Manifestations explained by the model.
- Manifestations that should have been observed.

A scoring mechanism awards points to the various possible models, a ranked set of disease hypotheses is created, and the highest rated become a differential disease hypothesis. Questions are then asked to

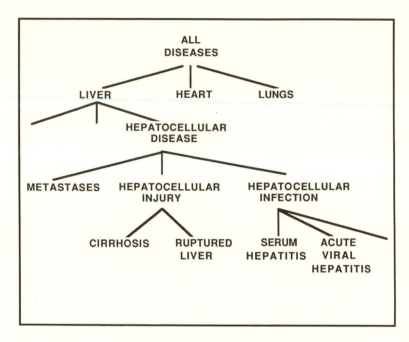

FIGURE 9. An INTERNIST disease tree.

help to discriminate between the entities in the problem set. Three major strategies are used—RULEOUT, DISCRIMINATE, and PURSUING (Pople, 1984). If there are five or more alternatives, the RULEOUT strategy is adopted, the program seeking negative findings to rule out one or more of the contenders. If there are between two and four alternatives, the program concentrates on the DISCRIMINATE strategy, choosing the leading two and seeking information to separate them in score. If only one alternative remains, the PURSUING strategy is adopted. Confirmatory data are sought to extend the lead of this leading alternative from its nearest competitors. All diseases are then reexamined and a new differential diagnosis is created. If the system runs out of questions while in a PURSUING strategy, it renders a peremptory conclusion. If this happens during a RULEOUT or DISCRIMINATE strategy, the current differential diagnosis is set aside so that another problem might be considered. (For an example of an INTERNIST diagnostic session, see Pople, 1984.)

The set-covering approach has proved to be successful. In terms of our earlier criteria in that knowledge is stored explicitly, the reasoning strategy based upon differential diagnoses does correspond to a natural diagnostic approach, explanations are provided quite naturally by way of the focus, and the system does handle uncertainty in the linkages. Finally, it is very easy to add new frames to the system to extend its power. It is the most experimental of the approaches and has not yet been sufficiently studied to allow a full assessment of the strengths and weaknesses of the method.

10. MULTIPLE PARADIGM APPROACHES

There is no reason why the rule-based and the frame-based approaches should not be combined in some way. This was done when the PUFF expert system (Aikens et al., 1983) was reimplemented as the CENTAUR system (Aikens, 1983). Aikins makes the point that it is not the kinds of knowledge structures used that are critical but that the chosen structures must be expressive enough to represent a variety of types of knowledge. The frames provide an explicit representation of the context in which sets of production rules are applied. Thus, the strategic knowledge is separated from the inferential knowledge and the latter can be applied differently in different situations. The production rule-sets are actually "methods" in the frames. The frame therefore consists of a set of values defining the context for the application of a set of rules. The system has three types of frame—prototypes, components, and facts. Controlling the interaction is a hierarchy of prototypes. Within these prototypes are slots that point to component frames, and facts in the system (name of a parameter, its value, certainty, etc.) are stored as frames as well. A typical prototype hierarchy is shown in Figure 10.

The top frame controls the consultation. The next level frames represent pathological states, and each of these is further specialized by type and severity. Each pathological state frame will have slots that point to component frames containing the tests to be carried out to identify the state. These component frames contain rule-sets for inferring values for the component. The complete system provides "context-specific" control. The control strategy used is determined by the context.

CENTAUR's control mechanism is fairly simple. An agenda of tasks to be performed is created as the consultation progresses. The interpreter simply takes the top task on the agenda list. When there are no more, the consultation terminates. Tasks include "fill-in" current prototype and "confirm" current prototype. The system begins with the task "fill-in" for the CONSULTATION prototype that obtains user options for the consultation. The confirm task then sets appropriate "if-con-

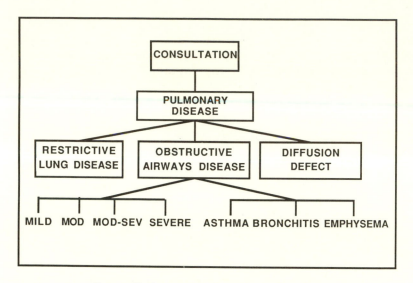

FIGURE 10. A prototype hierarchy in CENTAUR.

firmed" slots on other prototypes. Prototypes are ordered by certainty factors, the best scoring representing the best hypothesis. (For a concise readable account of the CENTAUR system, see Jackson, 1983.)

10.1. THE COMPASS SYSTEM

There are now a number of artificial intelligence workstations available to facilitate the multiple-paradigm approach. They are usually based on the object-oriented approach (Goldberg & Robson, 1983; Goldstein & Bobrow, 1980). An example is the COMPASS system developed at GTE (Goyal, Prerau, Lemmon, Gunderson, & Reinke, 1985). This paper is an interesting one since it goes into some detail on how the domain was chosen and why a multiple-paradigm approach was selected. Development was carried out on a Xerox LISP machine using INTERLISP-D and the KEE software environment.

A central office telephone switch controls many thousands of lines, both internal and external. GTE already had a monitoring and control system called RMCS to monitor, collect, and organize output messages. Experts then examined these messages and identified corrective actions. COMPASS contains the expertise to do this task, which requires a number of messages to be examined. The system is essentially a for-

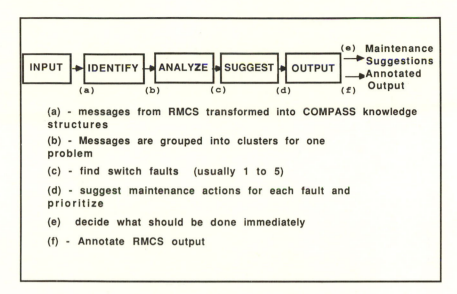

FIGURE 11. Subtasks in COMPASS.

ward-chained application, and observation of the experts at work revealed that the task could be broken down into a series of sequential subtasks, as shown in Figure 11.

The RMCS output is first converted into appropriate knowledge structures. Then these are analyzed by a set of rules to separate them into clusters, each for one fault. A further set of rules then analyzes these clusters to identify causing faults. Once the faults have been identified, other rules are used to suggest maintenance actions, and these are ordered by immediacy and concurrency. Finally, the system annotates the original RMCS output. At any point the system can explain and justify its reasoning.

The following knowledge structures are implemented using frames, demons, inheritance, and forward-chained rules in KEE:

- The generic structure of the switch.
- The structure of each individual switch.
- Maintenance messages.
- Message commonalities that facilitate clustering.
- Switch faults.
- Possible maintenance actions.
- Expert techniques for relating all of these.

A typical rule in COMPASS is:

> *if*   the analysis process, thus far, has identified a group of network recovery 20 maintenance messages as corresponding to a "NOT-CJ-NOT NO ADJACENCY" problem
>
> *then*
>
>   *if*   either of the involved network units is a mixed network
>
>   *then*   a possible site of the fault causing the messages is the circuit junctor between the two network outlet terminals with an estimated likelihood of 0.25
>
>   *and*   a possible site of the fault causing the messages is at the control points for the circuit junctor between the two network outlet terminals with a likelihood of 0.25
>
>   *and* . . .
>
>   *and* . . .
>
>   *else*   a possible site of the fault causing the messages is at the control points for the circuit junctor between the two network outlet terminals with a likelihood of 0.5
>
>   *and* . . .
>
>   *and*   a possible site of the fault causing the messages is at the pins and wiring on the back of the network units with a likelihood of 0.1

The ANALYZE knowledge base contains frames that represent generic hypotheses about problems in a switch in the form of a hierarchical structure, as shown in Figure 12. There are eight knowledge bases, six of which relate to the six stages in the consultation, one having the structure of individual switches, and the eighth collecting together a set of software tools. The frame paradigm is used throughout with sets of rules as methods in the frames. Special frames are created to represent the specific problem under investigation.

The initial field trials for COMPASS are reported as being successful. Field use has led the operating personnel to request that COMPASS be installed as soon as possible. It required several man-years of effort to complete, though the initial system was implemented and demonstrated in one year.

11. EXPERT SYSTEM SHELLS

Since expert systems rely heavily upon domain-specific knowledge, it might be expected that every system developed would be unique.

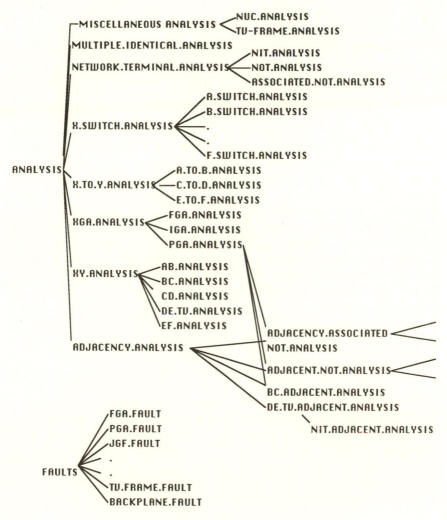

FIGURE 12. Analysis and fault hierarchies in COMPASS.

Each problem would have to be approached anew, and the possibility of providing general purpose building tools would be very limited. Fortunately, this is not the case. Over the past few years a considerable amount of interest and effort has been invested in what are termed expert system "shells." This section does make a rather arbitrary distinction between shells and the multiple-paradigm tools such as KEE and ART, discussed earlier. The latter are, of course, general-purpose expert system building tools, but they are very expensive and normally require special-purpose hardware. The systems discussed below will run on conventional systems.

11.1. THE SHELL CONCEPT

A shell is an expert system with its domain knowledge separated out—a shell, empty of knowledge. The possibility of doing this separation occurs because of two factors—one a property of the problem-solving process, the other an important design principle. The first factor arises from similarities that are present in apparently different problem-solving situations. Widely differing domains such as medical diagnosis and structural engineering calculations use knowledge represented in a similar fashion. Indeed, many diagnostic situations in a wide range of domains have very similar characteristics. Second, this similarity can be exploited by careful design. Provided the knowledge base (in production systems the facts, relations, and rules) can be separated out from the inference engine (control), a separation between the domain-dependent and domain-independent parts is achieved. The inference engine can then be used for a variety of problems. Thus, we have an "empty" knowledge base shell and a separate inference mechanism. Of course, the structure of the knowledge base still exists, and any knowledge placed into it will have to conform to its representational characteristics. Such an expert system building tool is not a general-purpose tool, but it will solve a class of problems.

The possibility of this approach was realized early in the development of expert systems. The knowledge contained in the MYCIN system was "emptied out" and the shell EMYCIN created (van Melle, Shortliffe, & Buchanan, 1981). This has been used over a wide range of domains. Out of PROSPECTOR came KAS (Reboh, 1981), which has been the basis of a number of microbased shells.

11.2. WHAT DOES A SHELL PROVIDE?

The shell is classified by two main sets of facilities—the services provided by the inference engine, and the representational scheme for the knowledge. Inference services include:

- Reasoning direction (forward or backward or both).
- Handling of uncertainty.
- Explanation facilities.
- Volunteering of information.

- Debugging aids.
- Explicit control of inference.

Representational facilities include:

- Types of objects and structures supported.
- Format of rules supported.
- Facilities for the creation of structures.

Before selecting a shell, therefore, the problem domain must be carefully studied and the essential inference and representational characteristics extracted to match the above characteristics.

11.3. What Sorts of Shells Exist?

There are now a large number of shells in the marketplace varying in cost from £200 to £50,000. The cost primarily reflects the facilities supplied, but it also relates to the target machine. Normally, a shell for a mainframe will cost much more than one for a microcomputer. It is difficult to provide a precise classification scheme, but they may broadly be separated into six types:

1. PROSPECTOR-like shell using backward reasoning based on Bayesian inference techniques.
2. Production system shells usually providing backward chaining but with some forward-chaining capability.
3. Multiple paradigm shells.
4. Inductive shells.
5. Special-purpose shells for particular applications.
6. Expansions of existing languages, such as PROLOG.

Shells of type 1 include SAVOIR, SAGE, EXPERT-EDGE, and ENVISAGE. Shells of type 2 include Xi-plus, EXSYS, PC plus, and M1. For type 3 there are KMS and KES. Type 4 shells include EXPERT-EASE, EXTRAN77, RULEMASTER, and TIMMS. An example of type 5 is ESP-ADVISOR, and shells such as APES and YAPES make up type 6 (both of these are based on PROLOG and extend the language by providing additional predicates for explanation, probability handling, etc.).

It is not possible in the limited space available to give a detailed account of their facilities. However, a few interesting points will be noted. One useful development has been the addition of explicit control facilities in systems such as KES and SAVOIR and by special rule constructs in Xi-plus. These facilities allow the designer to alter the control strategy as the consultation progresses. In SAVOIR, for instance, the INVESTIGATE verb triggers off a backward-chaining Bayesian analysis, but demons defined by ASSOONAS constructs will trigger off forward chaining (or INVESTIGATIONs). In Xi-plus rules can switch forward chaining on or off in the *then* part of a rule.

Most shells provide useful designer aids and debugging facilities (i.e., knowledge examination, probability logging or viewing, on-line modification, and *what-if* facilities). Most smaller shells will run on the IBM-PC, but for practical purposes a PC-AT is often required for good response times. Up to 500 rules can be handled even by the smaller shells, but for more than this one usually has to pay more.

The situation with shells is still developing, and it is not yet clear just how useful they will be, particularly for the small PC-based shells. However, if a shell is suitable, its use does considerably reduce the costs of development, and they are very useful in the knowledge-acquisition stage, where the deliberations of a domain expert can be coded up and viewed in a few hours.

12. RECENT DEVELOPMENTS

There are a number of ongoing developments in the expert systems field. These include:

- Nonmonotonic reasoning.
- Representation of deep knowledge.
- Commonsense knowledge.
- Better tools.

12.1. NONMONOTONIC REASONING

All the systems that have been described use essentially a monotonic reasoning technique; that is, facts once established are assumed to hold true for the rest of the consultation. In reality, of course, this is not a correct representation of an expert's approach to problem solving. Experts frequently make assumptions and gain insights from disproving them. Nonmonotonic reasoning systems already exist, such as AMORD (Doyle, 1979; de Kleer, Doyle, Rich, Steele, & Sussman, 1977). The main characteristics of such systems are:

- Propositional deduction from premises.
- Justification and explanation of deductions.
- Incremental updating of beliefs when premises are added or removed.

- Tracking down of premises underlying contradictions when they arise.

Such systems are often called "truth maintenance systems."

12.2. Deep Knowledge

Experts simultaneously use different levels of knowledge representation. Such levels have been characterized as "surface" or "deep" (Hart, 1982). Surface knowledge is now usually referred to as "shallow" knowledge. Such knowledge generally relies upon empirical associations between data typically in the form of *if . . . then* rules. It is a prescription for success but does not explain why such rules are relevant. It does not concern itself with the internal workings of the system but is rather an external view (or a high-level abstraction). Shallow knowledge is efficient to process. A connection is quickly made between symptom and remedy.

Deep knowledge is concerned with causality or the use of first principles. It is particularly useful when unexpected events occur for which no surface knowledge exists. There are good reasons why deep knowledge representations are needed (Chandresakaran & Mittal, 1982):

- Experts generally resort to deep knowledge in difficult situations.
- Surface knowledge can become too large when trying to deal with all possibilities.
- Explanation is often related to deep knowledge.

Guida (1986) has given a useful treatment of the connection between shallow and deep knowledge. In the last five years much effort has been concentrated in deep systems. Such approaches are particularly relevant to process control situations.

12.3. Commonsense Reasoning and Causality

This covers a whole spectrum of activity from qualitative reasoning about physical systems to causal modeling. Physical systems provide an excellent test bed for such approaches. Experts (such as physicists) often use a form of "common sense" when examining physical systems. An interesting example of the approach is given by Forbus (1986), where qualitative process theory is used to analyze raw data about boiling liquids. The goal of qualitative physics is to predict and explain behavior in qualitative terms, avoiding mathematics yet retaining key distinctions. Other key work in the area that is still very much in the research stage includes work using confluences (de Kleer & Brown, 1984) and on comparative statistics (Iwasaki & Simon, 1984).

12.4. BETTER TOOLS

A more detailed examination of the expert system shells on the market reveals serious limitations. Too often the representational schemes offered are primitive and the performance too slow. While at the larger end of the market the AI workstations provide rich representation schemes, they are expensive and the development system is often the final target machine. It is expected that in the near future the shell situation will improve by the addition of more realistic representation schemes and that cheaper target systems will be provided for systems such as KEE. General-purpose systems (such as the Sun and the Apollo) do provide a bridge between the general- and special-purpose areas but do require very considerable enhancement to support systems such as KEE. This situation should improve.

13. CONCLUSIONS

The application of expert systems techniques is still in the experimental stage. Although many systems have been reported, few have actually been carried through to real commercial use. The number of attempts can be assessed from reviews such as in Waterman (1986) or the *CRI Directory of Expert Systems* (Smart & Langeland-Knudsen, 1986), which lists over 600 systems. Of course, many of these systems were never intended for real use and were mainly concerned with exploring the technology. Indeed, there is some indication that when successful expert systems are developed for commercial applications they are not usually reported.

The key factor in determining success is the choice of the target domain. This should be as self-contained as possible, and not require commonsense knowledge. Time-varying data or reasoning processes should also be avoided. A cooperative expert should be available and the problem to be solved should require a few hours of expert time. Expert systems are not the panacea for all the ills of business and commerce; however, they do embrace some useful and powerful techniques that, if used in the right situation, can provide very cost-effective solutions.

14. REFERENCES

Aikens, J. (1983). Prototypical knowledge for expert systems. *Artificial Intelligence, 20,* 163–210.

Aikins, J. S., Kunz, J. C., & Shortliffe, E. H. (1983). PUFF: An expert system for interpretation of pulmonary function data. *Computers and Biomedical Research, 16,* 199–208.

Alty, J. L., & Coombs, M. J. (1984). *Expert systems: Concepts and examples.* Manchester, England: NCC Publications.

Bennett, J., Creary, L., Englemore, R., & Melosh, R. A. (1978). *Knowledge-based consultant for structural analysis.* Stanford, CA: Computer Science Department, Stanford University.

Bennett, J., & Goldman, D. (1980). CLOT: *A knowledge-based consultant for diagnosis of bleeding disorders* (Report HPP-80-7). Stanford, CA: Computer Science Department, Stanford University.

Brownston, L., Farrell, R., Kant, E., & Martin, N. (1985). *Programming expert systems in OPS5.* Reading, MA: Addison-Wesley.

Chandresakaran, B., & Mittal, S (1982). Deep versus compiled knowledge approaches to diagnostic problem solving. *Proc. AAAI Pittsburgh,* pp. 349–354.

de Kleer, J., & Brown, J. S. (1984). A qualitative physics based on confluences. *Artificial Intelligence, 29,* 3–72.

de Kleer, J., Doyle J., Rich, C., Steele, G. L., & Sussman, G. J. (1977). AMORD: A deductive procedure system. MIT working paper, 151 (August).

Doyle, J. (1979). A truth maintenance system. *Artificial Intelligence, 12*(3).

Duda, R. O., Hart, P. E., & Nilsson, N. (1976). Subjective Bayesian methods for rule-based inference systems. *Proceedings of the National Computer Conference, AFIPS, 45,* pp. 1075–1082.

Duda, R., Hart, P. E., Nilsson, N. J., Barrett, P., Gaschnig, J. G., Konolige, K., Reboh, R., & Slocum J. (1978, October). *Development of the PROSPECTOR consultation system for mineral exploration* (SRI Report). Menlo Park, CA: Stanford Research Institute.

Elstein, A., Shulman, L., & Sprafka, S. (1978). *Medical problem solving—An analysis of clinical reasoning.* Cambridge, MA: Harvard University Press.

Erman, L., Scott, A. C., & London, P. (1984). The HEARSAY-II speech understanding system: Integrating knowledge to resolve uncertainties. *Computing Surveys, 12*(2), 213–253.

Ernst, G. W., & Newell, A. (1969). *A case study in generality and problem solving.* London: Academic Press.

Forbus, K. D. (1986). Interpreting measurements of physical systems. *Proc. AAAI-86,* Pittsburgh, pp. 113–117.

Forgy, C. L. (1981). *OPS5 user's manual* (Report CMU-CS-81-135). Pittsburgh: Computer Science Department, Carnegie-Mellon University.

Goldberg, A., & Robson, D. (1983). *SMALLTALK-80: The language and its implementation.* Reading, MA: Addison-Wesley.

Goldstein, I. P., & Bobrow, D. G. (1980). Extending object-oriented programming in SMALLTALK. Stanford, CA: *Proceedings of the 1980 LISP Conference,* Stanford University.

Goyal, S. K., Prerau, D. S., Lemmon, A. V., Gunderson, A. S., & Reinke, R. E. (1985). COMPASS: An expert system for telephone switch maintenance, *Expert Systems, 2*(3), 112–124.

Guida, G. (1986). Reasoning about physical systems: Shallow versus deep models. In M.

Mamdoni & J. Efstathiou (Eds.), *Expert systems and optimisation in process control* (pp. 135–159). Aldershot: Unicorn Seminars Ltd., Gower Technical Press.

Hart, P. E. (1982). Directions for AI in the eighties. *ACM SIGART Newsletter, 79*, 11–16.

Iwasaki, Y., & Simon, H. A. (1984). Causality in device behaviour. *Artificial Intelligence, 24*, 7–83.

Jackson, P. (1983). *Introduction to expert systems* (Chap. 10). Reading, MA: Addison-Wesley.

Konolige K. (1979). Bayesian methods for updating probabilities. In R. Duda, P. Hart, K. Konolige, & R. Reboh (Eds.), *A computer-based consultant for mineral exploration*. Menlo Park, CA: Artificial Intelligence Center, SRI International.

Lesser, V. R., & Erman, L. D. (1977). A retrospective view of the HEARSAY-II architecture. Cambridge, MA: *Proceedings of the 5th Joint Conference on Artificial Intelligence* (pp. 790–800).

McDermott, J. (1981). R1's formative years. *AI Magazine, 2*(2).

McDermott, J. (1982). R1: A rule-based configurer of computer systems. *Artificial Intelligence, 19*(1).

Miller, A. M., Pople, H. E., & Myers, J. D. (1982). INTERNIST-1, an experimental computer based diagnostic consultant for general internal medecine. *New England Journal of Medicine, 307*, 468–476.

Minsky, M. (1975). A framework for representing knowledge. In P. Winston (Ed.), *The psychology of computer vision*. New York: McGraw-Hill.

Morrison, P., & Morrison, E. (1961). *Charles Babbage and his calculating engines*. New York: Dover.

Nii, H. P. (1986). Blackboard systems, blackboard application systems, blackboard systems from a knowledge engineering perspective. *AI Magazine, August*, 82–106.

Pople, H. E. (1984). Knowledge-based expert systems: The buy or build decision. In W. Reitman (Ed.), *Artificial intelligence applications in business*. Norwood, NJ: Ablex.

Reboh, R. (1981). *Knowledge engineering techniques and tools in the PROSPECTOR environment* (SRI technical note 243). Menlo Park, CA: Stanford Research Institute.

Reggia, J. (1981). *Knowledge-based decision support systems: Development through KMS*. Doctoral dissertation, Technical Report TR-1121, Computer Science Department, University of Maryland.

Reggia, J., Nau, D., & Wang, P. (1983). Diagnostic expert systems based on a set covering model. *International Journal of Man–Machine Studies, 19*, 437–460.

Shortliffe, E. H. (1976). *Computer based medical consultations: MYCIN*. New York: Elsevier.

Shortliffe, E. H., & Buchanan, B. G. (1975). A model of inexact reasoning in medicine. *Mathematical Bioscience, 23*, 351–379.

Smart, G., & Langeland-Knudsen, J. (1986). *The CRI directory of expert systems*. Oxford: Learned Information (Europe).

Teach, R., & Shortliffe, E. H. (1985). An analysis of physician attitudes regarding computer based clinical consultation systems, *Computers and Biomedical Research, 14*, 542–558.

van Melle, W., Shortliffe, E. H., & Buchanan, B. G. (1981). EMYCIN: A domain independent system that aids in the constructing knowledge-based consultation programs. In A. Bond (Ed.), *Machine intelligence* (Infotech state of the art report, Series 9, No. 3). Oxford, UK: Pergamon Infotech.

Waterman, D. A. (1986). *A guide to expert systems*. Reading, MA: Addison-Wesley.

7

Human Expertise

P. REIMANN and M. T. H. CHI

1. INTRODUCTION

The intention of this chapter is to provide the reader with a glimpse of the kind of questions and research that have been investigated on the nature of expertise in problem solving. For more detailed descriptions of the actual research results, the reader is referred to an edited volume on the nature of expertise by Chi, Glaser, and Farr (1988). This chapter is not meant to be an integrated interpretation of problem solving theories. Such a review may be seen in a chapter by VanLehn (in press). Instead, we view this chapter as an updated version of the review of the expertise literature in problem solving as provided in Chi, Glaser, and Rees (1982), and Chi and Glaser (1985). Descriptions of our own research in the context of problem solving are discussed more extensively in Chi, Bassok, Lewis, Reimann, and Glaser (in press), and Chi and Bassok (in press).

2. THE THEORETICAL FRAMEWORK: INFORMATION-PROCESSING THEORY OF PROBLEM SOLVING

The last years have seen the development of a psychology of experts' behavior that is based on a knowledge-level analysis. This analy-

P. REIMANN • Psychology Institute, University of Freiburg, D-7800 Freiburg, West Germany.   M. T. H. CHI • Learning Research and Development Center, University of Pittsburgh, Pittsburgh, Pennsylvania 15260.

sis in terms of experts' information processing has overcome the myth of experts' "intuitive" problem-solving wizardry by demonstrating over and over again that expertise is essentially related to experience—that is, experience acquired with specific domains. Thus, we might say that all of us are potential, if not actual, experts in one domain or another. Whether or not we can all develop our potential is still an open issue (see Chi, Bassok, Lewis, et al., in press, for possible differences among individuals and their potentials for becoming experts).

A general theory of problem solving has been developed within the context of information-processing theories of cognition (Anderson, 1976, 1983; Newell & Simon, 1972). Within this framework, one can discuss two issues: hypotheses about the form of cognitive action, and hypotheses about the form of cognitive representation (Greeno & Simon, 1984). Given a sequence in time, the problem solver starts out by analyzing the *task environment* (i.e., the problem statement and the context in which it is presented) and constructs an internal representation of the problem situation. The product of this encoding step is a problem representation that includes

> an individual's representation of the *objects* in the problem situation, the *goal* of the problem, and the *actions* that can be performed and *strategies* that can be used in working on the problem. It also includes knowledge of *constraints* in the problem situation: restrictions on what can be done, as well as limits on the way in which objects or features of objects can be combined (Greeno & Simon, 1984, p. 4).

The application of an operator to the *initial state* of a problem (the *initial state* is usually the givens of the problem) produces a subsequent problem state, and the application of a sequence of operators constitutes a solution path. The *problem space* is thus the space of all possible states generated by the application of all operators that can conceivably be applied to each state. Problem solving, then, by definition, is the *search* of the correct sequence of operators, from the initial state to the goal state, within the problem space. Sometimes the problem space differs for different individuals. This may result from a number of factors. Usually, it is due to the solver's failure to encode one or more aspects of the problem into his or her representation. For example, if the constraints on the operators are not encoded, then the problem space could be enlarged unnecessarily; alternatively, constraints not explicitly mentioned in the problem statement may be added implicitly, thereby omitting problem states that may need to be traversed in order to find the correct solution path. Thus, individual solvers' problem space may be more restricted or more extended than the actual permissible problem space.

Strategic knowledge includes processes for setting goals and employing general methods for the solution of a problem, thus controlling the search process. Strategic knowledge is procedural in nature and can be represented, for example, in the form of productions. It is a special form of procedural knowledge in that it is supposed to be general and global (Chi, 1984). By definition of its generality, we would expect to find only a small set of general strategies. And in fact only a small set of general strategies have been discussed in problem-solving research: generate-and-test, means–ends-analysis, best-first-search, planning, and subgoal decomposition, to mention the most prominent.

One of the basic functions of these general strategies is to provide the problem solver with criteria to *evaluate* a problem-solving step. Under the control of a *means–ends analysis*, for example, the evaluation consists of comparing the current state to the goal state, and actions are selected that reduce the difference between the current state and the goal state. The idea underlying *planning strategies* (e.g., Sacerdoti, 1977) is to abstract, by removing from the original problem statement, features that are considered to be inessential for solving the problem. The resulting problem space will be smaller and the search for a solution will take less time and/or effort. A crucial factor for the success of this class of strategies is the ability of the problem solver to correctly distinguish between relevant and less relevant problem features.

The preceding description of the content of a problem representation, taken primarily from the Newell and Simon theory (1972), is most characteristic of knowledge-lean types of problems, such as the Tower of Hanoi puzzle. Problem solving in semantically rich domains has two additional complexities: The first is that the representation of the problem is no longer straightforward—it requires the solver to inject a great deal of domain knowledge; the second complexity is that the operators that are actually used may also be domain-specific operators, such as knowing how to transform an algebraic expression, knowing how to draw a free-body diagram in the case of solving physics problems, and knowing the symptoms of meningitis in order to diagnose it in medical problem solving. Thus, the study of problem solving in knowledge-rich domains is not dominated necessarily by identifying the kind of strategies that are guiding search (although this has been the focus for some of the investigations), but rather, it centers on the analyses of (1) the kind of knowledge the problem solver brings to bear on the problem in order to build an enriched and adequate representation, as well as (2) the kind of specific procedural knowledge that is available for the problem solver to use. For instance, the *objects* in the problem representation can no longer be assumed to be those mentioned directly in the problem statement. The objects that are represented now depend on what configuration of features (such as pieces on the chessboard) or combinations of symptoms (as in medicine) are meaningful to the solver. Likewise, specific procedures include knowing when and how to transform an algebraic expression, and knowing how to draw a free-body diagram in the case of solving physics problems (in terms of knowing what forces to include and exclude). Thus, the nature of the problems (whether it is knowledge-lean or knowledge-rich) demands a shift in emphasis from understanding the kind of strategies that guide search (and its associated factors, such as memory for traversed problem states) to an emphasis on understanding the kind of knowledge that the solver can bring to bear on the problem in order to build an adequate representation that can lead to solution.

The trend in recent years has therefore been to examine knowledge-rich tasks that require huge amounts of learning and experience. As a result of this, the focus switched somewhat from studying general strategies in knowledge-lean domains to the analysis of the utilization of specific declarative and procedural knowledge in complex domains. Procedural knowledge about what forms of actions are permissible and appropriate in a knowledge-rich problem interacts with (and develops out of) a rich declarative knowledge base, involving knowledge about concepts, facts, and situations. A problem in medical diagnosis, for example, cannot be solved without knowing a lot about diseases and how they are manifested in symptoms; improving the crop production in a country requires extensive knowledge about agriculture, history, governmental regulations, and so forth. Thus, in order to elaborate on the problem statement successfully, the problem solver has to rely on a body of semantically meaningful information about the domain from which the problem is taken.

Our central concern for research in complex problem solving is what knowledge the problem solver brings to the task, and how it is used to solve a specific problem. This question has two aspects: (1) How is knowledge used to build up a problem representation, or how does it help to "understand" the problem? (2) What is its influence in the actual problem-solving process? Research on expert problem solving in recent years has become increasingly concerned with the first question since it is crucial for understanding expert problem-solving behavior. As Greeno and Simon (1984) summarize:

> Present findings indicate that a major source of expert performance is the expert's ability to represent problems successfully, and that this results from the expert's having a well integrated structure of knowledge in which patterns of features in the problem are associated with concepts at varying

> levels of generality, enabling the efficient search for hypotheses about the salient features of the problem that cannot be observed directly as well as methods and operations to be used in solving the problem. (p. 111)

Accordingly, work on experts' problem representation will be of pivotal interest in our chapter, although the research conducted on this topic is still preliminary. We present it from two points of view: as the *result* of a superior knowledge structure and as the major *factor* in successful problem solving. In Section 3, we illustrate the role that problem understanding plays in the performance of expert problem solvers and argue that it is the domain-specific knowledge structure that enables them to represent a problem effectively. In Section 4, psychological theories of knowledge representation are discussed as far as they are relevant for research on expertise. The role of strategies will be discussed in Section 5, and how expertise develops is the topic of Section 6.

We do not intend to provide an exhaustive review of research done in the area of expertise. The research domains we mainly draw on (mathematics, physics, social sciences, and medical diagnosis) are meant to provide the reader with a sample of prototypical research findings; furthermore, the range of examples allows us to see whether results and explanations from one domain are generalizable to another domain.

3. THE CONSTRUCTION OF A PROBLEM REPRESENTATION

As our analysis from the previous section indicated, problem solving must begin with the conversion of the problem statement into an internal mental representation. The contents of a problem representation are quite straightforward in puzzle-type domains since the initial and final states as well as the exact operators are well defined. Thus, the representation, by definition, is the specification of these objects, operators, and constraints, as well as the initial and final states. In complex domains like physics, however, even if the subject has a specific and sufficient repertoire of domain-specific operators, he or she may not be able to apply these directly to the objects given in a problem description. For example, when solving mechanics problems using Newton's laws, the ultimate problem-solving operators are mathematical ones: vector resolution, basic trigonometry, and algebraic transformations. However, problems are rarely formulated in terms of vectors, but in terms of objects like *strings, inclined planes, masses,* interrelated by concrete relations like *holds, slides down, is at rest.* Therefore, in order to apply the mathematical operators that constitute parts of the solution procedure, the solver has to transform the problem into a form that includes the appropriate problem objects; thus, the direct physical references mentioned in the problem statement have to be translated into physics entities that are related by physics principles (such as the relation between forces and bodies). Only then can a mathematical solution procedure (including points and vectors) be derived. This necessity of representing physics problems at different levels of abstraction makes them particularly interesting for analyzing the issue of representation.

The fact that building a representation is a key process in solving physics problems was noted by Larkin (1977, 1985), McDermott and Larkin, (1978), and Simon and Simon (1978). They found that experts spend more time doing a "qualitative analysis" of the problem, using their "physical intuition" prior to the actual retrieval of physics equations:

> Physical intuition might be interpreted in the following way: When a physical situation is described in words, a person may construct a perspicuous representation of that situation in memory. By a perspicuous representation, we mean one that represents explicitly the main direct connections, especially causal connections, of the components of the situation (Simon & Simon, 1978, p. 337).

The presence of this kind of activity prior to solving a problem algebraically can be seen by the use of diagrams. Simon and Simon (1978) found that experts tend to draw diagrams of the physical relationships between objects in a given problem more often than novices. One can interpret this diagram-describing activity as a means of representing the problem. A more elaborated problem representation, as embodied in a free-body diagram, can be used as a basis for generating equations (Simon & Simon, 1978) and checking errors (Larkin, 1977; Simon & Simon, 1978). Basically, it is a concise and global problem description that can be used as a starting point to draw further inferences about problem features not explicitly mentioned.

The processes of building a representation become much more transparent when one analyzes an ill-defined problem, as in social science. For example, Voss and his colleagues (Voss, Greene, Post, & Penner, 1983; Voss & Post, 1988; Voss, Tyler, & Yengo, 1983) analyzed the problem-solving behavior of novices and experts in a social science problem. The problem was: "Assume you are the head of the Soviet Ministry of Agriculture and assume crop productivity has been low over the past several years. You now have the responsibility of increasing crop production. How would you go about doing this?" It is a typical example for social science problems: An undesirable state exists and improvement is required. A typical solution strategy requires one to identify the cause(s) of the problem and solve the problem by eliminating the wrong cause(s).

Experts from three population groups were sampled: Faculty members from the political science department whose field of expertise was the Soviet Union represented the domain experts; undergraduates who were taking a course in Soviet domestic policy served as the novice group; a third group was made up of faculty members from the chemistry department. The last two groups were included in the study to control for one factor usually confounded with expertise in expert–novice contrast designs: academic training.

The subjects were given the problem and instructed to "think out loud" while solving it. Protocols were tape-recorded and analyzed using a combination of the problem-solving model as developed by Newell and Simon (1972) and the model of argumentation developed by Toulmin (1958). We report here only the results from a group comparison with respect to the process of problem representation (Voss, Tyler, & Yengo, 1983). In a comparison of the groups according to the relative amount of time spent on developing a problem representation (i.e., a formulation of the "cause(s)" for the low productivity that served as a starting point to solve the problem), both the domain experts and the groups of political scientists were found to spend a considerable amount of time working in this stage. Undergraduates and the chemistry faculty members both went directly to the development of problem solutions. The domain experts and the political scientists developed their representations by adding a lot of domain-specific constraints to their representation of the problem (such as the history, political ideology, climate), as well as more general constraints.

The distinction between a problem representation phase and a problem solution phase is somewhat arbitrary. Both processes seem to occur throughout problem solving. Also, it is not necessarily the case that only experts conduct a qualitative analysis of the problem while formulating a representation; a more accurate way of looking at this may be to say that both experts and novices form representations of a problem before executing the solution, only that the experts form a more abstract and enriched representation.

Chi, Feltovich, and Glaser (1981) investigated the process of problem representation by analyzing it independently from the problem-solving processes. Eight experts (advanced Ph.D. students in physics) and eight novices (undergraduates who had just completed a course on mechanics) were asked to categorize 24 problems selected from a stan-

dard physics textbook according to their similarities. Although the experts actually took longer to complete the sorting task than the novices,
other quantitative measures, such as the number of categories formed
and the category size, were equivalent between the experts and the
novices. The most noticeable difference was revealed by a cluster analysis
of the sorting categories, which showed that novices' categories were
characterized by the literal objects and entities explicitly stated in the
problem description, while experts' categories could be characterized
by principles of mechanics. The same picture emerged from an analysis
of the category labels provided by the subjects. For example, among
novices the strictly concrete object *spring* was the second most frequently used label for a problem category, but the least often used by
experts.

These observations indicate that both the experts and novices represent a problem as an instance of a more general problem category.
The crucial difference between experts and novices in this stage of
problem representation is that experts tend to classify the problem according to abstract categories related to physics, while novices classify
problems according to characteristics of the concrete objects and entities actually mentioned in the problems. Thus, both groups of solvers
represent the problems, except that the experts represent them in different contexts than the novices.

McDermott and Larkin (1978) claimed a taxonomy of representations that they have used to explain the differences between experts
and novices. According to this theory, a problem solver progresses
through one or more levels of representing a problem while studying
and solving it:

1. A *literal* representation, containing key words from the text.
2. A *naive* representation containing literal objects and their spatial
   and temporal relationships, often accompanied by a sketch of
   the situation.
3. *Scientific* representation containing idealized objects (points,
   bodies) and physical concepts (forces, momenta).
4. *Algebraic* representation, i.e., equations containing physical concepts and relationships.

McDermott and Larkin proposed that novices do not represent problems at a *scientific* level and are therefore not able to categorize them
appropriately. The implication of their theory is that the representation
must be developed *before* any categorization can take place, whereas it
now seems clear that categorization can occur prior to the complete
development of a representation at any level of the taxonomy. The em-

pirical evidence shows that categorization can be done on the basis of minimal information about the problem, often after reading only the first words of a problem description (see, for example, Hinsley, Hayes, & Simon, 1978; Lesgold et al., 1988). For example, in response to the first sentence in a problem statement ("a block of mass M is dropped from a height x"), an expert subject in the Chi et al. (1981) study reported her first hypotheses as: "My guess is this is Conservation of Energy and we're going to convert potential energy into kinetic energy." However, the category to which a problem is assigned determines to a certain extent the quality of the representation. Thus, we believe that the level to which a problem can be represented depends to a large extent on the problem schemata or categories that the solver has.

Thus, it appears that both experts and novices access knowledge in their long-term memory (their problem schemata) and attempt to instantiate the current to-be-solved problem into the accessed schema. This appears to be an ongoing top-down and bottom-up processing. That is, an initial cue (such as the first sentence in the problem statement) may trigger a particular schema, and once a specific schema is triggered, slots of that problem schema are then matched to the current to-be-solved problem. Any mismatch may result in the rejection of that schema, and another schema may be triggered. Hence, we view the development of a problem representation as the successive attempts at instantiating schemata. Once a schema with the optimal fit is found, then the solver derives and executes a solution, which requires the application of mathematical operators. As a general hypothesis about the nature of expertise, we claim that problem representation is this interplay between the triggering and the instantiation of schemata, which results in a characterization of the experts as spending more time planning, and producing processes that are more forward-working, more accurate, and more efficient. Differences between experts and novices with regard to the initial problem representation cannot be attributed to superiority in general problem-solving strategies since those are not applicable in this early stage. The problem representation is constructed by the solver on the basis of the structure of the domain-related knowledge. Thus, it seems to us that the critical issues to investigate in order to understand problem solving are how problem schemata are acquired in learning to solve problems and how they are represented (see Chi, Bassok, Lewis, et al., in press; Chi & Bassok, in press).

The interplay between a bottom-up and a top-down processing in the development of a representation can be seen more clearly in tasks that require perceptual processing, such as radiological diagnosis. Les-

gold, Feltovich, Glaser, and Wang (1981), for example, studied the diagnostic behavior of 11 novices (first- and second-year residency), 7
postnovices (third- and fourth-year residency), and 5 experts (10 and
more years of residency). Data were gathered by observing subjects
who analyzed X-ray films of specific cases of lung diseases. The subjects had to talk out loud while they made their first diagnosis. They
were then asked to indicate by drawing on the film anatomical features
that were used for their diagnosis, as well as all the anatomical con-
tours they could see in a critical area. Following this, they had to give
another diagnostic report. Only the main differences among the three
experimental groups can be reported here.

While studying the X-ray film of the chest, all subjects utilized
schematic knowledge about "normal" anatomy to identify irregularities
of the patient. In general, the more experienced subjects saw more anatomical features and perceived them more precisely than did less experienced subjects. Also, experts tended to relate one observation to
another, while the novices just listed them. Lesgold et al. (1981) concluded that "the data support the view of the expert as doing more
inferential thinking and ending up with a more coherent model of the
patient shown in the film. In contrast, novice representations, as manifested in their protocols, were more superficial, fragmented, and
piecemeal" (p. 8).

The relevance of the nature of the problem representation on problem solving can be seen directly in two computer-implemented programs that solve standard textbook problems in fluid dynamics (Larkin, 1983). The first program (a production system) implemented an
algebraic model and comprised four components: a representation of the
problem in the form of a list of quantities and associated units, a physics knowledge base containing basic equations sufficient to solve the
problem, a match algorithm that substitutes problem quantities for
variables of the same type, and an equation-solver. This model had no
real knowledge of physics. What it did was to substitute quantities for
variables with the only constraint that they had to have the same unit.
The search space for this model was very large since it had to consider
all possible combinations of variable substitutions. Not surprisingly, the
program produced many wrong solutions because it performed indis-
criminate substitution of any quantity for a variable of the same type
and was not able to invent quantities describing the problem situation.

The *physics representation* model tried to remedy the main deficiencies of the algebraic model. Three kinds of knowledge were added: (1)
The equations in the physics knowledge base were enriched, enabling
the model to distinguish between different variables of the same type;

(2) the model was further provided with knowledge of how to augment information from the problem statement with spatial and other relational information; and finally, (3) the match algorithm relating the knowledge base to the problem representation was extended to account for the new kinds of available information. This program exhibited considerably less search than the model with the knowledge-lean (mathematical) representation and solved more problems correctly. A comparison with human subjects for the same problems showed that differences between successful and less successful subjects corresponded to the differences in problem representation implemented in the two simulation models.

In light of empirical and theoretical accounts, it seems safe to conclude that the nature of the problem representations determines to a large extent the strategy used for search during problem solving, at least in the domains of physics and mathematics. Furthermore, the nature of the representations is determined by the knowledge that the solvers have, which allows them to represent problems in the form that is optimal for solving problems efficiently. Since problem-solving operators can presumably access the entities in the representation directly, the effect is that the problem-solving process appears to be data-driven and forward-working.

4. THE ROLE OF SCHEMATA IN PROBLEM SOLVING

Research in psychology and artificial intelligence has resulted in a variety of theories about how knowledge is represented in human memory (see Rumelhart & Norman, 1983, for an overview). The major categories are *propositional-based* representations, *analogical* representations, and *procedural* representations. Research on human expertise has utilized theories of semantic networks and schemata (both propositionally based), theories of mental models (a form of analogical representation), and production systems (a form of procedural representation). Many studies in the literature address the question of experts' memory structures independent of a problem-solving context. Since memory is not the focus of this chapter, we will discuss only the kinds of knowledge representations that have the most direct bearing on problem solving: schemata, mental models, and production systems. However, since a larger amount of research uses the schema framework, this particular representation will be emphasized here. Mental models and production systems frameworks will be alluded to in the context of specific models that are discussed throughout the paper.

Constructs such as *schemata* (Rumelhart, 1975) and *frames* (Minsky, 1975) have been useful frameworks for understanding the relation between problem solving and knowledge representation. Briefly, schemata are like models of the world; they embody prototypical expectations about objects, situations, events, and actions (Rumelhart & Norman, 1983). A cognitive system that uses schemata as its knowledge representation processes information by matching schemata to the incoming information. Information is understood, or an interpretation of it is developed, if it can be matched to a schema or a configuration of schemata. Some of the important features of schemata (see Rummelhart & Norman, 1983) are as follows:

- They contain *variables;* a schema of a concept has fixed parts, which are assumed always to be true for instances of the concept, and variable parts. Variables have two important properties: They have *default values,* values assumed to be true as long as the incoming information does not specify it otherwise, and they are augmented with knowledge of the plausible range over which possible fillers of the variable might vary.
- Schemata can *embed* one within another; a schema can consist of a configuration of subschemata.
- Schemata represent knowledge on all *levels of abstraction;* there are schemata for natural basic concepts like apples and trees, as well as for abstract concepts like love and cognitive psychology.
- Schemata are *active* processes, actively trying to evaluate incoming information and ascertaining the degree to which they are relevant to structuring the input.

Several findings in expert–novice research can best be interpreted within a schemalike framework. Hinsley et al. (1978) first presented evidence that schemata may play a role in solving algebra word problems by asking students to categorize problems. They were interested in the process of *understanding* a problem, the phase between reading a problem statement and attempting to solve it. The guiding question was: Is understanding basically driven by the formal and abstract knowledge of text comprehension or are specific problem schemas used? As we have discussed earlier, it was found that subjects do recognize problem categories. They can classify problems very early in reading, sometimes only after the first noun phrase. Their problem schemata include knowledge that is useful for solving a problem, such as equations, and procedures for making relevant judgments. In situations where the subjects were given unfamiliar problems, their understanding behavior was guided more by general knowledge about text forms. The effect of understanding a problem statement in relation to the complexity of the language in which it is presented was further explored by Hayes and Simon (1974).

The schema approach was further used to shed light on differences between experts and novices. Chi et al. (1981) used it to describe the problem-relevant knowledge organization of experts and novices in physics. The schema notion also proved to be useful for explaining differences between experts' and novices' categorization data. The first finding was that the organization and content of these schemata were basically different between the experts and novices. For example, the bases of the experts' categories tend to be major principles of mechanics, such as the conservation of momentum, the conservation of energy, and Newton's force law, whereas the bases of the novices' categories tend to be literal objects and concepts stated in the problem itself, such as inclined plane, a spring, and friction. Chi et al. (1981) also found differences between the experts and novices in the labels used to describe categories of problems. For example, the category label most often used by the experts (*Second Law*) does not even appear in the novices' label list. Furthermore, they found that although the schemata are organized hierarchically by both experts and novices, the experts have developed several layers of this hierarchy, whereas only the first level of the hierarchy seems to be developed for the very beginning novices. As skill is developed, the hierarchy develops into a complete tree with many levels of embedding.

A second finding is that the same problem may elicit different schemata for the experts and novices, even though both groups can basically identify the same set of key words as important. In fact, experts generally consider fewer key words as important cues than do novices. If novices can identify the relevant key words as the important cues, what causes the novices difficulty in solving the problem?

> We postulate that one reason that novices have difficulty in solving problems is that they have activated only a lower-level schema, whereas experts have activated a higher-level principle schema, which includes not only the lower-level schemata that the novices activate, but also additional knowledge about the relations between the embedded schemata and the high-level principle schemata (Chi & Glaser, 1982, p. 9).

In other words, the same key words trigger different inference processes in experts versus novices. As a result, the expert builds up a more abstract problem representation, which is—at least in the sciences—often related to relevant solution principles for the class of problems.

The third finding is that it is this difference in the content of the schemata that causes difficulty in problem solving for the novices. Thus, even if the "right" schema is activated, there may be differences with respect to the content of the schema. The method used to assess schema content was to ask subjects to elaborate on schemata that the researchers thought they might have (such as an Incline Plane schema). By coding the utterances of the subjects into *if . . . then* rules, the following differences emerged: (1) The experts' inference rules contain explicit actions (formulated as quantitative relations between problem entities), whereas the novices' inference rules contain general nonspecific actions (like *find knowns and unknowns*); (2) novices sometimes have rules that identify only the condition side without any action (this is consistent with the finding that novices can identify the relevant cues or key words, mentioned above, and yet they may not know what to do about them); and (3) experts also have more conditions in their rules, thereby constraining the application of rules more in accordance with the problem demands. In short, experts have a lot more precise procedural attachments to their problem schemata. Because both the experts and the novices can identify the same set of relevant explicit cues in the problem statement, it seems that the features that elicited this kind of knowledge are not given in the problem statements but are inferred features, which Chi et al. (1981) referred to as "second-order" features.

The existence of problem schemata has also been demonstrated in many other domains, such as programming (Weiser & Shertz, 1983), mathematics, and medical diagnoses. Using the domain of mathematics, the study by Schoenfelt and Herman (1982), for example, replicated the expert–novice differences in the nature of their problem schemata and, further, showed that the experts' schemata can be achieved with instruction. In that study, experts (professors) and novices (but not completely naive with respect to the problems) in mathematics had to sort 32 math problems according to the similarity in their solution procedures. The novices were then divided into two groups; the experimental group received a monthlong mathematics problem-solving course; the control group took a monthlong course in computer programming. Both groups then sorted the problems again. The sorting data revealed that experts agreed highly in their sorting criterion and—like the experts in physics—also used "deep-structure" features to sort problems—in this case general solution procedures. Novices' sorting behavior was mainly driven by surface features. The effects of training were also clear-cut. The novices who received training showed a clear shift in their problem perception toward the problem's "deep structure"; that is, they became more expertlike. There were, however, still differences between the trained novices and the real experts, differences that obviously cannot be remedied by a few hours of instruction.

The role of schemata in the form of classes of disease and their use in diagnoses is also explored in the medical domain. Clancey (1988) predicts the following differences in knowledge, on the basis of his observations of expert diagnosticians:

1. The links between findings (data) and diseases (hypothesis) are tuned in experts in a way that allows them to access disease knowledge "at the right level" of abstraction (vertical structure of concepts) and within the more probable class. This is the result of long experience, resulting in an index schema that accesses disease knowledge that is problem-oriented, not based mainly on textbook knowledge.

2. An expert may perceive classes of diseases as more related to each other than a novice (who learned basically "typical" cases stressing the differences between classes), which allows him/her to consider more alternatives in advance and/or behave in an opportunistic manner when encountering disconfirming evidence for the current main hypotheses.

3. The knowledge hierarchy in experts is more refined, resulting in more precise and specific diagnoses.

These expectations are substantiated by a set of empirical studies. Johnson et al. (1981) and Feltovich, Johnson, Moller, and Swanson (1984) concentrated their research specifically on the knowledge level of diagnostic reasoning. They used the notion of *disease knowledge* to describe the form of schematic knowledge that is represented by physicians for diagnosis: "Disease knowledge refers to a memory store of disease models, each of which specifies a particular disease, the pathophysiology of the disease and the set of clinical manifestations that a patient with the disease model should present . . ." (Feltovich et al., 1984, p. 280). Hypotheses about the character and structure of disease knowledge in experts and novices are formulated and related to behavior in diagnostic problem solving; the hypotheses are tested indirectly by observations about the problem-solving behavior of experts and novices.

The first hypothesis about novices' disease knowledge is that it is *classically centered*, that is, novices know—from textbooks and early hospital presentations—the most typical cases of a disease and use those as anchor points for subsequent elaboration. A second expectation is that novices' disease knowledge is *sparse* in the sense that connections between the different disease schemata are lacking. A final hypothesis is that each individual disease schema is *imprecise* in the sense that novices are either too general or too specific in their expectations about the range of findings connected with a disease. By contrast, experts' disease knowledge structure should be *prenumbral*, *dense*, and *precise*. Experts' expectations about what "goes" with a disease are shaped by thousands of hours of clinical experience, with the result that they have more generalized schemata for what seem to be superficially disconnected diseases as well as a more discriminated hierarchy of disease knowledge, allowing them to see small but important differences.

The assumption that novices have more imprecise expectations about manifestations of diseases in patients can be operationalized in the form of diagnostic reasoning errors (Feltovich et al., 1984). If novices overestimate the allowable range of variation for the findings of a given disease, they will not realize that a finding is at odds with the disease in question. On the other hand, if their expectations about the range of findings are too specific, they will reject a correct disease hypothesis even if the finding is within the range of possible variations. Further, they may not think about the correct diagnosis because the links between patient cues and the disease hierarchy are not well enough established. Finally, another possible reason for not thinking about the correct diagnosis results from missing interrelations between disease schemata themselves, so that the rejection of one hypothesis does not lead to the activation of the next plausible one.

To test their predictions about expert–novice differences with respect to disease knowledge, Johnson et al. (1981) compared the diagnostic behavior of experts, trainees, and students in a typical case of cardiovascular disease. Patient data were given to the subjects in the form of a patient file that included all information, and the subjects were advised to think out loud while they worked through the file. The analysis centered around two questions: (1) Which competing disease hypotheses come to mind? [Or in the Feltovich et al. (1984) terminology, what are the members of the Logical Competitor Set?] (2) How do the subjects select one presumably correct disease hypothesis from this set?

Johnson et al. (1981) found no quantitative differences among the three groups with respect to the number of hypotheses generated during the course of patient data evaluation, and no differences regarding the type of hypotheses. Analysis of strategic aspects of the problemsolving behavior showed a mixed picture. The two most experienced experts (who solved the problem correctly) both considered the full set of possible hypotheses, but in a different manner. The first expert searched in a "breadth-first" manner, first gathering all possible hypotheses and then trying to distinguish among them. That is, he behaved in a way that is in accordance with the classical hypothetico-deductive model. The second expert, however, implemented a "depth-first" search. He focused on one hypothesis and tried to verify it; he switched to another hypothesis only when he encountered contradictory data. The other subjects similarly showed the use of different strategies, with the distinction that they often did not succeed in finding the right hypothesis. The novices often could not even relate the findings to the diseases, due to a lack of knowledge about the relation between diseases and their symptoms.

Feltovich et al. (1984) concentrated their analysis of the same data on the specific *content* of the hypotheses uttered by the subjects. They found most of their expectations verified: Experts considered the full set of physiologically similar diseases (logical competitor set, LCS) and used it actively. They had enough knowledge to discriminate precisely between members of this set, often considering several hypotheses concurrently. Novices who did not have the full LCS had their disease concepts centered around "classical" cases, which are only loosely related. Several forms of evaluation errors (with respect to patient data) occurred. The trainees had a fully developed LCS but its members were more loosely related than in the case of the experts. They also showed less precise expectations. In short, experts do have more knowledge about (similar) diseases and have effective procedures to distinguish among them.

In summary, Johnson et al. (1981) and Feltovich et al. (1984) found no evidence for expert–novice differences on a strategic level. Both groups use a generate-and-test strategy. Differences do occur with respect to whether the hypothesis space is searched depth-first or breadth-first, but this also does not distinguish between experts and novices. Differences with respect to the correctness of solutions can be attributed to differences in the specificity of disease models, the degree of connectedness between these models, and the ease of access to the relevant knowledge. These results show once again that due to the structure of their knowledge, experts are able to come up with a better problem representation that potentially affects the quality of the problem solution and the way the problem is solved.

In sum, the schema theory [in the form presented by Rumelhart and Norman (1983) as well as extensions and elaborations provided by other researchers] explains various phenomena related to expert problem solving and related cognitive activities:

1. Rapid categorization (via pattern matching).
2. Inference or elaboration activities (relating to filling the schema slots with default values).
3. Top-down and forward-working processing (procedural attachments and expectations or hypotheses originating from information about a prototype drive the solution process).
4. Hierarchically organized knowledge (via embedding of schemata).

5. PROBLEM-SOLVING STRATEGIES

In this section, we focus on two problem-solving strategies: the way goal information is used to generate backward-working search, and the way problem givens are used to generate forward-working search.

An example for the forward-working strategy can be found in a study by Simon and Simon (1978). They compared one expert's and one novice's solution behavior for standard dynamics problems. Thinking-aloud protocol data from 19 problems were analyzed. To describe the solution paths more thoroughly, Simon and Simon wrote two production system programs that captured the basic difference between the subjects: The expert's system works according to a forward-chaining strategy; the novice's system works backward. In the expert production system, rules fired when all values for the independent variables (the givens) were known. For the novice system, two things were required to satisfy the condition part of the rules: (1) The values of all independent variables had to be known, and (2) the dependent variable (the one to be solved for) had to appear on a goal list with "wanted" variable values. This difference accounted for most of the variations in the solution behavior of the two subjects. The expert worked from the givens in the problem and did not attend to the specific variables the problem statement asked him to evaluate. The novice, on the other hand, wrote down equations in which the desired quantities were dependent variables. When all of the independent variables were not known, he set up a subgoal to solve for them. Similar differences in terms of forward/backward-working strategies have been reported by many authors (Bhaskar & Simon, 1977; McDermott & Larkin, 1978; Sweller, Mawer, & Ward, 1983) for physics and math problem solving.

Strategic differences of this kind are also found in the area of medical diagnosis. Patel and Groen (1986) address specifically the question of whether experts' diagnostic reasoning can be described as a form of hypothetico-deductive process, i.e., a form of means-end analysis, or as forward reasoning. They analyzed the behavior of seven experts in a difficult cardiology problem to find out more about the causal reasoning processes that lead to a diagnosis. A free-recall task was also used to see how experts represent the problem. In addition, in order to assess the causal models the subjects had about the disease, the subjects had to describe the pathophysiology of the case. Analyses of the subjects' causal model descriptions revealed that all the reasoning steps done by the *successful* subjects in this task (four out of seven) can be described as pure forward reasoning. These descriptions were captured by building a production system for each subject. The *unsuccessful* subjects basically used a subset of the rules found in the successful solver's production systems. But in addition, they had two other types of rules: irrelevant rules and backward-chaining rules. Specifically, they employed more backward reasoning from a goal than did the successful subjects.

The critical question is why working forward works for the experts. After all, it seems more intelligent to organize the solution process around the goal to find the desired quantities, and thus to work backward, instead of taking a chance and utilizing whatever information is given, hoping to end up with equations that will produce the finally desired values. But, as Larkin (1985) argues, working backward is more efficient only if one assumes that the problem is being solved in its mathematical representation. If one does not augment terms in an algebraic equation with additional meaning, the only reasonable way to solve for an unknown is a means–ends strategy—that is, to make the ultimately wanted unknown the dependent variable and to solve recursively for unknown independent variables until all of them are known. If, however, the solver tries to build up and utilize a "scientific" representation, the first thing he or she needs to do is to relate entities in the "naive" representation to entities in the scientific representation. For example, scientific concepts like forces (such as gravity) and energies have to be abstracted from naive representations like masses and heights. Scientific concepts are often related by equations such as $F = mg$ or $U = mgh$; these, then, would be the first equations utilized by a problem solver who strives to build a scientific representation of the problem, presumably an expert (Larkin, 1985).

One note of caution that we would inject is that working forward or backward has the characteristic of progressing in a linear way through a problem space, in which each problem state is "equivalent" in the sense of having the same status as the previous state. That is, each problem state is the result of applying an operator to the previous state.

This characterization seems to be quite adequate for knowledge-lean problems, or for problems in which one has to manipulate algebraic expressions. Solving a knowledge-rich problem like physics, however, has several properties that distinguish it from knowledge-lean problems. The first is that there is a difference in the way experts and novices solve them. Novices' solution processes may indeed be characterized as working backward in the ways that the equations are manipulated. Not only do experts' solutions, on the other hand, differ from those of the novices in that they work forward, but a more accurate characterization may be that experts' solution processes are composed of two intermingled subprocesses: building a representation, and deriving and executing the solution procedure. The representation-building phase cannot be accurately characterized as either forward- or backward-working, but perhaps more accurately as top-down and bottom-up (which we have discussed earlier). Because of the enriched representation that was built (as the result of processes of schema instantiation), the remaining solution derivation and execution phase appears to be forward-working. Hence, it may be misleading to grossly characterize the entire solution processes of the experts as forward-working.

Besides, experts also work backward. This expectation is confirmed by observations made in a study by Bhaskar and Simon (1977). They found that experts in thermodynamics work backward when they are confronted with an unfamiliar problem. The notion of "unfamiliar" is the crucial point: An unfamiliar problem is by definition one that cannot be categorized as an instance of a known problem class. Hence, a well-defined and prestored procedural solution cannot be derived by instantiating an existing schema. However, more research is needed to confirm this claim. We do not have enough data about how experts work on "difficult" problems, at least not in physics. The majority of the expert–novice research in math and physics deals with problems that are routine for the experts. A closer look at how experts solve complex problems might also shed light on the question of how general or specific the experts' skills are.

5.1. Interaction of Different Problem-Solving Strategies

In addition to discussing problem-solving strategies in an isolated way, one also needs to consider their interactions. Medical diagnosis seems to be a domain that is particularly suitable for studying the interaction of different problem-solving strategies. In order to talk about diagnostic problem solving (in medicine) within the terminology of the general problem-solving model as introduced in Section 2, one can assume that the problem representation is formed by some mental model of the patient. Problem solving relates this representation of symptoms to a hypothesis or a set of hypotheses considered as possible causes for the presented disease. Furthermore, it includes the process of finding out whether the proposed explanation, or another from a set of alternative explanations, is the actual cause.

The classical description of diagnostic thinking says that it is a hypothetico-deductive process: "Cues in patient data suggest hypotheses, which are, in turn, tested against subsequent data of the case" (Feltovich et al., 1984, p. 279). Pople (1982) mentions similar features: "One nearly universal finding is that the physician responds to cues in the clinical data by conceptualizing one or more diagnostic tasks which then play an important role in the subsequent decision making process" (p. 122). Early research in medical diagnosis (Barrows, Feightner, Neufeld, & Norman, 1978; Elstein, Shuylman, & Sprafka, 1978) has found no differences between experts and novices with respect to the use of this global (hypothetico-deductive) strategy. Also, various parametric characteristics of this process, such as the number of hypotheses maintained in active consideration or the percentage of patient data used before generating the first hypothesis, do not distinguish between experts and novices either (Feltovich et al., 1984).

While both novices and experts utilize cues (from patient's symptoms or test results), experts generate particularly appropriate diagnostic tasks to differentiate among the hypotheses (Feltovich et al., 1984; Pople, 1982). Furthermore, experts generate specific hypotheses very early after encountering some of the patient's data (Lesgold et al., 1988; Patel & Groen, 1986, Pople, 1982). This early formation of a hypothesis of a patient's illness and the resulting organization of the diagnostic strategy in the form of a specific *diagnostic task* serves the following functions (see Pople, 1982): (1) Competing hypotheses can be eliminated, (2) the diagnostic process can be organized in the form of a controlled, goal-directed sequence of further information gathering, and (3) a set of specific hypotheses allows one to evaluate costs and reliability of information. Thus, in this domain, the way experts arrive at their specific initial hypotheses can be thought of as analogous to reasoning forward from the problem description, where the diagnostic tasks that physicians request are guided by the goals (the set of hypotheses that are being entertained), so that the search is goal-driven and constrained. In short, an adequate way of understanding diagnostic reasoning is an interaction between the data-driven and goal-driven processing.

The real challenge in modeling diagnostic reasoning, however, is not in simulating the algorithms that physicians use to decide between a set of possible diseases (the *differential diagnoses*), which is what most of the research in analyzing diagnostic problem solving does. That is, the analyses start with the assumption that the problem solver has already constructed an initial set of hypotheses and probes the issue of how the problem solver verifies his hypotheses or eliminates the incorrect competing candidates. The real challenge lies in understanding how the physician arrives at the initial set of hypotheses in the first place, which is an issue that Pople's (1982) research addresses. He analyzed several computational models that perform this task: simple generate-and-test, direct evocation of hypotheses based on single symptoms (implemented as a system named INTERNIST-I), and a more complex search procedure based on an indexing scheme that allows for multiple representations of nosological knowledge (implemented in the program CADUCEUS). The only model that leads to tractable algorithms and has some similarity to experts' reasoning is the last one.

We are now in a position to integrate the observation of Patel and Groen (1986) reported earlier that expert diagnosticians work forward, which is at odds with the standard notion of diagnosticians working backward (using the hypothetico-deductive strategy). As Patel and Groen pointed out, the results from their study cannot be interpreted to mean that the hypothesis-generation strategy shown by the novices is the *cause* for the inaccurate diagnosis. A more plausible explanation for the wrong diagnosis is that certain critical rules have not been accessed or do not exist in the knowledge base of the unsuccessful subjects. In order to work forward successfully, certain critical rules have to be accessed. If they are not accessed, the physician might fall back to a hypothetico-deductive strategy. Another factor that might have contributed to the advantage of the forward-working strategy over a generate-and-test approach in Patel and Groen's task is the nature of the information supplied. In their study, *all* the information about the patient was summarized in one short description. In a more natural setting, the physician usually must gather data about a patient in an *incremental* fashion, with the possibility that new findings change his or her picture of the patient drastically; decisions about what data ought to be assessed under consideration of the benefits and risks for the patient are more effectively accomplished by considering alternative hypotheses in advance (see Pople, 1982). Thus, the extent of which forward changing occurs seems to depend on two factors: the degree of expertise and the nature of the task itself.

5.2. Switching Problem-Solving Strategy

While it is a fairly well established fact that at a gross level of characterization, experts use a forward-working strategy (in routine problem solving) and novices tend to work backward (Larkin, McDermott, Simon, & Simon, 1980; Simon & Simon, 1978; see also Section 4), no observations have documented *when* this switch occurs during the development of expertise. Another open question concerns what factors would facilitate this step. A series of empirical and theoretical investigations done in the last few years by Sweller and colleagues (Mawer & Sweller, 1982; Sweller, 1983; Sweller & Levine, 1982; Sweller et al., 1983) probes more directly into these questions. We will review some of the major results of this work.

The central hypothesis of Sweller et al. (1983) is that while novices often use means–ends analysis (MEA) to solve a problem, this strategy may actually prevent the acquisition of more problem-specific rules. Sweller, Mawer, and Howe (1982), using simple arithmetic problems, found that rule induction occurred only if subjects were provided with additional information (meaning in addition to the problem goal) either during or after problem solution. In two other studies, the degree of goal specificity was varied and its effect on rule induction observed. Mawer and Sweller (1982), again using arithmetic problems, found an increase in rule induction under conditions where many subgoals were given to the student. Sweller and Levine (1982) gave their subjects global goals ("Solve this equation for as many variables as you can") instead of ones formulated as a specific problem state ("Solve for x") and found that this form of treatment facilitated the induction of problem-specific solution rules. Sweller et al. (1983; see also Sweller, 1983) hypothesized that a crucial factor accounting for this finding is the kind of information a learner focuses on during problem solving. If an MEA-controlled regimen is used, the learner might focus mainly on moves designed to reduce the difference between the current problem state and the goal state (which in their types of problems is described as just another problem state). Hence, a problem solver will utilize to a smaller degree information about the problem structure and about moves undertaken so far. What gets potentially lost in this form of problem solving is information about the conditions that led to one specific path; this kind of information can be provided only if one analyzes the solution sequence backward. MEA, however, is more concerned with the next step in a forward direction, comparing the current state and the goal state. If this is true, the instructional consequence is obvious: "Under these circumstances, where knowledge or schema acquisition is an aim of problem solving, it may be useful to reduce the influence of the goal by altering its characteristics in a manner designed to reduce its function as a control mechanism" (Sweller et al., 1983, p. 641). In order to move control from the problem solving goal state to intermediate states, one can provide feedback on the level of single operator application, focus the student on subgoals instead of end goals, or reduce the specifity of the end goal.

Sweller et al. (1983) use the latter strategy to facilitate rule induction during problem solving. In the first experiment, this time using simple kinematics problems, they again establish the usual finding that novices use MEA to solve unfamiliar problems. Furthermore, by analyzing the solution strategies of their subjects during a long sequence of repeated encounters with the same simple problem type, they found a gradual shift from MEA to forward-oriented problem solving. This was associated with other indicators of expertise, such as a decrease in the number of moves required for solution. In addition, an interaction between time required to switch strategy and problem category was found. They then demonstrated that reduction of goal specifity can facilitate the switch from MEA to a forward-working strategy, in both kinematics problems and geometrical problem-solving tasks.

6. THE DEVELOPMENT OF EXPERTISE

Experts and novices can be distinguished by two major differences. Experts know more about the domain and can access and use their knowledge more efficiently than novices (Kolodner, 1983). Accordingly, considerations about how expertise develops must take into account modifications of the declarative knowledge base as well as changes of procedural knowledge. Below, we illustrate a couple of proposals about how knowledge is acquired and refined.

6.1. Acquisition of Episodic Knowledge Structures

When we say that experts have more declarative knowledge than novices, we have to distinguish among three alternative meanings of this statement: (1) Experts have more semantic knowledge than novices, (2) more episodic knowledge ("more experience"), or (3) both. In our discussion of the nature of medical knowledge differences, we have seen that an important difference between experts and novices seems to be that novices have structured their knowledge in a "textbooklike" manner, whereas the knowledge representation of experts is influenced by years of experience in applying that kind of textbook knowledge to real problems. Also, the commonsense meaning of an expert is one who is experienced in a domain. From this point of view, one aspect of the development of expertise consists of the continuous refinement of semantic knowledge about a domain through repeated experiences of using this knowledge. Kolodner's (1983) work, for example, describes the evolution from novice to expert as the development of domain-related factual knowledge and domain-specific reasoning strategies based on memory for specific experiences (i.e., episodic memory).

Episodic memory contains information about individual experiences that a person has had plus generalized episodes or types of events. Generalized episodes (more or less identical in meaning to Schank's *scripts*) (Schank & Abelson, 1978) are created by comparing different episodes and calculating similarities between them. For example, after having eaten two times in a restaurant, one may be able to come up with a concept of restaurant that encodes similar aspects between the two episodes. According to Kolodner (1983), "even if a novice and an expert have the same *semantic* knowledge (i.e., knew the same facts), the expert's experience would have allowed him to build up better *episodic* definitions of how to use it" (p. 499).

The structures that organize episodic memory in Kolodner's model are called E-MOPS, from *Episodic Memory Organization Packets*. "An E-MOP is a generalized episode and thus organizes generalized information about the individual episodes which comprise it. It also organizes those episodes by indexing them according to their deviations from those norms" (p. 503). E-MOPS are constructed for both declarative and procedural episodic knowledge. For example, a computer-implemented model of an E-MOP-based episodic memory structure named SHRINK (Kolodner, 1983) encodes knowledge about psychiatric disease categories, patient information, and diagnostic procedures in this domain.

How is episodic knowledge refined? Kolodner (1983) proposes a theory of incremental learning: "Previously learned knowledge is put to use. When it fails, the reason for the failure is established. In establishing why the failure occurred, previous knowledge is 'debugged' " (p. 507). Given the E-MOP's structure of episodic memory, new episodes are encoded in terms of deviations from existing memory concepts, i.e., generalized episodes. For example, a doctor may have diagnosed major depression on the basis of the evidence for three supporting symptoms, while the E-MOP structure for diagnosing major depression specifies that four supporting symptoms need to be established before the diagnosis can be made. Learning can take place in two ways. It can occur spontaneously on the basis of comparing similar E-MOPS stored in memory, and using the differences between the structures for building a new E-MOP that is more general (or more specific), that is, similarity-based learning. Learning can also be triggered by performance failures. For example, the diagnosis of major depression made on the basis of three symptoms may turn out to be wrong and the doctor may reason about what he or she did wrong.

Kolodner elaborates further on this second learning mechanism, using the computer model SHRINK as an example of how to improve diagnostic reasoning and knowledge in an incremental, failure-driven way. The basic strategy is to analyze a reasoning sequence that led to a failure, assigning blame to one or more components, and then to correct both the actual failure and the pieces of knowledge that caused the erroneous inference.

As we will see, there are striking similarities between Kolodner's model of refining knowledge through reflection on its application and Anderson's model of skill learning within a problem-solving context, despite many differences in theoretical assumptions and computer implementations.

6.2. ACQUISITION OF PROCEDURAL KNOWLEDGE

Anderson's (1983, 1986) theory (formulated in the form of the production system ACT*) is concerned with the question of how knowledge relevant for a skill (such as proving a geometry theorem or programming in a computer language) that is initially represented in a declarative form becomes proceduralized over time. *Proceduralization* is a technical term referring to the transformation of prestored declarative knowledge retrieved from long-term memory into a production or rule-like representation.

The process that accounts for this transformation is *knowledge compilation*. Knowledge compilation has two components: *composition* and *proceduralization* (Anderson, 1983, 1986). These learning mechanisms work as follows. Initially, a learner is viewed as having stored declarative information relevant to the execution of a skill. For example, a student might have read in a textbook about the properties of geometrical proofs. In a problem-solving context (for example, when asked to prove a geometry theorem) the solver must apply general problem-solving procedures, such as means–ends analysis, which takes as the condition certain declarative knowledge that has been encoded *a priori* as important and fundamental to the problem at hand. For instance, if a student is trying to solve a geometry problem that requires proving that two triangles are congruent, he might start by using means–ends analysis to set up the goal of transforming the current state (the givens) to the goal state. In order to transform the current state to the goal state, means–ends analysis sets out to reduce the largest difference between the current and the goal state, which the model notices to be that the corresponding sides of the triangle have not been proven congruent. Thus, in achieving this goal, the model in effect is *proceduralizing* the declarative knowledge that if the corresponding sides of a triangle are congruent, then one can prove the triangles to be congruent. The result of proceduralization is that it builds productions out of the domain-specific declarative knowledge so that the declarative knowledge will no longer be required to be retrieved from long-term memory the next time the solver solves a problem with similar conditions. Thus, proceduralization creates new productions so that the process of information retrieval can be omitted, and problem solving can be guided by production matching.

Composition, on the other hand, is simply the concatenation of separate procedures into one larger procedure. It "takes a sequence of productions that follow each other in solving a particular problem and collapses them into a single production that has the same effect as the sequence" (Anderson, 1986, p. 291). Such a composed rule is considerably faster to execute than the sequence of the original rules since it collapses a couple of steps into one operation. Also, composition seems to account for the switch to forward-working strategies since it eliminates search and the walk through intermediate steps.

Both the composition process and proceduralization can account for another observation made by experts. Experts are sometimes unable to report the details of a task they have just completed. Given this model of knowledge compilation, this may be the case because (1) experts skipped intermediate steps using a short-cut rule (and thus cannot report detailed steps) and/or (2) they lost the declarative representation (see Adelson, 1986).

Anderson's ACT* theory of skill acquisition can also account for memory phenomena known in the expert–novice literature, such as chunking and automization of skills. It should be pointed out, however, that the composition mechanism, while it can explain an impressive range of learning phenomena, may not be able to account for all forms of procedural learning (Neches, 1987). For example, Lewis (1981) has shown that certain differences in the ways expert and novices use strategies for solving algebra expressions cannot be produced by composition alone. There are many other examples (see Neches, 1987) that suggest that the development of experts' procedural skill often includes the *invention of new actions*, a process that has been difficult for any model to simulate.

7. CONCLUSION

We started out with the assumption that expert problem solving—as problem solving in general—can be described as an interaction between a problem representation and cognitive actions. Contrary to an intuitive notion of expertise, many studies show that the main differences between experts' and novices' problem-solving behavior cannot be attributed to superior domain-independent cognitive actions ("strategies") or a "better" memory, but are better explained by postulating that experts build problem representations that add information to the given problem statement in such a way that search for a problem solution is improved significantly. Specifically, experts elaborate upon the given problem formulation by drawing on their huge domain-specific knowledge base.

Probing deeper into the question of precisely what it is that makes experts' problem representations so effective, we found that they can be characterized as being coherent, complete, abstract, and functional. In particular, experts classify problems in terms of abstract principles of the respective domain, which in turn are—at least for the case of well-defined problems—directly related to problem-solving actions. In contrast, novices' problem perceptions are less articulated, include more surface features, and have a more remote connection to problem-solving activities.

Given that the elaborated problem representations the experts come up with are of pivotal importance for explaining differences in problem-solving behavior, an important issue was what enables experts to build a richer representation. An obvious candidate was domain-specific knowledge, in the form of memory schemata. We also summarized the differences in the strategies that experts and novices use to solve problems, such as forward versus backward working.

Our final discussion focused on how expertise is acquired. We perceive this also as a major issue for future psychological research. The learning theories we referred to have been applied to explain expertlike behavior for certain classes of problems. A question that remains to be answered is whether they can also account for long-term knowledge acquisition of the type that is required for real-world expertise—i.e., learning that often stretches over years of studying and gaining experience. Analyzing the development of expertise—i.e., the acquisition of a large body of knowledge, over a long period of time—also has the potential of telling us how individuals differ in becoming experts. The notion that everybody can potentially be an expert in some area leaves open the question of why it is that some people become experts more easily and rapidly than others. Our research on the varying degree to which students use self-explanations in studying new domain knowledge needed for solving problems may shed light on why some individuals can become experts more readily than others (Chi, Bassok, Lewis, et al., in press).

8. REFERENCES

Adelson, B. (1986). Constraints and phenomena common to the semantically rich domains. *International Journal of Intelligent Systems, 1,* 1–14.

Anderson, J. R. (1976). *Language, memory, and thought.* Hillsdale, NJ: Erlbaum.

Anderson, J. R. (1983). *The architecture of cognition.* Cambridge, MA: Harvard University Press.

Anderson, J. R. (1986). Knowledge compilation: The general learning mechanism. In R. S. Michalski, J. G. Carbonell, & T. M. Mitchell (Eds.), *Machine learning. An artificial intelligence approach* (Vol. 2, pp. 289–310). Los Altos, LA: Morgan Kaufmann.

Barrows, H. S., Feightner, J. W. Neufeld, V. R., & Norman, G. R. (1978). *Analysis of the clinical methods of medical students and physicians* (Final report to Ontario Ministry of Health). Hamilton, Ontario, Canada: McMaster University.

Bhaskar, R., & Simon, H. A. (1977). Problem solving in semantically rich domains: An example from engineering thermodynamics. *Cognitive Science, 1,* 193–215.

Chi, M. T. H. (1984). Representing knowledge and metaknowledge: Implications for interpreting metamemory research. In F. E. Weinert & R. Kluwe (Eds.), *Learning by thinking* (pp. 239–266). Stuttgart, West Germany, Kohlhammer.

Chi, M. T. H., & Bassok, M. (in press). Learning to solve physics problems by studying and using worked-out examples: Individual differences in self-explanations. In L. B. Resnick (Ed.), *Knowing and learning: Issues for a cognitive science of instruction.* Hillsdale, NJ: Erlbaum.

Chi, M. T. H., Bassok, M., Lewis, M. W., Reimann, P., & Glaser, R. (in press). Self-explanations: How students study and use examples in learning to solve problems. *Cognitive Science.*

Chi, M. T. H., Feltovich, P., & Glaser, R. (1981). Categorization and representation of physics problems by experts and novices. *Cognitive Science, 5,* 121–152.

Chi, M. T. H., & Glaser, R. (1982, December). *Final report: Knowledge and skill differences in novices and experts.* Pittsburgh: Learning Research and Development Center, University of Pittsburgh.

Chi, M. T. H., & Glaser, R. (1985). Problem solving ability. In R. Sternberg (Ed.), *Human abilities: An information processing approach* (pp. 227–250). San Francisco: Freeman.

Chi, M. T. H., Glaser, R., & Farr, M. J. (Eds.) (1988). *The nature of expertise.* Hillsdale, NJ: Erlbaum.

Chi, M. T. H., Glaser, R., & Rees, E. (1982). Expertise in problem solving. In R. Sternberg (Ed.), *Advances in the psychology of human intelligence* (Vol. 1, pp. 7–75). Hillsdale, NJ: Erlbaum.

Clancey, W. (1988). Acquiring, representing, and evaluating a competence model of diagnostic strategy. In M. T. H. Chi, R. Glaser, & M. J. Farr (Eds.), *The nature of expertise* (pp. 343–418). Hillsdale, NJ: Erlbaum.

Elstein, A. S., Shulman, L. S., & Sprafka, S. A. (1978). *Medical problem solving: An analysis of clinical reasoning*. Cambridge, MA: Harvard University Press.

Feltovich, P. J., Johnson, P. E., Moller, J. H., & Swanson, D. B. (1984). LCS: The role and development of medical knowledge in diagnostic expertise. In W. J. Clancey & E. H. Shortliffe (Eds.), *Readings in medical artificial intelligence*. Reading, MA: Addison-Wesley.

Greeno, J. G., & Simon, H. A. (1984). *Problem solving and reasoning*. Pittsburgh: University of Pittsburgh, LRDC.

Hayes, J. R., & Simon, H. A. (1974). Understanding written problem instructions. In L. W. Gregg (Ed.), *Knowledge and cognition*. Hillsdale, NJ: Erlbaum.

Hinsley, D. A., Hayes, J. R., & Simon, H. A. (1978). From words to equations: Meaning and representation in algebra word problems. In P. A. Carpenter & M. A. Just (Eds.), *Cognitive processes in comprehension*. Hillsdale, NJ: Erlbaum.

Johnson, P. E., Duran, A. S., Hassebrock, F., Moller, J., Prietula, M., Feltovich, P. J., & Swanson, D. B. (1981). Expertise and error in diagnostic reasoning. *Cognitive Science, 5*, 235–283.

Kolodner, J. L. (1983). Towards an understanding of the role of experience in the evolution from novice to expert. *International Journal of Man–Machine Studies, 19*, 497–518.

Larkin, J. H. (1977). *Group in science and mathematics education*. Berkeley, CA: University of Berkeley.

Larkin, J. H. (1983). *Mechanisms of effective problem solving in physics*. Unpublished manuscript.

Larkin, J. H. (1985). Understanding, problem representation, and skill in physics. In S. F. Chipman, J. W. Segal, & R. Glaser (Eds.), *Thinking and learning skills* (Vol. 2): *Research and open questions* (pp. 141–160). Hilldale, NJ: Erlbaum.

Larkin, J. H., McDermott, J., Simon, D. P., & Simon, H. A. (1980). Models of competence in solving physics problems. *Cognitive Science, 4*, 317–345.

Lesgold, A. M., Feltovich, P. J., Glaser, R., & Wang, Y. (1981). *The acquisition of perceptual diagnostic skill in radiology*. Pittsburgh: University of Pittsburgh, LRDC.

Lesgold, A., Rubinson, H., Feltovich, P., Glaser, R., Klopfer, D., & Wang, Y. (1988). Expertise in a complex skill: Diagnosing x-ray pictures. In M. Chi, R. Glaser, & M. Farr (Eds.), *The nature of expertise* (pp. 311–342). Hillsdale, NJ: Erlbaum.

Lewis, C. (1981). Skill in algebra. In J. R. Anderson (Ed.), *Cognitive skills and their acquisition*. Hillsdale, NJ: Erlbaum.

Mawer, R., & Sweller, J. (1982). The effects of subgoal density and location on learning during problem solving. *Journal of Experimental Psychology: Learning, Memory and Cognition, 8*, 252–259.

McDermott, J., & Larkin, J. H. (1978). Re-representing textbook physics problems. In *Proceedings of the 2nd National Conference*. Toronto: University of Toronto Press.

Minsky, M. (1975). A framework for representing knowledge. In P. Winston (Ed.), *The psychology of computer vision*. New York: McGraw-Hill.

Neches, R. (1987). *Learning through incremental refinement of procedures*. Cambridge, MA: M.I.T. Press.

Newell, A., & Simon, H. A. (1972). *Human problem solving*. Englewood Cliffs, NJ: Prentice-Hall.

Patel, V. L., & Groen, G. J. (1986). Knowledge based solution strategies in medical reasoning. *Cognitive Science, 10,* 91–116.

Pople, H. (1982). Heuristic methods for imposing structure on ill-structured problems; The structuring of medical diagnosis. In P. Szolovits (Ed.), *Artificial intelligence in medicine.* Boulder, CO: Westview Press.

Rumelhart, D. E. (1975). Notes on a schema for stories. In D. G. Borbrow & A. M. Collins (Eds.), *Representation and understanding.* New York: Academic Press.

Rumelhart, D. E., & Norman, D. A. (1983). *Representation in memory.* San Diego: University of California, Cognitive Science Laboratory, CHIP.

Sacerdoti, E. D. (1977). *A structure for plans and behavior.* New York: Elsevier North-Holland.

Schank, R. C., & Abelson, R. P. (1978). *Scripts, plans, goals, and understanding: An inquiry into human knowledge structures.* Hillsdale, NJ: Erlbaum.

Schoenfeld, A. H., & Herrmann, D. J. (1982). Problem perception and knowledge structure in expert and novice mathematical problem solvers. *Journal of Experimental Psychology: Learning, Memory and Cognition, 8,* 484–494.

Simon, D. P., & Simon, H. A. (1978). Individual differences in solving physics problems. In R. Siegler (Ed.), *Children's thinking: What develops.* Hillsdale, NJ: Erlbaum.

Sweller, J. (1983). Control mechanisms in problem solving. *Memory and Cognition, 11,* 32–40.

Sweller, J., & Levine, M. (1982). Effects of goal specifity on means–ends analysis and learning. *Journal of Experimental Psychology: Learning, Memory and Cognition, 8,* 463–474.

Sweller, J, Mawer, R., & Howe, W. (1982). Consequences of history-cued and means–ends strategies in problem solving. *American Journal of Psychology, 95,* 455–483.

Sweller, J., Mawer, R., & Ward, M.R. (1983). Development of expertise in mathematical problem solving. *Journal of Experimental Psychology: General, 112,* 639–661.

Toulmin, S.E. (1958). *The uses of argument.* New York: Cambridge University Press.

VanLehn, K. (in press). Problem solving and cognitive skill acquisition. In M. Posner (Ed.), *The foundations of cognitive science.* Cambridge, MA: MIT Press.

Voss, J. F., Greene, T. R., Post, T. A., & Penner, B. C. (1983). Problem solving skill in the social sciences. In G. H. Bower (Ed.), *The psychology of learning and motivation: Advances in research theory* (Vol. 17). New York: Academic Press.

Voss, J. F., & Post, T. A. (1988). On the solving of ill-structured problems. In M. Chi, R. Glaser, & M. Farr (Eds.), *The nature of expertise* (pp. 261–286). Hillsdale, NJ: Erlbaum.

Voss, J. F., Tyler, S., & Yengo, L. (1983). Individual differences in the solving of social science problems. In R. Dillon & R. Schmeck (Eds.), *Individual differences in cognition.* New York: Academic Press.

Weiser, M., & Shertz, J. (1983). Programming problem representation in novice and expert programmers. *International Journal of Man–Machine Studies, 19,* 391–398.

8

Machine Inference

R. A. FROST

From the early days of civilization, man has attempted to augment his ability to "think" by building machines that facilitate the processing of knowledge. Many such machines are primarily concerned with numerical computation. However, during the last few years, systems have been built that can "reason" in the sense that they are able to check a body of knowledge for consistency and are able to infer implicit knowledge from that which they have been given explicitly.

In this chapter, we introduce the reader to three approaches that have been used in the development of computer-based reasoning systems. The first is based on formal logic, the second makes use of techniques that have been developed in expert systems work, and the third makes use of techniques developed in natural language processing research. However, before we begin our discussion of these approaches, we consider how knowledge may be input to a computer.

1. INPUT OF KNOWLEDGE

1.1. FORMAL LANGUAGES

Before a computer can process knowledge, that knowledge has to be input. This can be achieved in various ways, for example: (1) through

R. A. FROST • School of Computer Science, University of Windsor, Windsor, Ontario N9B 3P4, Canada.

a keyboard, (2) through an optical character reader, (3) through sensors (e.g., patient monitors), (4) through a video camera. Irrespective of how input is achieved, it is useful to think of the knowledge being input as comprising *well-formed formulas* (wffs) of some formal language—that is, of a language that has a well-defined "syntax" and "semantics," where syntax is concerned with the structure of wffs and semantics is concerned with the meaning of wffs.

1.1.1. Syntax

As an introduction to the notion of syntax, we consider a relatively simple class of languages called context-free languages. The syntax of a language in this class may be described by a "grammar" called a *context-free grammar* (CFG), which consists of a finite set of *terminal* symbols, a finite set of *nonterminal* symbols (one of which is called the *distinguished* nonterminal), and a finite set of *productions*, each of which has a single nonterminal on its left-hand side and a sequence of one or more terminals or nonterminals on its right-hand side. Terminal symbols are *primitive* symbols, nonterminals denote *syntactic constructs*, and productions define how well-formed constructs may be built from simpler components. For example, if the input is text, then the terminals might be words, the nonterminals might denote noun phrases, verb phrases, sentences, etc., and the productions might define how sentences may be constructed from noun phrases and verb phrases, how noun phrases are built from words, and so on.

1.1.2. Notations for the Specification of Context-Free Grammars

Several notations have been developed for specifying CFGs. As an example, consider the following CFG, which is specified using a variant of a notation called Backus–Naur Form:

```
terminals = {peter, paul, sally, thinks, likes, knows}
nonterminals = {sentence, verbphrase, identifier, verb}
distinguished nonterminal = sentence
   productions:

 sentence   ::=  identifier verbphrase
verbphrase  ::=  verb
                | verb identifier
identifier  ::=  peter
                | paul
                | sally
```

verb ::= thinks
        | likes
        | knows

This notation may be explained as follows:

1. $n ::= \alpha$ means that the nonterminal n is composed of the sequence of terminals and nonterminals denoted by α.
2. $\alpha\,\beta$ denotes the sequence that consists of the sequence α followed by the sequence β.
3. $n ::= \alpha \mid \beta$ means that n is composed of α or β. This is shorthand for the two productions $n ::= \alpha$ and $n ::= \beta$.

Hence, according to the above grammar:

1. "peter," "paul," and "sally" are identifiers.
2. "thinks," "likes," and "knows" are verbs.
3. "thinks," "likes sally," and "knows peter" are examples of verb phrases.
4. "peter thinks," "paul likes sally," and "peter knows paul" are examples of sentences.

To show how these examples are obtained, we introduce the notion of a "derivation."

1.1.3. Derivations

In the following the Greek letters α, β, and γ denote sequences of terminals and nonterminals, and the abbreviation *iff* stands for "if and only if."

We say that α "directly derives" β in a grammar G; iff β can be obtained from α by replacing, in α, some nonterminal n by the right-hand side of some production in G whose left-hand side is n. We denote the fact that α directly derives β in a grammar G by:

$$\alpha \underset{G}{\Rightarrow} \beta \qquad \text{or, if G is known, by} \qquad \alpha \Rightarrow \beta$$

For example, in the grammar G1 above:

$$\text{identifier verbphrase} \Rightarrow \text{identifier verb}$$

If $\alpha \Rightarrow \gamma$ and $\gamma \Rightarrow \beta$, then we say that α derives β. More generally, we can say that α derives β if α directly derives β, or if α directly derives γ and γ derives β, i.e.:

$$\alpha \Rightarrow^+ \beta \text{ iff } \alpha \Rightarrow \beta \text{ or } [\alpha \Rightarrow \gamma \text{ and } \gamma \Rightarrow^+ \beta]$$

where $\alpha \Rightarrow^+ \beta$ denotes the fact that α derives β. For example, in the grammar G1 above:

$$\text{sentence} \Rightarrow^+ \text{sally likes peter}$$

If we let S, VP, V, and I stand for sentence, verbphrase, verb, and identifier, respectively, then we can explain this example by listing the steps in the derivation, together with the production used in each step:

Step	Production used
$S \Rightarrow I\ VP$	$S ::= I\ VP$
$S \Rightarrow^+ I\ V\ I$	$VP ::= V\ I$
$S \Rightarrow^+ \text{sally } V\ I$	$I ::= \text{sally}$
$S \Rightarrow^+ \text{sally likes } I$	$V ::= \text{likes}$
$S \Rightarrow^+ \text{sally likes peter}$	$I ::= \text{peter}$

1.1.4. Syntax Trees (Derivation Trees)

A *syntax tree* can be used to illustrate the structure of a wff with respect to a grammar. A syntax tree is a tree such that:

1. All leaf nodes are labeled with terminal symbols.
2. All nonleaf nodes are labeled with nonterminals.
3. The root node is labeled with the distinguished nonterminal.
4. If a nonterminal node is labeled with n and its children are labeled with α, β, γ, etc., then $n ::= \alpha\ \beta\ \gamma\ ...$ is a production in G.

As example, the syntax tree for "sally likes peter" in G1 is given in Figure 1.

1.1.5. Languages

Using the concepts above, it is now possible to give more precise definitions for the notions of *wff* and *language:* (a) A wff of a grammar

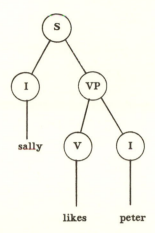

FIGURE 1. Syntax tree for "sally likes peter."

G is any sequence of terminals that can be derived from the distinguished nonterminal in G; (b) the language of a grammar G is the set of all wffs of G.

1.2. RECOGNITION AND PARSING

Recognition is the process of determining whether a given sequence of terminals is a wff of a given grammar. Parsing is recognition together with the implicit or explicit construction of the syntax tree.

1.2.1. Top-Down Parsing

There are various methods of parsing. We shall describe one method, called *top-down parsing*, with reference to an example. Consider the following grammar G2, which might specify a language whose wffs are signals consisting of electronic pulses from some sensor. That is, *i, c, h,* and *l* stand for different types of pulse and *;* stands for end of signal.

$$
\begin{aligned}
\text{G2} \qquad\qquad \text{terminals} &= \{i, c, h, l, ;\} \\
\text{nonterminals} &= \{S, P\} \\
\text{distinguished nonterminal} &= S
\end{aligned}
$$

Productions:
            S ::= P ;
            P ::= i
                | c P
                | h P l P

We now show how to parse the signal $c\ h\ i\ l\ i\ ;$ in G2 manually using a top-down approach:

1. Start by building a tree with the root labeled by the distinguished nonterminal S. Then attempt to reach down to the sequence $c\ h\ i\ l\ i$, as shown in step 1 in Figure 2. That is, start by applying 'S ::= P ;'.

2. There are now three possibilities. That is, there are three productions that could be applied:

   a.   P ::= i
   b.   P ::= c P
   c.   P ::= h P l P

   The alternatives (a) and (c) are inappropriate since application of (a) would lead to a tree corresponding to the wff i; and (c) would lead to a set of trees corresponding to sentences all of which start with h. Therefore, (b) is the only choice. Application of (b) is illustrated in step 2 in Figure 2.

3. Again, there are three possibilities, but (c) is the only valid choice this time. This gives the tree shown in step 3 in Figure 2.

4. Continuing in a similar fashion, we eventually obtain the final tree shown in Figure 2.

The following points should be noted: (1) The parse described above is top-down since we started with the distinguished nonterminal and worked down toward the sequence to be parsed. (2) The parse was relatively straightforward since at each stage, although there may have been more than one production that could have been applied, only one of these productions was valid in the sense that its application was compatible with the sequence $c\ h\ i\ l\ i\ ;$. (3) In the above example, and in all parses in G2, there is a simple method for determining which of the possible productions should be applied: We look at the next terminal in the sequence being parsed, which has not yet been linked into the syntax tree, and choose the production whose right-hand side starts with that terminal. This method works with G2 since this grammar is a "one-look-ahead" grammar. Notice, however, that the method would not work when parsing sequences with respect to the grammar G1 since G1 is not one-look-ahead.

1.2.2. Automatic Parsing

Much of the early work in computing science was concerned with the automation of parsing, and for many classes of language there are now well-defined techniques by which parser programs can be derived

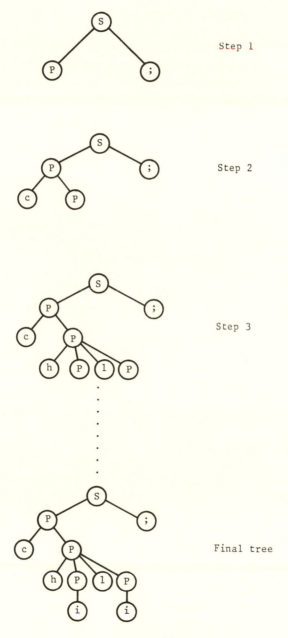

Step 1

Step 2

Step 3

Final tree

FIGURE 2. Top-down parse of the signal *c h i l i ;*.

from grammar specifications. For some classes of language, these techniques involve the manipulation of the grammar—for example, to make it one-look-ahead if possible—and the subsequent transcription of the productions to statements written in some programming language that, when taken together, constitute a parser program. In other cases, more complex techniques are required.

Discussion of how parser programs are derived is beyond the scope of this chapter. However, for those readers who are interested in this subject, a comprehensive introduction can be found in Aho and Ullman (1986).

1.3. Translation

Often, when knowledge is input to a computer, it is not in a form that is suitable for processing. However, if this knowledge is regarded as comprising wffs of some formal language, and if it is automatically parsed, then the result will be a syntax tree that is typically stored in the main memory of the computer as a linked structure. Since syntax trees explicitly represent the structure of the knowledge, it is often possible to process such trees in order to translate the knowledge into a semantically equivalent, but structurally different, form that is more suitable for processing. This translation typically involves the traversal and structural manipulation of the syntax tree. We illustrate this process with an example in Section 2.3.3.

1.4. Summary of Input of Knowledge

We began this section by pointing out that knowledge has to be input to a machine before it can be processed by that machine. We also stated that it is useful to regard the knowledge being input as comprising wffs of some formal language. We introduced the notions of syntax, grammar, and derivation and defined a well-formed formula of a grammar G as any sequence of terminal symbols that can be derived from the distinguished nonterminal in G using the productions of G, and the language of a grammar G as the set of all wffs of G. We then defined *recognition* as the process of determining whether a given sequence of terminals is a wff of a given grammar, and *parsing* as recognition together with the construction of the syntax tree corresponding to the wff. We followed these definitions with an example of how to manually parse a sequence with respect to a grammar using a technique called top-down parsing. We went on to state that much of the early work in computing science was concerned with the automation of parsing, and although we did not give details, we stated that for many classes of language, various techniques are now available by which parser programs can be derived from grammar specifications. We concluded this section with a brief discussion of translation and stated that even if the knowledge that is to be input to a computer is not in a form suitable for processing, this problem can often be overcome if the knowledge is regarded as wffs of some formal language. As such, the wffs can be automatically parsed and corresponding syntax trees constructed. These trees can then be manipulated in order to translate the knowledge to a more suitable form.

In the next three sections, we consider three approaches that have been used in the development of automatic reasoning systems. Various languages have been defined for encoding the knowledge that is to be processed according to each approach, and although we do not give details, several procedures that are based on the notions presented above are available for parsing wffs of these languages and for translating wffs to forms suitable for the processing prescribed by each approach.

2. MACHINE INFERENCE BASED ON LOGIC

2.1. INTRODUCTION

In order to facilitate the expression and justification of arguments, man has developed systems called *formal logics*. Each such system consists of (1) a formal language for expressing knowledge, (2) a *model theory*, which is concerned with the meaning of wffs and the semantic relationships between wffs, and (3) a *proof theory*, which is concerned with the structural manipulation of wffs in order to determine consistency and to "infer" new formulas from those given explicitly.

During the last 20 years or so, many computer scientists have been concerned with the automation of various reasoning processes prescribed by formal logics. Such automation typically requires (1) the construction of a parser program for the language of the logic concerned, (2) the construction of procedures for manipulating the syntax trees produced by the parser program in order to translate the knowledge to some "normal form" defined in the logic, and (3) the design and implementation of efficient consistency checking and inference procedures which are sound and complete, in the sense discussed later, and which are either closely based on existing methods in the proof theory of the logic or are new methods that may be regarded as extensions to the proof theory.

In order to give the reader a better understanding of this process, we describe how inference in a simple logic, called *classical propositional logic,* may be automated. We begin with a brief informal discussion of classical propositional logic.

2.2. CLASSICAL PROPOSITIONAL LOGIC

Classical propositional logic is concerned with the formulation of reasoning about propositions, where a proposition is a statement that can have a value of "true" or "false."

2.2.1. Languages of Propositional Logic

The wffs of all languages of propositional logic consist of symbols standing for propositions together with symbols standing for the logical connectives *and, or, not,* and *implies* concatenated in certain allowed ways. The following are examples of wffs of a particular propositional language:

$$S$$
$$P \rightarrow Q$$
$$\neg P \lor Q$$
$$P \land S$$

Where, for example, S stands for the atomic proposition "john is a man," P stands for "john is married to jane," Q stands for "jane is married to john," $\rightarrow$ stands for "implies," $\neg$ stands for "not," $\lor$ stands for "or," and $\land$ stands for "and."

All languages of logic are formal in the sense discussed in Section 1 and hence may be defined by grammars, and in many cases by context-free grammars.

2.2.2. The Model Theory of Propositional Logic

The model theory of propositional logic includes a specification of the semantics of propositional languages together with definitions of various semantic concepts such as *satisfaction, validity,* and *logical consequence.*

The semantics of propositional languages are typically defined using truth tables. For example, the semantics of the language exemplified above may be defined by the truth table in Figure 3, where A and B denote wffs and T and F stand for "true" and "false," respectively.

A	B	¬ A	A∨B	A∧B	A→B
T	T	F	T	T	T
T	F	F	T	F	F
F	T	T	T	F	T
F	F	T	F	F	T

FIGURE 3. Truth table definition of logical connectives.

The first row may be read as "A true and B true implies ¬A false, A ∨ B true, A ∧ B true, and A → B true." All columns except the last are intuitively appealing to most people. Although the last column may not be intuitively appealing to some people, it captures the semantics of → as defined in classical propositional logic.

The semantic notions of *satisfiability*, *validity*, and *logical consequence* may also be defined with respect to truth tables. For example, consider the following, somewhat informal, definitions:

1. A wff is satisfiable iff at least one row in the truth table has the value "true."
2. A wff is valid, or universally satisfiable, iff all rows in the truth table have the value "true."
3. A wff is unsatisfiable iff none of the rows in the truth table have the value "true."
4. A wff F is a logical consequence of a wff (or set of wffs) S iff F has the value "true" in all rows in which the wff S (or all of the wffs in S) are true.

As example, consider the truth table in Figure 4, which is derived from the definitions of ¬, ∨, ∧, and → given above. This truth table shows that P ∧ Q ∧ S is satisfiable, that [P ∧ S] → [Q ∨ P] is valid, that P ∧ ¬P is unsatisfiable, and that S ∧ Q is a logical consequence of P ∧ Q ∧ S.

S	P	Q	P∧Q∧S	[P∧S]→[Q∨P]	P∧ ¬P	S∧Q
T	T	T	T	T	F	T
T	T	F	F	T	F	F
T	F	T	F	T	F	T
T	F	F	F	T	F	F
F	T	T	F	T	F	F
F	T	F	F	T	F	F
F	F	T	F	T	F	F
F	F	F	F	T	F	F

FIGURE 4. Truth table for example wffs.

The fact that a formula F is a logical consequence of a formula, or set of formulas S, is denoted by:

$$S \models F$$

We see later that the notion of logical consequence is closely related to the notions of soundness and completeness of proof procedures.

2.2.3. The Proof Theory of Propositional Logic

All reasoning in propositional logic could be carried out through the construction of truth tables. However, in many cases the truth tables would be very large and the computation of truth values extremely time-consuming. Hence, various syntactic methods have been developed that involve the structural manipulation of formulas. Such manipulation involves the use of *logical axioms* and/or *inference rules*, where a logical axiom is some valid formula such as [A ∧ B] → A, and an inference rule is a rule that determines how a new formula may be syntactically derived from a given formula or set of formulas. For example, the rule called *modus ponens* is an inference rule which may be expressed as follows:

from A and A → B, infer B

Various formal deduction systems have been defined for classical propositional logic. Each consists of a (possibly empty) set of logical axioms together with a set of inference rules. These deduction systems are part of the proof theory of the logic. They may be categorized in various ways—for example, as

Axiom systems
Natural deduction systems
Sequent proof systems
Tableaux systems
Resolution-based systems

In some of these systems, the notion of "proof" may be defined as follows: A proof of a formula F from a set of assertions S in a deduction system DS consists of a sequence F1, F2, . . ., Fn of formulas such that F = Fn and for all Fi ($1 \leq i \leq n$) in the sequence, either Fi is a member of the set S, or Fi is a member of the logical axioms LA of the deduction system DS, or F*i* is generated by use of an inference rule in DS from formulas in LA and/or S and/or formulas appearing earlier in the sequence. For example, suppose that S = {P $\wedge$ Q, ¬ T, P $\rightarrow$ N} and that DS includes the logical axiom [A $\wedge$ B] $\rightarrow$ A together with the inference rules of modus ponens and substitution (we leave it as an exercise for the reader to formulate a definition of the substitution rule from the example of its use below). A proof of N from S in DS is:

$$[A \wedge B] \rightarrow A, [P \wedge Q] \rightarrow P, P, N$$

The first formula is a logical axiom, the second is obtained from the first by substitution, the third is obtained by the application of modus ponens to the second formula and the formula P $\wedge$ Q from S, and the last formula, N, is obtained by application of modus ponens to the third formula and the formula P $\rightarrow$ N from S. The notion of "proof" is different in some types of deduction system. Examples of other proof methods can be found in Frost (1986).

The existence of a proof of F from a set of assertions S in a formal deduction system DS is denoted by:

$$S \vdash_{DS} F$$

2.2.4. Soundness

A formal deduction system is sound iff:

$$S \vdash_{DS} F \text{ implies } S \models F$$

In a sound system, we are guaranteed that all proofs have a semantic justification. That is, if a formula F can be syntactically derived from a set of formulas S in a sound system, then we are assured that F is a logical consequence of S.

2.2.5. Completeness

A formal system DS is complete iff:

$$S \models F \text{ implies } S \vdash_{DS} F$$

In a complete system, we are able to provide proofs of all logical consequences of any set of assertions.

A formal system is of no use if it is not sound and is of limited use if it is not complete. The goal of many researchers who are working in the domain of machine inference is to design and implement efficient, sound, and complete deduction systems for the particular logics in which they are interested.

2.3. AUTOMATIC INFERENCE IN CLASSICAL PROPOSITION LOGIC

2.3.1. *Input of Knowledge*

Many languages of classical propositional logic may be defined by one-look-ahead context-free grammars of a particular kind for which it is a relatively simple process to construct parser programs. The syntax trees of wffs of propositional logic are binary trees and are consequently easy to manipulate. As example of a syntax tree, consider the tree in Figure 5, which corresponds to the formula:

$$[P \wedge \neg Q] \rightarrow \neg[S \wedge \neg T]$$

2.3.2. *Clausal Form*

Several of the sound and complete deduction systems that have been developed for classical propositional logic are based on an empty set of logical axioms and a single inference rule called the resolution

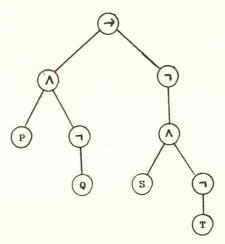

FIGURE 5. A syntax tree.

inference rule. Owing to their simplicity, these systems are amenable to automation. However, before the resolution inference rule may be applied, the formulas to which it is to be applied must be translated to a particularly uniform form called clausal form. A step in this translation involves converting the formulas to conjunctive normal form.

A formula is in conjunctive normal form if it consists of a conjunction of disjunctions of *literals*, where a literal is an atomic formula or the negation of an atomic formula. The following is an example of a formula in conjunctive normal form:

$$[P \lor Q \lor \neg S \lor \neg T] \land [R \lor T] \land S$$

This formula is a conjunction of three disjunctions, the first of which is a disjunction of four literals.

Since the order of literals in a disjunction is irrelevant, a disjunction may be represented by a set of literals. Similarly, since the order of disjunctions in a conjunction of disjunctions is irrelevant, a conjunction may be represented by a set. Using standard set notation, the formula above may be represented as follows:

$$\{ \{P, Q, \neg S, \neg T\}, \{R, T\}, \{S\} \}$$

Such a formula is said to be in clausal form.

2.3.3. Conversion to Clausal Form

Any formula of propositional logic may be converted to clausal form. The manipulation of syntax trees to do this is relatively straightforward and consists of the following processes applied in the order given:

1. Remove implication signs by application of the equivalence:

$$A \rightarrow B \equiv \neg A \lor B$$

2. Reduce the scope of negation signs by application of the equivalences:

$$\neg [A \land B] \equiv \neg A \lor \neg B$$
$$\neg [A \lor B] \equiv \neg A \land \neg B$$

Whenever two negation signs are encountered together, they cancel each other out.

3. Convert to conjunctive normal form by ensuring that no $\vee$ sign is above a $\wedge$ sign. This is achieved by application of the following equivalences, which are called distribution rules:

$$A \vee [B \wedge C] \equiv [A \vee B] \wedge [A \vee C]$$
$$[A \wedge B] \vee C \equiv [A \vee C] \wedge [B \vee C]$$

The branches of the syntax tree, and of all subtrees, are processed before the roots.
4. Convert to clausal form by traversing the tree in an appropriate order and reading off the nodes. (The exact details of the traversal algorithm are left as an exercise for the reader.)

An example of translation to clausal form is given in Figure 6.

A computer program that reads, parses, and translates propositional formulas to clausal form can be written in around 750 lines of well-structured, readable PASCAL (a simple block-structured high-level programming language). Such a program can be found in Frost (1986).

2.3.4. The Resolution Inference Rule

The resolution inference rule (Robinson, 1965) states that a clause C3 can be inferred from a pair of clauses $<$C1, C2$>$ if C1 contains a literal L and C2 contains the negation of this literal. The clause C3, which is produced by application of the resolution inference rule, is defined using standard set notation as follows:

$$C3 = \{C1 - \{L\}\} \cup \{C2 - \{\neg L\}\}$$

where $\cup$ denotes set union. For example:

C1	C2	C3: the resolvent of C1 and C2
{P, Q, R}	{S, T, ¬P}	{Q, R, S, T}
{P, Q}	{¬Q, S}	{P, S}
{T}	{¬T}	⊠
{P, Q, R, S}	{P, Q, ¬R, S}	{P, Q, S}

Thus, the "resolvent" of two clauses is any clause obtained by striking out a complementary pair of literals, one from each clause, and merging the remaining literals into a single clause. Note that, as exemplified in line 4 of the example above, redundant literals must be removed.

¬ P → ¬[S ∧ T]

parse and construct the syntax tree :

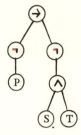

remove → sign, and cancel ¬ 's :

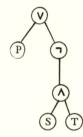

reduce the scope of the negation signs :

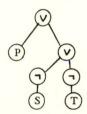

apply the distribution rules :

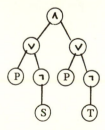

traverse and print out in clausal form :

{ { P,¬S }, { P,¬T } }

FIGURE 6. Translation to clausal form.

2.3.5. Inference-Using Resolution

As mentioned above, several of the sound and complete deduction systems that have been developed for propositional logic are based on the resolution inference rule. Some of these systems simply generate all formulas that can be proved from a given set of assertions S by repeated application of the resolution rule to formulas in S and to formulas that have been generated by earlier applications of the inference rule. For example, suppose that S consists of the following formulas:

$$P \vee Q$$
$$\neg P$$
$$Q \rightarrow S$$
$$[S \wedge \neg P] \rightarrow T$$

If we convert these formulas to clausal form, we obtain the following:

$$\{ \{P, Q\},$$
$$\{\neg P\},$$
$$\{\neg Q, S\},$$
$$\{\neg S, P, T\} \}$$

Application of the resolution inference rule to pairs of clauses from this set would generate the following new clauses:

$$\{ \{Q\},$$
$$\{P, S\},$$
$$\{\neg S, T\},$$
$$\{\neg Q, P, T\} \}$$

If we add these to S, we obtain a new set of clauses S'. Application of the resolution inference rule to pairs of clauses taken from S' would generate the following new clauses:

$$\{ \{P, T\},$$
$$\{S\},$$
$$\{\neg Q, T\} \}$$

If we add these to S' we obtain a new set of clauses S''. Application of the resolution inference rule to pairs of clauses taken from S'' would generate only the following new clause:

$$\{T\}$$

If we add this clause to S″ we obtain a new set of clauses S‴. Application of the resolution inference rule to pairs of clauses taken from S‴ would generate no new clauses; hence, we terminate the process.

The set S‴ contains the original set of clauses S together with all clauses that can be proven from S using the resolution inference rule. The set S‴ is called the "closure of S under resolution." Since the process described above is both complete and sound, we are assured that the closure S‴ contains all and only those clauses that are logical consequences of S. In other words, S‴ contains all and only those clauses that can be "reasonably" inferred from S.

The method exemplified above is called a *data-driven* method since we start with the *input* set S, which may be regarded as the given data, and proceed to generate all inferences that can be obtained from this data. Data-driven methods have limited use since they can be very inefficient when, for example, we wish to determine if a particular formula can be inferred from a given set of formulas. In applications such as this it is often more efficient to use a *goal-driven* method. In order to understand how the goal-driven method works, it is necessary to introduce the *resolution theorem*.

2.3.6. The Resolution Theorem

The resolution theorem states that a clause set S is unsatisfiable if its closure under resolution contains the *null* clause. The null clause is an empty clause, denoted by ⊠, which is obtained when two clauses containing a single literal of opposite sign are resolved. For example, if {P} is resolved with {¬P} the result would be the null clause.

2.3.7. Selected Literal Resolution

Selected literal (SL) resolution is a sound and complete goal-driven method that may be used to determine whether or not a particular formula, F, is a logical consequence of a given set of formulas S.

This method may be informally described as follows: First of all, the formulas in S are converted to clausal form, giving a set of clauses S′. The formula F is then negated and converted to clausal form, giving a clause G. G is then resolved against one of the clauses in S′ with which it can be resolved. The result of this resolution is a new clause G′. This clause is then resolved against a clause from S′ or against G, giving a new clause G″. This clause is then resolved against a clause from S′ or against one of its "ancestors," i.e., G or G′, giving a new clause G‴. This process is repeated, resolving the newly created clause against one from S′ or one of its ancestors until either the null clause is created or no further resolution is possible. If the null clause is generated, then the formula F is a logical consequence of S. If the null clause is not generated, then F is not a logical consequence of S.

There is a restriction on the resolution steps in this method: The literal in the newly created clause that is used in each resolution step must be one of the most recently introduced literals; i.e., it must be one of the literals that was most recently introduced to the new clause in a preceding step.

The following is an example of an SL proof: Suppose that we are given the following set of formulas:

$$S = \{K \rightarrow M, L \rightarrow K, K \rightarrow \neg L, M \rightarrow L\}$$

To prove that the formula $F = \neg[L \lor K]$ is a logical consequence of S, we proceed as follows: We convert S to clausal form, giving:

$$S' = \{\{\neg K, M\}, \{\neg L, K\}, \{\neg K, \neg L\}, \{\neg M, L\}\}$$

Now we negate F and convert to clausal form, giving:

$$G = \{L, K\}$$

We now form resolvents by the process described above (note that the clause below the line is the new clause that is derived by resolving the two clauses above the line):

Step 1 $\dfrac{\{L, K\}, \{\neg K, M\}}{\{L, M\}}$ using 1st clause in S

Step 2 $\dfrac{\{L, M\}, \{\neg M, L\}}{\{L\}}$ using 4th clause in S

Step 3 $\dfrac{\{L\}, \{\neg L, K\}}{\{K\}}$ using 2nd clause in S

Step 4 $\dfrac{\{K\}, \{\neg K, \neg L\}}{\{\neg L\}}$ using 3rd clause in S

Step 5 $\dfrac{\{\neg L\}, \{L\}}{\boxtimes}$ using the ancestor clause $\{L\}$, which was derived in step 2

Since the null clause was derived, we have shown that F is a logical consequence of S.

Note that we have not fully explained the relationship between SL resolution and the resolution theorem. The interested reader is referred to Kowalski and Kuehner (1971), Loveland (1969), and Reiter (1971) for more details.

2.4. Summary of Machine Inference Based on Logic

We began this section by defining formal logics as systems each of which consists of three parts: (1) a formal language, (2) a model theory, and (3) a proof theory. As an example, we described a simple logic called classical propositional logic and introduced the notions of satisfiability, validity, logical consequence, formal deduction system, soundness, and completeness with respect to this logic.

We then described an inference rule for classical propositional logic that is particularly amenable to automation. This rule, called the resolution rule, requires formulas to be converted to a uniform form called clausal form. We described how this conversion may be carried out and gave a reference to literature in which a program for automatic conversion may be found.

We concluded this section by showing how inference may be carried out using resolution-based deduction systems. We described two deduction systems that are appropriate for different types of application. This first was a data-driven system, which is appropriate when one wants to generate all formulas that can be inferred from a given set of formulas. The second system was a goal-driven system, which is appropriate when one wants to determine whether or not a formula can be inferred from a given set of formulas. Both of these systems are relatively easy to automate.

The logic, propositional logic, to which we have referred in this section is of limited expressive power. A more powerful logic, which has been used in many application areas, is called *first-order predicate logic*. The programming language PROLOG is based on this logic and uses an SL resolution theorem proving strategy minus ancestor resolution. A description of PROLOG, which has been hailed as heralding a new generation of programming languages, and of its relationship to first-order predicate logic, can be found in Frost (1986).

We now consider a different approach to machine inference, which was developed independently of the logic-based approach.

3. THE PRODUCTION-RULE-BASED APPROACH TO INFERENCE

3.1. WHAT IS A PRODUCTION-RULE-BASED SYSTEM?

A production-rule-based system consists of (1) a rule base module, (2) a rule application module, and (3) a database module.

The rule base module contains production rules (which are not totally unrelated to productions, as discussed in Section 1) that represent general knowledge about the problem domain. For example, the rule base might contain rules that are used in the diagnosis of diseases. In one class of production-rule-based system, each rule consists of a conjunction of conditions C1, C2, C3 . . . and a conclusion K, and is of the form:

$$\textit{if } C1 \textit{ and } C2 \textit{ and } C3 \ . \ . \ . \textit{ then } K$$

As an example, consider the following naive medical rule:

> *if* patient has blistery spots *and* fever *and* is of school age,
> *then* he/she has chicken pox

The database is used to store data about the problem at hand. For example, it may contain data about a particular patient whose disease is to be diagnosed.

The rule application module selects and "applies" rules, which may result in additions to the database. In classical production systems, the rule application module uses a data-driven approach whereby it cycles through the rules looking for one whose conditions are satisfied by the database. When it finds such a rule, it "infers" the conclusion K, which is then added to the database, possibly enabling other rules. The rule application module continues to cycle until either (1) the problem is solved (i.e., the goal is achieved; e.g., a diagnosis is determined) or (2) a state is reached where no more rules are enabled.

3.2. ORIGINS OF THE PRODUCTION-RULE-BASED APPROACH

The production-rule-based approach was originally proposed by Post (1943) and has since been used and adapted in various ways. In particular, in the late 1960s, the rule-based approach was beginning to be used in the construction of expert systems such as DENDRAL (Buchanan, Sutherland, & Geigenbaum, 1969) and MYCIN (Shortliffe, 1976).

Since then, the rule-based approach has been used extensively in the construction of computer-based reasoning systems.

3.3. RULE APPLICATION

There are many ways in which rule application modules can select and apply rules. An alternative to the data-driven approach briefly described above is called the goal-driven approach. In this approach, the system focuses its attention by considering only those rules that are relevant to the problem in hand. The user begins by specifying a goal as an expression G whose truth value is to be determined. The rule application module then looks in the database to see if G is present. If it is, then G is immediately given a value of "true"; otherwise, the rule application module identifies the set of rules S that have G as conclusion. It then selects one of the rules from S and checks the conditions C1, C2, C3 . . . of this rule by treating them as subgoals whose truth value it attempts to determine using the same method as it used for G. If all of these subgoals evaluate to true, then the goal G is true; otherwise, the rule application module selects another rule from S and checks to see if its conclusions are true. If none of the rules in S are satisfied, then G is given a value of "false."

Irrespective of whether the data-driven or goal-driven approach is used, the system may be regarded as trying to establish a *path of inferences* between the database and the goal. In many applications there may be several such paths. The totality of these paths is called the *search space*. For example, consider the following rule base and database:

Rule base
  (a) if D2 and D3 then D1
  (b) if D4 and D5 then D2
  (c) if D8 and D4 then D12
  (d) if D9 then D11
  (e) if D10 then D2
  (f) if D4 and D5 then D1
  (g) if D6 then D7

Database
  D3
  D4
  D5
  D9
  D10

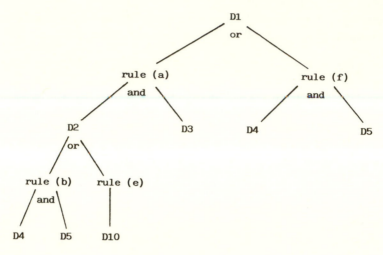

FIGURE 7. A search space.

Suppose that the goal is D1 and that the goal-driven approach is being used. The search space is given in Figure 7.

Various techniques have been developed for traversing the search space. For example, *depth-first* search would apply rules in the order: (a), (b), (e), (f), whereas *breadth-first* search would apply the rules in the order: (a), (f), (b), (e). A *heuristic* search would apply rules in an order dictated by criteria such as cost of rule application or past usefulness of the rule.

3.4. ACCOMMODATING UNCERTAINTY

In many of the domains in which rule-based systems are used, the knowledge available may be unreliable, incomplete, imprecise, vague, and/or inconsistent. Various theories have been developed to accommodate such uncertainties, for example: probability theory (Fine, 1973), certainty theory (Shortliffe and Buchanan, 1975; van Melle, 1980), the Dempster–Schafer theory of evidence (Schafer, 1976), possibility theory/ fuzzy logic (Zadeh, 1978), incidence calculus (Bundy, 1984), plausibility theory (Rescher, 1976), INFERNO (Quinlan, 1983).

Irrespective of which theory is used, the production-rule-based approach is extended to incorporate "certainty" values in the following way: (1) production rules are annotated with values (or pairs of values if the certainty is imprecise) that indicate the certainty of the relationship between the conjunction of conditions and the conclusion, (2) assertions in the database are annotated with values that indicate the certainty of their truth, and (3) some calculus is used to propagate certainty values through the search space. If the values attached to rules and assertions are probability values, then the equations of probability theory constitute the calculus used. However, if the values represent something other than probability values—for example, the confidence that an expert has in a rule—then one of the other theories listed above may be more appropriate.

3.5. SUMMARY OF THE PRODUCTION-RULE-BASED APPROACH TO INFERENCE

We began this section by defining a production system as comprising (1) a rule base module, (2) a rule application module, and (3) a database module. We then gave a simple example showing how a production-rule-based system might be used in medical diagnosis. We continued by explaining how rules may be selected and applied by rule application modules. We described two approaches: the data-driven approach and the goal-driven approach. We stated that, irrespective of which approach is used, the system may be regarded as attempting to establish a path of inferences between the database and some goal assertion. We then defined the search space as the totality of paths between a given database and a goal and stated that various techniques have been developed for traversing such search spaces. We illustrated two of these techniques—namely, depth-first and breadth-first search, with an example.

We concluded this section by stating that in many applications, the rules and/or data may be uncertain in some respect or other. We listed several theories that been developed to accommodate such uncertainty and briefly indicated how these theories are typically incorporated into production-rule-based systems.

4. THE FRAME-BASED APPROACH TO INFERENCE

The languages of formal logic and of production-rule-based systems allow us to represent various aspects of the universe of discourse. However, they do not in general allow us to structure this knowledge to reflect the structure of that part of the universe which is being represented. For example, suppose we want to represent the facts that "john is married to sally," "bill is married to jean," "john is employed by IBM," "bill is employed by IBM," "john has blue eyes," and "bill has brown eyes." In a language of first-order predicate logic we can represent these facts as follows:

married(john,sally)
married(bill,jean)
employedby(john,IBM)
employedby(bill,IBM)
eyecolor(john,blue)
eyecolor(bill,brown)

However, the order of these assertions is irrelevant and any other order would have been just as acceptable. The point is that in the languages of formal logic and production-rule-based systems there is no facility for clustering formulas such as the first, third, and fifth above, which are all related to a particular aspect of the universe of discourse (in this case, john).

The frame-based approach described in this section differs from formal logic and the production-rule-based approach in that it includes facilities for representing the structure of parts of the universe of discourse: All assertions about a particular entity are held together.

Some researchers believe that the advantage of clustering assertions in this way is not simply an improvement in access to associated facts. Additional advantages that are claimed for this approach are related to the fact that stereotype entities can be represented by structures that are often called slot and filler structures. These structures are so called since they contain slots that can be filled with values for a particular entity. It is claimed that these structures facilitate pattern recognition, inference of generic properties, handling of default values, inference by analogy, and the detection of errors and omissions in a body of knowledge.

4.1. SOME DEFINITIONS

4.1.1. Definition of a Frame

A *frame* is a data structure that represents an entity type. A frame consists of a collection of named slots each of which can be "filled" by values or pointers to other frames. Examples of frames are given in Figure 8.

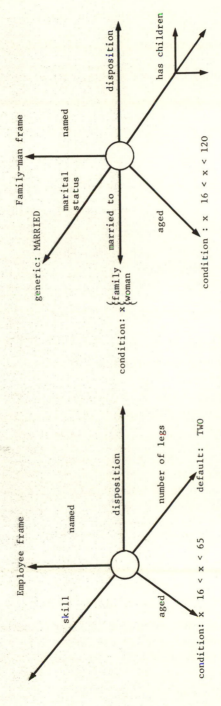

FIGURE 8. Examples of frames.

4.1.2. Instantiation

When the slots of a frame are filled, the frame is said to be instantiated and then represents a particular entity of the type represented by the unfilled frame. Examples of instantiated frames are given in Figure 9.

4.1.3. Representation of an Entity from Different Points of View

Frames may be used to represent the same entity from different points of view, as exemplified in Figure 9 in which the person called J. SMITH is viewed as an employee and as a family man.

4.1.4. Generic Properties

Preset values in a frame, such as the value MARRIED in the "marital status" slot in the "family man" frame in Figure 8, are called generic values or properties. They are values that occur in every instantiation of that frame.

4.1.5. Default Values

Default values in a frame, such as the value TWO in the "number of legs" slot in Figure 8, are values that can be assumed if no other value is known.

4.1.6. Slot Conditions

Conditions such as $16 \leqslant x \leqslant 65$ in the "aged" slot in Figure 8 restrict the values with which the slot can be filled. Conditions may be more complex than this example and may refer to values in other slots. For example, the allowed age of an employee may depend on whether the employee is male or female. This might be appropriate if there were different compulsory retirement ages for men and women.

4.1.7. Frame Structures

Frames may be linked to other frames in various ways:

1. A slot in one frame might be filled by another frame (or by a pointer to another frame). For example, in Figure 8 the "married to" slot in the "family man" frame can be filled by a "family woman" frame.

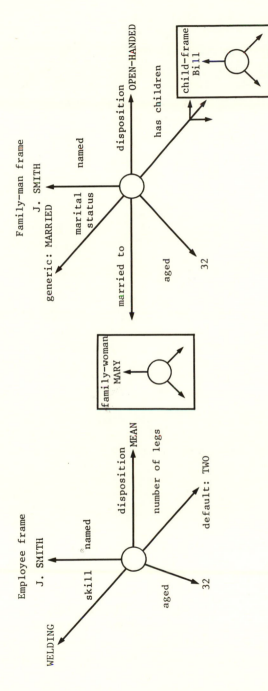

FIGURE 9. Examples of frame instantiations.

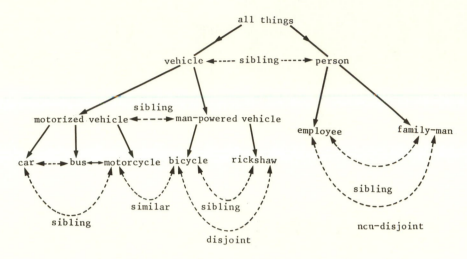

FIGURE 10. A frame structure.

2. Frames may be linked in taxonomical structures as illustrated in
   Figure 10. The father–son links in such structures (depicted by
   continuous lines in the figure) represent subset relationships.
   For example, the entity set "employee" is a subset of the entity
   set "person." Sibling links (represented by dotted lines in the
   figure) represent subsets that are similar in some application-
   specific sense of the word.

Such links between frames can be used to speed up matching and
for the inference of generic properties (see Sections 4.2 and 4.3).

4.2. MATCHING

In many applications of frames, the type of the entity under consideration is not always known. For example, we might know the name,
age, and disposition of a person but we do not know if he or she is a
family man, family woman, bachelor, spinster, etc. In such cases, it is
not always a straightforward matter of selecting a frame and then instantiating it to represent the entity concerned. We have to use the
properties that are known to select a candidate frame. The system then
tries to find values to fill the empty slots. If inappropriate values are
found, then another candidate frame must be selected. Identification
of useful candidate frames can be facilitated by reference to the frame
structure, as discussed below.

If sufficient slots of a frame, F, can be filled with appropriate val-

ues relating to some entity E, then F can be instantiated to represent E
and E can be categorized as being of type F. However, F might represent a "general" entity set such as "human." If we want to find a more
specific match, we must look lower down the subset hierarchy to see
if a specialization of F can be instantiated. For example, we might find
that the values related to an entity E are appropriate to fill the slots of
the "family man" frame. Such a match is more informative than matching E with the "human" frame.

In some cases, we may not be able to find an exact match. Some
slot values might not be known and others might be outside the allowed range. In such cases it will be necessary to find the best match.
This process is described next.

4.3. FINDING THE BEST MATCH

Suppose that we know the values of various properties of an entity
E. The system can use these values to select a candidate frame. This
can be done in various ways: (1) Start at the top of the subset hierarchy
and select the frame with the best match value (see below) at the first
level. (2) Index the frames by slot names. Select any frame that has a
slot name which is the same as any of the property names for which
there is a known value for E. (3) Select a frame arbitrarily. (4) Use other
contextual information to select a frame. For example, if it is known
that the entity E is some kind of human, then select the "human" frame
as the initial candidate frame.

When a candidate frame has been selected using one of the methods described above, the system partially instantiates the frame by filling as many of its slots as possible. In some applications, the system
may ask for additional knowledge in an attempt to fill more slots. A
match value is then computed which indicates the goodness of the match.
For example, if all slots are filled with appropriate values, then the
match value will be 1. If only half of the slots are filled, the match value
might be 0.5. The method of computing match values will differ from
application to application. In some cases the presence of an inappropriate slot value might set the match value to 0. For example, an entity
with "blood temperature COLD" would have a match value of 0 when
matched against a "human" frame. In other cases, inappropriate slot
values might not be so crucial and might simply reduce the match value.

Depending on the application, the match value will be regarded as
signifying various degrees of success. If the match value is high enough,
or the frame specific enough, for the application in hand then the system will not look at other frames. However, if the match value is not
high enough, or the frame not specific enough, then the system will

consider other frames. Rather than look at all other frames, the system can make use of the frame structure to identify relevant frames. It can do this in various ways:

1. The system could move up the subset hierarchy until it finds a perfect match. It could then search the subset hierarchy below the perfectly matched frame in order to find a more specific match. A depth-first, breadth-first, or heuristic search strategy could be used. For example, if we match an entity E with an "ape" frame and obtain a match value of 0.3, we could move up the subset hierarchy and find a perfect match with the "mammal" frame. We could then search the subset hierarchy below the "mammal" frame in an attempt to match E with a more specific frame, such as the "koala bear" frame.
2. The system could look at frames related to the current one by the similar or sibling relations. For example, if an entity E matches the "human" frame with a match value of 0.9, then the system might find a better match value by attempting to match E with the "male human" frame.
3. Complex relationships between frames can be used to identify candidates for matching. For example, if an entity matches a "car" frame except for its "number of wheels" slot value, then a relationship "similar but fewer wheels" could be used to iden-tify a "motorcycle" frame as a candidate frame.

4.4. Inference in the Frame-Based Approach

Frame systems carry out five types of inference: inference of the existence of an entity of a particular type, inference of generic proper-ties, inference of default properties, recognition of abnormal situations, and inference by analogy.

4.4.1. Inference of Entity Existence

When a sufficient match is made between an entity and a frame, the system is able to infer the existence of an entity of the entity type represented by that frame. The certainty with which this inference is made is related to the match value described above.

4.4.2. Inference of Generic Properties

When a match is made between an entity E and a frame F, the system can infer that E has all of the generic properties associated with

F and with all frames above F in the subset hierarchy. The certainty of this inference depends on the match value between E and F.

4.4.3. Inference of Default Properties

When a match is made between an entity E and a frame F, and the value for some slot S in F is not known for E, and there is a default value for S, the system can infer that E has this value for the property S. The certainty of such an inference depends on the match value and the certainty associated with the default value.

4.4.4. Recognition of Abnormal Situations

Since frames describe general or expected properties of entities that belong to some set, the absence of a value for a slot, or the presence of an inappropriate value, may signify an unusual situation. For example, if an entity matches a "car" frame except that it does not use gasoline or diesel as fuel, this signifies an unusual situation: possibly that the car is a veteran steam-powered car or a futuristic nuclear reactor-powered car.

4.4.5. Inference by Analogy

If the system is told, for example, that "the human Bill is like a bulldozer" it can use analogical reasoning to infer values for certain properties of Bill. For example, if both "human" and "vehicle" frames have slots for weight, and the bulldozer's instantiation of the "vehicle" frame has a relatively high value in this slot (relative, that is, to other vehicles), then we can put a relatively high value in the weight slot of Bill's instantiation of the "human" frame if no value for this slot is known.

Reasoning by analogy is discussed in more detail in Carbonell (1982), Rich (1983), and Winston (1980).

4.5. SUMMARY OF THE FRAME-BASED APPROACH TO INFERENCE

We began this section by explaining how the frame-based approach differs from the logic and production-rule-based approaches in that it allows all assertions about an entity to be held together. In addition, it allows stereotype entities to be represented. We then defined the notions of "frame," "instantiation," "generic property," "default value," "slot condition," "frame structure," and "matching." We followed these definitions with a description of how frame structures can be used to find the best match value between an entity and a frame.

We concluded this section with a discussion of the five types of inference that are supported by frame-based systems: inference of entity existence, inference of generic properties, inference of default properties, inference of abnormal situations, and inference by analogy.

The frame-based approach was developed and has been used extensively by people working on the automatic "understanding" of natural language text. Given a piece of text, a frame-based understanding system would begin by attempting to identify slot names and slot values occurring in the text. It would then attempt to identify the type of the entity to which the piece of text refers. When a sufficient match with a frame is made, the system can use information about the frame to help it search the text for values for unfilled slots.

Frames are primarily concerned with entities. However, a similar approach can be used for reasoning about sequences of events. The slot and filler structures that are used to represent frequently occurring sequences of events such as "going on a train journey" called scripts. Scripts include slots for frames representing the entities that are involved in the sequence of events (e.g., traveler, ticket inspector, porter) together with slots for properties of the sequence of events itself (e.g., distance traveled, journey time, cost). Scripts also have a structure that shows how the sequence of events is composed of simpler events and actions.

Discussions of the use of scripts may be found in Schank and Abelson (1977). An example of a script-based natural language text understanding system called IPP is described in Lebowitz (1980). This system reads and "understands" newspaper stories concerning international terrorism. In particular, it performs six tasks:

1. It parses natural language.
2. It adds new stories to a long-term script-based memory.
3. It recognizes similarities with previous stories.
4. It notices interesting (unusual) aspects of stories.
5. It makes generalizations based on collections of similar stories.
6. It predicts likely future events based on the generalizations it has made.

5. THE CURRENT STATUS OF MACHINE INFERENCE

In the preceding sections, we have explained how knowledge may be input to a computer, and we have given brief introductory descriptions of three approaches to the automation of inference. These approaches, at the simple level at which we have described them, were developed some time ago and have now been used in many various applications. This use has led to the identification of several problems. For example:

1. The logic-based approach, as described in Section 2, gives rise to systems that are slow, owing to the inefficiency of resolution theorem proving methods, and of restricted use, owing to the expressive limitations of classical logic.
2. The production-rule-based approach, as described in Section 3, does not have a well-defined semantics, hence, it is difficult to justify and/or explain the results obtained from its use. In addition, none of the various search strategies, which are used to establish a path of inferences between goal and database, are appropriate for all applications. Hence, the construction of a general-purpose production-rule-based system is more complex than was initially anticipated. Finally, there is no consensus regarding the value of the different theories that have been developed for dealing with uncertainty.
3. The frame-based approach does not have a well-defined semantics and is limited in the type of inference that it can undertake since it does not support the use of "chains" of inference.

In this final section, we give an indication of the type of work that is being carried out by researchers who are trying to overcome these problems.

5.1. The Status of the Logic-Based Approach to Inference

In order to overcome the expressive limitations of classical logic, researchers are automating the reasoning processes prescribed by non-classical logics such as modal logics, temporal logics, higher-order logics and intensional logics. At present, much of this work is at the research stage; however, it is likely that systems such as the following will become commercially available during the late 1990s:

1. "Intelligent" database systems whose deductive facilities are based on temporal logics, such as that described in Clifford and Warren (1983).
2. Automated natural language translators based on, for example, Montague's intensional logic. Such a system is described in Nishida and Doshita (1983).

3. Program verification systems based on temporal logics such as that described in Ben-Ari, Manna, and Pneuli (1981).
4. Artificial mathematicians based on higher-order logics with equality. A discussion of the use of such logics in automated mathematical reasoning is given in Bundy (1983).
5. Automated empathetic tacticians (i.e., systems that can make inferences based on their knowledge of other agents' knowledge and deductive capabilities) based on modal logics such as that described in Mays (1982).

Various methods for improving the efficiency of inference in formal deduction systems are also being studied. These include:

1. The "compilation" of the proper axioms of predicate logic theories together with formulas to be proved, in order to generate more efficient procedures based on relational algebraic operations. This approach is receiving a great deal of attention by people working on query evaluation in deductive database systems (e.g., see Zaniolo, 1986).
2. The use of sorted predicate logics to improve efficiency, as discussed in Cohn (1984).
3. The use of nonuniform techniques—that is, techniques that do not require the formulas to be converted to a uniform format such as clausal form. Examples of nonuniform techniques are discussed in Bibel (1983) and Bundy (1983).
4. The use of parallel processing capabilities available in some of the more advanced computer systems.

5.2. THE STATUS OF THE PRODUCTION-RULE-BASED APPROACH TO INFERENCE

The problem of production-rule-based systems not having a well-defined semantics can be easily overcome for those systems that do not accommodate uncertainty (i.e., those systems in which all facts and rules have a certainty of 1): the data and rules are simply regarded as proper axioms of a theory of some appropriate logic and the goal is regarded as a formula to be proven. The semantics of the logic can then be used. However, if the system is to accommodate uncertainty, then the provision of a well-defined semantics is more difficult since no logic has yet been developed that is ideally suited for this purpose. This situation may change in the near future since there are a number of researchers who are attempting to formulate suitable logics (e.g., Zadeh, 1983).

The problem of there not being a single search strategy that is effiecient for all applications has prompted a good deal of research, including (1) methods for the formal specification of search strategies (e.g., as discussed in Georgeff, 1982) in order to better understand, assess, integrate, and implement them, and (2) the extension of production-rule-based systems to include search control modules that decide which search strategy, or combination of strategies, to apply in a given situation. Examples of such systems are described in Aikins (1980) and Balzer, Erman, London, and Williams (1980).

5.3. The Status of the Frame-Based Approach to Inference

The problem of frame-based systems not having a well-defined semantics can also be overcome to some extent by use of the semantics of formal logic since much of the knowledge that can be represented in the frame-based approach can also be represented in languages of formal logic. For example, relationships involving frames, generic properties, and slot conditions can be represented as formulas of first-order predicate logic such as:

subset(human,mammal)
subset(employee,human)
fewerwheels(motorcycle,car)
$\forall x$ type$(x,$mammal$)\rightarrow$blood-temperature$(x,$ warm$)$
$\forall x\forall y\forall z[$type$(x,y)\wedge$sub-set$(y,z)]\rightarrow$type$(x,z)$
$\forall x\forall y\forall z[age(x,y)\wedge$type$(x,$maleemployee$)]\rightarrow$greaterthan$(y, 65)$

Default properties may be represented using nonmonotonic logics, as discussed in McDermott and Doyle (1980). However, little work has been undertaken to develop logics that can accommodate analogical reasoning.

5.4. Integration of Techniques from All Three Approaches

It is the author's opinion that advances in machine inference will result from an integration of concepts and techniques from all three of the approaches discussed in this chapter: (1) Concepts from formal logic will help to resolve semantic issues and can also be used to determine the soundness and completeness of the inference systems being built. (2) The methods that are being developed for dealing with uncertainty in production-rule-based systems can be used in other types of inference system, and the methods that are being developed for the control of search can also be used in other types of system. Finally, (3) the frame-based approach will provide insight into analogical inference.

A more detailed discussion of the approaches described in this chapter, and of their future integration, may be found in Frost (1986).

6. REFERENCES

Aho, A. V., & Ullman, J. D. (1986). *Principles of compiler design.* Reading, MA: Addison-Wesley.

Aikins, J. (1980). Representation of control knowledge in expert systems. *Proceedings of the First AAAI Conference,* Stanford: Stanford University.

Balzer, R., Erman, L., London, P., & Williams, C. (1980). Hearsay-III: A domain independent framework for expert systems. *Proceedings of the First AAAI Conference.* Stanford: Stanford University.

Ben-Ari, Manna, Z., & Pneuli, A. (1981). The temporal logic of branching time. *Eighth Annual ACM Symposium on Principles of Programming Languages.* Vancouver: Williamsburg.

Bibel, W. (1983). Matings in matrices. *CACM, 26*(11), 844–852.

Buchanan, B. G., Sutherland, G., & Geigenbaum, E. (1969). Heuristic DENDRAL: A program for generating explanatory hypotheses in organic chemistry. In B. Meltzer & D. Michie (Eds.), *Machine intelligence* (Vol. 5). New York: Elsevier.

Bundy, A. (1983). *The computer modelling of mathematical reasoning.* London: Academic Press.

Bundy, A. (1984). *Incidence calculus: A mechanism for probabilistic reasoning (Research Paper No. 216).* Edinburgh: Department of Artificial Intelligence, Edinburgh University.

Carbonell, J. G. (1982). Experimental learning in analogical problem solving. In *Proceedings of the AAAI 82.* Pittsburgh: University of Pittsburgh.

Clifford, J., & Warren, D. S. (1983). Formal semantics for time in databases. *ACM TODS, 8*(2), 214–254.

Cohn, A. G. (1984). A note concerning the axiomatisation of Schubert's steamroller in many sorted logic. In J. Alvey, *Inference workshop report.* London: Imperial College.

Fine, T. (1973). *Theories of probability.* New York: Academic Press.

Frost, R. A. (1986). *Introduction to knowledge based systems.* London: Collins; New York: Macmillan.

Georgeff, M. P. (1982). Procedural control in production systems. *Artificial Intelligence, 18,* 175–201.

Kowalski, R. A., & Kuehner, D. (1971). Linear resolution with selection function. *Artificial Intelligence, 2,* 227–260.

Lebowitz, M. (1980). Languages and memory: Generalization as a part of understanding. *Proceedings of AAAI 80.* Stanford: Stanford University.

Loveland, D. (1969). Theorem provers combining model elimination and resolution. In B. Meltzer & D. Michie (Eds.), *Machine intelligence* (Vol. 4). New York: Elsevier North-Holland.

Mays, E. (1982). Monitors as responses to questions: Determining competence. *Proceedings of the National Conference on Artificial Intelligence.* Pittsburgh: University of Pittsburgh.

McDermott, D. V., & Doyle, J. (1980). Non-monotonic logic I. *Artificial Intelligence, 13,* 41–72.

Nishida, T., & Doshita, S. (1983). An application of Montague grammar to English–Japanese machine translation. *Proceedings of the Conference on Applied Natural Language Analysis*, Santa Monica.

Post, E. L. (1943). Formal reductions of the general combinatorial decision problem. *American Journal of Mathematics, 65*, 197–215.

Quinlan, J. R. (1983). Inferno: A cautious approach to uncertain inference. *Computer Journal, 26*(3), 255–268.

Reiter, R. (1971). Two results on ordering for resolution with merging and linear format. *JACM, 18*, 630–646.

Rescher, N. (1976). *Plausible reasoning*. Amsterdam: Van Gorcum.

Rich, E. (1983). *Artificial intelligence*. New York: McGraw-Hill.

Robinson, J. A. (1965). A machine oriented logic based on the resolution principle. *JACM, 12*, 25–41.

Schafer, G. (1976). *A mathematical theory of evidence*. Princeton: Princeton University Press.

Schank, R. C., & Abelson, R. P. (1977). *Scripts, plans, goals and understanding*. Hillsdale, NJ: Erlbaum.

Shortliffe, E. H. (1976). *MYCIN: Computer based medical consultation*. New York: American Elsevier.

Shortliffe, E. H., & Buchanan, B. G. (1975). A model of inexact reasoning in medicine. *Mathematical Biosciences, 23*, 351–379.

van Melle, W. (1980). A domain independent system that aids in constructing knowledge based consultation programs. Doctoral dissertation, Department of Computer Science, Stanford University.

Winston, P. H. (1980). Learning and reasoning by analogy. *CACM, 23*(12), 689–703.

Zadeh, L. A. (1978). Fuzzy sets as a basis for a theory of possibility. *Fuzzy sets and systems*. Amsterdam: North-Holland.

Zadeh, L. A. (1983). Commonsense knowledge representation based on fuzzy logic. *Computer, 16*(10), 61–65.

Zaniolo, C. (1986). Safety and compilation of non-recursive horn clauses. *Proceedings of the 1st International Conference on Expert Database Systems*, Charleston, SC.

9

Human Inference

ANGUS R. H. GELLATLY

1. INTRODUCTION

The psychology of human inference making is a broad topic that embraces a tangle of difficult and interrelated issues, and that includes contributions from a variety of disciplines, including, in addition to psychology itself, linguistics, logic, philosophy, sociology, and anthropology. Some idea of the scope of the topic can be gained from Braine and Rumain (1983), Johnson-Laird (1983), Kahneman, Slovic, and Tversky (1982), Nisbett and Ross (1980), and Sperber and Wilson (1986). Given such breadth, a chapter of the present kind can only attempt to deal with a few selected issues and approaches that are of contemporary relevance. Foremost among these will be the relationship between logic and thinking, the question of whether logic is descriptive of thinking processes or merely prescriptive of what is considered to be sound reasoning.

The debate over this relationship is a longstanding one, and in current cognitive psychology it is associated with two different approaches to the explanation of human reasoning. On the one hand, there are those who argue for the existence of a natural, or mental, logic that is the basis of reasoning. Proponents of this view believe that the central component in reasoning is the application of natural rules of inference that closely resemble formal inference rules. They there-

ANGUS R. H. GELLATLY • Department of Psychology, University of Keele, Staffordshire ST5 5BG, United Kingdom.

fore conceive of logic as descriptive of normal thinking processes, although allowing that actual reasoning performance will reflect limitations imposed by other processing components involved in comprehension, selection of heuristics, short-term memory, and so on (Braine, 1978; Braine, Reiser, & Rumain, 1984; Osherson, 1974, 1975; Rips, 1983, 1986; Sperber & Wilson, 1986). On the other hand, there are theorists who argue that reasoning can be explained not by reference to special mental rules of inference but in terms of the usual information-processing operations that support other forms of cognition. A frequent claim is that people think in terms of mental models that represent important features of the relevant domain. Mental models are said to be essential for understanding normal discourse (Johnson-Laird, 1983), for probabilistic reasoning (Kahneman & Tversky, 1982), and for deductive reasoning (Johnson-Laird, 1983; Johnson-Laird & Bara, 1984; Johnson-Laird, Oakhill, & Bull, 1986).

The division between the supporters of mental logic and the supporters of mental models can be characterized as a division between those who favor a syntactic approach to the understanding of cognition and those who prefer a semantic approach. Each side to the debate tends to emphasize one of two contrasting facts about human reasoning (Rips, 1986). Supporters of mental logic point to the supposed universality of simple inference patterns like *modus ponens,* whether these are displayed during informal reasoning (Henle, 1962) or in the course of providing correct solutions to formal laboratory problems (Rips & Marcus, 1979). Conversely, proponents of mental models cite various well-known effects of content, or problem domain, on the ability of subjects to solve logically isomorphic problems (Griggs, 1983; Johnson-Laird, 1983). They argue that these effects demonstrate that reasoning must be conducted in terms of content-specific mental models and not by the application of abstract rules of inference.

This chapter provides a partisan account of the controversy surrounding mental logic and mental models. The bulk of the chapter is given over to a description of the two positions and to a review of some of the empirical evidence and arguments for and against each of them. The presentation of theories and data is intended to be fairly even-handed, but the author's preference for a mental models approach to reasoning will doubtless have influenced the manner in which the material is treated. In the final section of the chapter, all pretense of impartiality is abandoned and a further line of argument against mental logic is introduced.

Before launching into the debate over the relationship of logic and thinking, however, there are three short subsections in which some pertinent ideas and jargon and a little necessary background information are introduced. This is followed in the succeeding two main sections by accounts of the mental logic and mental model approaches.

1.1. What Is an Inference?

To make an inference is to pass from something that we know—or are prepared for present purposes to accept—to something else that seems to follow from it. Frequently this is phrased as moving from some given propositions (the premises) to a new proposition (the conclusion) that asserts information not contained in the premises. Such terminology tends to restricts inference making to those cases in which the relevant states of knowing are, or could be, expressed in language. For present purposes, however, it will be desirable to include within our definition also practical reasoning, the reasoning of action as well as of words. In this way questions about inference making in animals or prelinguistic children are not automatically excluded, although, in fact, the material to be covered in the chapter is concerned very largely with verbally stated reasoning problems.

Having defined inference making, it might seem that we now know the nature of the beast. But this is to overlook the problem, common to all definitions, of determining which individual cases do and do not fall under the definition. For example, in his great work on logic Mill (1875) argues that what sometimes pass for inferences should not be counted as inferences properly so called. Mill provides a number of examples, including the move from "All *A* are *B*" to "Some *A* are *B*." This, Mill argues, should not be classed as an inference because the second proposition does not go beyond the first proposition but merely repeats in different words part of what was already asserted. Similarly, the classic textbook example of syllogism:

All men are mortal, (1)
Socrates is a man,
Therefore, Socrates is mortal.

is rejected as an example of inference because, Mill argues, the first premise of the syllogism already includes the proposition that "Socrates is mortal." For if there were any doubt as to the mortality of Socrates, or any other individual, the same degree of uncertainty would hang over the assertion "All men are mortal," acceptance of which forms the basis on which the syllogism proceeds.

For present purposes it is unimportant whether or not one follows Mill in denying the status of inference to these examples. The point is that even when a definition has been adopted, examples of inference making are not self-evident; they have to be determined. This will prove to be of importance to the discussion in Section 4. More immediately, in Section 1.2 we will encounter a whole class of inferences that have come to be recognized only in recent years. These are known as implicit inferences, and they have particularly influenced the approach to reasoning in terms of mental models.

1.2. IMPLICIT AND EXPLICIT INFERENCES

The importance of what Helmholtz called "unconscious inferences" has long been recognized in theories of perception, for under at least some conditions of viewing the perceived size of an object depends on its perceived distance and vice versa. The reasons why one might or might not wish to recognize these perceptual processes as falling within a definition of inference making need not detain us at this juncture. The point is that although unconscious inferences have long been recognized in perception, the ubiquity of what have already been called "implicit inferences" is a more recent discovery, one that has come about largely as a result of attempts to write computer programs for natural language understanding.

It turns out that normal understanding of speech requires listeners to make all kinds of inferences of which they usually remain unaware. For example, to interpret the sentence "John needed some money and so he drove to Mary's house by way of the bank," it is necessary to infer that the pronoun *he* refers to the John mentioned in the first clause. One is also likely to infer that the bank was not a riverbank, that John not only drove by way of the bank but also stopped there, that he cashed a check or used a cash dispenser, that he was driving a motorcar rather than a horse and cart or a pedal car, and that (in Britain anyway) he was at least 17 years old. None of these things is explicitly stated, but linguistic communications would become infinitely protracted if speakers could not count on listeners to supply such added information for themselves.

Because a listener has to go beyond the information given in speech, language comprehension is seen to be an active process. This can be understood as the listener's constructing a representation of the discourse in which she is participating. In the above example, not only will John be assumed to have driven a car but, in the absence of contrary information, the car is likely to be assigned the default value of four-wheeler rather than three-wheeler. This, of course, is yet another form of implicit inference. The listener attempts to represent as plausibly as possible the events that have been described.

In what format discourse gets represented is itself a contentious issue between mental modelers and those who favor propositional representations only. Johnson-Laird (1983) argues that comprehension of language involves first a propositional analysis of sentences and then, where possible, the construction of an interpretative mental model. He takes the case of obscurity on the part of a speaker as evidencing that the second stage, although desirable, must remain optional. With only a propositional analysis available to the listener, the speaker's meaning is conveyed fragmentarily. Individual sentences will be understood but not the speaker's gist.

In general, language comprehension can be taken as the paradigm case for the existence of both implicit inferences and mental models, and a number of experiments supporting Johnson-Laird's theory have examined the way in which subjects interpret descriptions, especially descriptions of spatial relations (Ehrlich & Johnson-Laird, 1982; Mani & Johnson-Laird, 1982; Oakhill & Garnham, 1985). This emphasis on spatial representation is indicative of a continuity between modern mental models and the cognitive maps of an earlier generation (Tolman, 1932). But while implicit inferences are seen to be vital to ordinary language understanding, they are frequently regarded as something of a menace when it comes to verbal logic.

1.3. Logic and Comprehension

Logic is traditionally conceived as having to do with the validity of argument forms across different content matter. Argument forms such as "If p, then q; p; therefore q" or "All A are B; all B are C; therefore all A are C" are held to be valid regardless of the content with which the form is instantiated. The concepts of logical form and validity have been developed in a tradition of high literacy. They derive from a particular way of using language that is unfamiliar to nonliterate people. This is sometimes expressed as a distinction between ordinary comprehension and analytical comprehension (Braine & Rumain, 1983).

(During the course of the chapter, reference will be made sometimes to spoken language and sometimes to written language. The above distinction, inasmuch as it is a useful one, applies as much to one as to the other, and examples should be taken as interchangeable.)

Although sometimes we may, purposefully or otherwise, understand a speaker in a sense she did not intend, the usual aim of ordinary comprehension is to understand what a speaker means by a statement. We have already seen that interpreting statements requires a mass of implicit inferences derived from knowledge of how language and the world are. In addition, however, a listener (or reader) has to understand a number of conventions governing discourse, and also to appreciate how a speaker's temperament and sense of humor express themselves in the uses to which these conventions are put. It is only because we are skilled at ordinary discourse comprehension that we may understand the question "Were you born in a barn?" not as an inquiry concerning the circumstances of our upbringing but as a request to shut the door behind us. Ordinary comprehension thus relies upon inferences from social knowledge as well as from linguistic and world knowledge.

By contrast, analytical comprehension is supposedly very different from ordinary comprehension. Its purpose is said to be that of discovering not what a speaker means by a sentence but what the sentence itself means (Braine & Rumain, 1983). This is a distinction that is commonly expressed as a difference between the spirit and the letter of the law; it is assumed, for example, in the interpretation of tax laws. Sentences, or statements or propositions, are taken to have meanings of their own independent of the meaning intended by their author or of meanings read into them by others. The relevance of analytical comprehension to logic and reasoning is that in assessing the validity of an argument, ordinary comprehension is supposed to be supplanted by analytical comprehension. A subject who is given the syllogistic problem "All the people who live in Monrovia are married. Kemu is not married. Does she live in Monrovia?" is being requested to ignore the fact that the first premise is obviously untrue and that she knows nothing of the individual Kemu. To determine the validity of the syllogism, the usual rules of discourse comprehension must be suspended. The subject is required to attend to the exact words of the premises and to the relationships they express. The usual inferences from world knowledge and normal conversational practice have to be suppressed.

Children and nonliterate adults—and, frequently, literate adults as well—are said to perform poorly on verbal logic problems precisely because they are unable to slough off the habits of normal comprehension in favor of the rules for analytical comprehension (Donaldson, 1978; Scribner, 1977). Performance may be subverted in a number of ways by these well-established habits (see below), or the task may even be refused. Remarkably, as little as three years' schooling suffices to inculcate at least the rudiments of analytical comprehension (Luria, 1976; Scribner, 1977). A grasp is acquired of the rules of the new game, and there is a corresponding increase in the number of "correct" responses to simple syllogisms. However, degrees of analytical comprehension must be recognized. A child who can handle simple syllogisms may still be prone to fall back at times on normal conversational habits. For example, Geis and Zwicky (1971) distinguish between *necessary* inferences and *invited* inferences. The statement "If p, then q" invites the inference "If not p, then not q" because in ordinary language use the connective *if . . . then* frequently has the force of the biconditional "if and only if." Proper exercise of analytical comprehension is supposed to ensure that such "errors" are avoided, but schooled children and adults frequently commit them.

The purpose of this subsection has been to show how the habits of ordinary comprehension, involving as they do all manner of implicit inference, have to be set aside in favor of analytical comprehension when problems of verbal logic are tackled. In illustrating the difference between the two types of comprehension, two further distinctions were introduced. These were the distinctions between speaker's meaning and literal meaning, and between necessary and invited inferences. In Section 4 there will be occasion to reconsider all of these distinctions. For the present, they provide a background against which the debate over logic and thought can be understood.

2. THE MENTAL LOGIC APPROACH

This is the approach that assumes a correspondence between logical principles and ordinary thinking. Natural reasoning is taken to incorporate a mental, or natural, logic of some kind. Proponents of this view differ on the origins of the mental logic with some theorists, notably Piaget (1953), arguing that the individual acquires logic through a process of construction, while others, notably Fodor (1980, 1983), claim that there is no means by which logic could be acquired and that therefore mental logic must be innate. This, however, is not an issue with which this chapter will concern itself. Instead, we begin with a general argument for the existence of a mental logic.

2.1. HENLE'S ARGUMENT

In an influential paper, Henle (1962) urged a return to the position that logic is descriptive of thinking processes and not merely normative. Supporters of mental logic, it is interesting to note, present themselves as being in revolt against a mistaken view that has prevailed for the greater part of the present century (Braine & Rumain, 1983; Henle, 1962). By contrast, Johnson-Laird (1982, 1983) believes that the doctrine of mental logic enjoys an almost universal, if unreflective, adherence among psychologists, linguists, and computer scientists. Thus, both sides to the debate are able to characterize themselves as raising a banner in defiance of oppressive orthodoxy!

Henle's argument for the existence of a mental logic resembling the principles of formal logic begins from the problem of error. She claims that the errors that even heavily schooled subjects make on verbal syllogisms can be interpreted as evidence *for* rather than *against* a putative mental logic. As Scribner was later to do with respect to cross-cultural data, Henle suggests that error can always be explained as failures of performance rather than of underlying competence. Subjects may omit a premise or may incorporate an additional premise from their stock of general knowledge; universal premises may be illicitly converted, so that "All *A* are *B*" is taken as equivalent to "All *B* are *A*"; or a subject may shy away from a conclusion that follows from the premises but offends against common sense or general knowledge. In other words, where there is a failure of analytical comprehension, the subject may tackle a different problem to the one intended. But both Henle (1962) and Scribner (1977) argue that where it is possible to reconstruct the reasoning of a subject, this is invariably seen to accord with logical principles. Subjects may be inept at playing the game of verbal logic problems, but their actual reasoning is never at fault.

That Henle and Scribner are correct to emphasize the importance of the problem-as-interpreted rather than of the problem-as-intended is surely not open to question. Whether it is children failing apparently simple tasks or adults seemingly lacking statistical intuitions, there is an important rule of thumb in modern cognitive psychology which says that rather than attributing intellectual deficits to the subject, one should search for possible misunderstanding elicited by the problem (e.g., Donaldson, 1978; Evans, 1983; Gelman & Baillargeon, 1983). Moreover, Revlin, Leirer, Yopp, and Yopp (1980) have provided evidence that when illicit conversion of premises is blocked, educated adult subjects do indeed score better on syllogistic problems.

What is contentious in Henle's arguments is the move from a recognition of the influence of performance factors to the supposition of a universal mental logic. In effect, the argument is that people can sometimes be seen to reason in accord with the principles of deduction and are never seen to reason in contradiction of these principles, and therefore by analogy with linguistic competence they must be possessed of a logical competence (Henle, 1962, 1981).

In Section 4 there will be occasion to criticize this argument. For the present it should be noted, first, that it has been extremely influential among proponents of mental logic (e.g., Braine & Rumain, 1983; Revlin & Mayer, 1978) and, second, that a general form of the argument is commonly deployed. Thus, any system that generates deductive inferences is likely to be attributed an internal logic (Braine et al., 1984; Rips, 1986).

2.2. MENTAL LOGIC AND PROPOSITIONAL REASONING

Both Henle and Scribner argue for the universality of certain logical forms in the practical and verbal reasoning of daily life and in the protocols of subjects attempting to solve syllogisms. The same claim of universality is made by proponents of mental logic with respect to the ability to recognize the validity of elementary deductive steps. Subjects who are able to engage in analytical comprehension are claimed to invariably accept certain propositional argument forms. For example, Rips (1983) suggests that virtually any (literate) subject is likely to accept the following:

> If there is an M on the blackboard, there is an R.   (2)
> There is an M.
> _____
>
> Therefore there is an R.

Rips states that this argument has the form of *modus ponens,* and he asserts that it would be very hard to know what you could say to convince someone who affirmed the premises but denied the conclusion.

Later on, it will be suggested that argument (2) does not *strictly speaking* conform to *modus ponens* and that it is perfectly feasible to affirm its premises while denying its conclusion. At the same time, however, it is easy to see that, given the premises, an element of logical compulsion may appear to drive the unwary reader to accept the conclusion. It is this sense of compulsion that supporters of mental logic believe is universally experienced in respect to elementary deductive steps. The central assumption shared by such theorists is that deductive reasoning consists in the application of mental inference rules to the semantic representations of the premises of an argument—and in some theories also to the conclusion, so that reasoning backward becomes possible (Rips, 1983). If the mental rules yield a proof, then the argument is accepted. Thus, any propositional argument of the form:

$$\text{If } p \text{ then } q \tag{3}$$
$$p$$
$$\overline{}$$
$$\text{Therefore } q$$

should be accepted without regard to the complexity of the propositional content with which it is instantiated.

Since any logic can be formulated in a number of ways—for example, in terms of rules of inference and truth tables or in terms of
inference schemata—mental logicians have to specify the manner in
which a mental logic might be formulated. Those theorists who have
attempted to meet this stipulation have favored formulation in terms
of inference schemata based on the systems of so-called natural deduction. Individuals are assumed to have available a repertory of schemata
for the basic deductive steps that can make up a chain of reasoning,
and the psychologist's task is seen to be that of identifying which are
the elemental steps and schemata (Braine et al., 1984; Osherson, 1974,
1975, 1976; Rips, 1983). Although different theories posit different
numbers of elemental schemata, there is considerable agreement also.
Thus, all the theories include some kind of disjunctive schema like this
one from Braine et al. (1984):

$$p \text{ or } q; \text{ not } p \tag{4}$$
$$\overline{}$$
$$q$$

There is also a considerable degree of commonality in the attempts
to demonstrate the psychological reality of schemata. The most popular
technique is one in which subjects are given problems involving shorter
or longer chains of reasoning (Braine et al., 1984; Osherson, 1974, 1975,
1976; Rips, 1983). The simplest, or one-step, problems are those defined by one of the postulated elemental schemata. The more complex
multistep problems are built up from these so that their solutions require application of more than a single schema. Examples of a one-
step, (5), and a multistep, (6), problem used by Braine et al. (1984) are
shown below:

$$\text{There is a } D \text{ or a } T \tag{5}$$
There's not a D
? There is a T?

$$\text{There is a } Y \text{ or an } L \tag{6}$$
There's not a Y

If there is either an *L* or an *R*,
   then there's not a *W*
? There is a *W*?

The basis of the technique is that the difficulty of a multistep problem should be predictable from the sum of the difficulties of the component inferences thought to be involved in its solution. A further check on a theory is to show that the postulated steps in solving a problem are reflected in the solution protocols provided by subjects for that problem (Rips, 1983), but protocol analyses have not been extensively reported.

Difficulty of problems can be measured in terms of errors, or of reaction time to solve the problem, or of difficulty ratings assigned by subjects. In practice, however, the first two of these do not prove to be very useful measures. If the problems employed are simple, then insufficient error data are generated (Braine et al., 1984). On the other hand, if error data were plentiful, this would suggest that the supposedly elemental schema were not available to all subjects. Braine et al. say that reaction time data are also problematic because latencies include not only time to complete the chain of reasoning but also the time to check back on the premises and go through the reasoning again. They also point out that their latency data had undesirable psychometric properties, and that Osherson (1975) had also found latency to be a rather unsatisfactory measure. In practice, then, for studies of this kind the difficulty of problems has mostly meant rated difficulty.

To test a theory, rated difficulty is obtained for all problems, simple and complex. Predicted difficulty of a complex problem can then be calculated either in terms of the number of steps proposed for its solutions or in terms of the sum of the rated difficulties of those steps as assessed with simple problems. Rated difficulty of complex problems can then be compared with predicted difficulty. In their study of what they called direct reasoning problems, Braine et al. (1984) found that the rated difficulty of complex problems correlated highly with predictions from ratings of one-step problems, even with problem length partialed out. The correlation with predictions based on the assumed number of deductive steps was, however, only about .5 when problem length was partialed out. The correlations involving latency were also much reduced when length was partialed out.

The above account scarcely does justice to the complexity of the Braine et al. theory or to their method of making difficulty predictions for multistep problems. Nonetheless, some idea is provided of the nature of the evidence on propositional reasoning that is available to supporters of a mental logic of natural deduction. Rated difficulty of simple problems can be used to predict rated difficulty of more complex problems with considerable accuracy, and to predict latency to a lesser degree.

There are, however, at least two disturbing features of this evidence and of its relevance to the theories it supposedly supports. First, since the rated difficulty of complex problems correlates only about .5 with the number of reasoning steps posited by Braine's theory, there is some doubt as to what rated difficulty indexes. This links to the second worrying feature, which is that quite different theories of how people deal with problems of this sort would make very similar predictions about the relative difficulties of complex problems. For example, the theory of truth-functional reasoning to be described in Section 3.3 would most certainly do so. It is not clear, then, that the evidence supports the theories of mental logic rather than any other theory of propositional reasoning.

Much the same point applies to an experiment by Marcus (1982) on the recallability of lines from a natural-language proof. Rips (1983) is able to account for the Marcus results with his ANDS (A Natural Deduction system) model. But—and this is a common difficulty with theories incorporating a mental logic—his explanation appears to owe more to the processing components of his model than to the fact that the model is built around the application of logical schemata. To state the matter baldly, there is not a great deal in the data on propositional reasoning that is either surprising or especially confirmatory of mental logic. Yet, as we will see in Section 3.3, one main difficulty for opponents of mental logic is to show convincingly that it is possible to have an alternative theory of propositional reasoning in which schemata have not been smuggled in by the back door.

2.3. OTHER ARGUMENTS AND EVIDENCE FOR MENTAL LOGIC

Propositional reasoning is the area in which the major effort to support mental logic has been expended, but other evidence is also cited as confirming the hypothesis. As already mentioned, a number of attempts have been made to explain errors in syllogistic reasoning while maintaining an intact mental logic (see, e.g., Falmagne, 1975; Revlin & Mayer, 1978). Some of these attempts have enjoyed a measure of success, although it will be argued in Section 3.4 that a better account of syllogistic reasoning is available. There have also been proposals for how theories of inference schemata might be extended to handle syllogisms as well as propositional reasoning (Braine & Rumain, 1983; Osherson, 1976). However, evidence to support these proposals remains thin, or absent.

A more promising argument in favor of mental logic is based on the psycholinguistics of logical connectives. For example, the fact that people tend to paraphrase such statements as "Get out of my way or I'll hit you" as "If you don't get out of my way I'll hit you" (Fillenbaum, 1974) may be taken to show that they have schemata for both *or* and *if . . . then*, as well as an understanding of how the two are related. It is claimed that without the schemata it would be impossible to understand statements containing these two connectives.

The argument has been taken further through experiments on reasoning with conditionals, and it leads us back to the distinction remarked earlier between necessary and invited inferences (see Section 1.3). Given the major premise "If *p* then *q*," formal logic recognizes two valid (necessary) inferences and two fallacies (invited inferences) that may follow depending on the minor premise. With a minor premise *p*, the conclusion *q* follows by *modus ponens;* with "not-*q*," the conclusion "not-*p*" follows by *modus tollens;* with "not-*p*," the conclusion "not-*q*" commits the fallacy of denying the antecedent; with *q*, the conclusion *p* commits the fallacy of asserting the consequent. Children, and adults, frequently commit the fallacies, and the usual explanation is that they interpret the conditional *"if . . . then"* as the biconditional "If and only if" (Sternberg, 1979). This can be taken to suggest an inability to distinguish the supposedly logically necessary inferences of *modus ponens* and *modus tollens* from the invited inferences that constitute the fallacies. An alternative explanation is that children, and adults, *can* make the distinction but frequently accept the invited inference because a failure of analytical comprehension leads to the biconditional interpretation. Rumain, Connell, and Braine (1983) tested this alternative explanation by giving 7-year-old children problems in which the invited inferences were either explicitly or implicitly countermanded. For example, they announced the premises: *If there's a cat in the box, then there's an orange in the box; if there's a dog in the box, then there's an orange in the box.* Here the inference invited by the first conditional *(If there isn't a cat, there isn't an orange)* is said to be implicitly countermanded by the second conditional.

Rumain et al. found that the frequency with which the fallacies were committed was greatly decreased under these circumstances, and they interpreted their results as showing that children develop schemata for the valid inferences at an early age, and that their tendency to commit fallacies is due to performance failures rather than to a lack of logical competence. In other words, they have a reliable mental logic available to them, but this may be masked by a failure of analytical comprehension. Against this conclusion, however, are recent findings by Markovits (1985) and Byrne (1986). Markovits found that although implicit countermanding of invited inferences did reduce the number of fallacies committed by adult subjects, the effect was far from complete. He claims that adults differ in logical competence itself and not merely in performance on logical reasoning problems. More important, Byrne (1986) has shown that supplying additional premise information, in much the manner employed by Rumain et al., can lead undergraduate subjects to reject the supposedly necessary conditional inferences just as it can lead them to reject fallacies. So, for example, given the three premises *If it's raining, she'll get wet; if she goes out for a walk, she'll get wet; it's raining,* subjects were much less inclined to accept the conclusion *she'll get wet* than they were when the second premise was omitted. These results make it clear that the countermanding of inferences does not demonstrate the necessity for an underlying mental logic (see also Section 4).

A final argument for mental logic has been made by Rips (1986), who has pointed out that mental logicians have two options for dealing with the problem of content effects, as mentioned previously and discussed in greater detail in Section 3.2. First, they can add operators that formalize relations such as causality and temporal priority, thus absorbing content into mental logic (Osherson, 1976; Rips, 1983). Alternatively, they can regard content effects as resulting from the smuggling of additional premises by subjects, so that certain conclusions are illegally rejected. However, these proposals have yet to be elaborated into anything more concrete.

This completes our survey of the arguments and direct evidence for the existence of mental logic. A somewhat bleak picture has been painted. There are a number of phenomena that could conceivably result from the operation of a mental logic, but no one of them compels our assent to the hypothesis. In the next section the case for mental models is examined, and it will be urged that there is a greater weight of evidence favoring mental models than mental logic.

3. THE MENTAL MODELS APPROACH

That the idea of "mental models" is one whose time has come is witnessed by the recent publication in the same year of two books of that title (Gentner & Stevens, 1983; Johnson-Laird, 1983). The term is, however, used in a number of different ways by different authors. Rips

(1986) has provided an analysis of some of these usages and has identified what he terms "figurative" and "literal" mental models. Models of both kinds are motivated by a concern to explain the effects of world knowledge and domain-specific knowledge on problem solving and reasoning. But Rips asserts that in figurative models there is little attention given to the question of how knowledge is represented and no reason in principle why representation should not be in the usual propositional format associated with a syntactic approach to cognition. Literal models, by contrast, are those in which Rips detects a commitment to nonpropositional representation. Literal models are supposed to be analogues of the states of affairs that they represent; they are internal models that can be manipulated in the course of reasoning about or predicting about the represented matter or state of affairs.

Rips's critique of mental models largely excludes figurative models, and in what follows the term *model* is likewise to be taken as referring to literal models.

3.1. Simulation by Mental Model

As indicated above, one reason for the positing of mental models is the ability of people, particularly experts in a particular field, to apparently reason about and predict the functioning of physical systems, or the behavior of other people. A familiar example would be car engines. Many of us may feel that we have in our minds a rough model of the workings of an engine, and that this is what we use when trying to figure out why our car won't start. In a similar manner, when we are eventually forced to call upon the services of a mechanic, we may attribute his success at starting the engine to a more detailed and sophisticated mental model of its workings than our own. The acquisition of expertise can in this way be seen as essentially the development of such internal working models.

Kahneman and Tversky (1982) suggest that the same is true of understanding of the social world. They say that social behavior and political initiatives are anticipated by the running of mental simulations, and that these are also involved in the assessment of counterfactual statements such as "She could have coped with the job situation if her child hadn't become ill." Once again the idea appears to have intrinsic plausibility. Aren't we, after all, better able to predict the reactions of those we know well rather than of those we know only slightly? And do we not manage this by mentally simulating their behavior?

However, Rips expresses doubts as to whether simulations of this kind are truly practicable. He cites work in artificial intelligence indicating that mental simulation may just be too hard in most cases. It is more likely, Rips suggests, that people solve problems using simple rules of thumb; check the battery, check the points, check the ignition leads, and so on. Expertise would then consist in the accumulation and increased availability of numbers of such heuristics, and in experience of similar problems encountered in the past. The ability to solve wholly novel problems would be much less than ought to be expected if there were access to detailed analogue models.

This criticism appears to have considerable force. There is no body of evidence to show that people are capable of running dynamic simulations of any but very simple processes, while, on the other hand, there is an abundance of evidence that performance on novel problems is extremely poor unless an analogy with a familiar problem can be recognized (e.g., Griggs, 1983; see also below). However, although the criticism may count against mental models as dynamic simulations, it does not apply against mental models as an explanation of the comprehension of discourse or of reasoning about logical problems. The processes involved in these achievements seem much more amenable to mental modeling. These happen also to be the processes for which Johnson-Laird's (1983) theory of mental models was intended to account. Because his is also the most comprehensive theory yet developed in connection with mental models, the remainder of this section will be focused upon it.

3.2. Truth-Functional Reasoning

We have already, in Section 2.2, examined explanations of propositional reasoning in terms of the application of mental rules of inference. In this section we return to propositional reasoning, but this time to examine explanations of it offered by Johnson-Laird (1983).

At one time Johnson-Laird himself adhered to the doctrine of mental logic, and he was responsible for an early attempt to explain natural deduction with reference to a repertory of inference schemata (Johnson-Laird, 1975). Subsequently, he concluded that this was a mistaken approach. The view expressed in Johnson-Laird (1983) is that on rare occasions people tackle propositional problems by reasoning truthfunctionally, but that they more commonly employ mental models.

An example demonstrates what is meant by truth-functional reasoning. Given the premises:

> If the communications protocol is incorrect or the Baud rate is wrong then the printer won't work. The communications protocol is incorrect.

a reasoner may go through something like the following sequence of thoughts:

> The fact that the protocol is incorrect makes the antecedent of the conditional true. If the antecedent of a conditional is true and the conditional is true (which, because it is a premise, it is), then the consequent of the conditional follows. Therefore, the printer won't work.

This process may look very much as if it involves the application of formal rules of inference. Johnson-Laird denies that it does. He claims that the procedure depends on a knowledge of the truth conditions of conditional statements, on an ability to substitute a truth value for a proposition, and on the capacity to work out the resulting effects of such substitutions, but that it does *not* involve the application of inference rules. He cites the repeated reference that subjects make to truth values as evidence of this. Yet, needless to say, his protestations have not swayed the proponents of mental logic. Braine et al. (1984) state that the procedure "appears to include principles that are equivalent to" inference schemata, and it is certainly true that the sequence of reasoning given above could be recast into the form:

> If the antecedent of a conditional is true and the conditional is true, then the consequent of the conditional follows. The antecedent is true. *The conditional is true.* Therefore the consequent follows.

which looks very like the kind of propositional problems that Braine et al. set for their subjects. Notice, however, that this is exactly the kind of argument made by Henle. A piece of behavior is seen to be expressible in accord with one or more rules of formal inference, and application of the same rule(s) is then invoked to explain the behavior. In Section 4 the status of this argument will be further examined, and reasons for rejecting it will be proposed.

For the present, it should be noted that Johnson-Laird (1983) has developed a computer program which implements the procedure for truth-functional reasoning and which displays the added virtue of not drawing trivial conclusions. Given the premises "p" and "q," it declines to respond with the valid but trivial conclusion "p and q." The performance of the program thus resembles the performance of an ordinary speaker who observes conversational maxims (Grice, 1975, 1978). This is an important point in its favor, for none of the theories of natural deduction based on mental logic has yet been formulated in such a way as to account for the inferences that don't get made as much as for those that do.

3.3. Propositional Reasoning with Mental Models

The procedure for truth functional reasoning is particularly important because it offers an alternative explanation of the kind of reasoning that is at the heart of the mental logicians' enterprise. Propositional reasoning is the one area for which something approaching a detailed theory of mental logic has been developed. Yet although truth-functional reasoning provides an alternative to the application of inference schemata, Johnson-Laird (1983) says that it is only a possible, not a habitual, mode of thinking. Given the chance, he claims, people prefer to reason with mental models.

Two kinds of evidence are adduced to support this claim. First—and this is perhaps more evidence against mental logic than for mental models—there is the thoroughly documented effect of content on people's ability to solve problems. Content effects in syllogistic reasoning were well known to Aristotle, but in recent years they have been demonstrated also for reasoning with conditionals and other propositional forms (Evans, 1982; Griggs, 1983). An example is Wason's selection task. In the basic abstract version of this problem, subjects see four cards, the facing sides of which show "D", "E", "4", and "7." Subjects are told that each card has a number on one side and a letter on the other. They are then given the rule "If a card has 'D' on one side, then it has a '4' on the other," and they are asked to name those cards, and only those cards, that need to be turned over in order to check whether the rule is true or false. Very few subjects give the correct solution—the D card and the 7 card—to this abstract version of the problem.

However, if the content of the problem is changed so that subjects are told to imagine that they manage a department store and have to test the rule "If a purchase exceeds £30, then the receipt must have the signature of the manager on the back," they have a high probability of turning over the correct two receipts of four whose facing sides show £45, £15, a signed back, and an unsigned back, respectively (Mandler, 1981). Facilitation is also obtained, though to a lesser degree, with a nonsensible rule such as "If a purchase does *not* exceed £30, then the receipt must have the signature of the manager on the back" (Griggs & Cox, 1983). The effect of content on performance with the four-card problem is extremely difficult to predict. In general, it seems that facilitation occurs when the content is such that the rule expresses a relationship with which the subject already has some familiarity and which, therefore, is readily represented as a mental model. A similar effect of content on the way subjects reason with conditionals has been reported by Marcus and Rips (1979). They found that subjects were far more likely to interpret the rule "If the ball rolls left, then the red light flashes" as a biconditional than they were the rule "If there's a "B" on the left side of the card, then there's a "1" on the right side." As with children's reasoning about conditionals (see above), this can be interpreted as showing that the content of the premises influences the form of the mental model, and hence the inferences it allows.

The importance of content effects is really that they count against mental logic. If reasoning consists in recognizing the logical forms of arguments and problems, content should be irrelevant. Hypothetical inference schemata that operate only spasmodically and unpredictably do not pay their theoretical way, and their introduction leads to an asymmetry in the explanation of successful and unsuccessful reasoning.

Johnson-Laird's second line of evidence for a natural preference for reasoning with mental models concerns the sheer difficulty of truth-functional reasoning. Faced with a problem that can be interpreted either as a mental model of "real-world" relationships or truth-functionally, people show a consistent preference for the former interpretation. The example cited above from Marcus and Rips (1979) demonstrates this preference. And Wason and Johnson-Laird (1972, Chapter 7) found that even when subjects were encouraged to reason truth-functionally, they showed a strong tendency to be pulled in the direction indicated by a mental model.

Proponents of mental logic, such as Rips, retort to this argument by suggesting that they can enlarge their theories to include not only propositional logics but also logics of tense, time, causality, and intentionality. But as Johnson-Laird (1983) points out, the crux of the matter is that *natural deduction* is not achieved by recourse to inference schemata, or even to truth-functional reasoning. Natural reasoning is conducted on the basis of normal comprehension processes that yield mental models of states of affairs. These models are perceptual or conceptual in form rather than linguistic or abstractly symbolic. Other forms of reasoning, such as truth-functional reasoning, are acquired only with difficulty and are rarely used.

In this section we have examined Johnson-Laird's account of how people reason about propositions. Considerable space has been devoted to the topic because of its central role in theories of mental logic. Johnson-Laird's own theory of mental models has, however, been worked out most extensively for the case of syllogistic reasoning (Johnson-Laird & Bara, 1984; Johnson-Laird & Steedman, 1978; Johnson-Laird et al., 1986). In the following subsection we examine the mental models

account of reasoning with syllogisms and some of the criticisms that
have been leveled against it.

3.4. REASONING WITH SYLLOGISMS

To understand Johnson-Laird's theory of syllogistic reasoning, we
can begin with an example:

> None of the artists are beekeepers   (7)
> All of the beekeepers are clerks
> ───────────────────────────────
> Therefore?

How does one set about looking for a conclusion to this syllogism?
One way is to imagine a roomful of people who are acting out one or
more of the roles of artist, beekeeper, or clerk. To represent the first
premise, there are two distinct groups of people that must be kept
separate:

> artist   (8)
> artist
> ───────────
> beekeeper
> beekeeper

In the next step the representation can be extended to include interpretation of the second premise. All the individuals who are acting as
beekeepers must be free to act as clerks also, but allowance has to be
made for the existence of clerks who are not also beekeepers. This yields
the representation:

> artist   (9)
> artist
> ───────────
> beekeeper = clerk
> beekeeper = clerk
> (clerk)

The parentheses indicate the questionable existential status of clerks
who are not also beekeepers.

Four possible conclusions relating artists and clerks can be read off
this model. These conclusions are: "None of the artists are clerks,"
"none of the clerks are artists," "some of the artists are not clerks,"

and "some of the clerks are not artists." However, to be sure that these candidate conclusions are valid, it is necessary to search for alternative models of the premises that might render some or all of the conclusions false. For (7), though not for all syllogisms, a second model happens to be possible:

$$
\begin{array}{ll}
\text{artist} & \\
\text{artist} & = \text{clerk}
\end{array} \qquad\qquad (10)
$$

$$
\begin{array}{l}
\text{beekeeper} = \text{clerk} \\
\text{beekeeper} = \text{clerk}
\end{array}
$$

This model shows that the first two candidate conclusions from (9) are unwarranted, but it leaves both "Some of the artists are not clerks" and "Some of the clerks are not artists" as candidate conclusions. Once again, however, it is necessary to search for counterexamples. And, in fact, a third model consistent with the premises of (7) is possible:

$$
\begin{array}{ll}
\text{artist} & = \text{clerk} \\
\text{artist} & = \text{clerk}
\end{array} \qquad\qquad (11)
$$

$$
\begin{array}{l}
\text{beekeeper} = \text{clerk} \\
\text{beekeeper} = \text{clerk}
\end{array}
$$

This model excludes all except the conclusion "Some of the clerks are not artists," provided only that the class of beekeepers is assumed not empty (Boolos, 1984).

Johnson-Laird proposes that categorical syllogisms can be solved by setting up models in which, as above, individuals are represented by tokens. The notion of imaging individual actors provides a concrete illustration of how this could be done. What counts in the theory is the relational structure of a mental model. The theory makes predictions about the relative difficulty of all possible categorical syllogisms, depending upon whether they call for construction of one, two, or three models of the premises. The prediction is that, because of the increased load on working memory, there will be more errors for greater numbers of possible models. This prediction receives overwhelming support (Johnson-Laird, 1983; Johnson-Laird et al., 1986). The theory also predicts that when errors do occur, they will be congruent with a subset of possible models for the relevant problem, and this also has been confirmed (Johnson-Laird & Bara, 1984). Finally, the model also accounts for what are known as the figural effects in syllogistic reasoning

(Johnson-Laird & Steedman, 1978). These effects consist in a bias toward certain forms of conclusion and in differences in the difficulty of syllogisms dependent upon the form in which premises are stated (see Johnson-Laird, 1983). For example, syllogism (7) has premises of the form A–B, B–C. Subjects tend to formulate A–C conclusions, whereas the only correct conclusion is of the form C–A. Hence, both the figural effect and the need to construct three models make this a difficult syllogism.

The mental model theory of syllogistic reasoning must be the most detailed and best supported theory yet published for any form of human reasoning. Furthermore, research by Johnson-Laird and his associates has centered on how people actually draw conclusions from premises, whereas many other investigators have been content to test subjects' ability to evaluate given conclusions. Nevertheless, having given an outline of the theory and a sample of the empirical data it encompasses, we now turn to consider a number of objections that have been raised against it.

Rips (1986) gives four principal objections to mental models of this kind. A first objection, the claim that there is greater empirical evidence to support mental logic than mental models, strikes this author as being without foundation. It suggests wishful thinking. For while there are arguments for the existence of mental logic, few novel or convincing data have been generated on the basis of these arguments. A second objection raised by Rips is that in the case of syllogisms compatible with more than a single model, Johnson-Laird's theory does not give adequate specification of the order in which the models will be constructed. In the above example, models (9) or (10) might have been initially constructed rather than model (8), and Rips suggests that this would mean the syllogism would have Difficulty Level 2 or 1 rather than Difficulty Level 3. This criticism seems wrongheaded. For even if Model (10) were constructed first, because a conclusion is valid if, and only if, it is compatible with *all* possible models, it would still be necessary to check that the conclusion "Some of the clerks are not artists" held in the other possible models. So there would still be a greater load on working memory—and, therefore, greater risk of error—than for syllogisms that allow only one or two models. Furthermore, the empirical data demonstrate beyond all doubt that syllogisms which allow more models just *are* harder.

In this connection, it is worth noting that there are other theories of syllogistic reasoning that posit mental models having the form of Euler circles or Venn-like representations (Erikson, 1974; Guyote & Sternberg, 1981; Newell, 1981). These models can also explain difficulty in terms of the number of alternate representations required, but predictions from them have not been offered in detail and, if they were, would appear to conflict with the existing data (Johnson-Laird et al., 1986).

Rips's third objection is a familiar one. He points out that there must be procedures that manipulate mental models and allow the drawing of conclusions. He calls these procedures "rules" and says, "To the extent that the rules that operate on the models are sensitive to [these] logical constants, they just *are* inference rules." This is yet another version of the circular argument that if the behavior of a system includes segments that can be classified as according with various rules of inference, then the system must be guided by internal inference rules. As already promised, the shortcomings of this class of argument are examined in the next section.

The fourth objection to the theory offered by Rips is, on a first glance at least, more telling. He points out that according to the theory, the terms of a syllogism are interpreted simply as tokens within a mental model, and he argues that it is therefore no more obvious why content should influence reasoning with mental models than reasoning with mental inference rules. Since representations like (8) through (10) are quite abstract, Rips claims that they drift away from the notion of domain specificity that provides much of the motivation for mental models. The argument is correct inasmuch as a representation of the premises of a syllogism is not a dynamic simulation. But this says more about the nature of syllogisms than it does about the mental model theory of how people work with syllogisms. In fact, the theory allows content to influence performance with syllogisms in a number of ways. For instance, once a candidate conclusion has been derived, a subject may search more or less rigorously for counterexamples to it. Given the premises "All birds are feathered; No bats are birds," one may be inclined to accept the invalid conclusion that "No bats are feathered" without looking too hard for an alternative model that renders the conclusion false. But given the premises "All birds are living; No bats are birds," one might search diligently for a model in which the conclusion that "No bats are living" is falsified. Evidence of a content effect of exactly this sort has been reported by Oakhill and Johnson-Laird (1985; see also Johnson-Laird et al., 1986). The theory also allows for the possibility that content may influence the initial construction of a model of premises, or the formulation of a candidate conclusion from a model. So Rips's final criticism turns out to be unfounded.

In this section Johnson-Laird's theory of syllogistic reasoning has been described at some length, though in far from the full detail in which it has been worked out. The theory has a considerable base of empirical support, it has been implemented as a computer program, and it fares well against the criticisms that have been made of it. The essential feature of the theory is that it explains deductive reasoning as something that arises out of a number of cognitive processes no one of which can be identified as "the process of inference making." In this respect it contrasts with theories of mental logic that identify "the process of inference making" with the application of mental rules of inference. In the next section a general form of this argument against the plausibility of mental logic is developed.

4. THE NATURE OF INFERENCE

The mental models approach to cognition, especially as espoused by Johnson-Laird, offers an alternative to explanations of reasoning in terms of mental schemata. Having furnished a description of that alternative approach, I want in this section to offer some more general considerations against the possibility of a mental logic. In other words, having already presented evidence that people *do* not use a mental logic, the intention now is to argue that they in fact *could* not do so. The argument will also, though mainly by implication, place human cognition in relation to animal cognition and artificial cognition. The presentation will of necessity be highly compressed, but greater detail is given in Gellatly (1987, in press).

The point on which all else will turn is the unremarkable one that the terms *inference* and *inference making* do not have fixed extensions. As was described in Section 1.1, there is considerable latitude as to where the boundaries of such terms get drawn. Depending on their methodological and theoretical commitments, individuals will choose to site boundaries at different locations (Bloor, 1983). A corollary to this is that, although many psychologists assume the opposite, *inference* is a classificatory term that does not implicate any particular set of psychological processes or operations. The different types of inference are descriptive of the products of cognition, or thinking, not of underlying mechanisms. They are categories into which we organize our informal cognitions so as to be able to discuss them formally (Bloor, 1976). The remainder of this section is intended as a justification of these assertions.

4.1. THE ARGUMENT FROM OBSERVATION

As we saw in Section 2.1, both Henle (1962) and Scribner (1977) draw attention to the fact that it is frequently possible to give rational reconstructions of the thinking of people who produce "wrong" answers to formal logical problems. By invoking a variety of distinctions between speaker's meaning and literal meaning, ordinary comprehension and analytical comprehension, implicit and explicit inferences, and so forth, observed behavior can be brought into line with accepted logical practice. None of this is the least objectionable in itself. However, mental logicians take the fact as evidence for internal schemata, just as they do any behavior of a person or a computer program that can be judged to conform to an inference schema. This move is open to at least two objections. First, as has been pointed out by others (e.g., Gilhooly, 1982), it results in a wholly circular argument. Second, it requires taking a completely untenable position in respect to the relationship between rules and reasoning.

To see that the argument is circular, it is necessary only to think how examples of reasoning are identified. We identify as reasoning that behavior which can be characterized in terms of some logical schema (though see below for qualifications). The same schema is then invoked by mental logicians to explain the behavior. Whatever behavior is not seen to conform to an inference pattern is not classed as reasoning at all, but as fantasy or free association or somesuch (Henle, 1962). This means that it is impossible, by definition, to observe reasoning that flouts logical rules. Hence, the argument is circular.

The way in which mental logicians classify examples of inferential behavior also reveals how they conceive of the relationship between rules and behavior. For example, Braine et al. propose that everyone has a schema for disjunction that enables those who practice analytical comprehension to correctly answer problems such as (1) above. For those who are unable to exhibit their prowess in this manner, more informal evidence can be accepted, as with Henle (1962). A conversation of the form "Would you like your coffee black or white?" "Not white"; "Here you are then, one black coffee" might be taken to show possession of the disjunctive schema. However, mental logicians also distinguish "true reasoning," in which schemata are applied to make inferences, from what they consider to be only pseudo-inference making. Behavior that might appear to conform to a schema, or to a series of schemata, might in fact reflect only guessing a solution to a problem, or remembering the solution. Just as apparent logical failure can be explained away as due to inappropriate comprehension, so apparent logical success can be as easily invalidated if that seems theoretically desirable.

For example, mental logicians have not been explicit on the question of whether animals have schemata and make inferences. Yet suppose a rat has been taught to reach a goal box by running down either of two alleyways. Then on future trials one or other alleyway is always blocked, and each time the rat runs down the available path. Is this evidence of a mental schema for disjunction? If not, why not? Would it have been evidence if the experiment had involved an adult human subject rather than a rat?

Of course, many psychologists might want to postulate different, and simpler, mechanisms to explain rat behavior rather than human behavior. The important point is that if inferencelike behavior in rats can be explained by relatively simple mechanisms, and if inferencelike behavior in humans is sometimes due to simpler strategies like guessing or remembering, one may begin to wonder if there really is a core of "true inferences" that need to be explained in terms of schema application.

The same point can be made with reference to unconscious and implicit inferences. The fact that these inferences are made without awareness need not itself embarrass the mental logician, for mental schemata and the processes by which they are supposedly applied are held to be introspectively inaccessible (Braine, 1978; Braine et al., 1984). However, the multiplicity of such inferences looks more problematic. Visual perception and language understanding, particularly the filling in of default values, involve a continuous barrage of rapid-fire inferencelike processing. Can the application of inference schemata be at the heart of all of these? They certainly look like inference making. But perhaps they are not "true inferences," if they do not involve schema applications.

Once again the mental logician is seen to be occupying a bleak position. Internal schemata are postulated on the strength of inferencelike behavior. Then, to prevent the application of schemata getting out of hand (and even more radical possibilities are considered below), some inferencelike behaviors have to be invalidated on the grounds that they are generated by mechanisms other than schema application. Yet, as the debate over children's acquisition of transitivity illustrates (Gellatly, in press), there are no principled means by which true inferences can be distinguished from so-called pseudo inferences. Where the boundaries are drawn is a matter of theoretical convenience. In itself this is unimportant; it is the normal way of doing things. A problem arises only when the claim is advanced that a boundary sited by convention demarcates a real division in underlying processes.

By now the predicament should be clear. Mental logicians want to say that reasoning is *rule-generated* through a particular cognitive process; Braine and Rumain (1983, p. 270) refer to "the inferential process

itself . . ." and Gelman and Baillargeon (1983, p. 178) to "the operation of transitivity. . . ." But inference patterns are not rules in this
sense, they are descriptive categories. Behavior can instantiate one of
these descriptions, it cannot be generated by it. What the mental models
approach makes explicit, and what Johnson-Laird (1983, especially
Chapter 6) has stressed, is that there can be more than a single way to
make an inference. Even inferences of the same type, such as transitive
or syllogistic inferences, need not be produced by a single inference-
making mechanism.

The very idea of reasoning as rule-generated seems, in fact, to lack
coherence. This is better seen if we look more closely at how candidate
instances come to be judged as conforming with, or instantiating, particular schemata. Judgments of this kind turn out to be problematic.

4.2. ANALYTICAL COMPREHENSION REVISITED

The problem of determining exemplars of an inference class has
already been illustrated with the case of the rat and two alleyways. Is
this to be counted an example of disjunctive reasoning or not? More
radically, suppose one rolled a ball from the foot of a Y-maze, one of
the arms of which was blocked. Isn't there a sense in which the rolling
ball instantiates the schema for exclusive disjunction? In fact, could it
not be said that a Y-maze itself instantiates the schema for disjunction,
for it is surely a logical-*or* gate?

What counts as an exemplar of a pattern or class is not self-evident; it has to be agreed upon. Agreement depends in turn on the
sense in which a candidate instance is understood. There is a sense in
which a Y-maze might be accepted as instantiating disjunction but other
senses in which it would not. Just the same is true of verbal arguments
of the kind we have been considering in this chapter. We can see this
by returning to argument (2), reproduced here as (12), with the schema
it supposedly instantiates given as (13).

If there is an "M" on the blackboard, there is an "R"   (12)
There is an "M"

_____

Therefore there is an "R"

If p, then q (13)
p

_____

Therefore q

Rips (1983) says that anyone capable of analytical comprehension accepts the necessary validity of (12) because it is a simple example of *modus ponens*. But though one easily sees what he is getting at, disagreement is possible. One can argue that for *modus ponens*, the second premise of (12) would have to read "There is an 'M' on the blackboard." Mostly we accept (12) because we understand the sense in which it is meant. We make the two invited inferences, that the "M" of the second premise is indeed on the blackboard, and that therefore there is an "R." Notice that I am here calling the *modus ponens* inference invited, not necessary as Geis and Zwicky (1971) and others want to do. This is because we do not *have* to accept it.

Just as we can refuse to accept (12) until premise 2 is amended, so it is possible to go on refusing even after it is amended. We could question whether the blackboard of premise 2 was coreferential with the blackboard of premise 1. Alternatively, we could request a justification of the move from premises to conclusion (e.g., Carroll, 1895). What this means is that as language comprehenders we can withdraw our cooperation in the making of implicit inferences. And we can do so indefinitely. Nor is there anything perverse about such behavior. Bloor (1983, Chapter 6) demonstrates that this is exactly the manner in which logicians conduct their professional disputes. They deny the necessity claimed for an adversary's inference by calling into question the background assumptions and implicit inferences against which the claim functions. They refuse to accept the argument in the sense in which its proponents require it to be understood, for they are well aware that its necessity will arise only within that particular sense. This is true even of (13), which is sometimes pointed to as what *modus ponens* simply *is*. Until (13) is understood in a very special sense, one that is grounded in a familiarity with algebraic substitution, it remains a meaningless pattern of marks on paper.

The lesson to be drawn is that all the distinctions called upon by mental logicians—those between literal and speaker's meaning, between necessary and invited inferences, or between ordinary and analytical comprehension—are open to challenge. Of course, schooled literate people do understand verbal logic problems in a different way from the way they understand ordinary conversation, but this analytical comprehension is not a mechanical procedure that always delivers a unique reading of an argument. Analytical comprehension is a variant on ordinary comprehension; it is not something of a different order. And a listener is still free to choose in what sense to understand a speaker's words. Scribner (1977) more accurately indicated the nature of analytical comprehension when she described the use of language in verbal logic as a language *genre*. An equally applicable term is Witt-genstein's *language game*. What we call analytical comprehension is only ordinary comprehension with some of the rules altered, certain idio-syncratic implicit inferences being required in place of more usual ones.

What has this to do with the debate over mental logic? The answer is that because what is a necessary inference depends on the game being played, because indeed the very notion of logical necessity arises only in certain types of language game, there cannot be internal sche-mata that determine what inferences *have* to be made. The concept of mental logic comes about only because a particular language game, one that is well entrenched among academics, has misleadingly come to be regarded as enjoying a privileged status.

4.3. CONCLUSION

In this final section we have examined various theoretical objec-tions to the notion of mental logic. It has been argued that not only do people not employ a mental logic in reasoning but they could not in principle do so. The case for mental logic rests upon the setting up of a maze of theoretical distinctions that, while they may have their uses within a particular language game, are always open to challenge. Infer-ence patterns are part of a descriptive language; they are terms whose usage has to be negotiated among interested parties. Inference patterns cannot generate behavior; they provide a means of classifying behav-iors that result from activity in all manner of underlying mechanisms. It is the task of cognitive psychologists working in an information-pro-cessing tradition to identify these mechanisms, their components, and their interrelationships.

5. REFERENCES

Bloor, D. (1976). *Knowledge and social imagery.* London: Routledge & Kegan Paul.

Bloor, D. (1983). *Wittgenstein: A social theory of knowledge.* London: Macmillan.

Boolos, G. (1984). On "syllogistic inference." *Cognition, 17,* 181–182.

Braine, M. D. S. (1978). On the relation between the natural logic of reasoning and standard logic. *Psychological Review, 85,* 1–21.

Braine, M. D. S., Reiser, B. J., & Rumain, B. (1984). Some empirical justification for a theory of natural propositional logic. In G. H. Bower (Ed.), *The psychology of learning and motivation* (Vol. 18). New York: Academic Press.

Braine, M. D. S., & Rumain, B. (1983). Logical reasoning. In J. H. Flavell & E. M. Mark-man (Eds.), *Handbook of child psychology (Vol. 3), Cognitive development.* New York: Wiley.

Byrne, R. (1986). *The effects of contextual information on conditional reasoning.* Paper presented to the British Psychological Society, Sheffield.

Carroll, L. (1895). What the tortoise said to Achilles. *Mind, 4,* 278–280.

Donaldson, M. (1978). *Children's minds.* London: Fontana.

Ehrlich, K., & Johnson-Laird, P. N. (1982). Spatial descriptions and referential continuity. *Journal of Verbal Learning and Verbal Behavior, 21,* 296–306.

Erikson, J. R. (1974). A set analysis theory of behavior on formal syllogistic reasoning tasks. In R. Solso (Ed.), *Loyola symposia on cognition* (Vol. 2). Hillsdale, NJ: Erlbaum.

Evans, J. St.B. T. (1982) *The psychology of deductive reasoning.* London: Routledge & Kegan Paul.

Evans, J. St.B. T. (1983) Selective processing in reasoning. In J. St.B. T. Evans (Ed.), *Thinking and reasoning.* London: Routledge & Kegan Paul.

Falmagne, R. J. (Ed.). (1975). *Reasoning: Representation and process in children and adults.* Hillsdale, NJ: Erlbaum.

Fillenbaum, S. (1974). OR: Some uses. *Journal of Experimental Psychology, 103,* 913–921.

Fodor, J. A. (1980). Fixation of belief and concept acquisition. In M. Piattelli-Palmarini (Ed.), *Language and learning: The debate between Jean Piaget and Noam Chomsky.* Cambridge, MA: Harvard University Press.

Fodor, J. A. (1983). *The modularity of mind.* Cambridge, MA: MIT Press.

Geis, M., & Zwicky, A. M. (1971). On invited inferences. *Linguistic Inquiry, 2,* 561–566.

Gellatly, A. R. H. (1987). The acquisition of a concept of logical necessity. *Human Development, 30,* 32–47.

Gellatly, A. R. H. (in press). Influences on conceptions of logic and mind. In I. Hronszky, M. Feher, & B. Dajka (Eds.), *Scientific knowledge socialized.* Dordrecht: Reidel.

Gelman, R., & Baillargeon, R. (1983). A review of some Piagetian concepts. In J. H. Flavell & E. M. Markman (Eds.), *Handbook of child psychology (Vol. 3), Cognitive development.* New York: Wiley.

Gentner, D., & Stevens, A. (Eds.) (1983). *Mental models.* Hillsdale NJ: Erlbaum.

Gilhooly, K. J. (1982). *Thinking: Directed, undirected and creative.* London: Academic Press.

Grice, H. P. (1975). Logic and conversation. In P. Cole & J. C. Morgan (Eds.), *Studies in syntax (Vol. 3), Speech acts.* New York: Academic Press.

Grice, H. P. (1978). Further notes on logic and conversation. In P. Cole (Ed.), *Syntax and semantics (Vol. 9), Pragmatics.* New York: Academic Press.

Griggs, R. A. (1983) The role of problem content in the selection task and in the THOG problem. In J. St.B. T. Evans (Ed.), *Thinking and reasoning.* London: Routledge & Kegan Paul.

Griggs, R. A., & Cox, J. R. (1983). The effect of problem content and negation on Wason's selection task. *Quarterly Journal of Experimental Psychology, 35A,* 519–533.

Guyote, M. J., & Sternberg, R. J. (1981). A transitive-chain theory of syllogistic reasoning. *Cognitive Psychology, 13,* 461–525.

Henle, M. (1962). On the relation between logic and thinking. *Psychological Review, 69,* 366–378.

Henle, M. (1981). Another vote for rationality. *Behavioral and Brain Sciences, 4,* 339.

Johnson-Laird, P. N. (1975). Models of deduction. In R. J. Falmagne (Ed.), *Reasoning: Representation and process in children and adults.* Hillsdale, NJ: Erlbaum.

Johnson-Laird, P. N. (1982). Thinking as a skill. *Quarterly Journal of Experimental Psychology, 34A,* 1–30.

Johnson-Laird, P. N. (1983). *Mental models.* London: Cambridge University Press.

Johnson-Laird, P. N., & Bara, B. (1984). Syllogistic inference. *Cognition, 16,* 1–61.

Johnson-Laird, P. N., Oakhill, J., & Bull, D. (1986). Children's syllogistic reasoning. *Quarterly Journal of Experimental Psychology, 38A,* 35–58.

Johnson-Laird, P. N., & Steedman, M. J. (1978). The psychology of syllogisms. *Cognitive Psychology, 10,* 64–99.

Kahneman, D., Slovic, P., & Tversky, A. (Eds.). (1982). *Judgement under uncertainty: Heuristics and biases.* Cambridge: Cambridge University Press.

Kahneman, D., & Tversky, A. (1982). The simulation heuristic. In D. Kahneman, P. Slovic, & A. Tversky (Eds.), *Judgement under uncertainty: Heuristics and biases.* Cambridge: Cambridge University Press.

Luria, A. R. (1976). *Cognitive development.* Cambridge, MA: Harvard University Press.

Mandler, J. M. (1981). Structural invariants in development. In L. S. Liben (Ed.), *Piaget and the foundation of knowledge.* Hillsdale, NJ: Erlbaum.

Mani, K., & Johnson-Laird, P. N. (1982). The mental representation of spatial descriptions. *Memory and Cognition, 10,* 181–187.

Marcus, S. L., (1982). Recall of logical argument lines. *Journal of Verbal learning and Verbal Behavior, 21,* 549–562.

Marcus, S. L., & Rips, L. J. (1979). Conditional reasoning. *Journal of Verbal Learning and Verbal Behavior, 18,* 199–223.

Markovits, H. (1985). Incorrect conditional reasoning among adults: Competence or performance? *British Journal of Psychology, 76,* 241–247.

Mill, J. S. (1875). *A system of logic.* London: Longmans.

Newell, A. (1981). Reasoning, problem solving and decision processes: The problem space as a fundamental category. In R. Nickerson (Ed.), *Attention and performance* (Vol. 8) Hillsdale, NJ: Erlbaum.

Nisbett, R. E., & Ross, L. (1980). *Human inference: Strategies and shortcomings of social judgement.* Englewood Cliffs, NJ: Prentice-Hall.

Oakhill, J., & Garnham, A. (1985). Referential continuity, transitivity, and the retention of relational descriptions. *Language and Cognitive Processes, 1,* 149–162.

Oakhill, J., & Johnson-Laird, P. N. (1985). The effects of belief on the spontaneous production of syllogistic conclusions. *Quarterly Journal of Experimental Psychology, 37A,* 553–569.

Osherson, D. N. (1974). *Logical abilities in children (Vol. 2), Logical inference: Underlying operations.* Hillsdale, NJ: Erlbaum.

Osherson, D. N. (1975). *Logical abilities in children (Vol. 3), Reasoning in adolescence: Deductive inference.* Hillsdale, NJ: Erlbaum.

Osherson, D. N. (1976). *Logical abilities in children (Vol. 4), Reasoning and concepts.* Hillsdale, NJ: Erlbaum.

Piaget, J. (1953). *Logic and psychology.* Manchester: Manchester University Press.

Revlin, R., Leirer, V., Yopp, H., & Yopp, R. (1980). The belief–bias effect in formal reasoning: The influence of knowledge on logic. *Memory and Cognition, 8,* 584–592.

Revlin, R., & Mayer, R. E. (Eds.). (1978). *Human reasoning.* Washington, DC: Winston.

Rips, L. J. (1983). Cognitive processes in propositional reasoning. *Psychological Review, 90,* 38–71.

Rips, L. J. (1986). Mental muddles. In M. Brand & M. Harnish (Eds.), *Problems in the representation of knowledge and belief.* Tucson, AZ: University of Arizona Press.

Rips, L. J., & Marcus, S. L. (1979). Suppositions and the analysis of conditional sentences. In M. A. Just & P. A. Carpenter (Eds.), *Cognitive processes in comprehension.* Hillsdale, NJ: Erlbaum.

Rumain, B., Connell, J., & Braine, M. D. S. (1983). Conversational comprehension processes are responsible for reasoning fallacies in children as well as adults: *If* is not the biconditional. *Developmental Psychology, 19,* 417–481.

Scribner, S. (1977). Modes of thinking and ways of speaking: Culture and logic reconsider. In P. N. Johnson-Laird & P. C. Wason (Eds.), *Thinking: Readings in cognitive science*. London: Cambridge University Press.

Sperber, D., & Wilson, D. (1986). *Relevance: Communication and cognition*. Oxford: Backwell.

Sternberg, R. J. (1979). Developmental patterns in the encoding and combination of logical connections. *Journal of Experimental Child Psychology, 28,* 469–498.

Tolman, E. C. (1932). *Purposive behavior in animals and men*. New York: Appleton-Century-Crofts.

Wason, P. C., & Johnson-Laird, P. N. (1972). *Psychology of reasoning: Structure and content*. London: Butsford.

10

Machine Learning

I. BRATKO

1. INTRODUCTION

There are several forms of learning, ranging from *learning by being told* to *learning by discovery*. In the former type of learning, the learner is told explicitly what is to be learned. In this sense, programming is a particular kind of learning by being told. The main burden here is on the teacher, although the learner's task can be made more difficult by requiring that the learner *understand* what the teacher had in mind. So learning by being told may require intelligent communication, including a learner's model of the teacher. At the other extreme, in learning by discovery, as opposed to being told, the learner autonomously discovers new concepts merely from unstructured observations or by planning and performing experiments in the environment. There is no teacher involved here, and all the burden is on the learner. The learner's environment plays the role of an oracle.

Between these two extremes lies another form of learning: *learning from examples*. Here the initiative is distributed between the teacher and the learner. The teacher provides examples for learning, and the learner is supposed to generalize the examples, thereby inducing general rules, or a theory, underlying the given examples. The teacher can help the learner by selecting good training instances, and also by describing the examples in a language that permits formulating elegant general rules. Therefore, the task of the teacher is not trivial, although he does not

I. BRATKO • E. Kardelj University, Faculty of Electrical Engineering, and J. Stefan Institute, 61000 Ljubljana, Yugoslavia.

have to specify the targeted theory in complete detail but just provide illustrative examples instead. In this sense, learning from examples exploits the known empirical observation that experts (that is, "teachers") find it easier to produce good examples than to provide explicit and complete general theories. On the other hand, the task of the learner to generalize from examples can be difficult.

Learning from examples is also called *inductive learning*. Inductive learning has been dominating the research in machine learning in artificial intelligence, and this research has produced many solid results. Several types of task can be learned from examples. One can learn to diagnose a patient or a plant disease, or to predict weather, or to predict the behavior of a new chemical compound, or to predict mechanical properties of steel on the basis of some of its chemical characteristics, or to improve efficiency in solving symbolic integration problems. Machine learning techniques have been applied to all these particular tasks and many others (see, for example, Bratko & Kononenko, 1986; Quinlan, Compton, Horn, & Lazarus, 1987, for medical diagnosis; Michalski & Chilausky, 1980, for diagnosing plant disease; Lavrac, Varsek, Gams, Kononenko, & Bratko, 1986, for predicting properties of steel; Mitchell, Utgoff, & Banerji, 1983, for learning problem-solving strategies in symbolic integration). All these tasks can be formulated as learning concepts from examples. The stage of research is at a level where practical methods exist, implemented in computer programs that can be readily used in complex applications, in particular in the development of expert systems. Accordingly, in this chapter we will be mostly concerned with learning concepts from examples.

We will first define the problem of learning concepts from examples more formally. To illustrate key ideas we will then follow a detailed example of learning concepts represented by semantic networks. Then we will look at induction of decision trees, an approach to learning that has produced results of great practical interest.

2. LEARNING CONCEPTS FROM EXAMPLES: PROBLEM STATEMENT

2.1. CONCEPTS AS SETS

The problem of learning concepts from examples can be formalized as follows. Let U be the universal set of objects, that is all objects that the learner may encounter. There is in principle no limitation on the size of U. A concept C can be formalized as a subset of objects in U:

$$C \subset U$$

To learn concept C means to learn to recognize objects in C. In other words, once C is learned, the system is able for any object X in U to recognize whether X is in C.

This definition of concept is sufficiently general to enable the formalization of such diverse concepts as an arch, arithmetic multiplication, or a certain disease. The following paragraphs show how.

The Concept of an Arch in the Blocks World. The universal set U is the set of all structures made of blocks in a blocks world. *Arch* is the subset of U containing all the archlike structures and nothing else.

The Concept of Multiplication. The universal set U is the set of tuples of numbers. *Mult* is the set of all triples of numbers (a, b, c) such that $a \cdot b = c$. More formally:

$$\text{Mult} = \{(a, b, c) : a \cdot b = c\}$$

The Concept of a Certain Disease. U is the set of all possible patient descriptions in terms of some chosen repertoire of features. D is the set of all those descriptions that indicate the disease in question.

2.2. Description Languages for Objects and Concepts

For any kind of learning we need a language for describing objects, or possible events, and a language for describing concepts. In general, we distinguish between two kinds of descriptions: (1) structural descriptions and (2) attribute descriptions. In a *structural description*, an object is described in terms of its components and the relations between them. A structural description of an arch may say that the arch consists of three components (two posts and a lintel), that each of them is a block, that both posts support the lintel, that the posts are vertical and parallel and they do not touch, and that the lintel is horizontal. In an *attribute description*, we describe an object in terms of its global features. Such a description is a vector of attribute values. An attribute description of an arch may say that its length is 8 cm, its height is 5 cm, and its color is yellow.

Particular description languages that can be used in learning programs are, of course, of types similar to those that can be used for representing knowledge in general. Some formalisms often used in machine learning are as follows:

- Attribute vectors to represent objects.
- *If–then* rules to represent concepts.
- Decision trees to represent concepts.
- Semantic networks.
- Predicate logic.

Some of these representations will be illustrated in the discussion later in this chapter.

Once we have an object and a concept definition we need a rule, or a procedure, to establish whether the object belongs to the concept. Such a rule will determine whether the object satisfies, or *matches*, the concept description. This can be formalized as a matching predicate or a matching function of two arguments:

$$\text{match (object, concept\_description)}$$

The definition of matching depends on the particular learning system. In the case that *match* is a predicate it will just say that *object* does or does not satisfy *concept_description*. If *match* is a function, it may say to *what degree object* satisfies *concept_description*. Alternatively, in the case that *object* does not satisfy *concept_description*, *match* may produce a symbolic description of the differences, or reasons why not.

2.3. The Problem of Learning from Examples

The target of learning is a concept description, and the sources of information for learning are examples. An *example* for learning a concept C is a pair

$$\text{(object, class)}$$

where *object* is an object description and *class* is either "+" or "−." If *object* belongs to C then *class* = "+"; otherwise class = "−." We say that *object* is either a *positive example* or a *negative example*. The problem of learning concept C from examples can now be stated as follows: Given a set S of examples, find a formula F expressed in the concept description language, such that:

For all objects X:
(1) If X is a positive example in the training set S *then* X matches F
(2) If X is a negative example in S *then* X does not match F

As the result of learning, F is the "system's understanding" of the concept C as learned from examples. According to this definition, F and C

"agree" on all the given example objects in S. There is, however, no *a priori* guarantee that F will correspond to C on other objects as well. A major aim of learning is to learn to classify unseen objects (that is, those contained in U but not contained in S) with respect to C. Therefore, one important criterion of success of learning is the *classification accuracy* of F on unseen objects.

Sometimes we allow the construction of formula F that misclassifies some objects in S. This is sensible in cases when it is known that the learning data contain errors or other kinds of uncertainty. These properties of data are usually referred to as *noise*. Noise is typical of some application domains, such as medicine. Since the learning data are unreliable, the exact agreement between formula F and concept C on learning set S does not guarantee correctness, and it can therefore be abandoned in favor of some other advantage, such as conceptual simplicity of F. This sort of simplification in learning from noisy data will be discussed later in this chapter in the context of induction of decision trees.

2.4. Criteria of Success

Here are some usual criteria for measuring the success of a learning system.

Classification Accuracy. This is usually defined as the percentage of objects correctly classified by the learned formula F. We distinguish between two types of classification accuracy:

- Accuracy on unseen objects—that is, those not contained in the training set S.
- Accuracy on the objects in S (of course, this is interesting only when exact agreement between F and C on S is not required in the learning algorithm).

Transparency of the Induced Concept Description F. It is often important that the generated description be understandable by a human in order to tell the user something interesting about the application domain. Such a description can thus also be used by humans directly, without machine help, as an enhancement to humans' own knowledge. This criterion is also very important when the induced descriptions are used in an expert system whose behavior has to be transparent.

Computational Complexity. What are the required computer resources in terms of time and space? Usually we distinguish between two types of complexity:

- Generation complexity (resources needed to induce a concept description from examples).
- Execution complexity (complexity of classifying an object using the induced formula).

3. LEARNING CONCEPTS BY INDUCTION: A DETAILED EXAMPLE

Learning about structures in the blocks world, and about arches in particular, was introduced as a study domain by Winston (1975) and became a classical illustration of mechanisms involved in learning. We will use this domain as an illustration as well, although our treatment here does not exactly follow the behavior of Winston's program, called ARCHES.

Semantic networks are used in ARCHES as a description language to represent:

- Learning examples.
- Concept descriptions.
- Domain-specific background knowledge.

The program can be made to learn the concept of an arch from teacher-supplied examples and counterexamples, as shown in Figure 1. The given examples are processed sequentially, whereby the learner gradually updates the "current hypothesis"—that is, the current definition of the concept being learned. In the case of Figure 1, after all four examples have been processed by the learner, the hypothesis (that is, the learner's final understanding of an arch) may informally look like this:

1. An arch consists of three parts; let us call them *post1*, *post2*, and *lintel*.
2. *Post1* and *post2* are rectangles; *lintel* can be a more general figure, e.g., a kind of polygon, which may be concluded from examples 1 and 4 in Figure 1.
3. *Post1* and *post2* must not touch (this can be concluded from example 2).
4. *Post1* and *post2* must support *lintel* (this can be concluded from example 3.

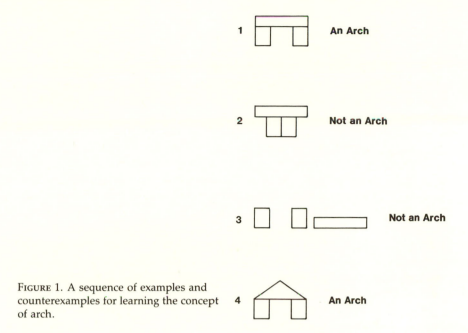

FIGURE 1. A sequence of examples and counterexamples for learning the concept of arch.

In general, when a concept is learned by sequentially processing the learning examples, the learning process proceeds through a sequence of hypotheses (H1, H2, etc.) about the concept that is being learned. Each hypothesis in this sequence represents an approximation to the target concept and is the result of the currently seen examples. After the next example is processed, the current hypothesis is updated, resulting in the next hypothesis. This process can be stated as the following algorithm.

To learn a concept C from a given sequence of examples E1, E2, . . . En, (where E1 must be a positive example of C) do:
1. Adopt E1 as the initial hypothesis H1 about C.
2. Process all the remaining examples:
   For each Ei (i=2, 3, . . .) do:
   2.1. Match the current hypothesis H(i-1) with Ei; let the result of matching be some description D of the differences between H(i−1) and Ei.
   2.2. Act on H(i−1) according to D and according to whether Ei is a positive or a negative example of C. The result of this is a next, refined, hypothesis Hi about C.

The final result of this procedure is Hn, which represents the system's understanding of the concept C as learned from the given examples.

Steps 2.1 and 2.2 above would in an actual implementation need some refinements. These are complicated and vary among different learning systems. To illustrate some ideas and difficulties, let us consider in more detail the case of learning about the arch from examples in Figure 1.

The first example, represented by a semantic network, becomes the current hypothesis of what an arch is (see H1 in Figure 2).

The second example (E2 in Figure 2) is a negative example of an arch. It is easy to match E2 to H1. Since the two networks are very similar, it is easy to establish the correspondences between nodes and links in H1 and E2. The result of matching shows the difference D between H1 and E2. The difference is that there is an extra relation, *touch*, in E2. Since this is the only difference, the system concludes that this must be the reason why E2 is not an arch. The action to take now to update the current hypothesis H1, producing a refined hypothesis, can be described by a condition–action rule that may look like this:

> *if*   example is negative and
>   example contains a relation R that is not in H
> *then* forbid R in H (add *must not R in H*)

The result of applying this heuristic rule about learning will produce a new hypothesis H2 (see Figure 2). Notice that the new hypothesis has an extra link, *must not touch*, which imposes an additional constraint on a structure should it be an arch. Therefore, we say that this new hypothesis H2 is *more specific* than H1.

The next negative example in Figure 1 is represented by the semantic network E3 in Figure 2. Matching this to current hypothesis H2 reveals two differences: two *support* links, present in H2, are not present in E3. Now the learner is faced with the guess between alternative explanations: Either (1) the sample E3 is not an arch because the *left* support link is missing, or (2) E3 is not an arch because the *right* support link is missing, or (3) E3 is not an arch because *both* support links are missing.

According to these three alternatives, the learner has the choice among three alternative ways of updating the current hypothesis. Let us assume here that the learner's mentality is more toward radical changes in this case, and it will therefore act according to explanation 3. It will thus assume that both *support* links are necessary and will therefore convert both *support* links in H2 into *must support* links in the new hypothesis H3 (Figure 2). The situation of missing links can be

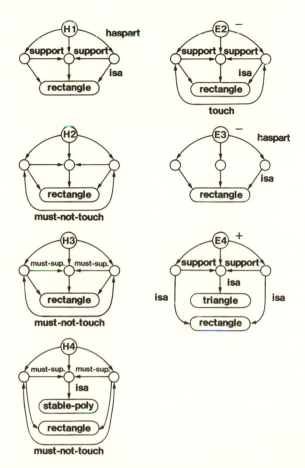

FIGURE 2. Evolving hypotheses about the arch. At each stage the current hypothesis Hi is compared with the next example E$(i+1)$ and the next, refined hypothesis H$(i+1)$ is produced.

handled by the following condition–action rule, which is another general heuristic about learning:

> *if*   example is negative and
>   example does not contain a relation R that is present in
>   the current hypothesis H
> *then* require R in the new hypothesis (add *must R in H*)

Notice again that, as a result of processing a negative example, the current hypothesis became still more specific since further necessary conditions were introduced: two *must support* links. Notice also that the learner could have chosen a more conservative action—namely, to introduce just one *must support* link instead of two. Obviously, then, the learning style can be modeled through the set of condition–action rules the learner uses to update the current hypothesis. By varying these rules the learning style can be varied between conservative and cautious to radical and reckless.

The last example, E4, in our training sequence is positive again. Matching the corresponding semantic networks E4 to H3 shows the difference: The top part is a triangle in E4 and a rectangle in H3. The learner may now redirect the corresponding *isa* link in the hypothesis from rectangle to a new object class: *rectangle or triangle.* Alternative (and more common) reaction in a learning program is to use a predefined hierarchy of concepts to find a common more general concept such that both rectangle and triangle are a kind of this superconcept. Suppose that the learner has as its domain-specific background knowledge a taxonomy of concepts as in Figure 3. Having found that, according to this taxonomy, rectangle and triangle are both a kind of *stable poly*, the learner may update the current hypothesis to obtain H4 (Figure 2).

Notice that this time a positive example has been processed that resulted in a *more general* new hypothesis ("stable polygon" instead of rectangle). We say that the current hypothesis was *generalized.* The new hypothesis now allows the top part also to be a trapezium, although

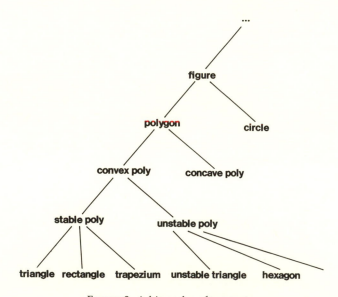

FIGURE 3. A hierarchy of concepts.

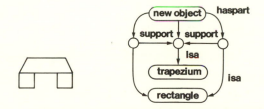

FIGURE 4. Left: a new object; right: its representation. This object matches the concept definition H4 of the arch in Figure 2, using the concept hierarchy of Figure 3.

no example of an arch with trapezium was ever shown to the learner. If the system was now shown the arch in Figure 4 and asked to classify it, it would declare it as an arch since its semantic network representation completely satisfies the system's understanding of an arch—that is, the hypothesis H4.

Here are some important points illustrated by the foregoing example:

- The procedure for matching an object to a concept description depends on the learning system. Matching can be complex owing to combinatorial processes. For example, in the case of semantic networks used as a description language, we may have to try all possible candidate correspondences between the nodes in the two networks that are being matched to establish the best fit.
- Concept descriptions can be compared with respect to their *generality* or *specificity*.
- Modifications of a concept description during the learning process enhances either (1) the generality of the description in order to make the description match a given positive example, or (2) the specificity of the description in order to prevent the description from matching a negative example.
- Concept modification principles for a given learning system can be represented as condition–action rules. By means of such rules, the "mentality" of the learning system can be modeled, ranging from conservative to reckless.

4. LEARNING DECISION TREES AND COPING WITH NOISE

4.1. THE TDIDT FAMILY OF LEARNING PROGRAMS

In this section we look at learning of concepts represented by decision trees. The corresponding learning procedures come under the

title *top-down induction of decision trees* (TDIDT for short; Quinlan, 1986).
The TDIDT approach to learning is well suited to handling uncertain
data usually attributed to noise of some kind. This is an important aspect from the practical point of view and will be discussed in this section in some detail.

The method uses attribute descriptions for objects. An attribute is
either symbolic or numerical. A symbolic attribute has an unordered
set of values. Such a set is typically small, practically never containing
more than ten values. An example of a symbolic attribute is the sex of
a patient. A numerical attribute has an *ordered* set of values. An example is the age of a patient, an integer, say, between 0 and 100. Attributes can be viewed as functions from objects to attribute values.

The statement of the problem is slightly more general than that
introduced in Section 2. Namely, instead of learning a single concept
(that is, to classify a given object into one of two classes: "yes" or
"no"), objects are to be classified into multiple classes. Classes are dis-
joint so that each object belongs to exactly one class. A learning example is a pair

(object, class)

where class is not restricted to "+" or "−" but can be any of a predefined set of class values. In medical domains, for example, class can
be one of possible diagnoses.

Figure 5 shows a simple example of a decision tree. The tree tells
by what means to go to work depending on weather attributes. In this
case the classes are *walk, bike, car, bus*. The attributes are *weather outlook*
(whose values are sunny, cloudy, rain, snow) and *temperature* (cold,
mild, hot).

TDIDT programs produce decision trees that "explain" the learning set of examples and can be applied to unseen objects. In the case
of noisy data, the learning procedure is allowed to generate a decision
tree that only partially explains the learning data; that is, it does not
necessarily classify the learning objects into classes as specified in examples. What the point is of this partial agreement of a synthesized
rule with the learning data and how this is done will be discussed later.

Some programs of the TDIDT family can cope with several types
of deficiency in the learning data. We allow objects in the learning set
S to be only partially specified (unknown attribute values). Also, we
tolerate the possibility of errors both in attribute values and in class
values. Therefore, we say that the learning data can be noisy. The object description language can be incomplete in that the available attri-

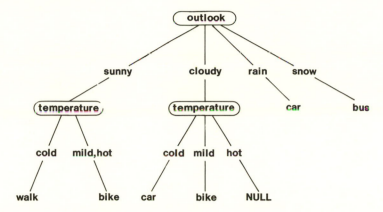

FIGURE 5. A simple decision tree about how to go to work. The leaf label NULL means that the corresponding situation never occurred in the learning examples.

butes are insufficient even in principle to reliably distinguish between the classes since some important features are simply not available. A learning set S can be incomplete also in the sense that it poorly represents the universe of all objects since S can be very small compared with the complete attribute space. Owing to this kind of incompleteness of S, it may be impossible for the learning system to generate a reliable rule for classifying new objects. Noise and incompleteness, of course, make the learning task more difficult. This sort of difficulty is, however, typical of many application areas, such as medical diagnosis. Several programs exist that induce decision trees and comprise special mechanisms to cope with noise and incompleteness in the above sense, for example, C4 (Quinlan et al., 1987). The discussion in this chapter is based on another such program called ASSISTANT (e.g., Bratko & Kononenko, 1986) and its successor ASSISTANT 86 (Cestnik, Kononenko, & Bratko, 1987).

Figure 6 shows a decision tree obtained from noisy data from an actual medical domain. The diagnostic problem here is locating the primary tumor in a patient. This tree was generated by ASSISTANT 86 (Cestnik, Kononenko, & Bratko, 1987) from a set of 170 examples—that is, medical records of 170 cancer patients. Internal nodes in the tree are labeled with attributes—that is, observable manifestations for this diagnostic problem. The leaves of the tree are labeled with diagnostic classes—that is, possible locations of the tumor. Arcs in the tree are labeled with attribute values. In classification of an object, a decision tree is used by following a path in the tree starting at the root node. In

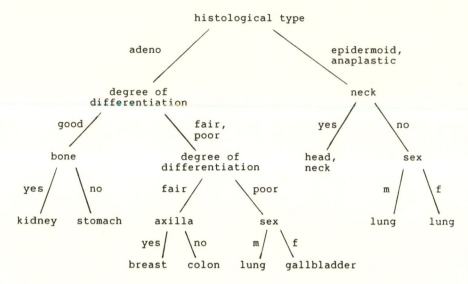

FIGURE 6. A decision tree for locating the primary tumor in a cancer patient with metastases as generated by the ASSISTANT learning program.

our example, the attribute at the root is "histological type of carcinoma" which can be either epidermoid, adeno, or anaplastic. If the histological type in the patient is either epidermoid or anaplastic, then look at the attribute *neck* (metastases found in the neck), and so on. Notice that the two rightmost leaves of the tree are both labeled "lung." This would superficially suggest that the parent node, *sex*, of these two leaves is redundant since, regardless of its value, the diagnosis will be "lung." The reason for including *sex* at this place in the tree is that the value of this attribute still considerably affects the *probability* of "lung," although "lung" is the most likely outcome in both cases (sex is either male or female). Closer inspection of this tree printed out in linearized form with additional information reveals that if the sex is male, "lung" is almost certain, whereas if the sex is female, lung is the most likely, but thyroid and vagina are also to be considered. This uncertainty arises from errors in learning data (usually referred to as noise) or incompleteness of the domain attributes. It should be noted that the tree in Figure 6 was generated while applying a high level of tree pruning. Pruning will be discussed later in relation to handling of noise in learning data.

The basic learning algorithm (Quinlan, 1979) shared by all the programs of the TDIDT family is as follows (it assumes completely specified examples and symbolic attributes only):

To construct a rule, in the form of a decision tree T, for a learning set S do:

begin
if   all the examples in S belong to the same class, C
then the result is a single node tree labeled C
otherwise
    begin
        select the most "informative" attribute, A, whose values
            are v1, . . .,vn;
        partition S into S1, . . ., Sn according to value of A;
        construct (recursively) subtrees T1, . . ., Tn for S1, . . .,
            Sn;
        final result is the tree whose root is A and whose subtrees
            are T1, . . ., Tn, and the links between A and the sub-
            trees are labeled by v1, . . ., vn; thus the decision tree
            generated has the form (linearized in the preorder fash-
            ion):

                    A
                v1: T1
                v2: T2

                . . . . .

                vn: Tn
    end
end

Even in its simplest implementation, this basic scheme needs some refinements:

1. We have to specify the criterion for selecting the "most informative" attribute. Usually this criterion is based on the information-
theoretic function. According to this criterion, the most informative attribute is the one that minimizes the "residual information"—that is,
the information content left in the example set after applying an attribute. The residual information of an example set after applying an
attribute A is:

$$\text{Ires } (A) = \sum_{v} p(v) \sum_{c} (p(v,c)/p(v)) \log (p(v,c)/p(v))$$

where v stands for values of A, and c stands for classes; probabilities
$p(v)$ and $p(v,c)$ are approximated by statistics on set S.

2. If S is empty, then the result is a single-node tree labeled NULL
(this is Quinlan's original label; Quinlan, 1979).

3. Each time a new attribute is selected, only those attributes are considered that have not yet been used in an upper part of the tree.

4. If S is not empty and not all the objects in S belong to the same class and there is no attribute left to choose, then the result is a single-node tree labeled SEARCH (Quinlan's original label again). Label SEARCH indicates the incompleteness of the set of available attributes: They are not sufficient to distinguish between class values of some objects (objects that belong to different classes have exactly the same attribute values).

This basic scheme was implemented in Quinlan's ID3 program (Quinlan, 1979). For efficiency reasons, Quinlan added a "windowing" mechanism. By that mechanism, if the learning set is very large, a subset called a "window" is randomly selected and a decision tree generated for this subset. This decision tree is tested on the rest of the learning examples. If objects are thus found that are misclassified by this tree, then these objects are added to the window and a new decision tree is generated for this extended window. These steps are repeated until a perfect decision tree is obtained.

More sophisticated versions of TDIDT extend the basic scheme with the following features: (1) handling partially specified examples (incomplete information is usual in some application areas); (2) handling numerical attributes; (3) refined attribute selection criteria that take into account the number of attribute values and their probabilistic distribution.

Experiments in complex domains (e.g., medical diagnosis; Kononenko, Bratko, & Roskar, 1984) revealed another major shortcoming of the basic TDIDT algorithm. Decision trees generated tended to be large (often with several hundreds of nodes) and therefore too complex for an expert to understand or to study; thus, it was hard to assess whether such a tree captured important regularities of the application domain. It can be easily shown that some of this tree complexity is only the result of noise in the learning data. As an example, consider a situation in which we are to construct a subtree of a decision tree and the current subset of objects for learning is S. Let there be 100 objects in S, 99 of them belonging to class 1 and 1 of them to class 2. Knowing that there is noise in the learning data and that all these objects agree in the values of the attributes already selected up to this point in the decision tree, it seems plausible that the class 2 object is in S only as a result of an error in the data. If so, it is best to ignore this object and simply return a leaf of the decision tree labeled with class 1. Since the original ID3 algorithm would, in this situation, further expand the decision tree, we have, in effect, by stopping at this point, pruned a subtree of the complete ID3 tree. Tree pruning is the key to coping with noise in TDIDT programs. A program may prune decision trees using a special criterion to decide whether to stop expanding the tree or not. The stopping criterion will be described in the sequel, as well as the effects of pruning. This kind of pruning, accomplished through stopping the tree expansion, is called *forward pruning* as opposed to another kind of pruning, called *postpruning*. Working in the postpruning regime, a learning program first constructs the complete tree and then estimates its subtrees with respect to their reliability and prunes those that seem unreliable.

4.2. TREE PRUNING IN TDIDT PROGRAMS

As stated above, there are essentially two types of pruning of decision trees: forward pruning and postpruning. We consider forward pruning first. Forward pruning is similar to pruning in game playing. A game tree is effectively pruned during search by simply stopping the expansion of the search tree. So a "pruned" subtree is in fact never generated. The critical question is when to stop expanding the tree. There are various sensible stopping criteria (e.g., Rutowitz & Shepherd, 1985). We here look in detail at one of them, used in ASSISTANT (Bratko & Kononenko, 1986). To decide whether to stop or not, ASSISTANT in a sense (for analogy with game-playing programs) performs a one-ply look-ahead and estimates whether such a one-ply expansion of the decision tree would be beneficial or not. This estimate is done as follows.

Suppose the decision to stop or not is to be made at some current node t in the tree into which a set S of learning instances falls. First, the situation is assessed in respect of what would be the classification accuracy if the tree was terminated at this node. In this case, the resulting leaf would be labeled with the majority class C in S, and we can estimate the classification error at this node as $1 - p(C|t)$, where the condition t denotes the event of an object falling into node t. We will call this error *static classification error*. The probability $p(C|t)$ can be estimated by statistic on S.

The static classification error is to be compared with the error that would result from applying one more attribute. This error is estimated using the following algorithm:

For each example x in S do:
begin
    $S' = S - \{x\}$;
    select the best attribute with respect to S';
    extend the tree with this attribute;
    classify x using this extended tree;

> determine the classification error for x
> end
Sum up the classification errors for all x

Now compare the estimated average classification error over all x with the estimated static classification error. If the static error is lower, then stop at node t; otherwise, continue expanding the tree below t.

The stopping criterion above is computationally expensive, but it can be implemented heuristically to improve efficiency. For example, instead of isolating from S a single element x each time, a random subset is selected from S for estimating the look-ahead classification error. This is repeated a few times and the error estimates are averaged.

The problem with forward pruning is its locality. The decision whether to prune or not is made on the basis of comparing the static error estimate and a *one-ply* look-ahead—that is, after applying one additional attribute. This may be misleading since the situation after applying one attribute may look bad, although it could improve after applying yet another attribute. Therefore, forward pruning may prune a beneficial subtree. Postpruning, which we consider next, does not suffer from this defect.

Postpruning is based on classification error estimates of decision trees. Such an estimator can be constructed as follows. Suppose we have a set of objects T, each of them belonging to one of k classes, and a set S of examples such that S is a subset of T. There are altogether N examples in S and the majority class in S is C; n out of N examples in S belong to C and other examples in S belong to other classes. Now assume that we choose to classify each object in T into class C. What will be the expected classification error? This error can be estimated probabilistically by assuming some prior distribution of the probabilities of classes in T. For example, for the uniform prior distribution of these probabilities, this error is (Niblett & Bratko, 1986):

$$E(S) = (N - n + k - 1)/(N + k)$$

Such an error estimator can be directly applied to estimate the classification error at each leaf of a decision tree. So if Node is a leaf of a decision tree with set S of examples falling into Node, then

$$\text{Error(Node)} = E(S)$$

This error estimator can be straightforwardly generalized to estimate classification errors of nonleaf nodes in a decision tree. Let Node be a nonleaf node of a decision tree and let Node's successors be Node1, Node2, etc. Let the probabilities of branches from Node to Node$i$ be Pi. Then

$$\text{Error(Node)} = \sum_i Pi * \text{Error(Node}i)$$

The probabilities Pi can be approximated by statistics on sets of examples that fall into nodes Node$i$. We call such a node's error estimate, obtained from the node's subtrees, the backed-up error. We can compare a node's "static" error with its backed-up error. In the case that the static error is lower, then we prune the node's subtree. Of course, to optimize the expected classification error, the subtrees must have already been optimally pruned with respect to their classification errors. Therefore, for postpruning, a complete (unpruned) decision tree is constructed first. Then the pruning algorithm has to start at the bottom of the tree and progress toward the root of the tree. This procedure guarantees that the tree will be pruned optimally with respect to the classification error estimates. As a result, it will minimize the expected error at the root of the tree—that is, the expected error of the whole tree. Of course, a pruned tree thus obtained is optimal only with respect to error estimates.

4.3. How Pruning Affects Accuracy and Transparency of Decision Trees

Pruning of decision trees is of fundamental importance because of its multiple beneficial effects when dealing with noisy data. Pruning affects two measures of success of learning: first, the classification accuracy of a decision tree on new objects, and second, the transparency of a decision tree. Let us consider both these criteria in the view of pruning.

The transparency of a concept description is important since we would like the synthesized rules not only to be used by a machine but also to be understood and used by a human. The latter is important in order to tell the human something about the problem domain by revealing yet unknown regularities or relationships in the domain. In this sense, inductive learning can contribute to the enhancement of human knowledge and can be viewed as one approach to the synthesis of new knowledge by a machine (see, e.g., Michie, 1986a,b). The comprehensibility of a description depends on its structure and on its size. A well-structured decision tree is, of course, easier to understand than a completely unstructured tree (for generating structured tree-based descriptions by means of "structured induction" see A. Shapiro, 1987). On the other hand, if a decision tree is small (consisting of just 10 or so nodes), then it is easy to understand regardless of its structure. Since pruning reduces the size of a tree, it contributes in this way to the transparency of a decision tree. As has been shown experimentally in several problem domains, the reduction of tree size can be dramatic so that the number of nodes can be reduced to, say, 10% of their original number, while retaining the same range of the classification accuracy (e.g., Cestnik et al., 1987).

Tree pruning can also improve the classification accuracy of a tree. This effect of pruning is somewhat counterintuitive since by pruning we throw away some information, and it would seem that as a result some accuracy should be lost. However, in the case of learning from noisy data, a proper amount of pruning normally improves the accuracy. This phenomenon can be explained in statistical terms: Statistically, pruning works as a sort of noise-suppression mechanism. By pruning we eliminate errors in learning data that are due to noise, rather than throw away useful information.

It is also interesting to compare the accuracy of the synthesized decision trees with the performance of human experts in particular domains. As shown, for example, in experiments in several medical domains (Bratko & Kononenko, 1986; Kononenko et al., 1984), the classification accuracy of decision trees learned from examples was at least in the same range as that attained by medical experts. Typically, the learned rules slightly outperformed the human experts when exactly the same information for diagnosis was available to both the human and the machine.

5. OTHER APPROACHES TO LEARNING AND BIBLIOGRAPHICAL REMARKS

An early attempt at machine learning is Samuel's learning checkers program (Samuel, 1959). This program improved its position evaluation function through experience obtained in the games it played.

Logic formalisms are used as a concept description language in several learning programs. First-order predicate logic is, for example, used in MIS (E. Y. Shapiro, 1981) and MARVIN (Sammut & Banerji, 1986). A large family of learning programs, known as the AQ family, was developed by Michalski and his co-workers (e.g., Michalski, 1983). This family of programs generates rules expressed in another logic-based formalism called VL1 (Variable-valued Logic 1). A pruning technique to cope with noisy data was also introduced into the AQ family, here named rule truncation (Michalski, Mozetic, Hong, & Lavrac, 1986). Another example of a program that successfully generates rules from noisy data is CN2 (Clark & Niblett, 1987).

An interesting approach to learning is *explanation-based learning* (e.g., Mitchell, Keller, & Kedar-Cabelli, 1986). Here the learning system uses background knowledge to reason about a given example to "explain" the example by a deductive process. Examples are so used to guide the learning system toward proper generalizations in forming a general rule from an example. The central role of explanation in AI in general is argued by Kodratoff (1987).

Some learning programs learn by autonomous discovery. They discover new concepts through exploration, making their own experiments. Celebrated examples of this kind of program are Lenat's AM (Automatic Mathematician; Lenat, 1982) and its successor EURISKO (Lenat, 1983). AM, for example, starting with the concepts of set and "bag," discovered such concepts as number, addition, multiplication, and prime number.

It has been realized that for complex domains it is essential to structure the domain by dividing it into subproblems and corresponding subconcepts. Then the overall problem can be solved in terms of subproblems, or the overall concept is expressed in terms of subconcepts. Subconcepts are learned separately, which makes the whole learning task much easier. The importance of this is studied in A. Shapiro (1987). Structuring information, expressed in terms of systems components and their interconnections, was also used in Mozetic's program, which learns a qualitative model of a system from examples of the system's behavior (Mozetic, 1987). Using a logic-based formalism, this program automatically derived a model of the electrical activity of the human heart from its overall structure and examples of its behavior. An important question in respect of structured learning is: Can the structuring of a problem domain be automated? Muggleton (1987) describes promising experiments to structure complex problem domains automatically.

Current research in machine learning is published in the AI literature, most notably in the journals *Machine Learning* (Boston: Kluwer) and *Artificial Intelligence* (Amsterdam: North-Holland). The following three books contain collections of research papers on machine learning:

- *Machine Learning: An Artificial Intelligence Approach* (eds. R. S. Michalski, J. G. Carbonell, & T. M. Mitchell). Palo Alto, California: Tioga Publishing Company, 1983.

- *Machine Learning: An Artificial Intelligence Approach* (Vol. 2) (eds. R. S. Michalski, J. G. Carbonell, & T. M. Mitchell). Los Altos, California: Morgan Kaufmann, 1986.
- *Progress in Machine Learning* (eds. I. Bratko & N. Lavrac). Wilmslow, England: Sigma Press; distributed by J. Wiley, 1987.

6. REFERENCES

Bratko, I., Kononenko, I. (1986). Learning diagnostic rules from incomplete and noisy Data. *AI Methods in Statistics, Proceedings of the UNICOM seminar*, London. [Also in *Interactions in AI and Statistics* (B. Phelps, Ed.). Gower Technical Press (1987).]

Cestnik, B., Kononenko, I., & Bratko, I. (1987). ASSISTANT 86: A knowledge elicitation tool for sophisticated users. In I. Bratko & N. Lavrac (Eds.), *Progress in Machine Learning*. Wilmslow, England: Sigma Press.

Clark, P., & Niblett, T. (1987). Induction in noisy domains. In I. Bratko & H. Lavrac (Eds.), *Progress in machine learning*. Wilmslow, England: Sigma Press.

Kodratoff, Y. (1987). Is AI a sub-field of computer science—or is AI the science of explanations? In I. Bratko & N. Lavrac (Eds.), *Progress in machine learning*. Wilmslow, England: Sigma Press.

Kononenko, I., Bratko, I., & Roskar, E. (1984). *Experiments in automatic learning of medical diagnostic rules*. International School for the Synthesis of Expert Knowledge Workshop, Bled, Yugoslavia.

Lavrac, N., Varsek, A., Gams, M., Kononenko, I., & Bratko, I. (1986). Automatic construction of a knowledge base for a steel classification expert system. *Proceedings of the 6th International Workshop on Expert Systems and their Applications*, Avignon, France.

Lenat, D. B. (1982). AM: Discovery in mathematics as heuristic search. In R. Davis & D. B. Lenat (Eds.), *Knowledge-based systems in artificial intelligence*. New York: McGraw-Hill.

Lenat, D. B. (1983). Eurisko: A program that learns new heuristics and domain concepts. *Artificial Intelligence, 21*, 61–98.

Michalski, R. S. (1983). A theory and methodology of inductive learning. In R. S. Michalski, J. G. Carbonell, & T. M. Mitchell (Eds.), *Machine learning: An artificial intelligence approach*. Palo Alto: Tioga.

Michalski, R. S., & Chilausky, R. L. (1980). Learning by being told and learning from examples: An experimental comparison of the two methods for knowledge acquisition in the context of developing an expert system for soybean disease diagnosis. *International Journal for Policy Analysis and Information Systems, 4* (2), 125–161.

Michalski, R. S., Mozetic, I., Hong, J., & Lavrac, N. (1986). The multi-purpose incremental learning system AQ15 and its testing application to three medical domains. *AAAI Conference 86*, Philadelphia.

Michie, D. (1986a). The superarticulacy phenomenon in the context of software manufacture. *Proceedings of the Royal Society, London, A 405*, 189–212. (Reprinted in D. Michie & I. Bratko, *Expert systems: Automating knowledge acquisition* (handbook to an AI Masters video). Reading, MA: Addison-Wesley.

Michie, D. (1986b). Towards a knowledge accelerator. In D. Beal (Ed.), *Advances in computer chess 4*. Oxford: Pergamon Press.

Mitchell, T. M., Keller, R. M., & Kedar-Cabelli, S. T. (1986). Explanation-based generalisation: A unifying view. *Machine Learning, 1*, 47–80.

Mitchell, T. M., Utgoff, P. E., & Banerji, R. (1983). Learning by experimentation: Acquiring and refining problem-solving heuristics. In R. S. Michalski, J. G. Carbonell, & T. M. Mitchell (Eds.), *Machine learning: An artificial intelligence approach*. Palo Alto: Tioga.

Mozetic, I. (1987). Learning of qualitative models. In I. Bratko & N. Lavrac (Eds.), *Progress in machine learning*. Wilmslow, England: Sigma Press.

Muggleton, S. (1987). Structuring knowledge by asking questions. In I. Bratko & N. Lavrac (Eds.), *Progress in machine learning*. Wilmslow, England: Sigma Press.

Niblett, T., & Bratko, I. (1986). Learning decision rules in noisy domains. In M. A. Brammer (Ed.), *Research and development in expert systems* (Vol. 3). Cambridge: Cambridge University Press.

Quinlan, J. R. (1979). Discovering rules by induction from large collections of examples. In D. Michie (Ed.), *Expert systems in the microelectronic age*. Edinburgh: Edinburgh University Press.

Quinlan, J. R. (1986). Induction of decision trees. *Machine Learning, 1*, 81–106.

Quinlan, J. R., Compton, P., Horn, K. A., & Lazarus, L. (1987). Inductive knowledge acquisition: A case study. In J. R. Quinlan (Ed.), *Applications of expert systems*. Reading, MA: Addison-Wesley.

Rutowitz, D., & Shepherd, B. (1985). ACLS versus statistical classifier in a biological application (Machine Intelligence Workshop 11, Ross Priory, Scotland). In J. Hayes, D. Michie, & J. Richards (Eds.), *Machine intelligence 11*. Oxford: Oxford University Press.

Sammut, C., & Banerji, R. B. (1986). Learning concepts by asking questions. In R. S. Michalski, J. G. Carbonell, & T. M. Mitchell (Eds.), *Machine learning: An artificial intelligence approach* (Vol. 2). Los Altos, CA: Morgan Kaufmann.

Samuel, A. L. (1959). Some studies in machine learning using the game of checkers. *IBM Journal of Research and Development*, No. 3, 211–229. [Also in E. A. Feigenbaum & I. Feldman (Eds.), *Computers and thought*. New York: McGraw-Hill (1963).]

Shapiro, A. (1987). *Structured induction in expert systems*. Reading, MA: Addison-Wesley.

Shapiro, E. Y. (1981). Inductive inference of theories from facts. Research Report 192, Yale University.

Winston, P. H. (1975) Learning structural descriptions from examples. In P. H. Winston (Ed.), *The psychology of computer vision*. New York: McGraw-Hill.

11

Human Learning

MICHAEL W. EYSENCK

1. INTRODUCTION

There have been considerable changes in theoretical approaches to human learning and memory over the past 20 years or so. During the late 1960s and early 1970s, the emphasis was on the basic architecture of the human memory system. This structural approach found its apotheosis in the multistore model proposed by Atkinson and Shiffrin (1968, 1971). Disenchantment soon became manifest with this type of theorizing, in particular because it appeared to deemphasize the processes involved in learning and retrieval. As a consequence, Craik and Lockhart (1972) put forward their levels-of-processing theory, which focused on processes rather than on structure. This approach also fell into disfavor, in part because of the dawning realization that general theories of learning and memory (such as the multistore and levels-of-processing models) are likely to be grossly oversimplified.

In recent years there has been a move toward theories that are less ambitious in terms of the data that they attempt to explain. Some of the fruits of this increased fractionation form the major part of this chapter. One influential approach has involved attempting to identify some of the structures in long-term memory that influence the comprehension and subsequent retrieval of information. The structures iden-

MICHAEL W. EYSENCK • Department of Psychology, Royal Holloway and Bedford New College, University of London, Egham, Surrey TW20 OEX, United Kingdom.

tified have been variously labeled: schemata, frames, or scripts. A second approach is the neuropsychological one, focusing on the amnesic syndrome. There are several potential advantages with this approach. Amnesia provides a testing ground for theoretical models of learning and memory, and the fresh insights obtained from amnesia research may affect our theoretical understanding of normal memory processes. A third approach has involved a focus on the processes involved in the retrieval process, i.e., output from the system. Of course, such an approach cannot ignore issues of learning and of storage. As Tulving and Thomson (1973) pointed out, "Only that can be retrieved that has been stored, and . . . how it can be retrieved depends on how it was stored" (p. 359). A fourth approach has considered concept learning. Concepts can be regarded as the building blocks of cognition. Earlier research investigated the learning of rather artificial and arbitrary concepts, whereas more recent research has focused on the concepts that we use in everyday life.

Before these contemporary approaches are explored in more detail, their theoretical antecedents in the early days of the "cognitive era" will be discussed. What was exciting about the multistore approach adumbrated by Broadbent (1958) and developed by Atkinson and Shiffrin (1968, 1971) was that it provided a plausible account of some of the structures and processes intervening between the presentation of a stimulus for learning and the subsequent response on a retention test. In essence, Atkinson and Shiffrin (1968) argued that there are three different kinds of memory store: modality-specific stores holding incoming information very briefly, a short-term store holding limited amounts of information for a few seconds, and a long-term store of essentially unlimited capacity. According to the theory, the process of attention transfers information from the modality-specific stores to the short-term store, and rehearsal plays a major role in transferring information from the short-term store to the long-term store.

The evidence still supports some kind of distinction among modality-specific, short-term, and long-term stores, but despite this the multistore approach is no longer held in the esteem that it once was. Why is this? One important reason is that the processes involved in learning are very much underspecified. For example, the theory assumes that information in the modality-specific stores is in a raw, uninterpreted form, whereas information in the short-term store is frequently in phonemic form as a result of rehearsal activities, and information in the long-term store is mainly in semantic form. Nowhere in the theory is it made clear how these substantial changes in the nature of the information are supposed to occur.

A further weakness with the multistore approach concerns the notion that the short-term store is unitary. The evidence increasingly indicates that the short-term store is *not* unitary (Eysenck, 1986), and that a variety of different processes occur within the short-term storage system. According to Baddeley and Hitch (1974), the concept of the short-term store should be replaced with that of the working memory system, which consists of several separate components: a modality-free central executive, an articulatory loop, an acoustic store, and a visuospatial scratch pad.

Perhaps the single most powerful reason for the decline in support for the multistore approach is that it is rather threadbare theoretically. In spite of the inclusion of the long-term memory store as one of the major memorial structures, multistore theorists had remarkably little to say about the organization of long-term memory, the different forms of representation in long-term memory, strategies for accessing long-term memory, and so on. In similar fashion, the account offered of the short-term memory store ignored a number of major issues.

Craik and Lockhart (1972) argued for a very different theoretical orientation. They claimed that memory traces are formed as by-products of perceptual and attentional processes, and that to understand memory we need to investigate these processes in detail. More specifically, they hypothesized that long-term memory was a direct function of the depth of processing, with deep processing involving semantic analysis and shallow processing remaining at the nonsemantic level.

The levels-of-processing theory proposed by Craik and Lockhart (1972) has not fared well. The reasons are spelled out by Eysenck (1984, 1986), so that only two or three of the main ones will be mentioned here. First, there is no adequate independent measure of the depth of processing. Second, deep encodings are usually more elaborate or extensive than shallow encodings, and they are also more distinctive or unique. It has proved extremely difficult to unconfound the three factors of depth, elaboration, and distinctiveness, so that their relative contributions to long-term memory remain unclear. Third, the theory is descriptive rather than explanatory, as argued by Eysenck (1984): "Why are semantic encodings usually better remembered than nonsemantic encodings? According to Craik and Lockhart (1972), the answer is that the retentivity is determined by the depth of processing. This obviously begs the question of *why* it is that deep processing is so effective, i.e., the observed relationship is not linked to any more general or fundamental ideas" (pp. 113–114).

Despite the criticisms that levels-of-processing theory has attracted, its general orientation still appears to be a reasonable one. It is indubitably the case that one of the most important determinants of long-term memory is the processing that the to-be-learned stimulus material receives at acquisition, and Craik and Lockhart (1972) were among the first theorists to emphasize this fact. A distinction can be drawn between the stimulus-as-presented and the stimulus-as-encoded. Previous theorists had focused largely on the stimulus-as-presented, whereas Craik and Lockhart (1972) quite correctly argued that it is the stimulus-as-encoded that is of fundamental importance to the memory theorist.

2. SCHEMATA, SCRIPTS, AND FRAMES

In general terms, the multistore and levels-of-processing theories both stress bottom-up or stimulus-driven processing in their accounts of learning. In other words, a to-be-learned stimulus is presented and is processed in various ways or proceeds through a number of memory stores. What is largely absent from these theories is any systematic consideration of top-down or conceptually driven processing. Top-down processing refers to processing that is affected by what an individual brings to the learning situation on the basis of knowledge and past experience.

The role played by top-down or conceptually driven processing in learning and memory was emphasized by Bartlett (1932) in a very influential book. According to Bartlett (1932), "Remembering is not the re-excitation of innumerable fixed, lifeless and fragmentary traces. It is an imaginative reconstruction, or construction, built out of the relation of our attitude towards a whole active mass of organized past reactions or experience" (p. 213). In other words, memory is affected both by the information presented for learning and by relevant prior knowledge.

Bartlett (1932) did not provide a precise theoretical formulation, but he apparently believed that the primary impact of prior knowledge on memory occurred at the time of retrieval. More specifically, he argued that remembering was affected by schemata, and he defined the schema as "an active organization of past reactions, or of past experience."

How can we investigate the role played by prior knowledge in the form of schemata on the processes involved in learning and memory? The answer suggested by Bartlett (1932) was to present stimulus material for learning that was inconsistent with the learner's knowledge of the world. In more concrete terms, what Bartlett (1932) did was to use stories taken from other cultures. The theoretical assumption was that the conflict between the actual story and prior knowledge would produce systematic distortions in the remembered version of the story, making it more conventional than the original from the learner's cultural perspective.

Bartlett (1932) reported considerable empirical support for his theoretical position. His subjects made numerous errors, and many of these errors involved what he termed "rationalization," i.e., making the recall more conventional than the original. Other distortions in story recall included flattening (i.e., failure to recall unfamiliar details) and sharpening (i.e., elaboration of some details).

Although Bartlett's (1932) theory and research have had a great influence, there have been several pertinent criticisms of his work. There is evidence (e.g., Gauld & Stephenson, 1967) that some of the recall distortions observed by Bartlett (1932) were produced by conscious guessing and confabulation rather than simply as a result of memorial malfunctioning. At the theoretical level, Bartlett (1932) claimed that prior knowledge affected learning and memory by influencing the retrieval process, whereas it is perhaps more plausible to assume that the main effect of prior knowledge is on the comprehension or initial encoding of presented information. The latter theoretical position was put forward by Bransford (e.g., 1979), who contrasted his constructive hypothesis with Bartlett's (1932) reconstructive hypothesis. The relevant evidence indicates that both of these hypotheses are partially correct (see Eysenck, 1984, for a review).

A further potential problem with Bartlett's approach is the fact that he observed memorial distortions attributable to prior knowledge under rather limited and artificial conditions. If it is necessary to use bizarre and incongruous stimulus material in order to obtain systematic distortions in memory due to schemata, then clearly Bartlett's approach is of relatively little general interest. However, the position has changed in recent years. Several studies (e.g., Bransford, Barclay, & Franks, 1972) have indicated that schematic information in long-term memory is used almost constantly to make inferences about the information that we hear or see, and that these inferences are then stored in memory and often mistakenly "remembered."

In sum, Bartlett's (1932) notion that past knowledge and experience have a pervasive influence on learning and memory has received substantial support. Despite the methodological deficiencies of Bartlett's (1932) own research, the basic phenomenon of systematic memorial distortions produced by prior knowledge can readily be demonstrated in methodologically sound experiments. However, Bartlett's (1932) emphasis on reconstructive processes seems somewhat misplaced. It is likely that prior knowledge usually affects encoding and comprehension processes rather more than subsequent retrieval processes.

Bartlett (1932) argued that remembering was affected by organized prior knowledge in the form of schemata, but his conceptualization of schemata was very amorphous. There have been various attempts in recent years to provide better-defined theoretical constructs to refer to relatively large, well-integrated chunks of knowledge. For example, Schank (1976) used the term *script*, whereas Rumelhart (1980) referred to *schema*, and Minsky (1975) to *frame*. Although these terms are clearly not synonymous, they do resemble each other in that scripts, schemata, and frames all consist of organized structures of stereotypical knowledge.

The meanings of some of these terms can be ascertained more closely if we considered definitions that have been proposed. According to Schank (1976), a script is

> a giant causal chain of conceptualizations that have been known to occur in that order many times before. . . . What a script does is to set up expectations about events that are likely to follow in a given situation. These events can be predicted because they have occurred in precisely this fashion before (pp. 180–181).

Rumelhart (1980) explained what he meant by a "schema" in the following definition:

> A schema, then, is a data structure for representing our knowledge about all concepts: those underlying objects, situations, events, sequences of events, actions and sequences of actions. A schema contains, as part of its specification, the network of interrelations that is believed to normally hold among the constituents of the concept in question. A schema theory embodies a *prototype* theory of meaning. That is, inasmuch as a schema underlying a concept stored in memory corresponds to the *meaning* of that concept, meanings are encoded in terms of the typical or normal situations or events that instantiate (i.e., provide concrete examples of) that concept (p. 34).

This definition can be clarified if we consider a specific example. The schema for "buying" obviously cannot be too detailed, because of the enormous variety of individuals and circumstances in which buying occurs. However, buying always involves a seller, a purchaser, some merchandise, a medium of exchange (e.g., money), and bargaining (i.e., the seller agrees to give the merchandise to the purchaser in exchange for a specified amount of the medium of exchange), and the buying schema incorporates these common elements.

Before elaborating on the role of schemata, scripts, or frames in learning and memory, it is useful to consider how schemata themselves are acquired. This issue was addressed by Rumelhart (1980), who proposed that learning can occur via accretion, tuning, and restructuring. Learning by accretion is based on the memory traces of comprehension processes, and these traces typically comprise partial copies of the instantiated schemata. Tuning involves the development and refinement of concepts as a result of experience. Restructuring involves the creation of new schemata, which can occur either by copying an old schema and adding some modifications (patterned generation) or by repeating a spatiotemporal configuration of schemata (schema induction).

Why are schemata, scripts, or frames useful? Perhaps their most obvious function is to reduce the demands on processing resources. Thus, for example, our restaurant script (Bower, Black, & Turner, 1979) contains information about the probable sequence of events when eating a meal in a restaurant (e.g., sitting down, consulting the menu, ordering, eating one or more courses, receiving the bill, paying the bill, and leaving the restaurant). The fact that the basic activities occurring in a restaurant are highly familiar ones means that nearly all of the available processing resources can be allocated to conversation and to enjoyment of the food.

It may be doubted whether we possess many scripts resembling the restaurant script in their structure. Eating a meal in a restaurant is a reasonably structured event having a number of almost invariant features. Most everyday events probably lack this structure and coherence, and so, presumably, do their underlying scripts.

Detailed information about the allocation of processing resources as a function of the currently activated frame was obtaining by Friedman (1979). She presented her subjects with line drawings of various scenes, such as a kitchen, a farm, and a living room. Each drawing contained mainly objects that one would expect to see in that particular setting—i.e., they were congruent with the activated frame—but a few unexpected objects were also present. Subjects spent longer processing the unexpected, or frame-incongruent, stimuli, with the duration of the first look being almost twice as long for unexpected as for expected objects.

Friedman (1979) also discovered that there was a substantial difference in recognition memory between frame-congruent or expected objects and frame-incongruent or unexpected objects. There was very poor detection of missing, new, or partially changed expected objects, but changes in, or replacements of, unexpected objects were usually detected. These findings demonstrate clearly the importance of the relevant frame to perception and to memory, and led Friedman (1979) to the following conclusion: "The episodic information that will be remembered about an event is the difference between that event and its prototypical frame representation in memory" (p. 343).

Similar findings with schematic passages were reported by Graesser, Woll, Kowalski, and Smith (1980). In their study there was better recognition memory for atypical than for typical actions; indeed, unstated typical actions were "recognized" as frequently as stated typical actions. These findings were replicated by Smith and Graesser (1981), who also discovered that the results were affected by the nature of the retention test. More specifically, typical events were less well recognized than atypical events, but better recalled at long retention intervals, a pattern of results that resembles the one often obtained in studies on distinctiveness of processing (e.g., Eysenck, 1979). The discrepancy between recall and recognition can be accounted for if we make the assumption that schemata guide the retrieval process far more in recall than in recognition, since a schema will enhance retrieval of schema-relevant information only.

The role that schemata can play in guiding the process of retrieval was demonstrated particularly clearly in a study by Anderson and Pichert (1987). A story was read from the perspective either of a burglar or of someone interested in buying a house, and it was then recalled. After that, the subjects were asked to adopt the alternative perspective for a second recall of the story. As predicted, the subjects' second recall contained more information that was directly relevant to the second perspective or schema than did their first recall.

A consideration of the available experimental evidence does not make clear the general usefulness of schemata. In particular, since schemata often lead to impoverished processing of schema-relevant information, and thus to low levels of retention, it might be argued that schemata reduce rather than promote learning. Such a conclusion is not actually warranted. What typically happens is that schemata allow us to capitalize on the regularities of situations, and thus to make accurate inferences and predictions in a very efficient fashion. Given our limited information-processing abilities, it makes sense to focus attention on those aspects of the environment providing information that is discrepant with our existing knowledge.

Schemata also serve the useful purpose of facilitating the process of bringing relevant knowledge to bear on the current environmental situation. Instead of numerous highly specific pieces of knowledge being accessed separately, it is often possible to access a single schema that will contain sufficient information to permit adequate interpretation of the situation. As a consequence, many situations can be interpreted very rapidly without apparent effort.

How useful have schema theories been in terms of increasing our understanding of human learning and memory? On the positive side, they have made it clear that top-down processes using previous knowledge and experience can influence what is learned and what is subsequently retrieved. Schema theories (or something very similar) seem required in order to account for the systematic distortions and inaccuracies that have been found in memory performance.

Another advantage of schema theories is that they have focused attention on the representation of information in long-term memory. The emphasis until quite recently was on individual words or other relatively limited units of storage (e.g., propositions), but schema theories indicate the value of considering much larger, well-integrated units of information in the form of schemata, frames, or scripts.

On the negative side, schema theories are usually rather imprecise. This imprecision revolves in part around the vagueness of the "schema" notion itself, and the fact that no independent measure of a schema is typically available. The most important consequence of the vagueness of most schema theories is that they do not make unambiguous predictions that are potentially falsifiable. Consider, for example, whether schema-irrelevant information should be remembered less well or better than schema-relevant information. Both results have been reported in the literature (Brewer & Treyens, 1981; Friedman, 1979; Smith & Graesser, 1981). These apparent inconsistencies have not been regarded as constituting a serious problem by schema theorists because both results can be accounted for in a *post hoc* fashion. Thus, schema-irrelevant information might be remembered particularly well because it is salient and receives extra processing, or it might be remembered poorly because it cannot be integrated with the currently activated schemata and because it does not benefit from schema-guided retrieval.

One of the few unequivocal predictions of schema theories is that the memory traces that are formed will be incomplete and inaccurate. This should be the case because what is stored and retrieved depends on the relationship between the incoming information and the schemata that are activated. The top-down processes emphasized by schema theories are of use in explaining memorial distortions but seem unable to account for the fact that long-term memory is often both accurate and detailed. For example, participants in a research-discussion group showed a good ability to distinguish between many of the actual utter-

298

ances made in the discussion and paraphrases of them at a retention interval of 30 hours (Keenan, MacWhinney, & Mayhew, 1977). Such detailed recollection of the actual form of incoming information appears to be inconsistent with the basic assumptions of schema theories. In a nutshell, schema theories overemphasize top-down processes and at the same time de-emphasize bottom-up processes.

In sum, schema theories have addressed fundamental issues about human learning and memory that had previously been relatively neglected. If the theories can be made sufficiently precise to permit unequivocal predictions, then their potential value will be able to be assessed more accurately.

3. AMNESIA

An approach to human learning and memory that differs considerably from other approaches is the neuropsychological one based on a systematic investigation of the amnesic syndrome. The essence of this approach consists in identifying those kinds of learning that are preserved in amnesics, and then comparing them against those types of learning that are substantially impaired. It is usually assumed that the intact system or systems underlying preserved performance differ importantly from the damaged system or systems involved in impaired performance. The hope is that the data collected from amnesics on learning and memory tasks will facilitate the testing of current theoretical formulations and lead to new theoretical distinctions.

The first point that needs to be made is that it is probably simplistic to assume that there is but a single amnesic syndrome. There is some evidence suggesting that the precise pattern of performance deficits varies somewhat as a function of the anatomical site of the lesion (Parkin, 1984). More specifically, a distinction can be drawn between amnesics who have suffered damage to the diencephalon and those whose hippocampus is damaged. In general terms, the former group (which includes Korsakoff patients suffering from advanced alcoholism) has a greater impairment of memory functioning than the latter group. Despite these complexities, the basic symptoms of most amnesics are broadly comparable, including some loss of ability to form new memories (anterograde amnesia), a partial inability to access old memories (retrograde amnesia), and essentially intact short-term memory. It is also worth noting that most research on amnesia has relied largely on sufferers from Korsakoff's syndrome, who appear to be reasonably homogeneous in their symptomatology. As a consequence, the learning data on Korsakoff patients are fairly definite and in most cases resemble the data from other amnesics.

It was believed at one time that amnesics were almost entirely unable to form new long-term memories, but there is now overwhelming evidence that this is not correct (see Cohen, 1984, for a review). What has now been reported numerous times is the surprising combination of clear evidence of learning despite a virtual absence of conscious recollection of that learning. For example, an amnesic known as H. M. was given training on the pursuit-rotor task, which requires the subject to attempt to keep a metal rod in contact with a target (a small metal disk) set into a rotating turntable. H. M.'s performance on this task improved progressively in terms of time-on-target, and he showed very good retention of this perceptual-motor skill over a period of one week (Corkin, 1968). However, during each learning session he showed practically no awareness of having seen the pursuit-rotor apparatus before.

This finding suggests the existence of two different systems, one underlying the perceptual-motor skill and the other relating to conscious awareness. However, since H. M.'s learning performance was inferior to that of normal controls, it could not be claimed that an intact system had been identified. Subsequent research (e.g., Brooks & Baddeley, 1976) has revealed that most amnesics have a learning rate on the pursuit rotor that is comparable to that of control subjects, so that H. M.'s discrepant performance may be due to poor rather than to impaired capacities.

Similar findings have been obtained with various tasks. Cohen and Squire (1980) found that amnesic patients showed as much retention as normal controls of the mirror-reading skill over a retention interval of three months. However, there were enormous differences in terms of conscious awareness of the fact that word triads were repeating during the mirror-reading task. All of the control subjects remarked spontaneously that some of the word triads were repeated, whereas none of the amnesics when questioned reported any awareness of the repetitions.

Cohen (1981) made use of the Tower of Hanoi puzzle. This is a complex task involving moving blocks from one peg to another under severe constraints, and the optimal solution requires 31 moves. Once again, the task performance of the amnesics was very good. The learning rate of amnesics on this task did not differ significantly from that of normal controls, and the amnesic patient H. M. showed very impressive retention of the task skills when tested one year after learning. Furthermore, the amnesics showed good transfer of skills when asked to solve a modified version of the puzzle after training on the original version, indicating that their learning was not simply confined to a particular set of moves. In spite of this high level of task mastery, the amnesics showed very little if any recollection of having worked at the task before, and they were unable to verbalize what they had learned. While these findings are undeniably very impressive, it has not been possible as yet for other investigators to replicate them.

We have seen so far that amnesics demonstrate an impressive ability to acquire and retain various different motor, perceptual, and cognitive skills. In addition, their performance on a number of tasks is affected as much as that of normals by prior exposure to, or priming of, relevant stimulus materials. These repetition-priming effects are illustrated in a study reported by Jacoby and Witherspoon (1982). The interpretation of homophones (e.g., *reed, read*) was biased in the first part of the experiment by hearing them in the context of questions that were to be answered. Then the subjects were simply asked to spell each homophone, with no reference being made in the instructions to the earlier part of the experiment. Finally, there was a recognition-memory test to determine whether the subjects remembered which interpretation of each homophone had been biased in the first part of the experiment. The amnesics were actually more likely than normal controls (63% vs. 49%) to spell the homophones in the way primed previously, but their recognition-memory performance was considerably inferior (25% vs. 76%). In other words, the amnesics showed a greater repetition-priming effect than normals, but their awareness of the primes was very poor.

What are the theoretical implications of these findings? The least interesting possibility is that those performance measures on which amnesics are comparable to normal controls are simply less sensitive than measures requiring conscious awareness. Thus, the pattern of results produced by amnesics may simply reflect their poor memory rather than exciting qualitative differences between amnesics and normals. This point of view was developed by Mayes and Meudell (1983), who argued that learning without conscious awareness can also be demonstrated in normals, provided that their overall level of remembering is reduced to that of amnesics. In a study of Meudell and Mayes (1981), amnesics and normal controls were asked to search cartoons for specific objects. Seven weeks later the amnesics demonstrated long-term retention of some of the knowledge acquired previously by their rapid rate of search on the same cartoons, but they were unable to decide accurately which cartoons they had seen before. The normal controls were tested 17 months after the first experimental session and showed the same pattern of fast searching coupled with very poor recognition memory.

Some of the data are consistent with the notion that the various measures of learning differ primarily in their difficulty or sensitivity, but this cannot be a complete explanation. If two measures of learning differ only quantitatively, then individuals who perform well on the more difficult measure should also perform well on the easier measure. In the study by Jacoby and Witherspoon (1982), the spelling and recognition measures were uncorrelated with each other; the fact that the two measures were independent of each other suggests that they reflect the workings of two different underlying systems rather than differentially sensitive measures of a single system.

An alternative explanation of the data has made use of Tulving's (1972) distinction between episodic and semantic memory. Episodic memory has an autobiographical flavor, since it refers to memory for specific episodes in our lives (e.g., the party we went to last night). Episodic memories usually contain spatial and temporal information, so that they can be "placed" in terms of time and location. In contrast, semantic memory is a mental thesaurus consisting of our general knowledge about the world, the meanings of words, and so on.

According to Parkin (1982), the pattern of preserved learning capability in amnesics "can be interpreted as an impairment of episodic storage with the relative sparing of what is often described as 'semantic memory' " (p. 436). If correct, the amnesia literature would greatly strengthen the theoretical argument for distinguishing between episodic and semantic memory. It is clear that the distinction can be defended on the basis of the different *content* of episodic and semantic memories, but it is far less obvious that the two kinds of memory depend on separate *systems*. Even Tulving (1972, 1984) has admitted that the systems involved are highly interdependent. Thus, amnesics may offer an opportunity of studying semantic memory relatively uninfluenced by episodic memory.

At first glance, it seems reasonable to argue that amnesics have intact semantic memory but grossly impaired episodic memory. In general terms, those tasks on which amnesics perform at the normal level have in common the fact that they do not require conscious awareness of specific earlier events in the patients' lives, i.e., episodic memory. In addition, amnesics typically have preserved language skills, and such skills constitute an important part of semantic memory.

Despite its intuitive appeal, the distinction between episodic and semantic memory cannot be regarded as a satisfactory basis for understanding the amnesic syndrome. First, even though the definition of "semantic memory" is rather vague, it still seems unwise to regard the particular skills acquired on the Tower of Hanoi or the pursuit-rotor task as forming part of a mental thesaurus. As we will see later in the chapter, there are alternative (and preferable) ways of conceptualizing what has been learned by amnesics on such tasks. Second, what has often been done (but rarely acknowledged) is to contrast amnesics' good premorbidly acquired semantic memory with their inferior postmorbidly acquired episodic memory. In order to disentangle the type of memory from the time of acquisition, it is obviously essential to consider postmorbidly acquired semantic memory and premorbidly acquired episodic memory.

Baddeley (1984) has considered some of the evidence relating to amnesics' ability to update semantic memory. He pointed out that amnesics frequently do not know the name of the current Prime Minister or President, which is hardly consistent with the notion that their semantic memory is unimpaired. The amnesic H. M. showed very little ability to learn the meanings of new words, despite receiving at least 15 learning trials on every word on each of 10 separate days (Gabrieli, Cohen, & Corkin, 1983).

Premorbidly acquired episodic memories were investigated by Zola-Morgan, Cohen, and Squire (1983). They found that amnesics were well able to recall specific premorbid events when provided with stimulus words (e.g., *flag, window*). The episodes recalled by the amnesic patients were indistinguishable from those recalled by control subjects, except that the average age of the memories was rather greater for the amnesics.

The evidence is reasonably clear-cut. It indicates that amnesia impairs the ability to acquire new information regardless of whether semantic or episodic memory is involved. On the other hand, most of the information acquired premorbidly is spared, again regardless of whether semantic or episodic memory is involved.

A more promising theoretical approach was outlined by Jacoby (1984). He argued that there is a useful theoretical distinction between incidental and intentional retrieval. As a first approximation, amnesics often perform adequately under conditions where there is no explicit and obvious retention test (i.e., incidental retrieval). In contrast, their performance is often markedly inferior to that of normals when definite instructions to retrieve are given before the retention test (i.e., intentional retrieval). At least part of the memorial superiority of normals over amnesics may be attributable to the greater variety of retrieval strategies that they use under conditions of intentional retrieval. If feelings of subjective familiarity or conscious awareness occur as a by-product of extensive processing, then the restricted processing engaged in by amnesics in intentional retrieval situations is directly responsible for their lack of awareness of remembering.

The strongest evidence in support of Jacoby's (1984) theoretical position was reported by Graf, Squire, and Mandler (1984). A list of words was presented for study. Subsequently the subjects were presented with word fragments, some of which came from list words and some of which did not. The word fragments were completed under conditions of either intentional or incidental retrieval. There was no difference between amnesics and normal controls in memory performance under incidental retrieval conditions, but controls performed better than amnesics with intentional retrieval. Of particular interest, the level of memory performance displayed by amnesics was essentially the same under intentional and incidental retrieval conditions. This suggests that amnesics cannot make effective use of intentional retrieval instructions.

A rather different approach is represented by context theory (reviewed by Mayes, Meudell, & Pickering, 1985). In fact, various context theories have been offered, although they all agree that the poor long-term memory of amnesics is due to a selective loss of (or failure to acquire) contextual information rather than of target information. The various theories differ in what they mean by "context," although the most popular view is that what is important is the background context consisting of the time and place of occurrence of the target learning material. This view received perhaps its strongest support from a study by Huppert and Piercy (1976). They discovered that amnesics were comparable to controls in their ability to recognize which pictures had been presented before, but the amnesics were very poor at judging on which day each picture had been presented. The suggestion is that the amnesics possessed target information about the pictures but not contextual information about time of presentation.

Context theories seem of some value in understanding the nature of amnesia. However, the notion of "context" needs to be defined more precisely. In addition, it seems important to address more closely the issue of *why* it is that amnesics apparently process some kinds of information (i.e., target) adequately, while they are unable to do this with other kinds of information (i.e., contextual).

Probably the most generally satisfactory theoretical account of the amnesic syndrome was proposed by Cohen and Squire (1980) and extended by Cohen (1984). Their starting point was a distinction emphasized by the philosopher Ryle (1949). He argued that "knowing that" requires the conscious direction of attention to the act of remembering, whereas "knowing how" is demonstrated simply by the performance of a skilled action. In more contemporary terminology, the distinction urged by Ryle (1949) can be reformulated as one between declarative knowledge and procedural knowledge. According to Cohen (1984), declarative knowledge is represented "in a system quite compatible with the traditional memory metaphor of experimental psychology, in which information is said to be first processed or encoded, then stored in some explicitly accessible form for later use, and then ultimately retrieved upon demand" (p. 96). In contrast, procedural knowledge accrues because "experience serves to influence the organization of processes that *guide* performance without access to the knowledge that *underlies* the performance" (p. 96).

The hypothesis that amnesics have suffered damage to the declarative system, and thus have great difficulty in adding to their declarative knowledge, but that their procedural system is intact provides a convincing explanation of most of the findings. Amnesics are able to develop a range of cognitive and motor skills such as those involved in the pursuit-rotor task and the Tower of Hanoi puzzle because they depend upon the acquisition of new procedural knowledge. They are able to demonstrate various repetition-priming effects because they involve relatively temporary activation of relevant procedures. Episodic memory and semantic memory, despite their differences, both belong to the category of declarative knowledge. As we have already seen, amnesics find it extremely difficult postmorbidly to acquire and retrieve new episodic and semantic memories, and this is exactly as predicted by the hypothesis.

In spite of the general plausibility of the declarative-procedural theory of amnesia, it leaves some issues unanswered. For example, while it facilitates interpretation of the data to assume that there can be conscious awareness of declarative knowledge but not of procedural knowledge, it remains unclear whether this assumption can be defended successfully. Another difficulty is that it seems to be assumed implicitly that the acquisition of cognitive and motor skills depends solely on procedural learning. In fact, declarative knowledge is typically used in the early stages of skill acquisition (e.g., a novice golfer may have heard that the left elbow should not be bent during the swing, and attempts to use this declarative knowledge to improve his or her swing). The same is almost certainly true of the initial learning on a complex problem such as the Tower of Hanoi.

If this characterization of skill acquisition is accurate, then it becomes a little problematical to explain how it is that amnesics show normal learning rates with many skills. On the assumption that their declarative learning abilities are damaged, the initial stages of skill acquisition should be retarded, and so the overall rate of learning should be significantly below that of normals.

Despite the remaining uncertainties, the recent history of amnesia research has been very much a success story. It used to be argued that the amnesic syndrome involved intact short-term memory but impaired long-term memory. This simple description made sense within the context of the multistore approach advocated by Atkinson and Shiffrin (1968) because it was assumed that long-term memory was unitary. The fact that long-term memory for some kinds of information is detrimentally affected, whereas that for other kinds of information is not, indicates that a more complex conceptualization of long-term memory is required. In essence, research into amnesia has revealed the importance of distinguishing between long-term memory for procedural knowledge and long-term memory for declarative knowledge. The minor role of that distinction in most theories of normal human learning and memory is obviously inappropriate in light of the evidence. Since the theoretical distinctions that are of importance in amnesia research differ markedly from those generally emphasized in conventional theories of learning and memory, it is likely that the neuropsychological approach will have a major influence on those theories in the future.

4. RETRIEVAL FROM LONG-TERM MEMORY

In order to assess what information the learner has acquired, it is necessary to make use of some form of retention test. Since the majority of the relevant research has investigated declarative learning, the most popular measures have been recall and recognition. There has over the years been a fair amount of controversy (see Eysenck, 1984, for details) as to whether or not recall and recognition involve the same processes. According to two-process theory (e.g., Anderson & Bower, 1972), different processes are involved in the two kinds of retention test. Recall involves a search or retrieval process, followed by a decision or recognition process operating on the information retrieved. In contrast, recognition is much simpler, making use of only the second of these two processes.

Two-process theory has been rejected, in part because it provides a greatly oversimplified view of recognition memory. It has been replaced by Tulving's (1979, 1983) theoretical approach. He has consistently argued that there are fundamental similarities between recall and recognition. This led him to propose the encoding specificity principle, which he claimed applies equally to recall and to recognition: "The probability of successful retrieval of the target item is a monotonically increasing function of informational overlap between the information present at retrieval and the information stored in memory." (p. 408).

Virtually all of the attempts to test the encoding specificity principle have made use of at least two encoding conditions and at least two retrieval conditions. In several cases, a crossover interaction has been obtained; i.e., one encoding condition leads to better memory performance than the other encoding condition in one retrieval condition, but the opposite happens in the other retrieval condition. This provides general support for the encoding specificity principle because it indicates beyond peradventure that memory performance depends on both memory-trace information and retrieval-environment information.

More precise tests of the encoding specificity principle require systematic manipulation of the "informational overlap" between the memory trace and the retrieval environment. Since Tulving (1979) assumed that contextual information is usually incorporated into the memory trace, the conventional procedure involves manipulating contextual information. High "informational overlap" is produced by ensuring that the context at study and at test is the same or highly similar, whereas low "informational overlap" is created by making the two contexts dissimilar. Most of the relevant literature supports the encoding specificity principle. This approach has even been extended to produce situations in which recall is superior to recognition memory (e.g., Tulving & Thomson, 1973). This counterintuitive finding is produced by maximizing recall by making the study and test contexts the same and reducing recognition by making the two contexts as dissimilar as possible.

Tulving (1983) had recently incorporated some of his earlier theoretical notions into a General Abstract Processing System. The essential idea behind the encoding specificity principle is retained, but it is now argued that the amount of informational overlap is not the only determinant of memory performance. Greater informational overlap is needed for recall than for recognition because recall necessitates the naming of some previous event, whereas recognition memory can be achieved simply on the basis of familiarity.

How useful is Tulving's (1983) theoretical analysis of retrieval? On the positive side, it is certainly correct that contextual information is usually contained in the memory trace, and Tulving's emphasis on "informational overlap" has achieved the valuable goal of focusing attention on the precise relationship between the information stored in long-term memory and the information available at the time of retrieval. As a consequence, it is now generally conceded that memory performance depends just as much on retrieval environment information as on stored information, whereas previously the overwhelming emphasis had been on the information in the memory trace.

On the negative side, Tulving's (1983) theoretical contribution is more paradigm-specific than is usually thought to be the case. The crucial problem can be seen if we consider the General Abstract Processing System in more detail. At the time of learning, according to the theory, the original event or to-be-learned stimulus is subject to an encoding process, and this encoding process is affected by the cognitive environment before an engram or memory trace is formed. This engram subsequently affects the process dealing with informational overlap. In contrast to this complexity, the retrieval stimulus or cue is processed in a very straightforward way. The retrieval cue (which is regarded as an "observable") enters directly into the process dealing with informational overlap.

The assumption that certain stimuli (called "original events") are processed in various complex ways, whereas other stimuli (called "retrieval cues") are minimally processed, seems rather dubious. Of course, the theory can be expected to be reasonably successful if the task is such that only very modest processing of the retrieval cue is required. This was probably the case with the main paradigm used by Tulving, in which pairs of words were presented as in paired-associate learning, with one member of each pair then being employed as a retrieval cue for the other member of the pair. However, the processing of the retrieval cue is likely to vary from one situation to another. As Reitman (1970) argued:

> To what extent can we lump together what goes on when you try to recall: (1) your name; (2) how you kick a football; and (3) the present location of your car keys? If we use introspective evidence as a guide, the first seems an immediate automatic response. The second may require constructive internal replay prior to our being able to produce a verbal description. The third . . . quite likely involves complex operational responses under the control of some general strategy system. Is any unitary search process, with a single set of characteristics and input-output relations, likely to cover all these cases? (p. 485)

Tulving's (1983) theory does not seem equipped to handle this variety of ways in which the process of retrieval can proceed, and he has explicitly excluded procedural knowledge, such as that involved in kicking a football, from the ambit of his theory. If we limit ourselves to declarative knowledge, consider a retrieval cue such as "What did you do last Wednesday evening?" According to the theory, this observable retrieval cue enters directly into the process dealing with informational overlap. In actuality, it is highly likely that the retrieval cue would set in motion a sequence of structured problem-solving activities that would ultimately produce the appropriate answer.

What is needed is a specification of the different retrieval strategies, together with an understanding of the circumstances in which each strategy is used. An interesting start in this direction was made by Jones (1982). Subjects were presented with a list of apparently unrelated cue-target pairs (e.g., regal–BEER), followed by cued recall (e.g., regal–?). Some of the subjects were told after learning but before recall that reversing the letters of the cue words would produce a new word that was meaningfully related to the target word (e.g., *regal* produces *lager*, which is closely related to BEER). Those subjects who were informed of this characteristic of the recall cues recalled more than twice as much as uninformed subjects. According to Jones (1982), a recall cue may lead to recall by producing immediate access to the target information (the direct route), or it may lead to recall via the making of inferences and the generation of possible responses (the indirect route). The uninformed subjects were restricted almost entirely to the direct route, whereas the informed subjects were able to make use of the direct and the indirect routes.

Jones (1987) had previously offered a distinction between two recall routes closely resembling the distinction between direct and indirect recall. He argued that recall could be based on intrinsic knowledge, which is information that is explicitly provided for retention (e.g., the cue in cued recall). Alternatively, recall can occur on the basis of extrinsic knowledge, which is additional information that can facilitate the recall process (e.g., realizing that *regal* backwards spells *lager*). In his theorizing, Tulving (1983) has emphasized the use of intrinsic knowledge at the expense of extrinsic knowledge.

It may well be the case that recognition memory can also occur in at least two different ways. According to Mandler (1980), recognition sometimes occurs simply on the basis of stimulus familiarity. If the level of stimulus familiarity is high, then the subject decides rapidly that he or she recognizes the stimulus. If stimulus familiarity is low, then it is clear that there is no recognition memory for the stimulus. However, if the level of stimulus familiarity is intermediate, then familiarity alone does not provide sufficient evidence to make a definite recognition decision. Under those circumstances, recognition involves identification based on a retrieval process. This retrieval process utilizes the organization of long-term memory to recover relevant contextual information about the stimulus (e.g., the contexts in which it has usually been encountered).

Mandler's (1980) hypothesis is intuitively appealing since we frequently convince ourselves that someone seen in an unfamiliar setting is known to us by remembering the setting (e.g., office, tennis club, restaurant) in which that person has previously been seen. There is some empirical support for this theory (e.g., Mandler & Boeck, 1974), and it appears that familiarity decays more quickly than does the organizational information involved in the retrieval process (Mandler, Pearlstone, & Koopmans, 1969). However, the theory is difficult to test empirically because the familiarity and retrieval processes are not specified in a precise fashion. In addition, while Mandler (1980) claimed that the familiarity and retrieval processes operate in parallel, the evidence is equally consistent with the alternative assumption that they operate seriatim, with the retrieval process occurring only after the inconclusive termination of the familiarity process.

In sum, the notion that there is a single process responsible for recall, or that a single process is involved in recognition memory, must be abandoned. The processes intervening between the presentation of a retrieval cue and successful recall or recognition depend on a variety of factors, such as the nature of the retrieval cue, the relevant knowledge possessed by the subject, and so on. Global theories such as that of Tulving (1983) have contributed greatly to our understanding of the phenomena of retrieval, but have de-emphasized the variegated strategies that are made use of in retrieval situations.

5. CONCEPT LEARNING

Bourne (1966) proposed that a concept exists "whenever two or more distinguishable objects or events have been grouped or classified together, and set apart from other objects on the basis of some common feature or property characteristic of each." There has been a constant interest in the ways in which concepts are acquired throughout the history of experimental psychology, but a major turning point was the work of Bruner, Goodnow, and Austin (1956). Their basic procedure involved presenting rectangular cards that varied in terms of four dimensions (the number of borders around the edges of the card, the number of objects in the middle of the card, the shape of the objects, and the color of the objects). They typically used conjunctive concepts, in which positive instances of the concept all had two or more specified features presented together (e.g., three red squares). The most interesting data were obtained form the selection paradigm, in which the subject selected one card at a time from a large array, with the experimenter indicating in each case whether it was a positive or a negative instance. The subject's task was to use this information to arrive at the concept.

The great advantage of the selection paradigm over previous experimental approaches to concept learning was that it provided much richer information about the thinking of the subject during the performance of the task. In particular, the pattern of selections and the hypotheses offered during the task often enabled the problem-solving strategies used by the subject to be identified. According to Bruner et al. (1956), only a rather small number of strategies was used with any frequency. Conservative focusing was an efficient strategy. It involved focusing on the first positive instance, and then selecting as the next card one that differed from it in only one attribute. If this second card was a negative instance, then the attribute that had been varied must have formed part of the concept. If, on the other hand, the second card was a positive instance, then the attribute varied must have been irrelevant to the concept. A similar strategy, but one carrying greater risk, was focus gambling. This strategy involved changing two or more of the attributes of the first positive instance when selecting the next card. Successive scanning was a rather different kind of strategy. The subject started with a specific hypothesis and then attempted to test the hypothesis by selecting cards that would produce relevant information.

Focusing tended to be a more successful strategy than scanning. There are various differences between these two types of strategy, but one of particular importance is in terms of what Bruner et al. (1956) referred to as "cognitive strain." Scanning tends to involve greater cognitive strain than focusing because it places greater demands on memory.

Despite the historical importance of the work carried out by Bruner et al. (1956), it suffers from various limitations. For example, they often asserted that a subject had made use of a particular strategy in spite of the fact that some of his or her selections did not accord with those that would have followed from consistent use of the strategy. More seriously, it may be very misleading to extrapolate from their findings to everyday life, where concepts are typically not well defined in terms of a small number of attributes or features. Since focusing permits only the gradual elimination of attribute dimensions, it would often be a very inefficient strategy in real life. Scanning was relatively inefficient when applied to the task of Bruner et al. (1956). However, the time pressures of everyday life may mean that action on the basis of the best available hypothesis is required, and this is what the scanning strategy provides.

The approach adopted by Bruner et al. (1956) is limited in another way. As Brooks (1978) pointed out, it is possible to distinguish between analytic and nonanalytic strategies of concept learning. Analytic strategies involve the abstraction of attributes, rules, or prototypes; the strategies involve the abstraction of attributes, rules, or prototypes; the strategies investigated by Bruner et al. (1956) are of this type. In contrast, nonanalytic strategies involve making use of a particular positive instance of a concept or category. Subsequent stimuli are regarded as members or nonmembers of that category on the basis of their overall similarity to the original positive instance.

What determines whether analytic or nonanalytic strategies of concept learning are used? Analytic strategies tend to be used when the positive instances of a category have one or more noticeable attributes in common (e.g., the red breast of a robin). They are also used when the rules defining membership in the category are salient. It is interesting to note that the Bruner et al. (1956) studies exhibited these characteristics, and their subjects primarily made use of analytic strategies. In contrast, nonanalytic strategies are used when someone is just starting to learn a new category (e.g., young children who call all adult males "Daddy"). Nonanalytic strategies also tend to be used when the relevant attributes of a concept are not obvious. While the distinction between analytic and nonanalytic strategies is a valuable one, it is often the case that concept learning involves a mixture of the two kinds of strategy. This is partially due to the fact that the knowledge obtained from one type of strategy can provide information that facilitates use of the other type of strategy.

If laboratory studies of concept learning are to be of direct relevance to ordinary concept learning, then it is clearly necessary for the concepts studied in the laboratory to resemble those of everyday life in their major characteristics. In fat, there are good grounds for supposing that the two sorts of concepts are not really comparable. For example, Bruner et al. (1956) used concepts that were arbitrary, that consisted of certain features, that were well defined, and whose positive instances were all equivalently "good" members of the category or concept. In contrast, as Mervis and Rosch (1981) have argued, most natural concepts are very different. They tend to be "fuzzy" rather than well defined, and different members of a category usually do not possess exactly the same features. In addition, some members of each category are usually "better" or more typical members than others (e.g., "robin" is a "better" member than "ostrich" of the "bird" category).

According to Mervis and Rosch (1981), concepts are represented as prototypes. A prototype best represents the total set of stimulus objects belonging to a category; it possesses most of the attributes that are characteristic of most of the category members, and fewest of the attributes belonging to nonmembers of the category. The reason some members of a category are rated as more typical than others is that they are more similar to the prototype of that category.

Evidence for the psychological reality of prototypes was obtained by Franks and Bransford (1971). They presented their subjects with visual stimuli that incorporated transformations of a prototype, but the prototype itself was not shown. On a subsequent recognition test, the more similar the test stimulus was to the prototype, the higher was the confidence rating it received. The most striking finding was that the subjects were most confident of having seen the prototype, despite the fact that it had not actually been presented.

A penetrating critique of prototype theory was offered by Osherson and Smith (1981). They distinguished between the core of a concept and its identification procedure. Whereas the core deals with the relationship of a concept to other concepts and to thoughts, the identification procedure specifies the information we make use of when required to make a rapid decision about the category to which a concept belongs. The crucial limitation of prototype theory is that it tells us about the superficial aspects of concepts relevant to their identification procedures, but tends to ignore the essential core elements.

In sum, it remains unclear whether concepts are more adequately described by prototypes or by attributes and rules. It may well be that some concepts are better described in one way, and other concepts in the other way. However, it is clear that a number of different processes are involved in concept learning. Current attempts to devise computer programs to model concept learning may founder on the sheer variety of strategies used. Different people attain concepts in different ways, and any given individual may shift his or her strategy during a concept learningtask (Dominowski, 1974). In other words, the search for an adequate general theory of concept learning may be doomed.

6. CONCLUSIONS

Recent research and theorizing on human learning and memory differ substantially from earlier approaches, most notably in terms of the questions that are addressed. The multistore and levels-of-processing theories basically addressed the question "How does learning occur?" Multistore theorists argued that rehearsal in the short-term store was crucial, whereas levels-of-processing theorists favored encoding processes of various kinds, but they dealt with similar issues. These theoretical approaches failed to consider seriously other questions, such as "What are the different forms of learning?" or "How is stored information retrieved from long-term memory?" These questions have been addressed in recent times, and answers are starting to be provided. Learning can be procedural or declarative, and declarative learning can be specific and detailed (e.g., in propositional form) or general and coherently structured (e.g., schemata). Retrieval usually follows the dictates of the encoding specificity principle, but more detailed accounts of the various retrieval strategies that are used are becoming available.

The theoretical limitations of previous theories are due in large measure to paradigm specificity. The learning of lists of unrelated words requires the acquisition of declarative knowledge, but scarcely involves either procedural learning or schemata. In similar fashion, the use of a single paradigm makes it extremely difficult to discover the great variety of retrieval processes that can be used. Research into concept learning was initially hampered by the reliance on a few laboratory paradigms lacking ecological validity, but a wider range of concept-learning tasks is now being utilized. The contemporary emphasis on exploring new issues in new paradigms offers real hope of expanding our knowledge of the human learner.

7. REFERENCES

Anderson, J. R., & Bower, G. H. (1972). Recognition and retrieval processes in free recall. *Psychological Review, 79,* 97–123.

Anderson, R. C., & Pichert, J. W. (1978). Recall of previously unrecallable information following a shift in perspective. *Journal of Verbal Learning and Verbal Behavior, 17,* 1–12.

Atkinson, R. C., & Shiffrin, R. M. (1968). Human memory: A proposed system and its control processes. In K. W. Spence & J. T. Spence (Eds.), *The psychology of learning and motivation* (Vol. 2). London: Academic Press.

Atkinson, R. C., & Shiffrin, R. M. (1971). The control of short-term memory. *Scientific American, 225,* 82–90.

Baddeley, A. D. (1984). Neuropsychological evidence and the semantic/episodic distinction. *Behavioral and Brain Sciences, 7,* 238–239.

Baddeley, A. D., & Hitch, G. (1974). Working memory. In G. H. Bower (Ed.), *The psychology of learning and motivation* (Vol. 8). London: Academic Press.

Bartlett, F. C. (1932). *Remembering: A study in experimental and social psychology.* Cambridge: Cambridge University Press.

Bourne, L. E. (1966). *Human conceptual behavior.* Boston: Allyn and Bacon.

Bower, G. H., Black, J. B., & Turner, T. J. (1979). Scripts in memory for text. *Cognitive Psychology, 11,* 177–220.

Bransford, J. D. (1979). *Human cognition: Learning, understanding and remembering.* Belmont, CA: Wadsworth.

Bransford, J. D., Barclay, J. R., & Franks, J. J. (1972). Sentence memory: A constructive vs. interpretive approach. *Cognitive Psychology, 3,* 193–209.

Brewer, W. F., & Treyens, J. C. (1981). Role of schemata in memory for places. *Cognitive Psychology, 13,* 207–230.

Broadbent, D. E. (1958). *Perception and communication.* Oxford: Pergamon.

Brooks, D. N., & Baddeley, A. D. (1976). What can amnesic patients learn? *Neuropsychologia, 14,* 111–122.

Brooks, L. R. (1978). Nonanalytic concept formation and memory for instances. In E. Rosch & B. B. Lloyd (Eds.), *Cognition and categorization.* Hillsdale, NJ: Erlbaum.

Bruner, J. S., Goodnow, J. J., & Austin, G. A. (1956). *A study of thinking.* New York: Wiley.

Cohen, N. J. (1981). Neuropsychological evidence for a distinction between procedural and declarative knowledge in human memory and amnesia. *Dissertation Abstracts International, 41,* 4733B.

Cohen, N. J. (1984). Preserved learning capacity in amnesia: Evidence for multiple memory systems. In L. R. Squire & N. Butters (Eds.), *Neuropsychology of memory.* New York: Guilford Press.

Cohen, N. J., & Squire, L. R. (1980). Preserved learning and retention of pattern analyzing skill in amnesia: Dissociation of knowing how and knowing that. *Science, 210,* 207–210.

Corkin, S. (1969). Acquisition of motor skill after bilateral medial temporal-lobe excision. *Neuropsychologia, 6,* 225–265.

Craik, F. I. M., & Lockhart, R. S. (1972). Levels of processing: A framework for memory research. *Journal of Verbal Learning and Verbal Behavior, 11,* 671–684.

Dominowski, R. L. (1974). How do people discover concepts? In R. L. Solso (Ed.), *Theories in cognitive psychology.* Hillsdale, NJ: Erlbaum.

Eysenck, M. W. (1979). Depth, elaboration, and distinctiveness. In L. S. Cermak & F. I. M. Craik (Eds.), *Levels of processing in human memory.* Hillsdale, NJ: Erlbaum.

Eysenck, M. W. (1984). *A handbook of cognitive psychology.* London: Erlbaum.

Eysenck, M. W. (1986). Working memory. In G. Cohen, M. W. Eysenck, & M. E. Levoi (Eds.), *Memory: A cognitive approach.* Milton Keynes: Open University Press.

Franks, J. J., & Bransford, J. D. (1971). Abstraction of visual patterns. *Journal of Experimental Psychology, 90,* 65–74.

Friedman, A. (1979). Framing pictures: The role of knowledge in automatized encoding and memory for gist. *Journal of Experimental Psychology: General, 108,* 316–355.

Gabrieli, J. D. E., Cohen, N. J., & Corkin, S. (1983). The acquisition of lexical and semantic knowledge in amnesia. *Society for Neuroscience Abstracts, 9,* 238.

Gauld, A., & Stephenson, G. M. (1967). Some experiments relating to Bartlett's theory of remembering. *British Journal of Psychology, 58,* 39–49.

Graesser, A. C., Woll, S. B., Kowalski, D. J., & Smith, D. A. (1980). Memory for typical and atypical actions in scripted activities. *Journal of Experimental Psychology: Human Learning and Memory, 6,* 503–515.

Graf, P., Squire, L. R., & Mandler, G. (1984). The information that amnesic patients do not forget. *Journal of Experimental Psychology: Learning, Memory and Cognition, 10,* 164–178.

Huppert, F. A., & Piercy, M. (1976). Recognition memory in amnesic patients: Effect of temporal context and familiarity of material. *Cortex, 4,* 3–20.

Jacoby, L. L. (1984). Incidental vs. intentional retrieval: Remembering and awareness as separate issues. In L. R. Squire & N. Butters (Eds.), *Neuropsychology of memory.* New York: Guilford Press.

Jacoby, L. L., & Witherspoon, D. (1982). Remembering without awareness. *Canadian Journal of Psychology, 36,* 300–324.

Jones, G. V. (1978). Recognition failure and dual mechanisms in recall. *Psychology Review*, *85*, 464–469.

Jones, G. V. (1982). Tests of the dual-mechanism theory of recall. *Acta Psychologica, 50*, 61–72.

Keenan, J. M., MacWhinney, B., & Mayhew, D. (1977). Pragmatics in memory: A study of natural conversations. *Journal of Verbal Learning and Verbal Behavior, 16*, 549–560.

Mandler, G. (1980). Recognizing: The judgement of previous occurrence. *Psychological Review, 87*, 252–271.

Mandler, G., & Boeck, W. (1974). Retrieval processes in recognition. *Memory and Cognition, 2*, 613–615.

Mandler, G., Pearlstone, Z., & Koopmans, H. J. (1969). Effects of organization and semantic similarity on recall and recognition. *Journal of Verbal Learning and Verbal Behavior, 8*, 410–423.

Mayes, A., & Meudell, P. (1983). Amnesia. In A. Mayes (Ed.), *Memory in animals and humans*. Workingham, UK: Van Nostrand Reinhold.

Mayes, A. R., Meudell, P. R., & Pickering, A. (1985). Is organic amnesia caused by a selective deficit in remembering contextual information? *Cortex, 21*, 167–202.

Mervis, C. B., & Rosch, E. (1981). Categorization of natural objects. *Annual Review of Psychology, 32*, 89–115.

Meudell, P., & Mayes, A. (1981). The Clarapede phenomenon: A further example in amnesics, a demonstration of a similar effect in normal people with attenuated memory, and a reinterpretation. *Current Psychological Research, 1*, 75–88.

Minsky, M. (1975). A framework for representing knowledge. In P. H. Winston (Ed.), *The psychology of computer vision*. New York: McGraw-Hill.

Osherson, D. N., & Smith, E. E. (1981). On the adequacy of prototype theory as a theory of concepts. *Cognition, 9*, 35–58.

Parkin, A. J. (1982). Residual learning capability in organic amnesia. *Cortex, 18*, 417–440.

Parkin, A. J. (1984). Amnesic syndrome: A lesion-specific disorder? *Cortex, 20*, 479–508.

Reitman, W. (1970). What does it take to remember? In D. A. Norman (Ed.), *Models of human memory*. London: Academic Press.

Rumelhart, D. E. (1980). Schemata: The building blocks of cognition. In R. Spiro, B. Bruce, & W. Brewer (Eds.), *Theoretical issues in reading comprehension*. Hillsdale, NJ: Erlbaum.

Ryle, G. (1949). *The concept of mind*. London: Hutchinson, 1949.

Schank, R. C. (1976). The role of memory in language processing. In C. N. Cofer (Ed.), *The structure of human memory*. San Francisco: Freeman.

Smith, D. A., & Graesser, A. C. (1981). Memory for actions in scripted activities as a function of typicality, retention interval, and retrieval task. *Memory and Cognition, 9*, 550–559.

Tulving, E. (1972). Episodic and semantic memory. In E. Tulving & W. Donaldson (Eds.), *Organization of memory*. New York: Academic Press.

Rulving, E. (1979). Relation between encoding specificity and levels of processing. In L. S. Cermak & F. I. M. Craik (Eds.), *Levels of processing in human memory*. Hillsdale, NJ: Erlbaum.

Tulving, E. (1983). *Elements of episodic memory*. Oxford: Oxford University Press.

Tulving, E. (1984). Précis of *Elements of episodic memory*. *Behavioral and Brain Sciences, 7*, 223–238.

Tulving, E., & Thomson, D. M. (1973). Encoding specificity and retrieval processes in episodic memory. *Psychological Review, 80*, 353–373.

Zola-Morgan, S., Cohen, N. J. & Squire, L. R. (1983). Recall of remote episodic memory in amnesia. *Neuropsychologia, 21*, 487–500.

12

Problem Solving by Human–Machine Interaction

J. C. THOMAS

1. PROBLEM SOLVING FOR THE REAL WORLD

1.1. What Is Problem Solving?

Let us define first a problem state as a state in which some system has a goal but no preexisting procedure to reach that goal. We define problem solving as the process by which a system goes from a problem state to a nonproblem state. There are several important corollaries to this definition and several critical areas of vagueness. These will be discussed in turn.

First, note that what is a problem depends upon the system and what its goals are. For you, determining the answer to 5 + 5 is not a problem. For a 4-year-old, it may be. On the other hand, if you ask the 4-year-old to find the answer and the child does not care and does not try to find the answer, then the child is not in a problem state. You are. If you have a procedure guaranteed to make the child want to learn, then, again, you do not have a problem.

It should be clear, then, that what constitutes a "problem" is not a "thing" but a relationship involving the system (e.g., a person, a corporation, a computer program, a team), the state of perceived reality and the state of desired reality. In this sense, then, proving the

J. C. THOMAS • AI Laboratory, NYNEX Corporation, White Plains, New York 10604.

four-color theorem* never was "a problem"; it was a problem only for some people. (And, for some, who do not accept the validity of computer proof, it still is.)

This definition is not introduced to make things difficult, only to make them realistic. In the real world, what constitutes a problem really does depend dramatically on the system and upon the goal structure of that system. As we grow up in the classroom and are given problems to solve, it is easy to overlook this. In the classroom, the various students are at least roughly in the same state of preparedness. Further, the students are conditioned to accept as their own the puzzles put forth by the teacher. Those students who are not willing are largely prevented from further education!

It is also useful to distinguish various kinds of problem solving. In problem solving, there is some initial state, a desired goal or final state, and some possible methods, transformations, moves, or means of moving from the initial state to the final state. If the initial state, final state, and transformations are all well defined, we have something like theorem proving, chess puzzles, or Rubik's Cube. While these situations are fun and certainly can provide mechanisms of use in the real world, more typically, we encounter situations where the initial state, final state, and allowable transformations are not so well defined. Examples include designing a house, designing a computer system, designing a governmental system, writing a novel, building a relationship, and organizing your office files.

This difference is absolutely crucial if we are to understand the profits and pitfalls in human–computer problem solving. If we are not careful, we may design systems that help people in school situations solve toy problems (well-defined puzzles) and miss all the most critical aspects of designing a system to help people with real-world problem solving. This is particularly tempting because it is easier to build computer systems if we (1) ignore individual differences, (2) ignore motivational considerations, and (3) stick with well-defined problems. Please note: Such systems can be very useful in some cases and can teach us something about the broader issues in human–computer problem solving. Even more, such systems can help people under certain conditions solve certain subparts of real-world problems. Common examples include linear programming, statistical packages, and simulations. Using

---

*The theorem states that four colors are enough to color any planar map and avoid having a border of two countries in the same color. An object of speculation for centuries, it was finally proven with the aid of a computer.

such tools can greatly improve the overall productivity of human–computer problem solving.

For example, a part of building a computer system is to test and debug the software. Computer programs themselves can be effective tools to aid in this process. For the past few decades, we have seen better and faster problem-solving tools to aid in well-defined problems. While we still have things to discover about how to make such tools better, I will concentrate in this chapter not on what has already happened in the world of computing but on what could happen: How we could use the computer to help people with the *rest* of problem solving.

In producing software, for instance, the most costly, most difficult problems are not in debugging. They come much earlier, during design. They deal with where requirements come from, how feedback from the field gets back to the designers and programmers, how the documentation is written, how and when the human interface is designed and tested, how one piece of software integrates with others, and how to keep people on track and committed to doing their jobs in a high-quality way. These are *not* well-defined problems; they are real-world problems. I believe computer tools can now be built to help people address these aspects of problem solving.

1.2. The Importance of Problem Solving

Our brains evolved over a long period of time to deal with a physical world that changed relatively slowly. Today, the rate of change is much more rapid than during most of our evolutionary history. Not only is the physical world changing but the social and the informational worlds are changing very rapidly. At the same time, the nature of the problems that we must solve is in many ways different, and certainly more complex, than many of the ones we had to solve during our evolution. The impact of all this is that if we are going to survive the next century, we are going to have to become much more effective problem solvers. We cannot simply rely on the slow pace of evolution to get us better brains, nor can we rely on the faster but still expensive and relatively slow process of learning. We will have to use insightful problem solving in many areas of human endeavor to "get it right the first time." The potential impact of mistakes in the design of chemical plants, nuclear reactors, disarmament plans—indeed, even perhaps aerosol cans!—may be disastrous.

In addition to this overwhelming particular reason for improving human problem solving, there is a philosophical, almost religious reason. Problem solving, as opposed to biologically programmed behavior or noninsightful learning, is what most makes us human; problem solving is quintessential humanity. To the extent that we can creatively comprehend and change our world, we are fully human. Using technology to help us do this more effectively does not detract from this; indeed, building and using tools to help us think more effectively is also a very human thing to do.

From a more scientific standpoint, a theory of human behavior—that is, a science of psychology—must at least incorporate a good account of problem solving. We cannot be satisfied with theories of classical conditioning, operant conditioning, and aberrant behavior as a complete account of human behavior. To do so, even if such theories are augmented with hand-waving accounts of how problem solving is an "extension" of conditioning, ignores what is most characteristic about us.

I would go so far as to say that a comprehensive theory of human behavior should *start* from an account of problem solving and, from that more complex view, derive learning and performance as degenerate cases. In constructing such a science, it is useful to do laboratory experiments under controlled conditions, but only in the service of furthering our understanding of phenomena that are observed in real-world problem solving. In the work reviewed in this chapter, there is a mixture of fairly uncontrolled observations of people working on "real" problems that they really care about and more conventional experimental studies. But even the experimental studies derive primarily from a consideration of what happens in real situations.

1.3. How Can Computers Help People Solve Problems?

We have established what problem solving is and that it is extremely important and becoming more important because of the speed of change in the world. We can now consider the general question: How might computers help people in doing problem solving more effectively?

Computers can make human problem solving more effective both directly and indirectly. The use of computers as direct aids to problem solving forms the focus of this chapter. It should be remarked in passing, however, that computers can also aid in human problem solving indirectly. For example, we can provide people with tools such as expert systems that will enable them to avoid spending large amounts of time on routine situations that do not require complicated human problem solving. This allows more time for creative problem solving. Computers can also help the problem-solving process indirectly by doing extremely routine tasks that the human would otherwise have to be concerned with (such as numeric computation), by providing access to data bases, or by providing communications facilities.

In considering the direct use of computer support of problem solving, we must first understand which aspects of problem solving are difficult and then consider the capabilities of both the computer and the human being. The difficult aspects of problem solving vary; they are different in different stages of the problem-solving process. Thus, as a further explication of how computers can help people do real-world problem solving, we will consider some of the strengths and weaknesses of human problem solvers at various stages of the problem-solving process. After explicating these and suggesting some ways in which computers can aid in each of these stages, we will then discuss in some detail a few examples of real-world problems and how computers aided the problem-solving process. We then describe another real-world problem and explain in some detail how computer tools *could* be built to aid solving that and similar problems.

2. PROBLEM SOLVING RECONSIDERED FROM A HUMAN FACTORS PERSPECTIVE

2.1. THE IMPORTANCE OF THE TASK

Problem solving is, for the purposes of providing a good interface, best thought of not as a task but as a series of interrelated tasks, each having its own characteristics. First, there are different kinds of problem solving, as discussed in the initial section. Most problem solving in the real world is somewhat different from the puzzles and games or abstract mathematical formulations that play such a large part in academic exercises. There are tendrils of the problem that extend outward from the neat formalisms and formulations into messier domains. Unless one considers adequately the implications of these tendrils of interactions with the messier domains, one can easily find oneself with a technically correct solution that cannot be implemented in the real world. One of the chief advantages of expert systems technology, which has led to widespread interest within industry, is the recognition that much human time is spent on fairly routine problems that nevertheless have a heuristic and arbitrary quality to them, relying on an extensive domain of application-specific knowledge in order to arrive at a reasonable solution.

The problem-solving tasks may be designated in formal terms according to whether or not the starting state, the ending state, and the allowable transformations are well or ill defined. In point of fact, however, nearly every real-world problem-solving domain has a subportion of creative design within it. That is, there are always exceptions—places where existing procedures do not work to advance the goals of the individual or organization. The insight that expert systems afford us in its application to the real world is that by providing computers to help the human being solve the more routine, more well-defined aspects of the task, a greater latitude is allowed for creativity to be applied to the small percentage of remaining problems that require the invention of new techniques, methods, and procedures.

While recognizing that there are some parts of nearly every type of problem that require creative design, it is nonetheless useful to distinguish diagnosis problems, design problems, configuration problems, induction problems, deduction problems, and classification problems. Additional task considerations that are important in interface design are the time constraints within which the problem must be solved, and the degree to which the problem involves understanding of people. The other major variable that is of extreme importance is the stage of the problem-solving process.

2.2. The Importance of the User

Another fundamental, but often overlooked, truth of human factors is that one must consider the nature of the user in order to provide a reasonable and effective system. Often one attempts to meet this goal by applying a series of classificational criteria to individuals in order to categorize them in terms of variables like age, sex, socioeconomic status, "left-brained" versus "right-brained," or cognitive style. Typically, such classifications are not particularly useful. Crossover interactions between user types and system types on performance are rare.

To pick one example, studies on the psychology of aging done at Harvard Medical School (Fozard, Thomas, & Waugh, 1976; Thomas, Fozard, & Waugh, 1977; Thomas, Waugh, & Fozard, 1978) demonstrate that age differences unrelated to medical problems or educational background are weak predictors of performance on most tasks. Individual differences within an age group are much better predictors of performance on tastes involving memory, problem solving, decision making, and complex perception. Even stronger predictors of performance are the environmental conditions, the task structure, the interface, and the instructions. In some cases, age effects are greater under conditions where the task is very complex, the instructions very ambiguous or poor, and the interface is not particularly well suited for the task. Age effects increase with complexity. However, there are very few documented cases of true crossover interactions between age and these variables. In other words, if you provide good human factors for old people, you will probably be providing good human factors for younger people as well.

As pointed out by Whiteside (S. Whiteside, ACM SIGCHI, Boston, April 1986), what one needs to consider to deal adequately with individual differences are the particular users of a particular application. It is not important to use demographic generic classification variables but rather to understand what it is about the users that is particularly relevant to designing the interface at hand. To take one obvious example, if one knows that the users of a particular system do not currently know touch-typing, then if the task requires a considerable amount of data entry, one needs to consider seriously the trade-offs among voice input, selection via touch screen or mouse, and the price of training people in touch-typing. In contrast to this way of looking at individual differences, as Whiteside pointed out, making general classificatory statements about people and attempting to design the interface on that basis without a careful analysis of the particular task can be worse than useless. It can, in fact, be counterproductive and detrimental to the individual.

An example of this phenomenon arises when people make the wrong attributions about IQ scores. On the one hand, people who find out that they have an exceptionally high IQ may come to believe that they need not work hard but should be rewarded merely on the basis of that potential, and to believe that IQ score, since it supposedly reflects general intelligence, perforce demonstrates that they are capable in every field. Conversely, people who receive feedback that they have a low IQ may feel as though hard work is pointless because they are limited by their capacity. Unfortunately, the school system and other social structures all too often reinforce this counterproductive set of attributional attitudes toward ability and work.

2.3. The Importance of the Interface

There are many sources of evidence within experimental and cognitive psychology and human factors that illustrate the importance of the interface and representations. The work in our laboratory on design problem solving further illustrates the importance of representation and extends these findings to the area of more ill-defined problems. For example, Carroll, Thomas, and Malhortra (1980) and Carroll, Thomas, Miller, and Friedman (1980) compared the ability of subjects to solve design problems depending upon whether the design was presented as a spatial or a temporal design problem. Subjects in the spatial condition spontaneously used a checkerboard-type layout as a representation for the problem and did much better on all performance measures. In the temporal case, subjects were far less consistent in their choice of representations. Their performance was worse. This performance difference between the spatial and temporal isomorphs was greatly reduce when subjects in the temporal condition were given a representation to work with that was appropriate to the problem.

Work by Thomas, Lyon, and Miller (1977) on problem-solving aids also illustrates the high correlation between representation and whether or not a solution was reached. This is also amply illustrated in verbal protocols collected by Paige and Simon (1966) on algebra word problems. The human factors literature provides numerous other examples of how tasks can be greatly changed in terms of their performance parameters by changes in representation, interface, or training sequence (e.g., Carroll, 1984).

2.4. RECOMMENDATIONS FOR HUMAN–COMPUTER PROBLEM SOLVING

There are some recommendations for human–computer problem solving that are independent of the particular stage of problem solving. In fact, there are important human factors considerations involving such things as hardware, furniture, menu structure, command language syntax, motivation, how to introduce systems into an organization, and how to develop a system. These considerations apply to *every* system—a problem-solving system is no exception. The interested reader is referred to some general works in the area (Schneiderman, 1986; Thomas & Schneider, 1984; Wickens, 1984). The focus of the recommendations in this chapter deal specifically with problem solving. It is felt that the tools to aid problem solving depend very much on the stage and type of problem solving that one is engaged in. Since the latter variable is highly related to the importance and difficulty of the various stages, I will discuss tools only from the perspective of stages.

3. STAGES OF THE PROBLEM-SOLVING PROCESS

Many writers about problem solving have set forth stage theories of problem solving (Stein, 1974). For present purposes it is not necessary to believe that there is anything magical or necessary about the particular steps in the problem-solving process that I will outline here. The stages given are based informally on a reading of the literature, my own experimental evidence, my experience in teaching courses in problem solving in a number of settings, and my experiences as a participant and observer in real-world problem solving in the computer science field over several decades. The purpose of the stages, however, is not to provide the framework for a scientific theory of problem solving but to focus the interface designer's attention on the real differences in requirements that can occur throughout the problem-solving process. It should also be clear that what follows is a normative rather than a descriptive model of problem solving. In particular, I believe that problem finding, problem formulation, and looking back later at the problem-solving process are extremely useful but seldom utilized. We will first describe the stages briefly and then revisit each in greater detail.

The first stage of problem solving is problem finding. Children seem to seek out problems spontaneously. Adults, by contrast, typically do not willingly engage in this type of behavior. This is illustrated by the language that many people use regarding problem solving in such expressions as "I've got enough problems" or "You've got a real problem."

Until a problem is found, however, it cannot be solved. Solving a problem means that we have found a way of achieving a set of goals. Yet often because of the initial discomfort caused by even *recognizing* a goal that is not currently met, people often prefer not to see problems that actually exist. Every time a person is angry or frustrated, somewhere there is a goal that is not being met. Somewhere there is the potential for a problem-solving process to be invoked. Somewhere, in fact, there is often the opportunity for a discovery, an invention, or a marketing opportunity. Much of the progress of Western civilization and the economic growth in the world can be traced to people first finding and then solving problems that were not quite seen by other people. Nevertheless, little research has been done on how people find problems.

The second stage of the problem-solving process as defined here is problem formulation. How does one define a problem? This often has a critical impact on the quality of solutions. Yet, all too often, people adopt a particular formulation by convention or out of habit and do not explicitly consider alternative formulations. There are several somewhat distinct aspects to the problem formulation process. These aspects are interrelated and no temporal sequence is necessarily implied.

One aspect is goal setting. How does one decide exactly what the goal is? A second is goal elaboration. This can be thought of as trying to clarify the goal or provide detail. Goal elaboration also involves some consideration of what, for the purposes of this particular problem, will be considered the context within which the problem-solving process is to take place. During the problem formulation stage, one also considers the consistency of various goals, the trade-offs, and the priorities. As in *problem finding*, little systematic research has actually gone into how people choose, elaborate, and cross-check their goals. Yet behavior is very largely determined by goals. Apart from deciding on goals, there are also decisions, all too often implicit, about the general approach that will be taken to solve this problem. As mentioned previously, a particular representation may be adopted for solving a problem merely because it is familiar or conventional; similarly, problem-solving strategies, such as a particular allocation of tasks to people and machines, may often be reflexively assumed.

Once the problem has been formulated, the next step is *idea generation*. Ample research illustrates that more creative ideas and more productive ultimate solutions can be generated if the evaluation of ideas is separated in time from the generation of ideas (Stein, 1974). Because of the associational structure of human thinking, it is almost guaranteed that the first few suggestions that someone makes in response to a problem will be solutions that have already been implemented or tried. It is further almost guaranteed that any truly new approach will initially have flaws. The typical response to a new idea is to point out the obvious flaws in the idea and all the reasons it will not work. This is a fairly trivial cognitive task for most of us. Much harder is to try to build creatively on a nascent idea in order to forge a more viable solution.

Eventually, ideas will need to be evaluated. After some preliminary evaluation of various ideas, one needs to more systematically match up the properties of an elaborated idea with the goals specified during problem formulation. One also needs to consider the implications of the idea for the environment. Typically, there are many constraints in the environment that have not been explicitly stated in terms of goals that the solution must address. One must therefore try to visualize the implementation of the idea in the environment. These aspects constitute *idea evaluation*.

Often, subparts of problems are worked on separately and the results must now be combined in the *integration stage*. The integrated solution must then be accepted or modified. Often this process of acceptance involves some type of formal testing or evaluation. At this point, the solution must be implemented; that is, the solution must be put in place, fielded, commercialized, or otherwise find a home in the real world. We label this the *implementation stage*. Finally, and often overlooked, one would ideally evaluate both the outcome (i.e., the product, the solution) and the problem-solving *process* (i.e., how could one have done things differently; how could one solve such problems better in the future?). We call this *retrospective evaluation.*

Let us now consider these "stages" in more detail and, for each, consider how computer systems might help.

3.1. Problem Finding

The first stage in the problem-solving process, as I have defined it, is *problem finding*. One might at first wonder why anyone would want to find problems. However, finding problems is certainly a prerequisite to solving them. Not recognizing problems does not protect one from the negative consequences. Unfound—that is, unnoticed—problems can produce even more disastrous results than found problems. As pointed out earlier, one person's problem is another person's product. While the solution of some problems requires advanced interdisciplinary teams to work over a period of several years to develop a complex technological solution, there are other problems that are solved with fairly simple ideas once the problem is recognized as such. It is now believed, for example, that written language may well have originated when merchants who traded across long distances wanted to verify orders. They hit upon the idea of putting small models of the things that they were trading inside a vase that would be broken open when delivery was made, and this invoice, in effect, could be compared against the goods delivered. Later, they simply stamped the outlines of the models onto a clay tablet. There could obviously be no "solution" requiring a written language until a problem existed for which written language would be useful. Similarly, several tribes of Indians used wheels and sticks in games but did not use them for more efficient transportation, presumably because this was not seen as a problem.

There are several very simpleminded methods that I can suggest for having a computer system that would help us find problems for potential solution. The first such idea is simply a reminder for people that when they are angry, or frustrated, to try to define the conditions giving rise to this and then seriously consider the possibility that there might be some invention that would solve the problem. The second notion is a quasi-random list of words that people look at which is supposed to remind them of a series of specific concrete problems that people run into as well as some more generic problems. The way in which this tool is to be used is to take a process, object, or system and hold it clearly in mind while perusing the various items on the list. For example, a person might be trying to think of improvements for an automobile. Keeping the particular automobile in mind, the person would then look through a list of items that would include both generic and specific concrete annoyances and frustrations that often come up. Some of these might be relevant to the design of an automobile—for example, barked shins, fogged vision, snagged panty hose, or no bathroom. Other specific items might not be related to the problem at hand. Similarly, generic items like "too heavy," "too fast," "too slow," "too expensive," "too ugly," or "too dangerous" might or might not be applicable to the particular problem at hand. The notion here is that it takes very little time to look through this list, and it is used as an aid to generate ideas for potential problems to work on.

An additional source of problem generation based on human–machine interaction is the diagnostic expert system. Although the primary purpose of the diagnostic expert system is to determine what is wrong with a particular piece of equipment, or to find breakdowns in communication, summarizations of diagnostic information could provide the stimulus to a new round of problem-solving design activity.

Naturally, there are numerous uses of computer-based tools that give pictorial or statistical summaries of operations. The purpose of such summaries is to alert people of "problems" or difficulties. While extremely useful, such tools are different in spirit from what has been proposed in this section. These alerting summaries are geared toward difficulties that have been identified *a priori* by human analysts. Such computer tools are not helping people to see problems for the first time.

3.2. Problem Formulation

The next stage of the problem-solving process outlined here is *problem formulation*. It is at this stage that people often go astray. People generally assume that they know what the real problem is and begin solving it. Peter Drucker (1966), for example, stresses that the most important thing is not so much making a decision as making the *right* decision—that is, deciding what it is that you need to make a decision about. There are some "problems" that will go away by themselves, or it may be the case that any possible solution will be too costly and/or painful to implement for the possible benefit gained. Similarly, people may try to address symptoms rather than the underlying problem.

The importance of formulating the problem correctly can be illustrated by the story of a New York City skyscraper where the people who had to use the building were continually complaining that the elevators were moving too slowly. Computer consultants and operations research teams were brought in to change the algorithm by which the elevators went from floor to floor. After months of study and attempts by several different teams, the net result was that the number of complaints had increased. At this point, with people threatening to move out, a structural engineering team was brought in to determine the cost of adding more elevators to the existing building. Plans were drawn up and people were about to launch into an extremely expensive reconstruction plan. Before this took place, however, mirrors were added in the lobbies near the elevators. The complaints stopped. The problem was solved. In this case, the problem was not that the elevators were actually moving too slowly; the problem was that people were complaining and threatening to move out. Once they had something more interesting to do while waiting for the elevators, the complaints stopped. Presumably, the solution could have been found more quickly if the problem solvers had initially spent more time formulating the problem rather than presuming a particular formulation.

Another example of poor problem formulation that is found in a large number of organizations is the global characterization of people as good or bad, poor performers or good performers, ones or tens, or the use of other similar classification systems. In order to simplify the data that one has to work with, it is a natural human tendency to attempt to put things into discrete classes rather than maintain more complex multidimensional spaces. However, if we categorize Joe as a poor performer, we may totally miss the fact that Joe is excellent at giving presentations. Presuming for a moment that Joe is excellent at giving presentations but poor in most other aspects of his job, the problem that we may wish to address is to find a procedure for improving performance in his current job. Alternatively, we may find a job within the organization where his excellent presentation skills can be maximally utilized to the mutual benefit of the individual and the organization. If, however, we stick with the more global characterization of Joe as a poor performer, we will probably formulate the problem as being one of how to terminate Joe with the least amount of friction.

Another widespread example of this general type comes from the field of computer–human interaction itself. All too often, the role assumed by the human factors group in an organization is to evaluate several alternative designs for the interface between people and the machine. Instead, a more fundamental look at the goals of the system might result in creating a different overall system design. In fact, in some cases no machine is necessary at all. What is needed may be better training, selection, or communication among the human beings now doing the job.

Another example comes from the arena of software design. A multiple regression study by Walston and Felix (1977) points out that a major problem with software development is the communication between the software designers and the people who want the product. A related point, that the importance of various goals influences the performance of programmers is made by Weinberg and Schulman (1974). Enormous expense and difficulty is incurred because clients change their minds about what it is that they really want. One way to formulate this problem is to find ways of ensuring that the client specifies completely and is legally bound by that initial specification. Studies on the psychology of design problem solving (Thomas & Carroll, 1979) indicate that attempting to do this will result in the development of software that still fails to meet the client's needs. Although it may be true that formulating the problem in this way will result in cheaper software development in the short run, it will almost certainly *not* result in satisfying the customer. Alternatively, one can accept that software development will involve evolution and redefinition. Then one may formulate the problem as being how to support this evolutionary development.

The point of all these examples is that proper formulation is extremely important. While there is no way to guarantee that solvers will hit on the best formulation, we can hypothesize some tools to increase the odds of doing so. A set of computer-based reminders could help encourage the problem solver to (1) imagine what the problem is from other people's viewpoints, (2) think about problems that may be "behind" the current problem, (3) try out various "scopings" of the problem from narrow to broad, (4) apply abstract labels like "attribute," "action," "good," "bad" to various pieces of the problem and then deliberately scramble these, (5) ask for a generic classification of the problem type (e.g., "diagnosis of equipment") and then suggest alternatives (e.g., "design of personnel selection system"). Each of these would have a small chance of providing a better formulation, but each would at least expand the problem solver's thinking. The main value would be in showing the solver that there are alternative formulations.

3.3. IDEA GENERATION

Our natural tendency, when confronted with a new idea, perhaps exacerbated by formal schooling, is to immediately find the flaws in the idea. Yet considerable research has now been amassed to demonstrate that separating the *idea generation* phase of problem solving from the *idea evaluation* stage can produce superior results (Stein, 1974). The computer can aid the process of idea generation in at least two distinct ways. First, if the overall control of the problem-solving process is linked to computer software, the software can *implicitly suggest* the separation of idea generation and idea evaluation. Second, fairly simpleminded computer software can help simulate certain aspects of synectics and brainstorming sessions. Studies in our laboratory indicated that subjects who were given a quasi-random list of words to look at produced more creative solutions on several problems than those who spent this same time directly working on the problem (Thomas, Lyon, & Miller, 1977). In many cases, it appeared that idea generation could be aided by access to a large database of visual, auditory, and semantic representations. If one were attempting, for example, to decorate a living room, it would be of fairly obvious benefit to be able to quickly scan through many, many examples of potentially relevant elements. In the not too distant future, we could imagine expert systems that would prioritize such items either according to a predefined preference that matched our particular profile or in terms of some optimality of covering the space of possibilities. Depending upon the degree of creativity that was required in a particular domain, we might also want to bring in metaphors from other domains. If one were interested in designing an extremely unusual interior, for instance, then one might want to consider not just examples of other interior designs but a much wider array of picture elements, or even musical arrangements.

If we expand our horizon beyond thinking of the individual user interacting with a computer to groups of individuals communicating partly via computer, more possibilities arise for using the computer to enhance the generation of ideas. For example, via computer networks, a wide variety of people from various backgrounds and cultures can be polled for potential ideas. The pool of ideas so generated will tend to be larger than that generated by a more centralized geographical group because the more centralized group will tend on the average to be more similar in background and culture. One can further imagine an expert system moderator who would bring people into the conversation on the basis of their unique potential contributions. Large screens combined with voice technologies and wide-band communications allow for the possibility of alternative means of coordinating the idea generation processes of many individuals. Projects to explore such technologies are under way at several research institutions (e.g., Xerox Park, MIT).

So far, we have been considering how the computer can support people in the production of new ideas. It is also possible, of course, using expert systems technology, to have the computer generate potential ideas. In fact, even "dumb" algorithms can be built to generate "ideas." Simpleminded programs using random number generators to pick out elements in an array that are appropriate to the syntax of sentences, for instance, have been used to construct science fiction story plots. While such stories themselves are lacking in substance, they could be used to trigger the thoughts of a human. In similar fashion, a whole series of quasi-random modifications on a basic plan could be generated for human perusal. This could be combined with an expert system to guide such variations to meet certain standards.

3.4. IDEA EVALUATION

Once ideas that would be relevant to solving a problem or a subproblem are generated, the computer could aid in the idea evaluation stage. One way of doing this is to use simulations. Even in cases where it is currently impossible for the computer to produce solutions to problems or designs, it is possible to apply an evaluation function to ideas generated by humans or by human–computer interaction. In many cases, these evaluations will be only part of the criteria that would be used in an overall weighting. For example, a stress and structural analysis of a bridge design might provide useful data about the mechanical engineering aspects of the design but would not be able to give an aesthetic judgment about the bridge. In addition to conventional simulations based on mathematical functions, today's technology allows evaluations of ideas based on expert systems.

Not only can the computer be used to give critical evaluations of a design, the computer can also be used to advantage as a communications medium. In areas where the evaluation of ideas has a subjective element, it is often useful to get inputs from many different people. Computer networks can be used to advantage for implementing the Delphi technique. In this technique, experts are polled for their opinions independently. These can be collected electronically and the data (in terms of evaluations or prioritizations) can be easily summarized by the computer and displayed in either tabular or graphic form. This summary information is then fed back to the individual participants and they are asked to give another judgment after seeing the judgments of other experts. In one variant, experts with opinions that are moderately to extremely discrepant from the group average are invited to give rationales.

In this idea evaluation phase, it is useful to have people involved from many different areas that might be affected by the final choice of approach. For example, if a computer program to accomplish a particular job within an application is evaluated by a panel of database and software experts along with experts from the application domain, they may reach a consensus fairly quickly about what the best approach might be. However, it may later turn out that this approach to the solution is inadequate from, say, an ergonomic perspective. It would have been far cheaper to have included ergonomic expertise at this preliminary idea evaluation phase. This general principle might be called "coverance."

The principle of coverance states that every "critical" aspect of the design should be considered early in evaluation. The cost of employing the principle of coverance is that it will take somewhat longer to reach an initial consensus. The advantage, however, is that one is more likely to obtain a solution that is feasible from every angle. One famous example of not following this principle is the story of a large building in Manhattan that was designed as an apartment building and for which no closet space was provided. In fact, in this particular case, no one noticed the problem until the building was finished, at which point the architect committed suicide by jumping off the building. A similar point is made by Drucker (1966) in his book on decision making. He cites the example of Harry Truman as someone who would bring in all the various federal agencies that would be required to implement a decision and ask them to think through the implications for their agency.

3.5. SOLUTION MATCH WITH GOAL

Showing the impact of tentative design decisions on desired utility functions is the major purpose and advantage of traditional simulations, linear programming systems, and spreadsheets. The limited treatment such systems are given here does not imply that they are unimportant. However, such human–computer problem solving systems abound. While they are extremely useful, as a consideration of the problem-solving process reveals, they address only a small part of the overall process and, worse, are often used *as though* they offered *accurate* and *complete* solutions merely because they offer *quantitative* solutions. (See Winograd & Flores, 1986, for further discussion of this issue.) Basically, one needs to have human beings responsible for these decisions and treat computer programs as tools—not as judges.

Problem solving according to the normative model presented in this chapter is a lengthy process containing many steps people are not used to taking. It is very tempting, and sometimes even appropriate, to short-circuit much of this process. One would not want to preface every use of Visi-Calc with a philosophical discussion of how best to measure success. I see little evidence, however, that people have a natural tendency to overquestion their fundamental assumptions. What seems common is the unthinking use of quantitative models year after year. These models typically address only a few aspects of the goal structure. The consequences of ignoring the harder-to-quantify goals can be stupendous. Companies and even whole industries (railroads, steel, automobile, oil) can "look good" for quite a while and "suddenly" they are in trouble when the mismatch between reality and goal becomes evident in quantitative measures. The view taken here is that by the time difficulties show up in the "bottom line," it may be too late to take effective action. Evaluation based on a broader range of criteria could demonstrate difficulties much earlier. One manner in which computer tools could help people make broader, more qualitative judgments about how the solution matches the goal would be a dialogue that forced the user's attention successively on various aspects of the goal. Expert systems technology could also be applied here to allow more qualitative assessments.

3.6. Solution Match with Environment

In our studies of design dialogues (Thomas & Carroll, 1979), we found two logically distinct ways in which people evaluated solutions and subsolutions. The first way was to compare the suggested solution with the criterion or criteria that had been defined. In other words, was the goal met? In addition, however, it is invariably the case that some prerequisites or requirements are not explicitly stated as goals; rather, they are a part of the context and background and, as such, are assumed on the part of people stating explicit goals and criteria. Since ideas may be generated by people not totally familiar with all aspects of that context and environment, even ideas that meet the formally stated criteria may still be inadequate or too costly, or may violate some unstated constraint. Therefore, in addition to evaluating the idea against the stated criteria, it is also necessary to try to visualize the suggested solution in the actual environment. Only in this way can one make a truly adequate preliminary judgment and evaluation.

One particularly important example of the impact of unstated goals is the design and implementation of user interfaces for computer systems. Rapid prototyping is highly desirable, largely for the reasons described in the paragraph above. Only by having real users interact with the interface can designers determine the adequacy of a proposed solution. By having people see a first prototype and attempt to interact with it, numerous faults at various levels will be found. For instance, there will invariably be terms which the designers implicitly assume will be well known to the users but which in fact they will not understand. Similarly, ambiguities in syntactic and logical structure of messages and documentation may not be apparent until offered to real users. At still higher levels, concepts presumed to be in the minds of end users may, in fact, not be present. Perhaps the most common and most serious failing in this regard is when designers have such a deeply embedded presumption about the goals of the system and the relationships of those goals to system-defined functions that no explanation is provided as to why the system is useful or how to incorporate it into the user's more general work flow. The "why" is obvious to the person who designs the system and works on it for several years. But it can be far from obvious to the user.

A simpler example of a solution's failing to match environmental criteria that we are all familiar with is the difficulty of providing verbal instructions for someone driving to a particular location. A person who is intimately familiar with a particular route and who has taken that route on numerous occasions will provide instructions that seem on the surface to meet all the criteria for being consistent and providing all the necessary information. In the actual context of real life, however, these instructions will almost invariably prove inadequate in several respects. For example, a traffic light that, because of the timing of the habitual driver, always appears green will frequently not be counted when the driver is giving instructions in which he or she counts the traffic lights. Similarly, if the driver is familiar with the name of a particular road, he or she may well not notice that the sign for this road cannot actually be read by the driver who is proceeding along a main highway. The sign that gives this information may actually be on an intersection a block down from the turn. Such discrepancies will typically be corrected only after the person who attempts to give these instructions gets feedback from someone attempting to follow them.

It is for this reason that design ideas that are evaluated against the formally stated criteria can sometimes fail to meet the real requirements. Tom Love, in his CHI tutorial in 1986, provided one particularly notorious example. A study done by the General Accounting Office in

1979 showed that a large proportion of the software that was paid for and delivered was never actually used. Another large proportion was used, but only after very extensive modifications were made. Here again, I believe the computer can help. By reminding evaluators of many concrete details of the environment in which something will be used, the computer (or videodisk) can help inform people about numerous previously unstated constraints. Here again also, the principle of coverance is important. Individuals with different backgrounds and with different roles and functions will tend to notice potential discrepancies between a proposed solution and their particular roles and functions.

3.7. IDEA INTEGRATION

One of the most difficult intellectual processes in many types of design is integrating ideas that each partially fulfill problem criteria or achieve some subgoal of a complex goal. An example problem that is simple enough to bring out this process in its essence is the following:

> There is a three-dimensional object with three orthogonal projections that are a circle, a square, and a triangle. In other words, if one were to shine a flashlight in back of the object and look at the shadow on a screen, from one angle that shadow would appear to be a square. If one turned the object in a different orientation, what appeared on the screen would be a triangle. If one turned the object yet again, what appeared on the screen would be a circle. The problem is this: What is the three-dimensional shape of the object?

Now here it is quite obvious what the three subgoals are. It is also quite easy to imagine a wide variety of shapes that will fulfill one or even two of the criteria simultaneously. How might the computer be used to help the person find the integration of these subsolutions into an overall solution? Depending on the structure of the problem domain, it should be noted that the solution that fulfills all the criteria of a particular problem may contain conceivably as few as zero elements of a solution to any subset of the criteria. Our intuitions about the domain of physical three-dimensional space, however, lead us to believe that there will be a great deal of similarity between the solution that fulfills all three of the criteria stated in this problem and the subsolutions that fulfill two of the criteria simultaneously. Certainly, one simple aid that might prove effective in increasing the probability that a person would be able to solve a problem of this type would be to have a graphics system that would simultaneously show the three subsolutions. In this case, the circle–square constraints would be satisfied by a cylinder, the circle–triangle pair of constraints would be satisfied by a cone, and the triangle–square constraints would be satisfied by a wedge. Viewing these three shapes in three-dimensional projection on the screen simultaneously might make the problem solver's task easier than if it were necessary to mentally visualize these subsolutions. Could the computer be used to do more than this, however? I believe that it could.

Suppose that the computer could parse the three-dimensional objects into the points, lines, and planes that made it up. Now suppose that a similarity match is done among the subsolutions. Further, imagine that the computer now begins putting together partial subsolutions in such a way as to maximize the similarity of corresponding parts. In effect, the computer finds the circle as a common element between the cone and the cylinder and identifies and puts together the bottom circle of the cylinder and the bottom circle of the cone. If it continues to match similarities in this manner while simultaneously checking back to make sure that the projections still meet the three constraints, we could imagine a system that might automatically integrate the three subsolutions. (The solution is difficult to describe in words. It is approximately like the bottom inch of a full tube of toothpaste or a short, fat chisel point.)

Consider now database retrieval mechanism. A researcher, lawyer, or doctor is interested in retrieving documents that fulfill multiple constraints. The researcher could provide, perhaps, examples of articles that would fulfill some of these constraints. The computer could either query the user for these constraints or induce them by looking at similarities among the descriptors of the partially relevant articles. The criteria so generated could then be used as items in a conjunctive search. The difficulty of this integration task depends to some extent on the complexity of the mapping between the constraint space and the solution space. In the case of finding articles with certain descriptors, the relationship is fairly straightforward and the task fairly easy. In the case of the spatial reasoning puzzle, the task is slightly more difficult. In some domains where there may be strong interactions among elements, the integration task becomes still more difficult. It might be interesting to speculate, for example, how one might use a computer to help write jokes or help solve Rubik's Cube.

3.8. ACCEPTANCE OR MODIFICATION

On the basis of how well subsolutions can be integrated and on how well they match the problem goals and environment, we may accept the proposed solution or use the information about mismatches as additional input to earlier stages (e.g., problem formulation, idea generation, idea evaluation, idea integration). The major new tool I see as possible for this stage (*acceptance/modification*) is one that helps keep track of the various matches and mismatches over versions (retries) of the solution and forces the problem solver to some disciplined overall evaluation. The chief value of storing and displaying such information would be to enable the solver to see whether he or she is really converging toward a solution. This would help avoid a tendency that humans fall prey to, the "illusion of progress" (Thomas, 1977). Basically, this illusion arises when we are focused on the mismatch we are currently working on and overrate its relative importance. A tool that would keep asking us to rate the solution on *all* important dimensions could help avoid this problem. There is the possibility, of course, that we change our evaluation function as we learn more, and the tool should be flexible enough to accommodate such changes but keep us aware of them.

3.9. Planning for Implementation

Just because a workable (in principle), elegant solution to a design problem has been found does not, of course, mean that the problem is solved in reality. In order for the proposed solution to become a reality, a very specific plan with measurable goals and objectives and deadlines should be put in place. This is not to say that plans should preclude flexibility or that goals that are important but not quantifiable should be ignored. However, other things being equal, to the extent that goals are clearly defined and measurable, they will tend to become a reality. In attempting to implement a solution, it will be necessary to have the cooperation of many people. There may be some sales involved in this activity. This sales activity will be much easier if the people whose cooperation must be enlisted have been involved in the design process from the beginning. Apart from the purely intellectual advantages of the principle of coverance cited earlier, having all relevant functions represented in the problem solving process will make it much easier to implement the solution. PERT charts, Gantt charts, and variants can be useful computer-based tools in this *planning for implementation* process.

3.10. Measuring the Outcome

No matter how carefully thought out a design solution is, there are bound to be places for improvement once it is put into the real world. To err is human, but to learn from mistakes is our evolutionary responsibility. It is extremely important for long-term learning within an organization that a measurement process be put in place that is as honest as possible in terms of providing feedback on the product of the problem-solving process. An overall computer system to help control a project can go beyond the scheduling of activities, to the statement and refinement of goals and to guidance of the evaluation process. In cases where quantification of results is difficult, the computer can again be used as a mediator for the Delphi technique as one means of reaching a consensus about the value of a project.

3.11. Evaluating the Process

While it is important to evaluate the outcome of a design process, it is also important to examine the process that was used. One may look back over the process and find ways in which it could have been improved even if the overall outcome was favorable. For example, at the beginning of a project, it might be valuable to bring in four or five consultants with different viewpoints. After the project is over, one will be in a much better position to look back at the advice that those consultants gave and determine in retrospect which particular consultants really added to the process, or even whether consulting as a whole was valuable. Similarly, a variety of analyses of data may have been tried at various points. One may now look back with the wisdom of hindsight and see which of these analyses was in fact useful. One can further try to relate what it was about this particular problem that made certain analyses useful or useless. Of course, it is quite typical to look back at the people who were involved in a project and try to assess the value of their contributions. It might well be possible, however, to go beyond this simple person evaluation process. Ideally, one should be able to relate the skills and other characteristics of the person as they relate to the characteristics of the problem. It may be that a person who turned out not to have made much of a contribution to this project might be suited to other projects. Conversely, someone who was particularly valuable on this project may have been valuable primarily because of special skills and aptitudes that may not be relevant to the next project. In this entire process, it is vitally important that people try to avoid the simpleminded attitude of blaming and crediting. Rather, what is needed is an honest, nondefensive evaluation of the product and process. If we treat evaluations as learning experiences, they will be quite valuable in making us more productive in the future.

We have examined each stage of the problem-solving process and suggested ways the computer might help in each of these stages. We can also imagine putting the suggested aids into an overarching "problem-solving manager" that would orchestrate the problem solver's progression through the stages. This problem-solving manager would also provide for data communication among the stages—probably based on a blackboard architecture. Such a system would also be designed to allow domain-specific versions that incorporated human expertise in various areas.

Let us now examine human–computer problem solving from another perspective: some specific examples of real-world problems. I will summarize each case and then examine how computer tools helped or might have helped.

4. HUMAN–COMPUTER PROBLEM SOLVING: CASES

4.1. Speech Synthesis as an Interface Problem

Speech synthesis (having a computer translate unlimited text into speech) provides an interesting example of several ways in which computer systems can be useful in problem solving. Speech synthesis provides a tool that can aid problem solving indirectly by providing access to information when it is otherwise difficult to get at. For example, people can understand spoken language who are unable to use written language. This includes a large number of people who have never learned to read, children who are too young to read, and people who are visually impaired. In addition, because of the ubiquity of the telephone, people may access information more readily when it is available by voice than when it is available only via a computer terminal. Speech synthesis also allows the play-out of verbal instructions when the eyes are otherwise engaged. Synthesis can thus be useful in situations where people are already using their eyes and hands.

In addition, it seems reasonable that people can process more total information when that information comes in over more channels, thus enabling them to use the nonreallocatable hardware within their own brains that is devoted to the processing of sensory-specific information. Therefore, when appropriately designed, information can be learned more readily when it is presented over both visual and auditory channels. Speech synthesis, therefore, is a useful adjunct to human problem solving and computer-aided instruction. Another potential, but largely unexplored, application is the use of speech synthesis as a motivational channel for people. In this regard it could be used to keep the person focused on a task and/or keep him or her motivated.

In addition to the ways in which speech synthesis can aid the human problem solver, we can consider the process of building an effective speech synthesis system to be an interesting example of design problem solving. From 1982 to 1984, the author was managing a project whose goals were to produce high-quality synthetic speech and transfer this technology to a product division.

Let us examine the different stages of the problem-solving process presented earlier. In terms of problem finding, a perusal of the literature and our own informal observations suggested that even when synthetic speech was perceived correctly enough to be transcribed by the listener in an accurate fashion, such speech placed heavy cognitive and/or perceptual demands on the listener. In addition, synthetic speech, even when intelligible, was not aesthetically pleasing. We felt that for the market and context that we would be interested in—namely, office principals using synthetic speech from remote locations and as an adjunct to their terminals under complicated situations—it would be important to have a system that met four criteria:

1. Speech as intelligible as human speech.
2. Speech that produced no additional cognitive load.
3. Speech embedded in a system with useful and usable functions.
4. Aesthetically pleasing speech.

In the context of this overall problem, there are a number of subproblems that are interesting in their own right. In some cases, the computer itself provided a useful tool to help in this problem-solving process. For example, one challenge in providing a high-quality speech synthesis system is to provide prosody (or intonation) that mimics human prosody. There are several ways that the computer can aid in this process. In order to mimic human prosody, we must first understand what human prosody is. The computer has proven to be a valuable tool for running experiments, collecting data, analysing data, and presenting data in this arena. Several commercially available pitch trackers are of interest to anyone attempting to do research into providing a system with adequate prosody. In our case, both a PC-based version and a VM-based version of pitch tracker were used.

At another level, solving the problem of adequate speech synthesis involves the translation of orthography into phonetic symbols. These are popularly known as letter-to-sound rules. While this is a necessary step for every language, the English language provides a special challenge in this regard. While every computer-based text-to-speech system utilizes some form of rules on the computer, we also found it useful to use the computer as a tool for the analysis of these rules. In the past, letter-to-sound rules were created by linguists, more or less by trial and error. This process was time-consuming and did not guarantee any convergence. Typically, the linguist would try out a set of rules, find some exceptions that were not well handled, and try to change the rule set again. Instead, we used programs to analyze the on-line dictionary in order to extract the regularities of English letter-to-sound rules. The computer was found to be useful in the areas of the letter-to-sound arena as well.

Another difficulty with most existing synthesizers is the handling of proper names. Preliminary results in our laboratory with commercially available synthesizers indicated that, on the average, only about 50% of the proper names were pronounced with what a human being would consider a feasible pronunciation. We therefore began using a computer program to analyze regularities as a function of etymology and to determine distinguishing features of etymology based on letter digraph, trigraph, and other more global characteristics of the word in question. In this way, a preliminary analysis of a name could be obtained and from this analysis a guess made as to the etymology. Once the etymology was guessed at, a more reasonable hypothesis could be generated concerning the pronunciation of the name.

One of the advantages of our synthesis system was that we used a parser in conjunction with a large on-line dictionary to discriminate words in sentences such as: "Please *record* the *record*" and "*does* he see the *does* by the edge of the wood?" However, there are some remaining nonhomophonic homomorphs that are not distinguished by this technique. For example, the bow of a boat and the bow on a package are both nouns. In a full natural language understanding system, these discriminations would be made on the basis of semantic and pragmatic understanding of the full sentence. However, such a complete analysis is still some years away. We determined, however, that a first pass at disambiguating pronunciation of *bow* could be accomplished by a contextual analysis based on Markovian models.

In all the aforementioned cases, the use of a computer greatly aided us in solving the problem. Nevertheless, all of these cases basically involved using the computer to perform analyses that could be done more slowly by hand. We also used the computer to help us provide representations of speech for the purposes of developing the library of stored segments of control signals. The sound spectrogram invented in the 1930s has proven to be an extremely useful tool in the analysis of speech and the development of speech recognition, speech synthesis, and speech-coding algorithms. However, modern technology provides additional opportunity for alternative representations that can be made more task dependent. We explored in some detail the use of three alternative representations.

In the first of these representations, we use Chernoff faces (Chernoff, 1973) to describe or represent various aspects of the speech or the input parameters to the synthesizer. In a second and somewhat more fruitful line of investigation, we used a set of cylindrical coordinates to represent the phase relations among harmonics within voiced sounds. It is an oft-repeated, though false, "truism" to state that the ear is monaurally phase-insensitive. What does seem to be true is that people classify phonemes identically regardless of shifts in the phase of relative harmonics. However, this does not prove that the ear is monaurally phase-insensitive, any more than the fact that we see the similarity among red, green, and blue triangles as evidence that the eye is color-insensitive. One problem with trying to analyze any possible regularities in phase relations with an ordinary Fast Fourier Transform is that the phase components in speech appear as a random jumble. If, however, one limits analysis to those sounds that have a harmonic structure—i.e., the voiced sounds—and then preprocesses the speech in terms of taking a pitch track to determine the fundamental frequency, a clearer picture emerges. This picture can be further clarified by plotting the speech in cylindrical coordinates. A much more natural representation for phase relations results. In the system devised, increasing frequency is indicated going away from the observer. The magnitude of harmonics is illustrated by the length of error vector. Finally, the phase angle is indicated by the angle around the central axis. When looked at in this way, similarities in human speech over time in the phase relations of lower harmonics are quite apparent. The next step in trying to make more natural speech based on these results is to try to ensure that the synthesizer also shows these same phase relationships. In addition, phase signatures, if further research bears out their consistency for a particular speaker, could be used to enhance the capability of speaker-dependent speech recognition. We found, for example, that N and M had quite different phase relations among their lower harmonics.

A final example of the ways computers could be used to help problem solving by providing alternative representations comes from the work of Pickover (1985) on "speech flakes." Sounds from a human voice and sounds from the synthesizer that appeared nearly identical on traditional speech spectrographs were nonetheless quite distinct and discriminable to the listener. For example, nasalized and denasalized vowels appeared very similar and difficult to classify accurately on the basis of the sonogram alone. Yet when these denasalized and nasalized vowels were shown in the speech spectrograph in the speech flake representation, the differences were quite obvious.

The basic idea of the speech flakes is to capitalize on the structure and redundancy of the feature detectors in the human visual system. The algorithms start with input in the form of the time wave form and take successive adjacent pairs of points, which we will call Point X and Point $X + 1$. Point X is used to fix the angle in polar coordinates of a point. The amplitude of point $X + 1$ is used to determine the length. Scaling factors are applied so that the angles of the resulting points all lie within a 30-degree arc and so that the points fall in a convenient part of a computer display. If one looks at such a plot, subtle differences are just as hard to detect. If, however, a mirror image is formed so that 60 degrees is subtended and the pattern repeated six times around a point, the resulting hexagonal snowflake pattern makes subtleties emerge in an obvious fashion.

4.2. The Computer as an Active Communications Medium

In the 1986 panel on computer–human interaction in the year 2000, presented at the Computer–Human Interaction Conference in Boston, one thing that all members agreed on was that we would see a continuing expansion of the use of computers as a communications medium. Within IBM, for example, the use of VNET is extremely important as a tool for coordinating the work of people across locations, divisions, and international boundaries. At MIT's Sloan School, Tom Malone is exploring the way computers might be used to support alternative methods of organization and decision making. At Xerox Park and at MCC, work is under way to facilitate groups of people working cooperatively on a project by the use of large displays that several people can influence and interact with simultaneously. Extensive research programs have been carried out at Bell Laboratories to understand various types of communications and the relative contributions of various media of communications. Clearly then, the computer has one role in problem solving as a medium of communication.

4.2.1. A Model of Communication

In cases mentioned above, however, the computer serves as a passive communications medium. Thomas (1980) suggested that the computer could also be usefully utilized as an active communications medium. In the active mode, computer programs themselves would be used to filter, enhance, or reformat information in order to improve the communication process among human beings. In some cases, additional semantic and pragmatic information could be added or deleted. To understand the rationale for such a proposal, we need to examine communication in some detail. This may seem to be a diversion. However, the author's view is that the main reason computers enable higher productivity in problem solving is their role as a new communications medium.

Many writers in both the popular and the scientific press presume an underlying model of communication that might be called the encoding/decoding model of communication. In this model, Person A has some idea or concept that is to be communicated. This idea must be encoded into some suitable format for transmission across some transmission medium. The encoded idea, according to this model, is then transmitted across the communications medium. At that point, Person B decodes the message into the internal representation appropriate to that person's internal thought processes. In this model, communication is "good" to the extent that there is an isomorphism between the idea originally present in Person A's head and the idea as it finally exists in Person B's head. As amply illustrated by Thomas (1978) and Winograd and Flores (1986), such a model of communication is inadequate for understanding human–human communication.

To fundamentally understand human communication, one must first realize the preeminence of the following concepts. Human communication exists for a purpose. People communicate in order to achieve goals. There are many types of goals that people may be trying to achieve by communicating. In some cases, people may be speaking to another person in order to clarify their own thoughts. In some cases, they are attempting to persuade the other person of something. Two or more people may also be involved in a joint exploration and problem-solving process. Even in the case where Person A is trying to inform Person B as clearly and directly as possible, it would be a very *poor* communicator who would not take into account the preexisting mental state of person B while determining what was to be said.

A more thorough model of communication might be called the design-interpretation model of communication. In this model, communication is best thought of as a design problem-solving process. Person A has a model of the world as it currently exists. Person A further has certain goals that are desired. The model of the world typically includes some presuppositions about what already exists in the head of Person B. Person A then *designs* a message giving the constraints of the goal that he or she is trying to reach, the presumed characteristics of the transmissions medium, the interpretation properties of Person B, and the current internal state presumed to be true of Person B. Once the message is transformed (not encoded) into a means suitable for transmission, and received at the boundary of Person B, Person B then interprets the message. This interpretation, in turn, will depend upon Person B's knowledge of the world, including a model of Person A's state of knowledge, goals, and internal model of Person B, as well as Person B's understanding of the transmission medium and Person B's goals. Even in the simplest cases, such a model is necessary to understand the fundamental aspects of human–human communication. The main quibble with the terms *design* and *interpretation* is that they may connote too self-conscious a process. In typical communication, all these factors are taken into account rapidly and smoothly.

Human–human communication has two further aspects that need to be addressed. First, it evolves in *interactive* situations. A whole set of problems arise when we attempt to communicate something *nonin*teractively (e.g., printed instructions, statistics textbooks, user interfaces). The computer medium must allow interactivety.

Last, when a human being says something, some *commitment* or *responsibility* accrues to that human being. When we read something in a computer manual, or use some software, who is responsible? The issue of responsibility is the most critical unaddressed issue in the use of computers. If the expertise of people who know about communication is used to make an active communications medium, the users should know who those people are.

4.2.2. Human Communication Difficulties

While human language (and other media, such as pictures) allows people to communicate in more effective and flexible ways than any other known species, very significant problems with human–human communication still exist. One of the problems with the sequential presentation of ideas using the spoken or written word is that language evolved for many thousands of years to allow communication in cases where both the designer and the interpreter of a message shared a common cultural framework. Indeed, in our complex, highly diversified society today, it is probably difficult for us to imagine the degree of cultural similarity shared by the members of a primitive tribe such as the ones where spoken communication occurred and evolved for countless generations. Language having evolved in such situations is very efficient for communicating about small differences within a generally accepted framework. However, language is not very effective at all for communicating about differences in general frameworks. Not only is language itself, by its linear nature, not very well suited to this type of communication, but the vast majority of people hold a set of beliefs about themselves and their world that makes changing general frameworks extremely difficult.

Most people believe that if they make a fundamental change in their belief structure and framework, it indicates there was something of less value about them. Further complicating the picture, most people hold a set of nonempirically based beliefs about communication itself. For example, people will say that they stated something clearly and therefore that any miscommunication must have been the fault of the other person. Or conversely, a listener may attempt to fix blame on the speaker by saying that the speaker was unclear. Once we realize that communication is an interactive process and involves both design and interpretation rather than reference to a predefined external standard, it becomes clear that any attempt to fix "blame" on one party or another is miscommunication is fruitless.

Another problem that often arises in cooperative human activity is a confusion about the hierarchy of goals. To illustrate this, let us take the example of two people playing tennis doubles. At one level, both the tennis partners may want to win the game. To both partners this may be more important than the particular strategy and tactics they adopt. Nevertheless, observation suggests that it is not uncommon for two tennis partners to get into an argument about the tactics to such an extent that it diminishes their chances of winning the game to a point far below what could reasonably be expected regardless of which tactics were employed. Similarly, all four tennis players, in typical situations, at least, are primarily playing in order to have fun. The goal of having fun is probably of higher importance than who wins. Yet many people will get so involved in trying to reach the lower-level and less-important goal of winning that they will destroy the chances for having fun. We can observe similar mechanisms at work when people work cooperatively on large-scale problem solving within organizations. The difficulty here seems to be that people have trouble keeping in mind the relative importance of various goals. If their attention is focused on meeting some lower-level goal, they may do almost everything in their power to meet this lower-level goal and, in so doing, defeat their own higher-level goals.

4.2.3. Computer as an Active Medium

A computer system that behaved as an active communications medium could help avoid this type of suboptimization by visually presenting to all the problem solvers and communicators the entire goal structure at all times. This is not, of course, a guarantee that people will keep in perspective the relative importance of various goals. We could imagine, though, that such a pictorial presentation of the entire goal structure would at least facilitate people's ability to keep the various levels of goals in proper perspective.

Another similar example concerns people working on problems that require an interdisciplinary solution. The reason for bringing in people of various backgrounds early in the problem-solving process is to bring to bear their various perspectives, viewpoints, and experiences on a complex problem. While this should result in a superior overall design solution, it also increases the probability of conflict during the initial stages of problem solving. It is precisely because these people have different backgrounds that they are unlikely to agree initially. In fact, even the same terms may connote or even denote different things to experts in different domains. The presuppositions, priorities, and methodologies of experts in different fields are also probably different. Conflict at this stage is not in and of itself bad; rather, it is from this dialectic that creative new ideas may spring. A difficulty arises, however, when people begin to take personally disagreements about perspectives and methods and therefore become emotionally upset.

While labeling the computer as an active communications medium may be new, the actual use of computers as an active medium is not. In fact, software is precisely this: It provides an active medium of communication between the software engineers and domain experts who built the software and the end users. The main difficulty with conventional software is that it has not been viewed as a communication process. Hence, the necessities for adequately providing for the *interactivity* and *responsibility* requirements of human communication have not been met. The use of iterative design, rapid phototyping, and involving end users early in the design process help address the interactivity aspects of communication. Society has still not evolved adequate ways of dealing with the responsibility issues in this domain.

5. A RETROSPECTIVE EXAMPLE

5.1. DESIGNING A STRATEGY FOR HUMAN FACTORS

We have tried to analyze problem solving; let us now try to synthesize. As a final example of human–computer problem solving, I would like to recount the experience of developing and implementing a strategy for human factors within the IBM Corporation. This particular example is illustrative of many real-world problems and in contradistinction to many problems found in school and laboratory. For example, the problem does not have clearly defined boundaries. Second, it was never "presented to me" as a "problem to be solved." Rather, awareness and activity level grew together over time. We will briefly set the scene for the reader, then we will examine how computers were in fact used, and finally, we will show how they could have been used.

Soon after I joined IBM in 1973, it became apparent that the future success of the company would depend on paying much greater attention to the quality of the human–computer interface. Nevertheless, formulating a strategy in this area was far beyond the scope of my research assignment in 1973. Furthermore, it is doubtful that formulating such a strategy at that time would have had any impact, even assuming that I had known enough about the corporation to formulate a reasonable strategy. Instead, my awareness of the problem and its magnitude grew slowly as a kind of background activity over the next few years. What my colleagues and I did during this time was conduct research aimed at trying to improve computer–human interaction. We also attempted to generate interest in universities in this area.

The only additional relevant activity we engaged in during the 1970s was to mention the magnitude of the problem in various internal meetings, forums, trip reports, and the like. These communications had an unknown effect. Nevertheless, for whatever reasons, by the late 1970s, several key IBM executives became aware of the seriousness of the problem. At about this time, an attempt was made to organize a scientific symposium within IBM on human–computer interaction. The papers submitted also lent further credence to the notion that some drastic changes were needed. A management conference was held at which product developers, executives and human factors engineers attempted to formulate the problem. At this time, external consultants, including Dick Pew and Alfonse Chapanis, also became heavily involved. A plan was formulated and carried to the top management committee of the company and approved. Several top IBM executives were charged with jointly making sure the plan was carried out.

In May of 1980, I went to work for one of these executives, the chief scientist, Lewis Branscomb. At around that time, I began to understand, implement, enhance, and reformulate the strategy for ergonomics. In terms of the stream of activity that I was engaged in over the next few years, there were a number of factors that make this rather typical of problem solving within corporations. It was problem solving in the sense that there were goals that I wanted to achieve, and I did not have any preexisting method of achieving those goals. However, unlike a puzzle problem, not only was the problem ill-defined at the boundaries, but clearly, a large part of the problem had to do with the interactions and interrelations with other people. In terms of tactical implementation, given my particular position as a staff person in the organization, rather than taking one or two critical or top priority items and attempting to push them through regardless of resistance, I found it more useful to subtly influence the activities of a large number of interacting parts simultaneously. In fact, some of the activities that I witnessed would lead me to believe that this would be an effective strategy for actually implementing change, even for top executives. In any case, this type of strategy seemed suited to both my personal style and the nature of the organizational problem.

The organizational problem could be characterized as a case of "organizational gridlock." The human factors professionals said that they would like to get involved earlier in the process but they didn't have enough head-count to meet their existing obligations to fix existing products. In addition, many experimental psychologists and even some human factors professionals were mainly experienced in pointing out what was wrong with existing products, not in being part of the initial design team. Product managers said they would pay more attention to human factors except that this was not part of the marketing requirements statement. Marketing said that ergonomics might be important but they couldn't quantify it. People in forecasting said that they would be willing to give a higher forecast for better human factors if the human factors people could make a good case for quantifying the increased sales due to having products that were easier to learn and easier to use. But the human factors people had no time to do it and were not involved early enough. And so it goes. Everyone seemed willing to change the way they were doing business provided that everyone else changed first. Attempting to move only one "top priority" part of this gridlock did not seem to be the optimal strategy.

5.2. The Actual Use of Computers in Solving This Problem

In attempting to produce the changes that I thought would be important for the corporation, it was necessary to employ organizational and interpersonal as well as technical skills. This is an oversimplified, personal, and greatly summarized view of what happened. The strategy was first presented publicly in 1982 and subsequently published in Thomas (1984). The results were outlined in Thomas (1985). What is interesting about the development and implementation of this strategy is that computers themselves played a very minor role in the problem-solving process (and I believe this is typical). In actuality, the computer was used in five ways. First, it was used as a word processor. Second, it was used as an information retrieval device. Third, at several points I used a quasi-random word list file to help stimulate the generation of ideas for possibilites. Fourth, and probably most uniquely important, it was used to communicate electronically to individuals throughout the corporation. The internal corporate network, VNET, allowed a much more efficient communication process than internal mail. Fifth, IBM's Audio Distribution System also proved useful in communicating.

What is interesting about these cases of actual use is that all of these essentially involved human–human communication. The computer was a fairly transparent medium of communication. In the case of the quasi-random word list, and, to some extent, the case of using the Audio Distribution System, the computer was useful as a tool for me to communicate with myself over time. The lack of use of a computer as a computational device during this problem-solving process was not because of the lack of facilities (at least in the traditional sense) or an absence of programming ability. At that time I had had approximately 15 years' experience as programmer in a variety of available languages. Perhaps it was my own lack of imagination, but I could simply not see a way in which using any existing application programs would help me generate or implement a strategy other than the ways listed above. There were a few simple computations involved in trying to show the dollar value of introducing human factors considerations earlier in the design process. These computations, however, were easily carried out with a hand-held calculator.

Consistent with the ideas of Winograd and Flores (1986), most of the real activity involved in the development and implementation of this strategy was determined by me "on the fly." That is, I was in the condition of "throwness." Only a small fraction of the time that I spent on this project was I able to sit back and think reflectively in anything like the problem-solving mode that is characteristic of the artificial situations in which we put people in the psychological laboratory. Much of the activity that I engaged in was of an opportunistic nature. That is, I had certain goals in mind, and a certain general approach, combined with relevant background in a number of areas. In addition to activities that were decided upon as being in the service of these goals, a large number of requests on my time were made, a large number of communications were directed to me that were initiated by other people, and I became aware of a large number of potentially relevant ongoing activities. A great deal of judgment was involved in selecting

from this array of information and activities, those for which interven-
tion on my part would prove relatively fruitful. Given the nature of
this problem solving process, which I believe to be fairly characteristic
of real problem solving in the real world, I see little available software
that would have aided me in the ongoing problem solving process. I
believe that such human–computer problem-solving systems, however, are possible. There are a number of tools which I believe would
have been technically feasible, and which I also believe could have aided
me in the process outlined above. These are described below in some
detail. Although I believe I could see my way clear to design such tools
as described, I am not making a claim that they would be financially
justifiable commercial products at this point.

5.3. The Potential for Human–Computer Problem Solving

Much of what I did was to communicate with other individuals.
Throughout the IBM company, a great deal of hard-copied or original
paper documentation flows. Much of this is logged in mail logs. In
addition, there is a great deal of communication by phone that could
potentially be logged. Finally, a great deal of communication takes place
over the internal VNET. If I could have had a view into the overall
flow of communication within the corporation at various levels in the
hierarchy, my task (as well as the tasks of thousands of other people)
could have been made much easier. I envision seeing an overall map
of the corporation from various views available on a large, high-reso-
lution color graphics terminal. I envision being able to zoom in on various portions of this and query for a variety of parameters using discrete word voice input in conjunction with a touch screen. In this way,
I could quickly find the critical information paths for changes that I
wanted to have brought about.

Similarly, there is a financial record of virtually everything that
takes place within a corporation at a fine-grained level of detail. It would
have been invaluable to have had access to the financial structure of
the corporation in an analogous fashion so that the financial impact of
various decisions about allocation of resources could have been documented and summarized. I envision the integration of such views of
the corporation with a document-processing capability so that summaries could be easily incorporated into documents of various forms.

A serious objection to such a system might be not so much its
technical feasibility or even its cost. A serious objection might be that
indeed it *would* enable the individual within a corporation to have tremendous power to effect change. If such power were misused, the

argument might run, individuals could greatly hamper the effectiveness of the corporation or even destroy it. Such an argument, if carried to the extreme, should also suggest that we forgo communicating by computer at all, or even using natural language! Indeed, it is true that social structures changed much more slowly before the invention of spoken, and later written, language. I believe, however, that in the near future, organizations that have these kinds of capabilities and secure the trust and cooperation of the people working within the organizations will be able to move on a competitive field so much more quickly and effectively that organizations who limit themselves to conventional means of intracompany communication will quickly find themselves extinct. This is not to deny that there are numerous and vital details of implementation for such systems that have to be worked out. Human nature is human nature. There must be thought given to how to prevent an individual from misusing this type of power to advance personal ends at the expense of the corporation. Nonetheless, given the proper implementation, such tools could empower the corporation by empowering the people with the corporation. Indeed, I would argue that such tools could actually help *clarify* shared goals and commitments.

In the process of developing and implementing a human factors strategy, a large amount of personal interaction was necessary. Different people have different goals, communication styles, and relevant backgrounds. It would have been extremely helpful to have had available, as another problem-solving tool, something to aid in these interactions. For instance, it would have been useful to have had an information file on various people that specified their personal goals, backgrounds, assignments, schedules, and preferred methods and styles of communication. Over time, such a file would be augmented with the history of our own interactions. Again, thought needs to be given about how to do this so *all* the people involved feel empowered and not exploited.

I also imagine that a variety of office tools would be useful indirectly by organizing the calendar and helping to keep track of project management. In fact, an on-line calendar facility was available to me and was used for several months during the management of a different project. After a few months, I stopped using this calendar facility. Basically, it was not worthwhile, given the degree of functionality, the lack of interconnection with other people's calendars, and the fact that many commitments were made or had to be referred to while the computer was not accessible. In addition, it was simply easier and more convenient to write appointments in a calendar book. This had the additional advantage that it was easier to see multiple heirarchical views of time with the traditional appointment book than with the computer calendar facility. In order for an on-line calendaring facility to be worthwhile, it should be available from nearly all places and at all times. It should also be possible to query other people's calendars and to use this calendar coordination to set up meetings. Further, the entry, access, and revision of calendar data needs to be made quite simple.

One would also hope that planning, project management, and documentation would be automatically integrated with such a facility. In other words, if there were a meeting scheduled in New York City for July 21, and this meeting was attended, an automatic default expense report should be generated for the principal so that only unusual expenses would need to be specifically entered. Similarly, knowledge in the system should be used to automatically generate tickler files. For example, if the principal were scheduled to give a talk on October 15, then at various intervals before this date, based on a model of the talk composition process, the principal should be reminded of the need to prepare the talk. Only when such facilities are available from virtually anywhere would the on-line calendar prove worthwhile as an actual tool to aid efficiency and thereby indirectly aid in the problem-solving process.

If a project planner and a calendar facility like the one described were connected to a knowledge-based system that knew about general planning schemes as well as a specific knowledge about the organization and the individual, then one could imagine that such a calendar could take a more active role in human–computer problem solving. For example, suppose that the principal had a number of commitments for work during the month of September. Now let us suppose that a phone call was received asking the principal for an additional commitment that would require a substantial amount of work during the month of September. While the principal was on the phone, the automated calendar/project manager would be called up, and as the principal began entering a target date in October into his calendar, the active project manager could, at that point, perhaps using speech synthesis, remind the principal that either some other commitment would have to be broken or it would be impossible to take on this additional responsibility without extensive delegation or detracting from the quality of committed activities.

In addition, one could imagine that the active calendar planner could also query the principal for the relationship between the activity under discussion and the long-range goals and strategies that had been decided upon. Note, however, that the scenario described plays into the notion mentioned earlier of "throwness." That is, most, if not all, of the true value of such a facility would be lost if it were merely something that could be used as an off-line planning tool. In real life, principals are continually engaged in conversation and the handling of paper work. A tool that would allow one to periodically update and reflect on one's activities would be far less valuable than one that would allow flexible and smooth integration into the ongoing stream of activities.

Another tool that might have been useful, and is more in line with what is traditionally thought of as human–computer problem solving, would have been an expert system to actually help formulate the human factors strategy. Such an expert system, however, would be far beyond the state of the art in expert systems in several important respects. First of all, such an expert system would have to have a base of commonsense knowledge. On top of that base, we would have to imagine a tremendous amount of knowledge about the planning process, how to implement change in organizations, what constitutes good human factors, and a vast amount of specific information about the state of the IBM Corporation. In addition, the effectiveness of a strategy would depend heavily upon interpersonal skills and characteristics of the people involved. The system would thus have to have a model of interactions among people and the specific characteristics of the person or persons attempting to implement the plan.

Of course, one could imagine that there would be some utility gained from a less ambitious project. For example, a more content-free version could nonetheless be useful in reminding the person developing and implementing any strategy of various general considerations. For instance, we could imagine that in any situation where one was attempting to influence a large organization, it is important to understand the goals and payoffs of the people that one is attempting to influence. One could imagine a sort of on-line help system based on Dale Carnegie's book, for example, or the writings of Peter Drucker. It seems clear, however, that such a facility would be far less useful than having internalized the principles by study and continued practice. A recognition of this fact implicitly underlies our insistence on practical supervised training for professionals such as clinical psychologists, surgeons, airline pilots, and executives. Even if all the relevant information were available instantaneously on line via effective computer searches, one would not desire to have one's surgeon perform an appendectomy using information available solely from this computer source. This is basically because additional learning is required to translate from the abstract verbalized knowledge that might exist in a book into operational practice and skill.

What might be ideal, then, for someone trying to develop and implement a strategy would be the ability to try out various strategies in simulation mode and see what the effects might be as a function of various hypothesized conditions in the organization and the external world. In such a scenario, the computer is used not so much to actually solve a problem as to help train the human being in the necessary skills for solving the problems. Simulation programs have been written to teach people the rudiments of flying, bridge building, and financial management. Few simulation programs exist at this point to train people in interpersonal skills.

The advent of interactive videodisks makes the possibility for teaching interpersonal skills via computer-based training more feasible. However, some technical difficulties remain. First of all, a live supervisor of clinical psychologists or salespeople can take into account the personal styles and skills of the individual students and alter the modeling and feedback process accordingly. There exists no way currently for the computer to have as input the actual raw behavior of the trainee in a meaningful fashion. Via wide-band networks, however, we can envision the trainee being videotaped and having this information transmitted to a remote site where a human observer skilled in giving feedback in interpersonal skills could react to the trainee's performance with a combination of free-form and preprogrammed materials. In addition to specific free-form comments, for example, the instructor could select segments of videotape or selection sequences from a videodisk to illustrate the particular changes in behavior that were requested. Such a system comes from the perspective of viewing a computer as a method of communication among individuals, and from this perspective it is perfectly reasonable to leverage the human teacher's ability to effectively monitor and guide a larger number of students.

The computer itself could also conceivably be used to help monitor the ongoing behavior of an individual according to parameters that were jointly set by a trainee and a trainer. For example, let's suppose that the trainer told the trainee not to use so much esoteric language. One could then imagine selecting parameters from a style-checking text editor in such a way that the student would be given immediate feedback while typing a report or set of projection materials for a talk. One could even imagine a speaker-trained speech-recognition device that would give feedback when too high a proportion of the speaker's words fell outside a predefined simple vocabulary of 5000 words. Apart from technical challenges, it would be vital that such systems were embedded in a social framework that continually reminded the "students" that simulations are not reality, that the computer is a *medium* of communication, and that the instructor and the student share social responsibility—that is, the computer has none.

An additional tool that would have proven useful in helping to formulate and implement a human factors strategy (and, moreover, whose usefulness would increase greatly over time) would be a system that would automatically track the progress achieved in meeting the goals. An ongoing record, viewable in graphical format, would be useful in an informational sense and also as a motivational aid. In addition, it would be nice to have such a system integrated with a text editor so that progress reports for management could easily be prepared.

Of further value would have been the ability to retrieve earlier relevant examples of attempted changes within the corporation from a corporate database. In this way, I could have reviewed a vast number of case histories of successful, partially successful, and unsuccessful attempts to change the way in which the corporation worked. Conceptually, one can fairly easily imagine how such a system might operate. The difficulty in building such a system is to implement it in such a way that the overhead of data entry on the part of the principal is not overwhelming.

One way to accomplish this is to make expressing specific goals and objectives to the system useful in a wide variety of applications. For example, an intelligent help system, mail screener, and calendar facility could all operate much better knowing the principal's goals and priorities. Periodic checks of progress against these goals and objectives would be a normal part of project management. Beneath the overview layer, it would be useful to have voice annotation of the specific details of projects. This would be useful because it would provide for easier data entry on the part of the principal and because voice annotation would give later reviewers of these case histories a better flavor for the emotional tone and interpersonal interactions that were important in the implementation of a particular strategy. Subjectively, it appears to me that being able to review 10 to 20 cases of previous attempts to implement strategies would prove invaluable in formulating a new strategy for introducing change within a corporation. Aside from review of these cases by a human being, one can also imagine that as the corporate database of such records grew, there would come a point at which a computer program would be able to draw some rather interesting inferences about which plans were likely to be successful or unsuccessful. Such a program could begin with traditional statistical

regression analysis, and be enhanced by a knowledge-based approach.
In both cases, of course, a human problem solver would be the responsible individual.

While the tool described in the preceding paragraph would be invaluable, again, a tremendous additional benefit would be gained if the
system were automatically apprised of the ongoing activity stream that
the principal was engaged in and could automatically generate cases
and parts of cases that were particularly relevant to this ongoing stream
of activity. For example, if I made a phone call whose purpose was to
meet a particular subgoal within an overall goal structure, it would be
useful if I could see a computer display during that telephone conversation. Such a display could have several expandable windows, each
showing a similar activity that had proven successful or unsuccessful
in the past. Ideally, one could even imagine that the machine itself
could induce skeletal plans for a conversation based upon an inductive
rule-learning procedure from a number of previous case histories of
similar phone calls.

6. SUMMARY AND CONCLUSIONS

Problem solving, by its very definition, implies that we are doing
something new. In the past, the main use of computers has been in
helping human beings do things that are routine. However, computers
have also been used to help people solve problems. This has largely
been in terms of enabling people to retrieve information or to make
lengthy computations quickly and accurately. More recently, computers have been used to simulate complex phenomena, including even
the reasoning process of experts within certain limited domains. In this
chapter, I have tried to show some of the additional ways in which
computers could be used to aid human problem solving. I have tried
to do this in several ways.

First, I stressed the importance of considering human factors in the
design of computer human systems to solve problems. What this means
is that human capabilities must be taken into account in designing such
systems. Second, I tried to break down the problem-solving process
into a number of stages. Heuristics allow us to focus on tools that are
appropriate to the various stages. No serious attempt is made to demonstrate empirically the validity of these stages; rather, thinking about
separate stages is merely a tool to help generate ideas about problem-
solving aids. After presenting some specific ideas for tools (e.g., to aid
in problem finding, problem formulation, and idea generation), I then

went through some specific cases and showed how various problem-solving aids either improved or could have improved the problem-solving process.

For the last 25 years, I have been intrigued with the question of whether a computer could have helped Albert Einstein develop his theory of relativity sooner. Or, to put it more boldly, how could a computer system have enabled an average physicist to have formulated this theory? To put the question in more operational terms, how could one design a computer program that would simply help people score higher on a standard (speeded) IQ test (apart from the obvious tricks of providing a calculator and a dictionary)? All three of these are probably beyond the state of the art at this time.

I believe, however, that with the advent of expert systems, interactive representations, and using the computer as an active communications medium we are on the threshold of being able to fundamentally enhance human problem-solving capabilities and to build a system meeting the tests above.

To enhance human problem solving is essential if we are to survive the coming centuries and continue to enjoy an increased standard of living. There are more and more people on earth wanting more and more things. Yet certain physical resources are diminishing. The rate of change and the complexity of problems that we face continue to increase while the human brain evolves very slowly, if at all. First the spoken word, and then the written word, greatly increased our ability to solve problems. The computer is most appropriately thought of as a third revolution in our ability to communicate with ourselves and with each other over time, space, and a variety of viewpoints. It is key to remember, as the computer becomes more important in human problem solving, that the knowledge and expertise that enable an increase in human problem-solving capability always comes from other human beings. If we have access to a computer system that magnifies our ability to solve problems, it is only because we are leveraging our own brain power with the expertise of engineers, computer scientists, human factor specialists, and computer programmers. It is these unseen colleagues that will soon enhance our ability to solve problems in new ways.

7. REFERENCES

Carroll, J. (1984). Minimalist training. *Datamation, 30*(18), 125–136.
Carroll, J., Thomas, J., & Malhotra, A. (1980). Presentation and representation in design problem solving. *British Journal of Psychology, 71*(1), 143–155.

Carroll, J., Thomas, J., Miller, L., & Friedman, H. (1980). Aspects of solution structure in design problem solving. *American Journal of Psychology, 93*(2), 269–284.

Chernoff, H. (1973). The use of faces to represent points in a K-dimensional space graphically. *Journal of the American Statistical Association, 68*, 361–368.

Drucker, P. F. (1966). *The effective executive.* New York: Harper & Row.

Fozard, J. L., Thomas, J. C., & Waugh, N. C. (1976). Effects of age and frequency of stimulus repetition on two-choice reaction time. *Journal of Veractology, 31*(5), 550–563.

Paige, J. M., & Simon, H. A. (1966). Cognitive processes in solving algebra word problems. In B. Kleinmuntz (Ed.), *Problem solving: Research, method, and theory.* New York: Wiley.

Pickover, C. A. (1985). On the use of computer generated symmetrized dot-patterns for the visual characterization of speech waveform and other sampled date. *IBM Research Report, RC-11110.*

Schneiderman, B. (1986). *Designing the user interface.* Reading, MA: Addison-Wesley.

Stein, M. (1974). *Stimulating creativity.* New York: Academic Press.

Thomas, J. C. (1977). Cognitive psychology from the viewpoint of wilderness survival. *IBM Research Report, RC-6647.*

Thomas, J. C. (1978). A design-interpretation analysis of natural English. *International Journal of Man–Machine Studies, 10*, 651–668.

Thomas, J. C. (1980). The computer as an active communications medium. *Proceedings of the 18th Annual Meeting of the Association for Commutational Linguistics*, 83–86.

Thomas, J. C. (1983). Psychological issues in the design of data base query languages. In M. E. Simes & M. J. Coombs (Eds.), *Designing for human–computer communication.* London: Academic Press.

Thomas, J. C. (1984). Goodness (human factors) does not equal degree (quantification). *Contemporary Psychology, 29*(2), 119–120.

Thomas, J. (1985). Organizing for human factors. In Y. Vassilou (Ed.), *Human factors and interactive computer systems.* Norwood, NJ: Ablex.

Thomas, J. C., Lyon, D., & Miller, L. A. (1977). Aids for problem solving. *IBM Research Report, RC-6468.*

Thomas, J., & Schneider, M. L. (1984). *Human factors in computer systems.* Englewood Cliffs, NJ: Ablex.

Thomas, J. C., Waugh, N. C., & Fozard, J. L. (1978). Age and familiarity in memory scanning. *Journal of Gerontology, 33*(4), 528–533.

Walston, C. E., & Felix, C. P. (1977). A method of programming measurement and estimation. *IBM Systems Journal, 16*, 54–73.

Weinberg, G. M., & Schulman, E. L. (1974). Goals and performance in computer programming. *Human Factors, 16*(1), 70–77.

Wickens, C. D. (1984). *Engineering psychology and human performance.* Columbus, OH: Merrill.

Winograd, T., & Flores, R. (1986). *Understanding computers and cognition.* Norwood, NJ: Ablex.

8. FURTHER READING

Anderson, J. R. (1983). *The architecture of cognition.* Cambridge, MA: Harvard University Press.

Bolt, A. (1984). *The human interface: Where people and computers meet.* Belmont, CA: Lifetime Learning Publications.

Branscomb, L., & Thomas, J. (1984). Ease of use: A system design challenge. *IBM Systems Journal, 23*(3), 224–235.

Buxton, W., Bly, S. A., Frysinger, S. P., Lunnery, D., Manxur, D. L., Mezrich, J. L., & Morrison, R. C. (1985). Communicating with sound. *Proceedings of the '85 Computer Human Interaction Conference.* Baltimore, MD: ACM.

Card, S. K., Moran, T. P., & Newell, A. (1983). *The psychology of human–computer interaction.* Hillsdale, NJ: Erlbaum.

Cross, N. (Ed.), (1984). *Developments in design methodology.* Chichester, UK: Wiley.

Ellis, A. E., & Harper, R. A. (1961). *A guide to rational living.* North Hollywood, CA: Wilshire Books.

Furnas, G. W., Landauer, T. K., Gomez, L. M., & Dumais, S. T. Statistical semantics: Analysis of the potential performance of keyword information systems. In J. Thomas & M. Schneider (Eds.), *Human factors in computer systems.* Norwood, NJ: Ablex.

Hayes-Roth, F. (1984). The knowledge-based expert system: A tutorial. *Computer, 17*(9), 11–28.

Hollan, J. D., Hutchins, E. L., & Weitzman, L. (1984). STEAMER: An interactive inspectable simulation-based training system, *AI Magazine, 5,* 15–27.

Johnson, P. E., Duran, A. S., Hassebrock, F., Moller, J., Prietula, M., Feltovich, P. J., & Swanson, D. B. (1981). Expertise and error in diagnostic reasoning. *Cognitive Science, 5*(3), 235–283.

Jones, J. C. (1969). *Design methods.* London: Wiley.

Kidd, A. L., & Cooper, M. B. (1985). Man–machine interface issues in the construction and use of an expert system. *International Journal of Man–Machine Studies, 22,* 91–102.

Malhotra, A., Thomas, J., Carroll, J., & Miller, L. (1980). Cognitive processes in design. *International Journal of Man–Machine Studies, 1*(12), 119–140.

Newell, A., & Simon, H. A. (1972). *Human problem solving.* Englewood Cliffs, NJ: Prentice-Hall.

Pickover, C. A. (1983). The use of vector graphics system in the presentation of alternative representations of synthetic speech data. *IBM Research Report, RC-10084.*

Pickover, C. A. (1984). Spectrographic representations of globular protein breathing motion. *Science, 223,* 181.

Poincaré, H. (1952). Mathematical creation. In B. Ghiselin (Ed.), *The creative process.* New York: Mentor Books.

Reitman, W. R. (1965). *Cognition and thought.* New York: Wiley.

Rosson, M. B. (1985). Using synthetic speech for remote access to information. *Behavioral Research Methods, Instruments, and Computers, 17,* 250–252.

Rubinstein, R., & Hersh, H. (1984). *The human factor.* Maynard, MA: Digital Press.

Sackman, H., Erickson, W. J., & Grant, E. E. (1968). Exploratory and experimental studies comparing on-line and off-line programming performance. *CACM, 11,* 3–11.

Schoenfeld, A. H. (1983). Beyond the purely cognitive: Belief systems, social cognitions, and metacognitions as driving forces in intellectual performance. *Cognitive Science, 7*(4), 329–363.

Schwartz, S. (1971). Models of representation and problem solving: Well-evolved is half solved. *JEP, 91,* 347–350.

Sime, M. E., & Coombs, M. J. (1983). *Designing for human–computer communication.* London: Academic Press.

Sleeman, D., & Brown, J. S. (1982). *Intelligent tutoring systems.* London: Academic Press.

Thomas, J. C. (1974). An analysis of behavior in the hobbits-orcs problem. *Cognitive Psychology, 6,* 257–269.

Thomas, J. C. (1976). A method of studying natural language dialogue. *IBM Research Report, RC-5882.*

Thomas, J. C., & Carroll, J. M. (1981). Human factors in communication, *IBM Systems Journal, 20*(2), 237–263.

Thomas, J., Klavans, J., Nartey, J., Pickover C., Reich D., & Rosson, M. B. (1984). WALRUS: A development system for speech synthesis. *IBM Research Report, RC-10626.*

Williges, B. H., Schurick, J. M., Spine, T. M., & Hakkimen, M. T. (1985). Speech in human–computer interaction. In R. C. Williges & R. W. Ehrich (Eds.), *Human–computer dialogue design.* Amsterdam: Elsevier.

Witten, I. H. (1982). *Principles of computer speech.* Academic Press: London.

Yetton, P. W., & Vroom, V. H. (1973). *Leadership and decision making.* Pittsburgh: University of Pittsburgh Press.

13

Human and Machine Problem Solving

A Comparative Overview

K. J. GILHOOLY

1. INTRODUCTION

In this chapter I will be reviewing, with a comparative eye, the substantive pairs of chapters in the body of this book. I will be particularly concerned with questions of mutual influences between research on human and machine problem solving and with general principles that emerge from a comparative reading of Chapters 2 through 12.

2. NONADVERSARY PROBLEMS

The chapters by Mayer and du Boulay indicate interesting differences and similarities between approaches to human and machine solving of nonadversary problems. The machine work, discussed by du Boulay, has focused on "postrepresentation" processes of search. That is, *given* a problem representation, execute a search process (blind or heuristic, state space or problem reduction). On the other side, Mayer focuses very much on problem representation, and numerous studies cited in his chapter attest to the importance of representational pro-

---

K. J. GILHOOLY • Department of Psychology, University of Aberdeen, Aberdeen AB9 2UB, United Kingdom.

cesses in the course of human problem solving. Moreover, he points out that much of human problem solving (particularly of nonroutine problems) consists of seeking useful representations that lead ideally to solution, with little or no further search being required. Indeed, it is a fairly safe generalization to say that humans are not well suited to extensive mental searches of problem spaces, because of limitations on working memory storage and on retrieval from long-term memory. Models discussed elsewhere by Polson and Jeffries (1982) indicate that only limited look-ahead seems to be involved in human attempts to solve transformation tasks, such as missionaries-and-cannibals. So, the elegant techniques for extensive state-space search, which can be applied very effectively to machine solving of well-defined problems, are not evident in human solving, because such techniques are not compatible with the architecture of the human information-processing system.

Mayer points to the importance of general beliefs in the human approach to problems—for example, the belief that all mathematics problems can be solved in 10 minutes or not at all, and the belief that there is one and only one way to solve a given mathematics problem. Most such beliefs prevalent in the area of mathematical problem solving are unfortunately rather dysfunctional! (It would be interesting to see some studies of *useful* beliefs, possibly from expert solvers.) The programs discussed by du Boulay do not exhibit such stop rules or dysfunctional beliefs. Since the programs were aimed at good performance, the absence of dysfunctional rules is not surprising. Stop rules in computer problem solving would normally be implicit, in terms of time and CPU limits requested before program compilation and execution.

As regards mutual influences between machine and human approaches, there was little explicit sign of influences from psychology to computing, except perhaps a very general influence of Gestalt analyses on the Newell, Shaw, and Simon (1958) pioneering general problem solver project. There has clearly been a strong influence in the other direction, at least at the level of terminology and metaphor. The information-processing approach to human problem solving, in which the solver is seen as a computerlike system, has been dominant since the early 1960s and looks set to continue so for the foreseeable future.

The types of tasks considered by the two approaches have not exactly coincided. The computer approach has focused on very well-defined transformation and rearrangement tasks, while the psychological studies have considered less well-defined puzzles in which general semantic knowledge has a role to play (e.g., the X-ray task). In order to tackle the X-ray task by machine, considerable real-world knowledge of human anatomy, physiology, properties of rays, etc., would have to be encoded in a manageable way. Not surprisingly, this does not appear to have been attempted.

Overall, my comparative reading of the two chapters in this book on nonadversary problem solving indicates support for the general principle that solving methods reflect system architecture. Computer memory characteristics facilitate extensive search procedures; human memory characteristics militate against extensive search; and this leads to searches for representations permitting solutions with as little further search as possible. However, to do this effectively, rich real-world knowledge is necessary to provide alternative ways of representing or modeling problems.

3. ADVERSARY PROBLEMS

The theme of extensive search reappears in the domain of adversary problem solving. As Clarke's chapter shows, virtually all of the highly rated chess-playing programs carry out extensive searches through vast trees of possibilities. In contrast, human players search considerably less, considering at most hundreds of possible states rather than the millions considered by the typical chess-playing program. However, it must be emphasized that search is still important in human play. Holding's chapter provides good evidence that increased skill at chess is closely linked to increased breadth and depth of mental search. The role of search in human play was neglected until recently, following the pioneering results of de Groot (1965), which indicated that more skilled players engaged in no more search than less skilled players. However, these results were based on small samples of subjects, and the subjects were not widely different in skill levels. Holding's more extensive studies, using larger subject samples and wider ranges of skill, clearly show skill effects on the quantitative aspects of mental search. The neglect of search in human play led to an emphasis on *pattern recognition* as a possible explanation of chess expertise. This type of explanation fitted the robust finding of superior memory for briefly presented chess positions in skilled players compared with less skilled players. The pattern-recognition model was most fully articulated by Chase and Simon (1973) and appears to have influenced Wilkins's (1980) AI program, PARADISE, aimed at finding winning combinations. It may also be noted that the pattern-recognition model dovetails nicely with production system formalisms, and this compatibility probably facilitated acceptance of the model.

Given the importance of search in human play, it is of course still true that the sheer volume of search is considerably less in human players than in the typical high-performance chess program. Thus, humans can achieve the same or better performance with much less search. How might this be achieved? Apparently, the answers lie in greater use of general chess knowledge and better positional planning. Although this is plausible and some supporting evidence exists, relatively little research has gone into human planning in chess (particularly planning in playing entire games as against that in choosing single moves in positions presented without their natural buildup).

Regarding mutual influences, computer analyses have provided useful terminology and examples of well-defined processes for tackling chess. These have been taken up in psychology and used to describe human performance. In the other direction, psychological influences have had little impact on computer chess, except for the development of pattern-recognition-based programs (which, so far, have not rivaled the overall success of search-based programs).

The differences between human and computer approaches are reminiscent of the differences in the nonadversary areas. In the computer case, there is much greater use of extensive search, while the human player displays much less search but more planning. "Planning" in chess may be regarded as corresponding to "formulating the problem" in the nonadversary case.

Overall, my comparative reading of the two chapters on adversary problem solving again suggests support for the general principle that solving methods reflect system architecture. Current computer architectures facilitate extensive search; human cognitive architecture does not. Knowledge of chess principles and "lore" is used in the human case to facilitate the development of problem representations or plans that permit solutions with relatively little search. Interestingly, Clarke notes that the impending development of parallel architecture computers may well simply lead to yet more extensive search in AI-oriented chess programs. However, possibly such machines will also facilitate better simulations of human play since human play is built on some form of parallel architecture.

4. EXPERTISE

Alty, and Reimann and Chi, discuss efforts at synthesizing and analyzing expertise. On the machine side, it is clear that much progress had been made, leading to commercially successful systems such as the VAX configuring system, XCON. Human research has uncovered some of the complex differences between expert and novice solvers in a range of domains. However, the transition from expert to novice is not yet well understood.

Regarding mutual influences, the overall impact of psychological studies of expertise on machine expert systems appears to have been modest. However, studies of human experts have been used to guide the design of some expert systems, sometimes by suggesting an overall order of attack (XCON) or by providing detailed rules from interviews and other techniques (MYCIN). The problem of knowledge extraction from human experts is a bottleneck in developing expert systems. (This is one motivation for the development of learning programs; see Bratko's chapter in this volume.) In research on human expertise, the machine-inspired production system formalism has been influential. As was noted in the case of chess, production systems fit well with pattern-recognition- or schema-based approaches to expertise.

The importance of problem representation again emerges strongly from the psychological research. Experts have much better representations of problems in their fields than do novices. These rich representations help make the experts' preferred "working forward" approach feasible. Experts' representations serve to minimize search and lead to rapid solutions. If, however, unfamiliar problems are presented, then the expert reverts to the "working backward" approach typical of the novice.

It is noteworthy that human expertise in any complex field takes years of experience to develop. This makes for difficulties in studying the skill acquisition process. Also, there are implications for machine expertise in that the result of years of experience is presumably a truly vast knowledge base. This suggests that expert systems will be restricted to fairly narrow domains of knowledge that can be extracted and coded in a reasonable length of time.

Rather direct comparisons of human and machine approaches to expertise can be made in certain fields of medical diagnosis. Human experts seem to rely on very well differentiated, yet interrelated, sets of disease concepts to provide candidate hypotheses for testing when faced with a new patient's symptoms. These hypotheses are then tested in a flexible way involving both forward and backward search. The INTERNIST system mimics the human approach to diagnosis in internal medicine to a large extent.

Regarding connections with other problem-solving areas, the machine work relates quite closely to inference and to general strategies in nonadversary problem solving. The human work relates to learning and also to nonadversary problem solving.

In general terms, the importance of problem representation again emerges from a comparative reading of the chapters. Expert system programs without the rich representations of the human expert engage in long searches (e.g., MYCIN, PROSPECTOR); similarly, human novices may attempt such searches (often failing) while human experts short-circuit search and, guided by their extensive knowledge bases, work forward directly to solution.

5. INFERENCE

Frost and Gellatly discuss deductive inference in machines and humans, respectively. There appear to have been few mutual influences between the two fields. Indeed, the two fields appear to be heading in opposite directions! In the machine case, Frost outlines logic-based approaches and the non-logic-based production system and frame approaches. The context-free "semantically lean" logic-based approaches have a number of advantages for machine reasoning in terms of their formal properties (consistency, completeness). However, the more content-dependent production rule and frame-based approaches can tackle a broader range of problem areas, but at the cost of doubts about their formal properties. Ultimately, Frost argues that the production system and frame approaches will be absorbed by extended logic-based approaches, which will have desirable formal properties *and* broad application.

Gellatly points out serious problems with the logic-based approach to human reasoning, i.e., the "mental logic" approach. A "mental model" approach seems more fruitful and accounts better for the observed patterns of human responses to syllogistic and other reasoning tasks. The mental models approach stresses content-dependent processes rather than the content-independent processes of mental logic. Human inference is seen as a *product* of many diverse processes rather than as a single *process* in its own right.

In general, then, while research on machine inference stresses content-independent, logic-based processes, current research on human inference stresses the use of content-rich mental models.

6. LEARNING

Comparison of the chapters by Bratko and Eysenck on machine and human learning suggests little mutual influence between the two areas. Bratko concentrates on *concept learning*, which has been a major focus of machine learning research. Certain techniques are now well established for developing conceptual rules from noiseless complete data. Bratko outlines strategies for dealing with the more interesting cases of noisy and/or incomplete data. Some considerations, such as minimizing storage loads, are pertinent to human learning. It is notable that concept learning has been a major area of study in human learning and that some of the classic human strategies described by Bruner, Goodnow, and Austin (1956) are similar to a number of the algorithms described by Bratko. However, while the machine work has focused on attribute-value examples and rule-based concepts, psychological research has recently emphasized notions of "prototypes" and "global similarity among instances" as the bases of concepts rather than deterministic rules.

Eysenck's review indicates a range of concerns not reflected in the machine learning literature, i.e., information structures in long-term memory, amnesia, and retrieval processes.

In general, in the human case we are dealing with a vast information system that is constantly interpreting new information in the context of current activities, goals, and available schemata. This context-linked processing can lead to difficulties when the context at retrieval is different from that at encoding. Computer learning systems, on the other hand, tend to be context-independent and implement general routines that are applied to specific learning tasks. There is no equivalent of the continuing context within which human learning takes place. In a sense, the machine learning field has focused on the acquisition of "timeless" semantic information, while the study of human learning has concentrated much more on context-linked episodic information.

7. SOLVING PROBLEMS BY HUMAN–COMPUTER INTERACTION

Thomas considers possible modes of collaboration between humans and computers especially in tackling ill-defined problems typical of real life. The lesser susceptibility of the machine to "set" effects could help ensure a wider "coverance" of constraints, goals, and options. Use of randomized lists of cues may help in the production of novel ideas in the human part of a human–computer system. Computerized records of communications among group problem solvers could be the subject of useful retrospective analyses to improve future problem-solving endeavors.

In principle, it could be argued that the architectures of human and computer information processing are largely complementary, and so an integrated system should be able to exploit the strengths of both (for example, for extensive search in the machine component and for rich representational capability in the human component). However, before this promise can become a reality, the many problems of human–computer interfacing will need to be overcome, presumably by using many of the problem-solving methods discussed in this book.

8. CONCLUDING COMMENTS

Over a broad range of problem areas, humans typically display an avoidance of extended mental search, while computer problem solving typically displays extensive search. Humans typically focus on the representational aspects of problem solving, seeking representations that will permit solutions with minimum further search. The avoidance of search is presumably to minimize cognitive strain, since the human memory system is poor at encoding and retrieving long sequences of similar events (including the imagined events of mental search). This generalization needs to be qualified to take account of practice effects. Practice in chess, for example, permits chess experts to handle more extensive mental searches than can novices. The explanation is probably that practice facilitates "chunking" of move sequences into meaningful large units. Similar chunking effects have been reported in studies of practices in immediate memory for digit series (Ericsson, Chase, & Falloon, 1980).

The human tendency to focus on seeking good representations is supported and made possible by the extremely rich and interconnected knowledge bases built up through years of everyday life and through formal education. These rich knowledge bases facilitate the development of alternative representations, for example, through the use of analogy (see Keane, 1988). Computer systems, on the other hand, are well equipped for search. However, computer systems are very limited in their knowledge bases and thus are less able to use possibly distant analogies that may suggest new ways of representing the task and lead to rapid solutions.

An overall conclusion, which is supported by a comparative reading of the chapters in this book, and which may have been less evident if only human or only machine solving were considered, may be stated as follows:

"Solving processes are a function of system architectures, knowledge bases, and task demands (where task demands include effort minimization as well as attainment of good solutions)."

9. REFERENCES

Bruner, J. S., Goodnow, J. J., & Austin, G. A. (1956). *A study of thinking.* New York: Wiley.

Chase, W. G., & Simon, H. A. (1973). The mind's eye in chess. In W. G. Chase (Ed.), *Visual information processing.* New York: Academic Press.

de Groot, A. D. (1965). *Thought and choice in chess.* The Hague: Mouton.

Ericsson, K. A., Chase, W. G., & Falloon, S. (1980). Acquisition of a memory skill. *Science, 208,* 1181–1182.

Keane, M. (1988). *Analogical problem-solving.* Chichester, England: Ellis Horwood; New York: Wiley.

Newell, A., Shaw, J. C., & Simon, H. A. (1958). Elements of a theory of human problem-solving. *Psychological Review, 65,* 151–166.

Polson, P., & Jeffries, R. (1982). Problem-solving as search and understanding. In R. J. Sternberg (Ed.), *Advances in the psychology of human intelligence* (Vol. 1). Hillsdale, NJ: Erlbaum.

Wilkins, D. (1980). Using patterns and plans in chess. *Artificial Intelligence, 14,* 165–203.

Author Index

373

Subject Index

379